Date Due

Museum of Fine Arts, Boston

A Centennial History

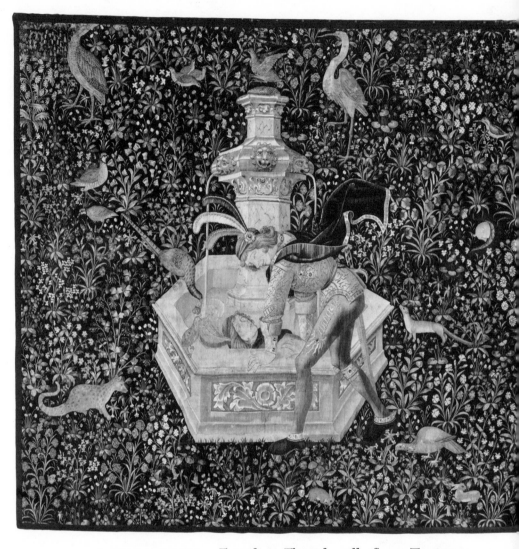

A GOTHIC NARCISSUS. French or Flemish mille fleurs Tapestry, ca. 1500. *Charles Potter Kling Fund. 68.114*

De quo consultus, an esset
Tempora maturae visurus longa senectae,
Fatidicus vates "si se non noverit" inquit.
OVID. Metam. iii. 346–348

Museum of Fine Arts
Boston
A Centennial History

Walter Muir Whitehill

VOLUME ONE

Quamquam ridentem dicere verum
Quid vetat?

HOR. *Sat.* i. 24

THE BELKNAP PRESS OF HARVARD UNIVERSITY PRESS
CAMBRIDGE, MASSACHUSETTS 1970

Preface

THE RIVER NYMPH LIRIOPE, HAVING BEEN FORCEFULLY ravished
by the curving stream and waves of Cephisus, brought forth a son,
so Ovid relates, whom she named Narcissus. When the proud mother
inquired of the blind seer Tiresias whether this most beautiful boy
would live to a ripe old age, he replied: "Yes, if he does not come to
know himself." We all know the sad sequel. By the time the child
of Cephisus and Liriope had reached his sixteenth year, he was so
beautiful that many lads and many girls fell in love with him, notable
among them the nymph Echo, who pined away, when her consuming
affection was unrequited, until finally her voice alone remained. At
last one of his scorned male admirers prayed that Narcissus might
experience an unrequited love, such as he had caused many others
to suffer. Accordingly, Narcissus, wearied with hunting in the heat
of the day, sought to quench his thirst in a forest pool. Seeing his
beautiful reflection in the clear water, he fell in love with it. After
much wooing of this insubstantial shape, finding himself scorned as
he had scorned poor Echo, Narcissus laid down his weary head on
the greensward and died of unrequited love. Although the nymphs
of the spring and wood mourned him, and Echo sang her refrain to
their lament, his body was nowhere to be found. In its place was only
a flower, with a circle of white petals around a yellow center. So the
beautiful Narcissus died in his teens because he had come to know
and to love himself too well.

The frontispiece of this volume reproduces a *mille fleurs* tapestry of about the year 1500, which depicts the climax of the story as it was imagined by late medieval French or Flemish weavers. A very fully clothed Narcissus, with velvet cloak and plumed headgear, admires his reflection in the waters of a Gothic fountain, set in a flowering meadow, peopled by animals and small birds, that must have been only an echo distant from the abode of *La Dame à la licorne* of the Musée de Cluny tapestries. This enchanting *survivance des dieux antiques* — a metamorphosis that only Ovid could have taken in his stride — is chosen for this position because it is one of the most remarkable works of art recently acquired by the Museum of Fine Arts to honor the completion of its first century.

When one ponders upon Tiresias' prophecy that Narcissus would live to a ripe old age "if he does not come to know himself" — *si se non noverit* — the wisdom of having such a centennial history as this comes into question. It may prove very dangerous for an institution to come to know too much about itself, but as the Museum of Fine Arts has safely reached the age of one hundred, it is hopefully tougher than the young Narcissus, and less likely to be fatally deranged by contemplating its own image.

When Perry T. Rathbone became Director in 1955, he hoped that each department of the museum would take steps to record its own history over the previous eighty-five years. Dows Dunham's admirable book, *The Egyptian Department and Its Excavations,* which appeared in 1958, was the only result of that hope to reach publication. As there seemed little likelihood of this plan for a cooperative record, prepared by the curators, being achieved before the museum's hundredth birthday, the Director asked me in the summer of 1968 to write this history, as one element in the celebration of the forthcoming centennial. I agreed with enthusiasm, for I have known the institution fairly intimately for more than half of its life, in addition to having been one of its trustees since 1953. I stipulated only that I should write the history as it looked to me, and that the book should be published by the Harvard University Press, at no expense to the museum either for preparation, printing, or distribution. As with Samuel Eliot Morison's *History of the United States Naval Operations in World War II,* this is a work in which I have been given full access to all the resources of the Museum of Fine Arts, as well as the most helpful and generous assistance by its staff. It is, however, in no sense an official history. The form, style, and character are my own, as are the opinions expressed and the conclusions reached. Many of the works of art reproduced are ones for which I have a particular affection; they include both very old and more recent friends.

I have never so thoroughly enjoyed writing any book as this, for a variety of reasons. I have long intended to write a history of the Boston Athenæum, where I have spent twenty-three happy years, and which was the predecessor of the Museum of Fine Arts as the artistic center of an earlier and simpler Boston. Logically I should have done that first, but Perry Rathbone's desire to have this history appear as part of the museum's centennial celebration in February 1970 led me to put the cart before the horse. Once again I invoked the dignified precedent of Rear Admiral Morison, the second volume of whose *History of United States Naval Operations* was the first to appear. Because of these two similarities I venture to appropriate the "tag" of Horace that he placed in 1930 upon the title page of his *Builders of the Bay Colony*. But beyond the family relationship between the Athenæum and the museum, almost every day that I have spent on this book has been rewarded by some happy recollection of people or of works of art that reach back to my earliest memories.

Of the Copley Square building, which the museum abandoned a few weeks after my fourth birthday, I remember nothing, although my mother assured me that I had been taken there. I was not only taken to the new museum in Huntington Avenue with great frequency, but from the time that I entered the Boston Latin School in 1918, began to go there equally often under my own power. As a Harvard undergraduate absorbed in Spanish Romanesque matters, I was not only greatly excited by the museum's purchase of the apse paintings from Santa Maria de Mur, but came to know Dr. Denman W. Ross. W. G. Constable was my supervisor of studies at the Courtauld Institute from 1932 to 1934 while I was working for a doctorate at the University of London. When I returned from Spain and settled at the Peabody Museum of Salem I made the acquaintance of Kojiro Tomita, who frequently came there, in his capacity of Honorary Curator of Japanese Ethnology, accompanied by his then-young disciple, David Britton Little. Soon after I went to the Boston Athenæum, George Harold Edgell arranged an assembly in the temporary exhibition galleries of works of art collected by the library before the establishment of the museum. Since 1953, I have had a perennial excuse for going to the museum, on the ground that I was perhaps doing some useful business as well as enjoying myself. This then is the record of a lifelong love affair with an institution.

As my chief sources have been the published annual reports and *Bulletins* of the museum and unpublished recollections furnished by various members of its staff, there seemed little need of encumbering the chapters with detailed footnotes, so I have summarized them in an appendix. If any justification for this practice is needed, I invoke two sentences from the preface of Samuel Eliot Morison's 1965 *The Oxford History of the American People*: "Since this is not a textbook, but a history written especially for my fellow citizens to read and enjoy, footnote references, bibliographies, and other 'scholarly apparatus' have been suppressed. Readers may take a certain amount of erudition for granted!"

The Poet Laureate Robert Bridges in 1916 invited readers of his anthology *The Spirit of Man*, "to bathe rather than to fish in these waters." So do I, for this is not an encyclopedic work of reference but a continuous narrative in which certain themes are interwoven. By frequent quotations, I have tried to allow the chief actors of various decades to explain what they thought they were doing and why, and to show how unforeseen circumstances have altered stated purposes, often for the better. At every stage I have had to choose examples of opinions and works of art that seemed reasonably to represent the mood of the times; ideally the book should be read from beginning to end to understand the context in which material is presented.

Illustrations are small and numerous, for they are intended as reminders rather than as ideal representations of works of art. As their size attempts to suggest the scale of the objects reproduced, some are very small indeed, for although the importance of the diminutive Minoan *Snake Goddess* richly deserves a full page, rather than an area hardly larger than a postage stamp, it would convey a false impression were she to be reproduced on an equality with the colossal alabaster statue of King Mycerinus, builder of the Third Pyramid at Giza. In the captions all works of art owned by the Museum of

Fine Arts are identified by their accession numbers, the first two digits of which indicate the year of acquisition. These numbers are valuable not only for precise identification but as indications of the growth of the collections. Such a number as 90.95 indicates, without reference to the text, that William Blake's drawing of *The Creation of Eve* became the property of the Museum of Fine Arts only fourteen years after the Copley Square building was opened.

So many people have been helpful to me in the course of the work that I could hardly list them without duplicating most of the roster of the trustees and staff. I must, however, especially thank the sixth Director, Perry T. Rathbone, for having asked me to write the book, and his Special Assistant, Diggory Venn, for constant help in locating materials that did not spring to the eye. Henry P. Rossiter, Curator Emeritus of Prints, has been a constant encouragement in the last strenuous weeks of completing the manuscript. His highly sympathetic response to the early chapters, which were sent to him for reading by the Harvard University Press, led me to inflict further drafts upon him as they were completed. Each letter that he has written me from Hopkinton, New Hampshire, has made the effort seem worthwhile. I owe special thanks also to Dr. and Mrs. Cornelius C. Vermeule, Miss Mary B. Comstock, and Miss Sarah C. Dublin of the Department of Classical Art for constant help; to Dows Dunham, Curator Emeritus of the Department of Egyptian Art, to Miss Gertrude Townsend, Curator Emeritus of the Department of Textiles, and to Kojiro Tomita, Curator Emeritus of the Department of Asiatic Art, for personal recollections that go back well beyond my own.

I am especially grateful to my secretary at the Boston Athenæum, Miss Jane A. Ramsay (now Mrs. William H. Key), for invaluable help in typing the manuscript, and to the staffs of the Harvard University Press and the Meriden Gravure Company for their greatly appreciated assistance in transforming that manuscript into type and pictures.

WALTER MUIR WHITEHILL

Boston Athenæum
4 August 1969

Contents

Museum of Fine Arts, Boston

A Centennial History

CHAPTER I

The Foundation

Most frequenters of the Boston Athenæum have at one time or another read the two handsome brass tablets in the vestibule, flanking the front door, which summarize the history of the institution. These were made by the Birmingham Guild in England in 1928, following a typographical design by Daniel Berkeley Updike of the Merrymount Press, and read:

THE BOSTON ATHENÆUM

HAD ITS ORIGINS IN THE LIBRARY OF

THE ANTHOLOGY SOCIETY

INSTITUTED OCTOBER 17, 1805

THE ATHENÆUM WAS INCORPORATED

FEBRUARY 17, 1807

AND HOUSED IN SCOLLAY'S BUILDINGS

UNTIL 1809

WHEN THE TRUSTEES PURCHASED

A ROUGH CAST WOODEN HOUSE

NEAR KING'S CHAPEL BURIAL GROUND

ONCE THE DWELLING

OF HENRY CANER, LOYALIST RECTOR

IN 1822

THE COLLECTIONS WERE MOVED

TO THE MANSION OF JAMES PERKINS

IN PEARL STREET

*   *

THIS BUILDING
DESIGNED BY EDWARD CLARKE CABOT
WAS DEDICATED TO THE
CULTIVATION OF LETTERS AND THE ARTS
ON APRIL 17, 1847
OPENED IN JULY OF THE SAME YEAR
AND ENLARGED IN 1913
THE CABINET OF NATURAL HISTORY
AND LECTURE HALL OF THE ATHENÆUM
NO LONGER EXIST
BUT ITS GALLERIES OF ART FORMED
THE NUCLEUS OF THE
BOSTON MUSEUM OF FINE ARTS

*   *

HERE REMAINS A RETREAT FOR
THOSE WHO WOULD ENJOY
THE HUMANITY OF BOOKS

The closing lines, quoted from an essay written by Barrett Wendell on the centenary of the library in 1907, are as pertinent today as they would have been at any time in the past one hundred and sixty-three years. The tablets, however, like many historic markers, contain an error of fact. Although the cornerstone of the present building was laid on 17 April 1847, it was not opened in "July of the same year," but in July 1849.

As originally built from Edward Clarke Cabot's designs, the Beacon Street building was a combined library and art gallery, for the Athenæum was at the time the principal repository of the fine arts in Boston. Soon after the Athenæum moved to James Perkins' house in Pearl Street in 1822 a subscription was undertaken to raise funds for an addition that would provide space for lectures and art exhibitions. In consequence a three-story brick building, 60 feet long and 50 feet wide, designed by Solomon Willard, was erected at the rear of the property at the cost of some $13,000. It contained rooms on the first floor to be rented for small exhibitions and meetings. On the second floor was a lecture hall, 18 feet high, with 500 seats

BOSTON ATHENAEUM IN 1885.

placed in a curve on an inclined plane. The skylighted third story, 20 feet high, provided the gallery for paintings, which caused the whole structure to be known as the Athenæum Gallery. As the Athenæum owned only seven paintings, five of which were by Gilbert Stuart or copies of his work, at the time the gallery was completed, Washington Allston, Stuart, and Thomas Sully painted in it for a time. In May 1827 the first public loan exhibition was held in the Athenæum Gallery, which was followed for nearly half a century by annual exhibitions that included both the works of contemporary American artists and European paintings, sculptures, and casts. By gift and purchase the institution had, moreover, begun to assemble a permanent collection of some distinction. The record of this activity is summarized in Mabel Munson Swan's book, *The Athenæum Gallery, 1827–1873: The Boston Athenæum as an Early Patron of Art*, published by the Athenæum in 1940.

As originally constructed in 1847–1849, 10½ Beacon Street was a three-story building with skylighted picture galleries on the top floor and the principal library space on the second. The rear of the first floor was divided between a reading room for current news-

BOSTON ATHENAEUM SCULPTURE GALLERY IN 1855. Woodcut from *Ballou's Pictorial.*

papers and a sculpture gallery. The latter was necessary because the Athenæum had received eleven full-length plaster casts of classical sculpture in 1822, and had acquired original works by Horatio Greenough, Richard S. Greenough, John Frazee, Hiram Powers, Shobal Vail Clevenger, Thomas Crawford, and other contemporary sculptors. To the left of the entrance hall, the room looking onto Beacon Street was for several decades occupied by the American Academy of Arts and Sciences. To the right of the entrance a monumental staircase led to the upper stories. As this had been a pet project of Charles Sumner, a member of the building committee in 1845, who had glowing memories of Bernini staircases in Rome, it was long known as the "Sumner Staircase."

The library was moved from Pearl Street and installed in the new building by July 1849, but some months passed before the works of art were similarly transferred. At the annual meeting on 7 January 1850, it was reported that "the Statuary (with the exception of Crawford's Orpheus, which has been removed to the new building while the snow favored its transport) still remains in the Gallery in Pearl

Street." By late spring the moving was completed, for the twenty-third Athenæum exhibition opened on 27 May 1850 in "the new Gallery in Beacon Street, which proves to be admirably adapted to its purpose."

Institutions outgrow their buildings with remarkable regularity. In less than twenty years the new Athenæum, which had seemed so spacious when planned in 1847, was already becoming overcrowded. The Fine Arts Committee, of which Edward N. Perkins was chairman, reported in January 1866: "The picture galleries are good as regards light, but they are badly situated, being at the top of a lofty staircase. The Athenæum possesses so many valuable and interesting pictures, that, if they were in a gallery on the first floor, easily accessible, and warmed in winter, it would be constantly resorted to by the proprietors as well as citizens and strangers . . . If the Athenæum should hereafter become possessed of a suitable site, or if one now in its possession could be used for the purpose, it would, in the opinion

BOSTON ATHENAEUM, THE SUMNER STAIRCASE. Removed in 1888 to make way for bookstacks, as it occupied nearly a quarter of the cubic content of the building.

of the Committee, be well to surrender the present galleries to the library, and erect a building adapted in all respects to the Fine Arts." Here is the germ of the idea that led to the creation of the Museum of Fine Arts.

A year later, on 8 January 1867, the Library Committee stated: "The room used as a statuary gallery was originally designed for the use of the library. Its alcoves are now imperatively needed for books and its open space for a reading room." As the books had doubled in number since they had been placed in the building in 1849, "everything points to the erection of an addition to our present building on the land now owned by the Corporation in Tremont Place." The Fine Arts Committee, through Mr. Perkins, recognized the inevitability of the move but pointed out that "the appropriation of the Sculpture Gallery to its original and useful purpose . . . will break up our collection of valuable casts from the antique and marbles, the only one existing in New England." The Trustees, at a special meeting of 4 February 1867, approved the Report of the Joint Committee of Proprietors and Trustees on the proposed enlargement of the accommodations for the Library and the Fine Arts Department, which recommended the construction of a new gallery in Tremont Place.

In the course of 1868 the first-floor Sculpture Gallery was refitted for books. Although the principle of separate buildings for the library and the art gallery was generally accepted, even in 1867, there was doubt that the adjacent Tremont Place property was sufficiently ample as a site for the new gallery. This doubt was greatly increased when Colonel Timothy Bigelow Lawrence (1826–1869) bequeathed to the Athenæum an extensive collection of armor and weapons, and Mrs. Lawrence offered to fit up a room for its proper exhibition. As no room was available, this bequest inspired wider thoughts upon the future of the Fine Arts in Boston. When President John Amory Lowell reported the Lawrence bequest to a special meeting of the Athenæum trustees on 15 November 1869, the following vote was passed:

> Whereas the late T. Bigelow Lawrence, Esq., generously bequeathed his large and valuable collection of arms and armour to the Boston Athenæum and his widow, Mrs. Lawrence, has in the

same liberal spirit expressed her intention, not only that the bequest should come free from the legacy tax, but also to fit up a room in a suitable manner and style for its reception at her own expense, to the end that it may be properly exhibited and kept and also to make provision for its permanent care and custody;

And, whereas, she has also in furtherance of the same object, and in the same enlarged spirit, considering that this institution has not at its disposal a suitable place for the reception and exhibition of that collection, nor for its other works of art, and considering also the great importance of establishing in this city a gallery for the collecting and exhibiting on a scale larger than is now possible, paintings, statuary and other objects of virtu and art, expressed her willingness to contribute the sum of twenty five thousand dollars in addition to the foregoing donations, provided the sum of seventy five thousand dollars in addition thereto should be raised from other sources, for the erection of a building adapted to such uses and to the exhibition of the above mentioned collections;

And, whereas, it is understood that a large and valuable piece of land, in a good location, now in the possession of the city of Boston, is dedicated to the purpose of erecting such a structure, which can be made available in this connection without cost, therefore

It is voted: that the present is a proper time for making an appeal to the public and especially to the friends of the Fine Arts, to raise the sum required to make available Mrs. Lawrence's proposed donation, and, if possible, to provide even larger means to carry out so noble a design in the confident hope that it may be attended with success, and that the President and Treasurer with the Committee on the Fine Arts Department be a committee to devise a plan of proceeding and to make such an appeal with full power to receive subscriptions and to carry out the plan suggested under the organization and auspices of the Boston Athenæum.

Less than two months later, the minutes of the annual meeting on 10 January 1870 state:

In reply to a question from Mr. Matthews whether any steps had been taken toward the erection of a Museum of the Fine Arts, the President replied that a committee of the Trustees now had that matter in charge and was conferring with similar committees representing other public institutions; that an Act of Incorporation would speedily be applied for, and, if the expectations of the Trustees were fulfilled a meeting of proprietors would be called to authorize the Trustees to remove the art collections of the Athenæum to the Museum hereafter to be erected.

The need of more space for the Athenæum Gallery and the Lawrence bequest when noised about in the city made other institutions aware of the magnitude of the problem. Harvard College had no adequate means of making available to the public the collection of prints bequeathed to it by Francis Calley Gray (1790–1856). The recently founded Massachusetts Institute of Technology had insufficient room for its collection of architectural casts, while the American Social Science Association had notions of the public usefulness of a collection of plaster reproductions of sculpture.

The latter idea sprang chiefly from the pedagogical theories of Charles Callahan Perkins (1823–1886), a grandson of the China Trade merchant James Perkins, who had been the benefactor of the Boston Athenæum in 1822. Charles C. Perkins' mind turned more naturally to the studio than the counting house. After graduation from Harvard in 1843, he went abroad determined to study art. In Rome he became friendly with the sculptor Thomas Crawford. Although in Paris he studied painting with Ary Scheffer and etching with Bracquemonde and Lalanne, his life was to be spent in the criticism and interpretation of art rather than its creation. His love of music equaled his enthusiasm for painting and sculpture. Not only long the president of the Handel and Haydn Society, he wrote creditable music for them, and on occasion conducted their concerts. He was the largest single contributor to the construction of the Music Hall in 1852, as well as the donor of a great bronze statue of Beethoven by his friend Crawford. He lectured in 1857 at Trinity College, Hartford, on "The Rise and Progress of Painting," and later on Roman and Greek art before Boston schoolteachers. During thirteen years' service on the Boston School Committee, he brought to Boston the South Kensington methods of teaching drawing and design to children, and was instrumental in founding the Massachusetts Normal Art School. His *Tuscan Sculptors* (1864) and *Italian Sculp-*

tors (1868), published in London and illustrated by his own etchings, gave C. C. Perkins a European reputation. In 1869 the American Social Science Association appointed him chairman of a special committee to consider the subject of art from an educational point of view. The other members were William R. Ware, the first head of the new architectural school of the Massachusetts Institute of Technology; Edward Clarke Cabot, architect of the Boston Athenæum and president of the recently founded Boston Society of Architects; James M. Barnard of Boston; and the New York sculptor John Quincy Adams Ward.

On behalf of this committee, Perkins prepared a report for the second volume of the association's *Journal*, suggesting "the feasibility of establishing a regular Museum of Art at a moderate expense." The general argument was "that nations as well as individuals should aim at that degree of aesthetic culture which, without passing the dividing line between general and special knowledge, will enable them to recognize and appreciate the beautiful in nature and art." Although suggesting that Greeks and Orientals had special capacities for such appreciation, Perkins argued that

> there exists a modicum of capacity for improvement in all men, which can be greatly developed by familiarity with such acknowledged masterpieces as are found in all great collections of works of art. Their humblest function is to give enjoyment to all classes; their highest, to elevate men by purifying the taste and acting upon the moral nature; their most practical, to lead by the creation of a standard of taste in the mind to improvement in all branches of industry, by the purifying of forms, and a more tasteful arrangement of colors in all objects made for daily use.

Perkins' immediate proposal was "the establishment of a Museum of Art of the character of that at South Kensington." The plan, as one might have expected from an organization devoted to the forward-looking but suspect field of "social science," was didactic rather than aesthetic in its approach, for Perkins stated resolutely:

> In regard to the class of art objects with which we should propose to stock the proposed Museum, there can be but one opinion. As its

aims are educational, and its funds are likely to be for some time limited, these objects must be such as are to be obtained at once at a moderate expense, and of such a nature as to place the institution on a high ground in the esteem of the community as a means of culture to the public, of education to artists and artisans, and of elevated enjoyment to all. Original works of art being out of our reach on account of their rarity and excessive costliness, and satisfactory copies of paintings being nearly as rare and costly as originals, we are limited to the acquisition of reproductions in plaster and other analogous materials of architectural fragments, statues, coins, gems, medals, and inscriptions, and of photographs of drawings by the old masters, which are nearly as perfect as the originals from which they are taken, and quite as useful for our purposes.

One suspects that, had the Prince Consort survived a few more years, he would have highly approved of these elevated yet practical sentiments.

Another very practical consideration, of a kind likely to appeal to frugal New Englanders, entered the picture. In the development of the Back Bay, then in the course of being converted from water to land, certain plots of land were set aside for institutional use with the thought of raising the tone of the new area. In this newly filled desert, on the south side of what later was to become Copley Square, was a tract of land belonging to the city which, under suitable circumstances, might become available for a purpose connected with the arts.

All these disparate interests came together when the Massachusetts Legislature, on 4 February 1870, passed an act establishing "a body corporate by the name of the Trustees of the Museum of Fine Arts for the purpose of erecting a museum for the preservation and exhibition of works of art, of making, maintaining, and establishing collections of such works, and of affording instruction in the Fine Arts." In anticipation of this act, the Trustees of the Athenæum had already, on 17 January 1870, authorized its Fine Arts Committee to make the use of the third-floor galleries available "in case of an art loan exhibition being gotten together in the spring to forward the movement in favor of the proposed Museum of the Fine Arts."

The act of incorporation named twelve men — Martin Brimmer,

Charles C. Perkins, Charles W. Eliot, William Endicott, Jr., Samuel
Eliot, Francis E. Parker, Henry P. Kidder, William B. Rogers, George
B. Emerson, Otis Norcross, John T. Bradlee, and Benjamin S. Rotch.
These, with three persons to be appointed annually by the President
and Fellows of Harvard College, three by the Trustees of the Boston
Athenæum, and three by the Massachusetts Institute of Technology,
and, *ex-officiis*, the Mayor of Boston, the President of the Trustees of
the Public Library, the Superintendent of Public Schools, the Secretary of the Board of Education, and the Trustee of the Lowell
Institute, constituted a Board of Trustees, empowered to hold real
and personal estate to the value of one million dollars. Vacancies
occurring among the twelve trustees named in the act, or their successors, were to be filled by the whole board at an annual meeting.

Martin Brimmer (1829–1896), the first named in the list, was
elected president on 17 March 1870 and held the office for the next
twenty-five years. Son of a mayor of Boston, he was a member of the
Harvard class of 1849, where he led his class in Latin and Greek, and
was graduated with highest honors. Although admitted to the Massachusetts bar, he found European travel and the study of art more
congenial than the practice of law. Disqualified for military service
because of lameness, he served for a time in the Massachusetts
Legislature. Although he was a member of such boards as those of the
Boston Athenæum, the Massachusetts General Hospital, the Perkins
Institution for the Blind, the Provident Institution for Savings, and
the vestry of Trinity Church, his consuming interests were the Museum of Fine Arts and Harvard College, of which he was a Fellow
1864–1868 and 1877–1896. By his happy marriage to Miss Mary
Ann Timmins, he had no children. John Jay Chapman, who married
his niece, wrote of Martin Brimmer:

He was the best of old Boston; for he was not quite inside the Puri-
tan tradition and was a little sweeter by nature and less sure he was
right than the true Bostonian is. He was a lame, frail man, with
fortune and position; and one felt that he had been a lame, frail
boy, lonely, cultivated, and nursing an ideal of romantic honour.
There was a knightly glance in his eye and a seriousness in his deep
voice that told of his living, and of his having lived always, in a

little Camelot of his own. He was not quixotic, but he was independent. There were portcullises and moats and flowered gardens
around him. He was humble with a kind of Hidalgo humility — the
humility of a magnificent impoverished Portuguese Duke. There
was nothing sanctimonious about his mind, and this is what really
distinguished him from the adjacent Boston nobility. There was in
Mr. Brimmer nothing of that austere look which comes from holding on to property and standing pat. And besides this he was warm;
not, perhaps, quite as warm as the Tropics, but very much warmer
than the average Beacon Street mantel-pieces were.

Chapman himself, anything but a patient man, observed that "Mr.
Brimmer's most powerful quality was his patience." "His power of
patience impressed me and awed me." As he saw the elements of a
situation more quickly than others, he often became the controlling
force. It was remarked that John Hay's description of Abraham
Lincoln — "that he could see around the corner while the rest were
looking down the street" — might well be applied to Martin Brimmer. This then was the man who led the Museum of Fine Arts during
its first quarter-century of life: a thoughtful and perceptive student
of the arts, who once remarked: "So accustomed have men become
to books as the storehouses of facts and ideas, so limited are we to the
use of words as the only vehicle of thought, that we have lost touch
with the earlier and more natural mode of expression by images."
  To the 30 October 1880 issue of *The American Architect and
Building News*, which was devoted to the Museum of Fine Arts,
Martin Brimmer contributed a few paragraphs on the aims of the
new institution. He pointed out the growth and multiplication of
great collections of art, as well as the change in their character.

They were formerly the private property of sovereigns, and were
confined to what may be called the luxuries of art — the pictures
of the masters, the remains of Greek and Roman sculpture, engraved gems, examples of the best goldsmith's work. The museums
of today open their doors to all the world, and the scope of their
collections has broadened to meet the public needs. None the less,
however, are the best pictures and marbles their prizes. The master's hand, expressing the master's mind, gives that which fills the

eye and touches the imagination as nothing else can, and no opportunity should be neglected to procure for our museums works of this original and permanent value. The fact that such works of the older painters and sculptors are daily becoming more rare and costly, as they are gradually being gathered into the public collections of Europe, should be rather a stimulus than a discouragement; for at the rate at which they are now being absorbed, they will, in another generation, be almost unattainable.

Along the lines that had guided the Boston Athenæum during the previous half-century in its collecting of the works of contemporary American artists, Brimmer wrote:

> Our Museum, too, has its local duty to perform in gathering together adequate examples of the artists associated with this neighborhood. A public gallery at The Hague, which failed to show us Paul Potter, a public gallery at Birmingham in which David Cox was ignored, would be justly censured. A Boston collection would be singularly deficient if it did not contain a full representation of Copley and Stuart, of Allston and Crawford, of Hunt and Rimmer.

He further pointed out the "new wants" and "fresh resources" resulting from the spread of public interest in the Fine Arts, and indicated the archaeological activities of Schliemann and Cesnola in uncovering the records of old civilizations, of which "America should not lose a share . . . for lack of enterprise." Only after alluding to the works of art from Japan, India, and China, which are becoming increasingly known "within our time," does Martin Brimmer allude briefly to the reproductions of works of art, "which are themselves obtainable with difficulty or not at all."

In concluding he touched upon decorative art, which "may almost be said to have come into existence among us within fifteen or twenty years," and the many industries, still in their infancy, which are dependent upon designers skilled in line and color. "The designer needs a museum of art, as the man of letters needs a library, or the botanist a herbarium."

The second trustee named in the act of incorporation was Charles Callahan Perkins. As he had been in the forefront of the effort to create the new museum, he was in 1876 designated as Honorary Director, a post that carried with it, *ex officio*, the chairmanship of the Committee on the Museum, which had supervision of the collections and responsibility for purchases of works of art and acceptance of gifts. Among the other ten incorporators were men of substantial position in both the learned and the financial activities of Boston: Charles William Eliot (1836–1926), who had become president of Harvard the previous year; his first cousin Samuel Eliot (1821–1898), a former president of Trinity College, Hartford; William Barton Rogers (1802–1882), founder and first president of the Massachusetts Institute of Technology; and George Barrell Emerson (1797–1881), educator and naturalist, ably represented the learned community. The financial probity of the enterprise was ably guaranteed by the presence on the board of such men as Henry P. Kidder (1823–1886), head of the investment firm of Kidder, Peabody and Co.; William Endicott (1826–1914), partner in the dry goods firm of C. F. Hovey and Co., and president of the New England Trust Company and the Suffolk Savings Bank; and the merchant Otis Norcross (1811–1882), Mayor of Boston in 1867, a man of great experience in municipal matters, whose opinion had great influence in the conduct of affairs. Henry P. Kidder, elected treasurer of the museum on 17 March 1870, held that office until his death, ably managing the finances of the institution through its leanest and most difficult years.

In less than four months after the incorporation of the museum, a building site was in hand. The city of Boston on 26 May 1870 awarded the museum a tract of land, facing what was later to become Copley Square, at the corner of Dartmouth Street and St. James Avenue. A decade earlier the site had been mudflats that lay within the Receiving Basin of the ambitious but unsuccessful Mill Dam scheme of 1814–1821. The filling of the Back Bay, begun in the late eighteen fifties, had by 1870 progressed as far west as Exeter Street. Houses and churches began to line the newly created streets. Early in the filling, Mathias Denman Ross, a businessman whose interests involved real estate, waterpower, wharves, surveying, textile manufacturing, and banking, pointed out to the Legislature the financial advantages of reserving certain areas in the Back Bay for open spaces or the use of public institutions. Demonstrating the higher prices paid for house lots adjoining the Public Garden or on Commonwealth Avenue, he reasonably alleged that by reserving certain blocks for public use, higher prices would be obtained for the lots that adjoined them. In accordance with this logic, the Legislature in 1860–61 granted land on Berkeley Street extending from Boylston to Newbury to the Boston Society of Natural History, while the remainder of that block was devoted to the newly incorporated Massachusetts Institute of Technology, of which Ross had been one of the founders. Through the influence of Mathias Denman Ross, the Boston Water Power Company had been persuaded to convey to the city in trust the land subsequently awarded the museum, to be used either for an Institute of Fine Arts or for an open space. The 91,000 square-foot lot, surrounded by streets on every side, was granted to the trustees on condition that they erect upon it a building to the value of $100,000 within three years — a period subsequently extended to six years when fundraising dragged — and that the museum should be open free of charge four days in each month. Mathias Denman Ross was, incidentally, one of the first three trustees appointed to the museum board by the Massachusetts Institute of Technology. He continued his valuable services to the museum until his death in 1892. The family tradition long continued, for his nephew Denman Waldo Ross (1853–1935), painter, collector in many fields of art, and Lecturer on the Theory of Design at Harvard, who was elected a trustee on 17 January 1895, during the next forty years proved to be one of the great donors of works of art to the museum.

At the time of the award, the site was encumbered by a vast temporary wooden Coliseum in which a gargantuan musical National Peace Jubilee had been held in June 1869. This was, however, no great inconvenience, for the trustees of the museum needed time to raise funds for whatever they were to build. Thus, before it had to be demolished the Coliseum survived long enough to house a similar International Peace Jubilee in June 1872, celebrating the conclusion of the Franco-Prussian War.

At a public meeting held in the Music Hall on 3 February 1871, a large committee was appointed to solicit funds for construction. Through smaller meetings held in private houses the committee

NATIONAL PEACE JUBILEE COLISEUM IN 1869. This stereoscopic view suggests the frontierlike aspect of the Back Bay in its first decade of filling. On the left is the Rogers Building of the Massachusetts Institute of Technology. The streets were filled to a higher level than unoccupied lots; the thoroughfare in the center is Clarendon Street, while a bit of Newbury Street appears in the lower right corner.

moved forward with such energy that before the summer of 1871 about a quarter of a million dollars had been pledged. Meanwhile architects had been asked to submit designs. Out of fourteen submitted, the trustees chose Messrs. Sturgis and Brigham's plan of a red brick and terra-cotta Gothic structure in the manner made popular by John Ruskin's visits to Italy.

During the six years that were to pass between incorporation and the opening of the new Museum of Fine Arts, the third-floor galleries of the Boston Athenæum provided a crowded but congenial setting for the exhibitions of the new institution. The two gifts of the year of incorporation were works of American art by artists long associated with the Athenæum: the first was Washington Allston's 1812 painting of *Elijah in the Desert*, given by Mrs. Samuel Hooper and

THE ATHENAEUM GALLERY. Oil by Enrico Meneghelli, showing two of the third-floor rooms at 10 1/2 Beacon Street during their temporary occupancy by the Museum of Fine Arts, 1870–1876.

ELIJAH IN THE DESERT. Washington Allston. *Gift of Mrs. Samuel Hooper and Miss Alice Hooper.* 70.1 The first gift to the museum in the year of incorporation.

Miss Alice Hooper, the second was Thomas Crawford's group of *Hebe and Ganymede*, from his friend and patron, Charles C. Perkins. In 1871, following the February auction of the luxurious contents of the Deacon house in the South End, Miss Deacon gave the museum a large Brussels allegorical tapestry representing *Victory*, while the heirs of Peter Parker (the father of Mrs. Edward P. Deacon) gave two pictures by François Boucher, *La Halte à la Fontaine* of 1765 (formerly in the Hôtel de Richelieu, Paris) and *L'Aller au Marché* of 1767. With a view to providing a handsome setting for the collection of armor and weapons that her late husband had bequeathed to the Athenæum, Mrs. T. Bigelow Lawrence bought from a Mr. Wright in Wardour Street in London carved oak paneling

VICTORY. Brussels tapestry, late 17th or early 18th century. *Gift of Miss Ida Deacon*. 71.1 One of the sumptuous adornments of the Deacon house in the South End, 1848–1871.

LA HALTE À LA FONTAINE. François Boucher. *Gift of the Heirs of Peter Parker.*
71.2 Bought in Paris in 1852 for the Deacon house.

from a sixteenth-century room. These panels, in which were set portraits supposedly representing Henry VIII, Edward VI, Queen
Elizabeth, and others, were given to the museum in 1871, in anticipation of the construction of the new building.

The first public exhibition in the name of the Trustees of the
Museum of Fine Arts was held, not at the Boston Athenæum, but in
a room lent by the jewelers Messrs. Bigelow, Kennard, and Co., in the
rear of their store in West Street. It consisted of a small collection of
Cypriote antiquities, sent to this country by the United States Consul
at Cyprus, Brigadier General Luigi Palma di Cesnola (1832–1904).
Cesnola, born near Turin, served in the Sardinian Army of Revolution and the Crimean War before coming to the United States to win
his highest rank in the Union Army during the Civil War. Appointed
to the Cyprus consulate on condition that he become an American
citizen, Cesnola spent eleven years there, during which, at his own
expense, he explored sixty-five necropoli and numerous other sites.
Returning eventually to the United States, he became secretary of

the Metropolitan Museum in New York, and its director in 1879, both of which posts he held, against violent partisan criticism, until his death. The more than five hundred objects from his excavations, chiefly vases and terracottas, that he sent to Boston were acquired for the Museum of Fine Arts in 1872 by the subscription of friends, and became the genesis of the classical collection. Included in the Cesnola purchase were four archaic Cypriote stone heads of men that still find a respected place in the galleries after nearly a century of collecting.

HEADS OF MEN. Marble, Cyprus. 72.325 *and* 72.320 Sculptures from the Cesnola Collection that are still exhibited nearly a century after purchase.

A *Catalogue of the Collection of Ancient and Modern Works of Art, given or loaned to the Trustees of the Museum of Fine Arts, at Boston* was published in 1872, with a preface by Charles C. Perkins, dated 16 June 1872. Of the 539 objects listed, 349 were the Cesnola Cypriote collection, by then the property of the museum. Some forty Greco-Italian vases, found by Alessandro Castellani in Etruscan and Campanian tombs, were lent for exhibition by Thomas G. Appleton, as were a variety of examples of European pottery, glass, and bronzes from various private owners.

By the time the second catalogue, with preface dated 10 April 1873, had appeared, the museum had acquired the nucleus of an Egyptian collection, assembled by Robert Hay of Linplun, East Lothian, who had been a frequent visitor to Egypt in the eighteen twenties and thirties. After Hay's death, it was offered for sale by his son and exhibited in the Crystal Palace at Sydenham until 1871, when it was bought by Samuel A. Way of Boston, whose son, C. Granville Way, gave it to the museum in June 1872. The Way collection contained not only seven mummies, which to small boys and the idly curious have always been the most fascinating product of Egypt, but some hundreds of small objects of considerable rarity and beauty. Among those of particular interest are a charming little wooden statuette of a dancing girl of the Eighteenth Dynasty and a tiny stone tablet of the New Kingdom with an unfinished sketch of a king engaged in the congenial occupation of slaying foreign captives.

The need of installing the Way collection temporarily in one of the third-floor galleries of the Boston Athenæum attracted to the museum a remarkable Bostonian who, with Martin Brimmer and Charles C. Perkins, played a highly significant role in the development of the institution. Charles Greely Loring (1828–1902) of the Harvard class of 1848, because of delicate lungs, had spent one winter in Málaga and another on the Nile, where he devoted himself to the study of Egyptian art and archaeology. In 1855 he visited the Sinaitic Peninsula, Arabia Petraea, and Palestine, returning by way of Constantinople and Greece. On coming home, as his health was far from robust, he devoted himself to laying out and planting the seaside farm at Prides Crossing that had been since 1844 his family's summer home. Nevertheless, in 1861 he joined the Union Army as a first lieutenant on General Burnside's staff and served throughout the war, receiving three brevet promotions, first to colonel, then to brigadier-general, and finally to major-general. In 1868 and 1869 he returned to Egypt to continue the archaeological and historical studies for which previous visits had given him so considerable an enthusiasm. When the Way collection was received, Charles C. Perkins persuaded General Loring to undertake its installation and cataloguing; the following year he was elected a trustee. In 1876 he was made Curator, then the chief executive head of the institution, a post that he filled for more than two decades. When Charles C. Perkins died in 1886, his office of Honorary Director was abolished, and General Loring's title was changed to Director. In that capacity he served until six months before his death in 1902. Thus, even before the first building of the Museum of Fine Arts was completed, the *dramatis personae* that were to play the principal roles in the museum for its first quarter-century had appeared on the stage.

The year 1872 brought setbacks as well as progress, for the great fire of 9 November, which destroyed so many blocks in the center of Boston, obliterated the Pearl Street warehouse in which the Lawrence collection of arms and armor had been stored by the Boston Athenæum, pending the availability of space for its proper exhibition. The insurance received from this loss was devoted by the Art Committee of the Athenæum to the purchase of a collection of Italian textile fabrics and embroideries, carved wood, and metalwork of the Renaissance period from the Italian collector and dealer Alessandro Castellani. Among these objects, which were thought to be of considerable potential usefulness to designers, were various altar cloths and vestments, including a superb red and gold sixteenth-century Italian chasuble, ornamented with the golden bees of the Barberini family.

In 1874 the museum trustees borrowed, for exhibition at the Athenæum, a group of Spanish paintings belonging to the Duc de Montpensier, son of Louis Philippe, who had married Luisa Fernanda, sister of Isabella II of Spain. Third and fourth catalogues of the objects shown in the Athenæum Picture Gallery were published in 1874 (with prefaces dated 1 March and 23 October); fifth and sixth catalogues came out in 1875 (1 January and 12 July). The will of Senator Charles Sumner, who died on 11 March 1874, left the museum 94 pictures, a number of framed engravings, and a bust of himself by Thomas Crawford. Most of Sumner's pictures were sold, and the $3,856 that they realized was invested in the ordering of plaster casts. In 1875 Quincy Adams Shaw lent 28 paintings, chiefly French, and gave the museum Corot's large canvas of *Dante and Virgil entering the Inferno* (1859), the snarling animals of which were painted by A. L. Barye. Thus interest was sustained in the new museum, even though the construction of its building progressed slowly.

CHASUBLE. Red and gold brocade, Italian, 16th
century. *Ath.* 237 One of the objects bought by
the Boston Athenæum for the new Museum of
Fine Arts.

Losses sustained in the Chicago fire of 1871, the Boston fire of
1872, and the business confusion brought about by the panic of 1873,
had impeded fundraising. The architects Sturgis and Brigham had
proceeded rapidly enough with their plans for the building. Indeed,
at the December 1872 meeting of the Boston Society of Architects,
John H. Sturgis, the partner chiefly responsible, had exhibited them
for comment and discussion. The lot extended 350 feet along Dartmouth Street, and 260 feet along St. James Avenue. The plans called
for a building that, save for a 30-foot setback from the street-line on
all sides, would eventually cover the entire space. One series of
galleries ran around the outside of the building; another gave upon
two interior open courts. The ground plan, which could most easily
be described as an H with the ends closed, provided for entrances
and staircases in all four façades; the cross bar of the H contained on
the first floor a restaurant and dining room, and on the second floor

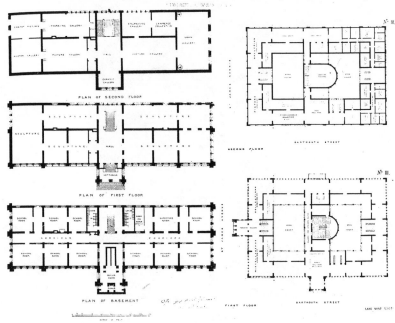

PLAN OF SECOND FLOOR

PLAN OF FIRST FLOOR

PLAN OF BASEMENT

N° IV.

SECOND FLOOR

DARTMOUTH STREET

N° III.

FIRST FLOOR

DARTMOUTH STREET

STREET 40 FT WIDE

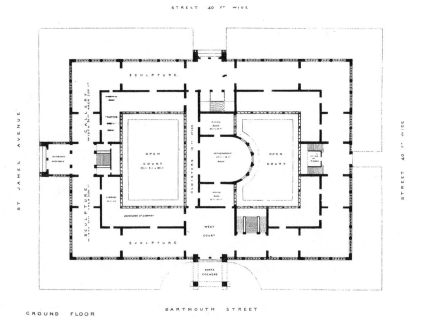

GROUND FLOOR

DARTMOUTH STREET

ST JAMES AVENUE

STREET 40 FT WIDE

THE MUSEUM OF FINE ARTS, BOSTON, MASS.

STURGIS & BRIGHAM, ARCHITECTS.

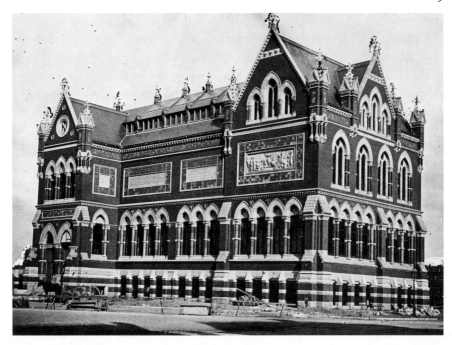

MUSEUM OF FINE ARTS IN COPLEY SQUARE. The first section, opened on 3 July 1876.

a lecture hall. As Dartmouth Street was expected to be the principal thoroughfare in the region, the main entrance, adorned with a porte-cochère, was placed there. The building, which was of fireproof construction, was of red brick, with profuse employment of terra-cotta decoration in two colors, designed by the architects and produced in England by the Blashfield Terra-Cotta Company. By the use of terra cotta for the arches of doors and windows, columns, string-courses, cornices, copings, and ornamental work, including large decorative panels, a physical affinity was suggested with the institutions in South Kensington which had inspired the founders of the Museum of Fine Arts.

Not all of this ambitious plan could be achieved in the first building campaign. It was intended only to build the shorter façade along St. James Avenue, which amounted to approximately one-fifth of the whole, but financial stress made it difficult to obtain even the funds for that portion. While the foundation and basement walls of the entire façade were laid, it was decided for the time being to complete only the central pavilion and the wing that ran west from it to Dartmouth Street.

Beginning in 1876, the Boston Society of Architects adopted the practice of devoting meetings to the examination and criticism of their members' recent work. On 4 February they applied their minds to the New Old South Church, recently completed at the corner of Boylston and Dartmouth streets, by Cummings and Sears. On 7 April they went to Cambridge to consider Ware and Van Brunt's Memorial Hall at Harvard, and on 15 May to Brookline to dissect William G. Preston's Town Hall. On 2 June, John H. Sturgis' nearly completed Museum of Fine Arts was the subject of the fourth of these critiques.

Mr. Tilden waded in with a radical objection. He did not like the Italian Gothic style and would have preferred the classical! His second criticism was equally vigorous; he did not like the combination of ordinary red brick with terra-cotta trimmings. Robert S. Peabody came to Mr. Sturgis' rescue with the observation that the contrast in materials would undoubtedly be decreased by age, as had happened in London both to the Albert Hall and the South Kensington Museum. Henry Van Brunt, although considering terra cotta a valuable material, and the present example of its use interesting, thought the central division of the façade did not differ enough from the pavilions at the end. Charles A. Cummings criticized the general plan as being a confused series of rooms approached through each other, and thought the main staircase quite inadequate in design to its position and uses. This was, of course, the result of having completed at this time less than two-thirds of the first one-fifth of the entire plan.

To all of this criticism Mr. Sturgis amiably pleaded not guilty. The museum's building committee, he stated, chose the style and the terra cotta because of its cheapness and its proof against extremes of weather. Blashfield's terra-cotta panels (even though imported from England) cost $41,000 less than freestone without any decoration. The secretary noted: "Mr. Sturgis closed his defense by defiantly mentioning several weak points in the plan which escaped the keen scent of the critics." In short, he passed the buck to his clients!

At the opening of the museum on 3 July 1876, Charles C. Perkins, whose Italian sojourns, one suspects, had had more than a little to do with the choice of the style, neatly side-stepped the buck when he stated:

It was within the possibilities of any rich and liberal community to erect a handsome and suitable building; but to fill it worthily, which is a much more important matter, might have been impossible without a concurrence of fortunate circumstances. It is not the building which makes the Museum, but the works of art which you place in it. You see before you what these are, and if you examine many of them carefully and intelligently, you will agree with me that to have obtained some of them at all, and all without spending a dollar of the money given by our subscribers, is little short of miraculous.

Some $230,268 had been spent on account of the building, out of $261,425 received from the general subscripton. The largest single gift was that of $25,000 from Mrs. T. Bigelow Lawrence, as long previously promised. Thomas Gold Appleton had subscribed $15,000 and Nathaniel Thayer $10,000. Out of close to a thousand subscriptions, there had been thirteen of $5,000 each, six of $2,000 but the remainder had come in smaller sums, meticulously listed down to three gifts of 50 cents and one of 35 cents. The workmen of Chickering and Sons' piano factory had subscribed $1,404; teachers in public schools, $764; Mayor Gaston and City officers, $362; the employees of the Smith Organ Co., $361. The *Boston Journal* contributed $500 and its employees $76 more, as against $100 each from the *Daily Advertiser, Evening Transcript, Evening Traveller, Commercial Bulletin,* and *Waverley Magazine,* while *The Congregationalist, The True Flag,* and the *Youth's Companion* came in with only $50 each. An anonymous "Believer in Fine Arts" contributed one dollar.

The nucleus of the exhibits was of course the collection assembled over the previous half-century by the Boston Athenæum lent to the new museum. Among these works of art were the unfinished Stuart portraits of George and Martha Washington, Benjamin West's *King Lear,* John Trumbull's *Sortie from Gibraltar,* five Washington Allstons, Albert Bierstadt's *Arch of Octavius,* the Duplessis portrait of Benjamin Franklin, Greuze's enchanting *Femme au chapeau blanc,* a pair of fine Panninis, and such marbles as Thomas Crawford's *Orpheus,* Richard S. Greenough's *Carthaginian Girl,* and a copy of the *Venus de Medici* that Thomas Crawford had greatly admired. Many of these works of art are still lent to the Museum. Others

MARTHA AND GEORGE WASHINGTON. Gilbert Stuart. *Ath. 2 and Ath.* 1 Bought by the Boston Athenæum in 1831 from the artist's heirs and lent to the Museum of Fine Arts since 1876.

BENJAMIN FRANKLIN. Joseph Silfrède Duplessis. *Ath. 4* Bought by the Boston Athenæum from the heirs of Thomas Jefferson in 1828.

CHAPEAU BLANC. Jean Baptiste Greuze. *Ath. 58* Bequeathed to the Boston Athenæum in 1856 by the Cambridgeport leather-dresser Thomas Dowse.

ROMAN PICTURE GALLERY. Giovanni Paolo Pannini. *Ath. 18* One of a set painted
in 1756–57 for the Duc de Choiseul, bought by the Boston Athenæum in 1834.

THE GOLDEN AGE. Attributed to Luca Giordano. *Ath. 42* Given to the Boston
Athenæum by George Washington Wales in 1862; lent to the Museum of Fine
Arts in 1876; now hangs in Newspaper Room at 10 ½ Beacon Street.

borrowed in 1876, like the vast allegorical *Golden Age*, attributed to Luca Giordano, showing the immortal gods picnicking on the greensward in a happy state of nature, and Greenough's *Carthaginian Girl*, eventually wandered into storage and came back to 10 ½ Beacon Street. But John Neagle's great portrait of *Pat Lyon, the Blacksmith, at his Forge*, which the Athenæum bought in 1828, was not wanted by the museum until well into the present century! In 1876 a blacksmith in his working clothes did not appeal to the creators of the Museum of Fine Arts, even though their latter-day successors have happily borrowed and exhibited it.

With space to exhibit, numerous works of art of varying quality were borrowed from private owners. Turner's *The Slave Ship*, which

THE SLAVE SHIP. Joseph Mallord William Turner.
99.22

John Ruskin characterized as "the noblest sea that Turner has ever painted, and if so, the noblest certainly ever painted by man," was lent by Miss Alice S. Hooper, and in 1899 was purchased by the museum. Pottery, porcelains, textiles, embroideries, tapestries, and other examples of decorative arts were borrowed in considerable numbers. It was assumed in the beginning that sculpture other than contemporary would necessarily be represented mostly by plaster casts.

Twenty-five casts were lent by the Athenæum for the opening, while the proceeds of the sale of Charles Sumner's pictures were devoted to the purchase of more. The delayed arrival of casts coming from England prevented the opening of the museum on 1 May 1876 as originally planned, for the ship *Daisy M. Boynton*, which had sailed the previous December with fifty cases of casts, put into the harbor of St. Thomas, Virgin Islands, on 12 February, dismasted and leaky. However, the cases were in good condition, and in due course they arrived, in time to help fill the Sculpture Gallery for the 3 July 1876 opening.

The Committee on the Museum, making preparations for the opening, became troubled about the explicitness of some of the classical casts. The minutes of their meeting of 22 April 1876 conclude thus: "Discussion then ensued on the use of fig leaves, and the question was laid over till the next meeting. Adjourned." In recording the meeting of 18 May, General Loring noted: "The Committee then went to the Sculpture Gallery and on motion it was Voted, That Mr. Ware [William R. Ware, head of the M.I.T. Architectural School] be a committee to procure fig leaves where desirable." This did not settle the matter, for on 29 May the committee returned to the Sculpture Gallery "and motion being put whether fig leaves should be placed on all the statues it was declared lost." Mr. Ware evidently had too much sense of humor to concern himself with the problem, for on 9 June "the matter of putting on fig leaves was referred to Dr. Bigelow [Dr. Henry Jacob Bigelow, Professor of Surgery, Harvard Medical School] with full power." An undated note from C. C. Perkins to General Loring states: "Now that the fig leaf question is settled I wish you would order it done decently and in haste."

Thus on 3 July 1876, pictures being hung and fig leaves in place, the new museum was formally opened. At noon President Brimmer welcomed the guests, Mayor Samuel C. Cobb, Dr. Samuel Eliot, and Charles C. Perkins spoke with creditable brevity, and the company then proceeded to examine the newly installed galleries. The section of the building then finished was only two galleries deep, and extended from the middle of the St. James Avenue frontage west to Dartmouth Street. Entering the pavilion that was to be center of the completed building, one mounted eight steps into the stair hall, where Crawford's *Orpheus*, Harriet Hosmer's *Will-o'-the-wisp*, and Giulio Monteverde's contemporary Italian marble *Il Colombo Giovinetto* were the chief attractions.

At the rear of the hall, to the right of the staircase, was the entrance to a long Egyptian Room that contained not only the Way collection, and a number of Egyptian casts given by General Loring, but some monumental pieces of Egyptian sculpture that had, surprisingly, been in Massachusetts for more than a third of a century already, because of the romantic travels of John Lowell (1799–1836). He, after the death of his wife and daughters from scarlet fever, had in 1831 abandoned the textile business, and set out for the Mediterranean and the East. At Luxor, in Upper Egypt, he bought granite sculptures from the ruins of the great temple of Karnak; there also he fell ill and made a will establishing the Lowell Institute, which became effective when he died at Bombay. Although he never returned to New England, his cumbersome purchases safely arrived. In 1875 his heirs gave the museum — with, one suspects, some pleasure and relief — a great black granite seated statue of the

BLACK GRANITE STATUE OF THE GODDESS SEKHMET. Egypt, 18th Dynasty, from Karnak. *Gift of John A. Lowell and Miss Lowell.* 75.7

EUROPA ON THE BULL and HERAKLES STRANGLING THE NEMEAN LION. Attic
black-figured amphoras. *Gift of Thomas Gold Appleton.* 76.42 and 76.41

goddess Sekhmet, two fine fragments from the broken red granite
obelisk of Queen Hatshepsut, and a colossal royal head of the Eighteenth Dynasty from Karnak.

From this Egyptian Room opened the First Greek Room, containing the Cesnola collection of antiquities from Cyprus, 47 Etruscan
vases, found at Chiusi, given by John James Dixwell in 1876, and 41
Greco-Italian vases given in the same year by the wit Thomas Gold
Appleton, a trustee appointed by Harvard College. His gift included
a pair of entirely respectable late sixth-century Attic black-figured
amphoras, one representing *Europa on the bull* and the other
Herakles strangling the Nemean lion. Here also were casts from
Aegina, Mycenae, Athens, Rome, and London, acquired with the
Sumner bequest. Along the front of the building the Second and
Third Greek rooms contained nothing but casts. Most of these had
been procured through the Sumner bequest, but one, a cast of the

portico of the Caryatides from the Erechtheum, had been presented
by George B. Dorr. The Roman and Renaissance Room, again chiefly
of casts, occupied the remainder of the front of the building.

As one climbed the staircase to the second floor, the walls were
decorated with the Athenæum's *Golden Age,* Miss Deacon's large
Brussels tapestry of *Victory,* by thirty casts from the walls of the
Alhambra, presented by the Spanish Commissioner to the Centennial Exhibition at Philadelphia — who presumably had not found
room for them there — and electrotype reproductions of trophies of
arms and armor, "presented by a former citizen of Boston."

THE LOAN ROOM IN COPLEY SQUARE. Oil by Alice M.
Frye. This view of the northeastern corner of the Loan
Room shows the entrance to the original Picture Gallery
of 1876–1879.

The walls of the Upper Hall were hung with paintings. Along the front of the building was a skylighted Picture Gallery, that led into the Loan Room. This gallery with windows on Dartmouth Street, was devoted to tapestries, pottery, and porcelain of various kinds, a few Japanese bronzes, and other oriental objects, a few cloisonné and Limoges enamels, embroideries, silks, and laces, as well as some

WALL PANELS. Claude-Nicolas Ledoux. *Lent by the Boston Athenæum and* 79.327 Eight panels from the Hôtel de Montmorency in Paris, later installed in the Deacon house, were lent by Harleston Parker in 1876; in 1879 the Museum of Fine Arts and the Boston Athenæum each bought four.

examples of German and Venetian glass. A conspicuous ornament was the series of eight carved oak panels, painted and gilded, nearly 12 feet high, from a room of the Hôtel de Montmorency in Paris, designed by Claude-Nicolas Ledoux between 1770 and 1782. These magnificent examples of Louis XVI decoration, brought from Paris to adorn the Deacon house in Boston, were lent by Harleston Parker. Circular staircases led from the Loan Room to a third-story Photograph Room, where were exhibited a series of Braun's photographs of old master drawings and of Arundel Society chromo-lithographs, lent by the Athenæum.

After returning from this photographic detour, the visitor passed from the Loan Room into the Lawrence Room, which, with the adjacent Engraving Room, occupied the space on the rear of the building behind the Picture Gallery. In the Lawrence Room were

THE LAWRENCE ROOM. Oil by Enrico Meneghelli. 57.675 This shows the appearance of the room between 1876 and 1879; through the door to the Loan Room two of the Hôtel de Montmorency panels may be seen.

THE PICTURE GALLERY, NORTH WALL, 1876–1879. After the enlargement of 1879 this room became the Textile Gallery.

displayed the oak panels, purchased in London, and other examples of carved wood of somewhat dubitable importance, bought by the Athenæum from Signor Castellani, together with various Italian Renaissance bronzes, with the insurance money received from the destruction of the Lawrence collections of arms and armor. Here too were a miscellany of picturesque loans, including a Philippine Island chain cuirass, mounted with buffalo horn, an Igorot shield and lance, various Zulu small arms, and an old Friesland sled with a bas-relief representing Solomon and the Queen of Sheba! In the Engraving Room were housed the collection of prints bequeathed to Harvard University by the late Francis Calley Gray, which were rotated from time to time, while engravings bequeathed by Charles Sumner were hung permanently on the walls. Returning to the Picture Gallery,

the visitor had completed the circuit of the building. Whatever offices
and working spaces there were at this stage must have been in the
basement, for the two main floors were entirely devoted to exhibition.

Even this first section of the museum was a noble accomplishment
for six and a half years of work, for there was clearly three times the
gallery space that had been available on the third floor of the Boston
Athenæum, and this represented only a little more than half of the
portion of the building that it was hoped soon to complete. As Martin
Brimmer pointed out at the dedication: "We have the terra cotta
needed for the rest of the façade, so that the east wing could be
completed and the capacity of the Museum almost doubled for a
comparatively small outlay." The foundations, it will be remembered,
were already laid.

Thomas G. Appleton concluded an anonymous pamphlet, *Boston
Museum of the Fine Arts: A Companion to the Catalogue*, in which
he took an imaginary friend called Starbuck on a tour of the galleries,
with this pitch.

We have made a brilliant beginning, but there is very much to
be done before the Museum is complete. So favorable is the present
opportunity for building the Museum's unfinished front, labor and

MUSEUM OF FINE ARTS AS ENLARGED IN 1879.

materials being low in cost, that it is thought an effort should be
made to do so at once. Sixty or seventy thousand dollars only is
necessary for that which at a more flourishing period might cost a
hundred thousand. May we hope that, if your visit to this little
section of our future great home of Art shall have made you really
its friend, you not only may be tempted to a liberality which you
are sure will be wisely used, but that you will urge your neighbors
and friends to join with us in cordial efforts to complete our plan,
and thus add to our many public institutions and our noble series
of schools this one, which, if our hopes are justified, may prove the
crowning glory of the city we love.

This and similar appeals were heeded, for within three years the
St. James Avenue façade was finished, and the enlarged building
opened on 1 July 1879.

CHAPTER II

The First Decade

The Museum of Fine Arts opened its doors to general visitors on 4 July 1876, centennial of American independence, and was thereafter open on every weekday during the year, except Thanksgiving. Admission was free on Saturdays; on other days the number of paying visitors during the remainder of 1876 was 5,551, an average of 43 a day. Saturdays proved to be quite another matter, for the number admitted then was 33,147, an average of 1,274. The smallest number of visitors on any Saturday was 402; the largest, 2,125, distinctly strained the capacity of the building. To accommodate this demand, after 1 March 1877 the trustees began opening the museum without charge on Sunday afternoons. The total attendance for the year 1877 reached 158,446. This, however, brought little financial assistance to the institution, for less than a tenth of this large number paid admission. The weekday average of visitors was only 63, while the free Saturday average was 1,601 and that of Sundays 1,429. During the next decade total attendance fluctuated between a low of 131,305, in 1878 and a high of 183,155 in 1882, but always with a trickle of paid admissions from Monday to Friday, and a mob on the free weekends. Paid admissions showed a daily average, ranging from 43 to 81; Saturdays fluctuated between 799 (1883) and 1,601 (1877), while Sunday afternoons, which soon became the most popular time in the week, varied from 1,255 (1883) to 1,690 (1881). In addition to the general openings on Saturdays

and Sundays, free admission was given at all times to professional
artists, to students of the department of architecture of the Massachusetts Institute of Technology, of the Free School of Design at the
Lowell Institute, of the State Normal Art School, and of the School
of Drawing and Painting that had been promptly established in the
museum.

As "affording instruction in the Fine Arts" had been one of the
purposes stated in the 1870 charter of the museum, provision had
been made in the basement of the new building of rooms suitable for
drawing classes. While various proposals for such instruction had
been discussed since the autumn of 1874, they had foundered for
lack of the suitable quarters which became available with the opening
of the museum in July 1876. With space to be had, it soon appeared
that, if $5,000 could be raised at once, a school could be opened
before winter. As nearly $3,000 was in hand by mid-September, a
permanent committee was constituted to fit up the rooms and appoint
a teacher of drawing. This committee consisted of the three principal
officers of the museum, Messrs. Martin Brimmer, C. C. Perkins, and
Charles G. Loring; three architects, Edward Clarke Cabot, Robert
S. Peabody, and William R. Ware (also a trustee of the museum);
five painters, William Morris Hunt, John La Farge, Francis William
Loring, Francis D. Millet, and Frank Hill Smith; and Edward W.
Hooper, Treasurer of Harvard College. Although the museum provided the quarters and was eminently represented on the committee,
the School of Drawing and Painting was an independent venture,
responsible for its own finances and operations. Edward C. Cabot
became chairman of this Permanent Committee, William R. Ware
its secretary, and Edward W. Hooper its treasurer. Millet, Hunt,
La Farge, and Smith, designated to appoint a teacher of drawing, engaged Millet's former fellow-student, Otto Grundmann, who arrived
in Boston from Antwerp on 16 December 1876. The school opened
punctually at 9.00 A.M. on 2 January 1877, with eighty pupils.
Edwin G. Champney assisted Grundmann. The sculptor-physician
Dr. William Rimmer offered a course in anatomy in a lecture hall at
the Massachusetts Institute of Technology, around the corner in
Boylston Street, while Professor Ware's M.I.T. lectures on perspec-

tive were available on payment of a small fee. The school offered instruction in painting, drawing from the cast and from life, with exercises in sketching and in drawing from memory, at a moderate price to those who could afford it, as well as free tuition to five students, selected by competitive examination. During the summer of 1877, the museum's trustees permitted the school to complete two additional rooms in the basement of the unfinished east wing. Furnished with skylights, these made admirable painting studios; moreover they made it possible to accommodate as many as 150 students.

The School of Drawing and Painting was an object of particular interest to the founders of the museum; indeed Charles C. Perkins, in the report of the Committee on the Museum for 1877, wrote:

Nowhere has the wisdom of giving works of art an educational bearing been more completely shown than in our Museum since the establishment of the Drawing School, whose busy, earnest life permeates the whole building, gives animation to its halls, and convinces those who have labored to make it promote the artistic growth of this commonwealth, that they have not labored in vain. Without the Drawing School, the Museum was like a body without a soul; with it, it is alive. The objects of beauty in its collection attract the students, and even when they are not directly engaged in copying them, give them new ideas of form, color, and design. Casts, stuffs, pictures, engravings, are constantly utilized, and a never-ceasing influence for good goes out from them, to charm, to elevate, to instruct, and to delight those who are brought in contact with them, day after day, and week after week. Thanks to the present advantages for study offered at the Museum, the number of absentees among our artists has diminished. Formerly it was out of the question for anyone who wished to study art seriously to remain in Boston, if he could afford to cross the Atlantic. A few determined spirits frequented the spasmodic Life School opened in the cellar of the Art Club, and here and there isolated efforts showed the need of more ample care for artistic needs, but none of an adequate character was taken until the Museum and the Drawing School joined hands, and made this city as good a place of residence for the art student as any of the cities of Europe, excepting the great capitals.

The Museum ran in the most modest way, relying heavily upon the voluntary services of its trustees, and especially of Charles C. Perkins, its Honorary Director. Charles G. Loring as Curator received the modest salary of $2,000, raised to $3,000 in 1879. In the first year the paid staff consisted of six persons: a janitor and engineer, at $65 a month; an assistant to relieve the janitor on Sundays and one evening in the week, at $10; a ticket-seller, at $12 per week; a male custodian, at $12.50; a female custodian, at $9, and a doorkeeper at $6. In 1877 it became necessary to employ a clerk for General Loring at the modest salary of $500 a year, while the cost of the Sunday openings added another $500 to the ordinary expenses. Even with this frugal staff, the museum was far from being self-sufficient, for the general operating expenses amounted to $16,330, while receipts from admissions were only $3,879, income from investments $3,500, and proceeds from the sales of catalogues $1,896. The excellent descriptive catalogues, which were often reprinted, paid their way, for they cost only $1,222 to produce, but the huge numbers of free visitors, however welcome they were, led to a persistent annual deficit that could only be offset at some time in the future by raising an endowment fund.

The most pressing need, however, was to complete the St. James Avenue façade of the building, for, with the burgeoning attendance and the increase in the collections through loans and gifts, there simply was not room enough to turn around in the section completed in 1876. Thus at the annual meeting in January 1878 the trustees appointed a committee to appeal for funds for this purpose, with the stipulation that the addition not be undertaken until $100,000 had been subscribed. Within a few months $126,003 had been subscribed and paid. On 2 April 1878, when the $100,000 mark had been reached, the Building Committee was authorized to let contracts for the completion of the front, according to the plans of Messrs. Sturgis and Brigham. The work was soon undertaken; by November the new galleries were roofed in, and before the end of the year the basement rooms were already in use. The new east wing was completed in the spring of 1879; after a month's closing in June to complete the rearrangement of collections, the enlarged museum was reopened on 1 July 1879.

Charles C. Perkins, in the Committee on the Museum's report for 1878, commented on the manner in which the external completion of the new wing had improved the appearance of the building.

> Many who were slow to recognize its beauty when the façade was half finished, now frankly acknowledge it; and certainly, as a structural and decorative manifestation of an intended use, it merits admiration. No intelligent person, seeing it for the first time, could possibly take it for anything but a Museum; and such revelation of the end in the aspect is a cardinal virtue in any piece of man's work, whether it be a teacup or a cathedral, a salt-cellar or a museum.

There were, unfortunately, at the entrance, three vacant pedestals that were to have been occupied by terra-cotta figures of Architecture, Sculpture, and Painting, modeled by the local sculptor Frank Dengler, who had, for a short time, been in charge of the modeling class in the Drawing School. He had, however, died suddenly, leaving models that were too incomplete to permit their use as intended.

The architect Arthur Rotch, describing the museum in the 30 October 1880 issue of *The American Architect and Building News*, noted that

> A visitor to the Boston Museum of Fine Arts usually finds waiting before it hackney carriages, which are evidently those of tourists, and by this we are reminded that the institution is of more than local interest. The foreign tourist will not, to be sure, be greeted by an obsequious and shabby individual who offers to explain the collections in one's native tongue, spoken more fluently than intelligibly; this height of civilization we have not yet reached.

Nor, thank heaven, have we reached it in the ninety years that have followed! Arthur Rotch's hypothetical foreign visitor then offers some of his impressions of the institution.

> As he pauses before the portion of the proposed building, which for the present constitutes the Museum, he will perhaps be startled by the contrast of the red brick and yellow terra-cotta against the pitiless American sky, and wonder what prejudice favored a granite

basement, whose crude white strikes a harsh note in the façade. The architecture, however, is good in character, and needs no inscription to announce the purpose of the building.

The enlargement of the building permitted considerable expansion of the collections. The large new room at the east end of the first floor, higher ceilinged than the others, was set aside for plaster casts of architectural subjects, deposited by the Massachusetts Institute of

A RICH PROFUSION OF PLASTER CASTS. Copies of the Aegina pediments as exhibited in Copley Square.

Technology. Some 614 casts fell into the following divisions: Greek and Roman, 95; Byzantine, 19; Gothic, 299; Moorish, 143; and Renaissance, 58. The other adjacent new rooms were devoted to casts of Italian Renaissance sculpture, and to the Greek collection of vases, the Cypriote glass and pottery, and Tanagra figurines, which had been removed from the First Greek Room. As Perkins remarked: "Making the circuit of the rooms on the first floor of the Museum, a peripatetic lecturer might now discourse upon the history of sculpture in Egypt, Assyria, Greece and Rome, with examples before him of almost every phase of its rise and decline." As new casts had come from London, Paris, Berlin, Rome, and Athens to fill chronological gaps, the whole collection had been rearranged, to such purpose that, he stated:

We have now by far the best collection of casts in the United States, and one of the best in the world. Among them are such masterpieces as the splendid Hermes with the Infant Dionysus, by Praxiteles, lately discovered at Olympia; the noble Amazon bas-relief from the Villa Albani; several fine sarcophagi from the Vatican; one of the great bas-reliefs from the Arch of Titus; and a number of stêles and fragments, some of which are not to be found in the great collection of casts at Berlin or Paris.

THE PRINT ROOMS IN COPLEY SQUARE.

On the second floor, the Gray engravings were transferred to two specially fitted rooms on the back of the new wing. The prints were arranged first by nationality; all the works of Italian, German, French, Dutch, and English engravers were kept in separate divisions, in each of which the prints were arranged chronologically, according to the dates of the engravers. In one room several hundred of the finest specimens, such as the Rembrandts and Dürers, were kept permanently on exhibition in glazed showcases, while in the adjoining room the contents were changed every six weeks, making the entire collection available by rotation. In the room formerly occupied by the Gray engravings, and in the adjacent Lawrence Room, "the South Kensington aspect," as Arthur Rotch put it, developed. Here, he wrote:

The halls to the left of the vestibule are filled with different kinds of bric-à-brac which in spite of a name associated with *dilettanti* collectors, includes objects of the greatest importance to industrial interests. A recognition of this fact is found in the recent creation of the Hôtel Cluny. The narrow and mistaken views of art which made directors of French museums overlook inestimable opportunities of collecting treasures of medieval art may be measured by the importance now attached to the fine museum of Gothic art in Munich.

The former Picture Gallery, on the front of the west wing, had been converted for the display of textiles. The walls were hung with tapestries, separated from each other by the eight splendid carved panels from the Hôtel de Montmorency, earlier lent by Harleston Parker, which the Museum and the Boston Athenæum bought from him. "On this acquisition," Perkins remarked, "we may well congratulate ourselves, for it may be safely said that an opportunity of purchasing objects of like character and excellence will not probably soon occur."

The Loan Room, now rechristened the West Room, continued to be used for the exhibition of a great variety of objects — pottery, porcelain, bronzes, and the like — lent to the museum. Before long it began to contain remarkable examples of Japanese art. In 1880 Dr. William Sturgis Bigelow, the son of Dr. Henry Jacob Bigelow (the trustee charged with the application of fig leaves), lent 111 pieces of Japanese lacquer, 35 pieces of stuff and embroideries, 6 examples of wood and ivory carving, 19 bronzes, 18 pieces of pottery and porcelain, 116 swords and 177 *netsuke*, mostly of ivory. The following year he lent 509 Japanese objects. As Edward Cunningham of Milton, whose family had China Trade connections, lent more than 100 Chinese porcelains, lacquers, bronzes, and jades in 1881, the West Room began to have a distinctively Oriental quality.

In the new wing, opening from the front of the upper hall, was the new picture gallery. In addition to numerous paintings lent by the Athenæum and private owners, there were now a visible number permanently owned by the museum, such as Corot's *Dante and Virgil entering the Inferno* and *Nymphs Bathing* (given by James Davis,

THE FIRST PICTURE GALLERY, AFTER 1879. Oil by Enrico
Meneghelli. 61.238 This sketch shows the view from the Hall,
looking through the gallery to the steps leading to the Allston
Room.

1876), Millet's *The Sewing Lesson* and *Woman Milking a Cow*
(both from Martin Brimmer, 1876), Gustave Doré's *Summer* (gift of
Richard Baker, 1873), and the *Wood Interior* by François Louis
Français (given by Edward Darley Boit, 1879). Beyond this gallery,
on the front of the building, opened the Allston Room, by no means
completely devoted to that artist, for it contained various Italian
paintings, as well as the Stuart portrait of Mayor Josiah Quincy,
given by his daughter, Eliza Susan Quincy, in 1876, and the John
Trumbull portraits of Mr. and Mrs. Stephen Minot, given by Susan
I. Minot in 1879. The Water-Color Room, in the back of the build-

PRIAM RANSOMING THE BODY OF
HECTOR. Jacques Louis David.
Gift of Mrs. John Cheney. 77.151

ing, was equally imprecisely named, for it contained a strong preponderance of oil paintings. Among those that permanently belonged to the museum were Albert Cuyp's *The Artist's Daughter*, bequeathed by Senator Sumner and kept rather than sold, David's sketch *Priam Ransoming the Body of Hector*, given by Mrs. John Cheney in 1877, and a School of Rubens representation of a very fat, drunken, and naked Bacchus, with attendant satyr and faun, that had been bought in 1879 from the income of the Everett Fund. This fund, the principal of which amounted to $7,500, had been given to the museum by a committee who had been so successful in raising money for a statue of Edward Everett that they had funds left over; until 1880, when Benjamin P. Cheney bequeathed $5,000 for similar use, it was the only fund whose income was available for the purchase of works of art.

The slender income available for purchases led Charles C. Perkins in the 1881 report to lament, in a manner still common today among museum directors, the steadily rising prices of the art market.

Knowing that other chances of equal importance may arise, we could wait with greater patience, did we not also know that every year increases the number of purchasers, and raises the scale of prices which objects of any merit will bring in London or Paris. Within a year we have seen a rare Syracusan coin, the full-faced Arethusa, valued at fifty pounds according to previous sales, sold at auction for one hundred and thirty pounds; an enamelled locket of rock crystal, esteemed by an excellent judge at thirty pounds, brought two thousand pounds; and a Kylix of uncommon interest acquired by the British Museum for four hundred pounds, which some years ago might have been bought for a third of that sum. Such instances show that there is really no limit to the prices which museum officials and rich amateurs are ready to pay for objects which they wish to acquire.

The history of auction sales in the years that have passed since Perkins' death bears out the truth of his statement. Alas, there was all too little likelihood of being able to buy before further increases, for Martin Brimmer had pointed out in 1880, when the operating deficit was $7,242, that in view of the large annual cost of maintaining the museum, the trustees would hardly be justified in adding to the collections beyond what could be achieved with the income of the Everett and Cheney funds, whose combined capital was only $12,500. A bequest of $10,000 was received from Nathaniel C. Nash in 1880. The following year John Lowell Gardner had given a welcome fund of $20,000, the income only of which was to be used. Although this gift was encouraging, the annual yield of $900 was far from eliminating the alarming deficits that occurred annually. Similarly, the bequest of $5,000 received in 1882 from Otis Norcross, one of the original trustees, was helpful without really solving the problem. Larger sums were needed to achieve solvency.

In his *Art in Education*, prepared for the American Social Science Association, C. C. Perkins had proved himself a poor prophet by predicting that a museum of the type that he proposed "would rapidly become self-supporting, even with one to two days' free admission a week." He had, moreover, quoted "the pertinent words" of an unnamed "American writer" in support of this view. This optimistic and promotionally minded precursor of the ad-man had written:

Were one of our great towns to own a great museum, visitors would flock there from all parts of the Union in such numbers as would soon repay its outlay, and leave it, as it were, a free gift to posterity, with a prolific income for the benefit of the citizens at large. The pecuniary gain would be none the less, because chiefly flowing in from indirect sources. Providence so regulates cause and effect that the best things morally, intellectually, and aesthetically, are certain of the best consequences, in not merely these respects, but ultimately in material well-being. To use an expressive American phrase, Central Parks "pay." So do national museums, as that city will discover which is the first to found one on a Central Park scale of organization and administration.

Whatever the intellectual and human dividends from Central Parks and great museums may be, their financial returns are seldom encouraging. Private citizens of Boston had built a museum and filled it with collections. The only public support that they had received was the gift of the land on which the museum stood. Visitors *had* flocked there in great numbers, but those who arrived in hackney carriages and paid admission on weekdays were too small a group to insure "a prolific income for the benefit of the citizens at large," or even bare solvency for the museum.

In spite of unbalanced budgets and pitifully slender funds for acquisition, the 1879 addition to the museum permitted considerable expansion both in school instruction and in temporary exhibitions. As the completion of the east wing deprived the School of Drawing and Painting of its temporary skylighted studio in the unfinished basement, the third-story room in the west wing, fitted out in 1876 for the exhibition of photographs, was given as a substitute. The Museum of Fine Arts provided basement space for other educational ventures than the School of Drawing and Painting. Rooms were given to a School for Art Needlework and a School of Carving and Modelling directed by John Evans, both of which were founded by the Women's Educational Association. These, which like the School of Pottery and Painting on Porcelain, sponsored by the Society of Decorative Art, were created chiefly as a means of teaching crafts to women obliged to support themselves, proved impermanent. The School of Art Needlework faded away in 1879; the other two soon followed, for lack of enthusiasm.

The School of Drawing and Painting, however, proved to be not only useful but permanent, in a modest and economical way. When it opened, William R. Ware, as Secretary of the School, gave the class of 1877 a talking-to about standards of decorum. H. Winthrop Peirce, one of the class, fifty years later recalled Ware's warning that it had not been easy to obtain consent to have a School installed in the Museum; that there were very grave doubts of the wisdom of exposing the valuable collections of the Museum to the possible depradations of irresponsible young people who, if nothing worse happened, would soil the floors with their paint and charcoal and probably break the glass cases, and that it behooved the class to be most circumspect in their conduct while in the Museum.

This was heeded for, continued Peirce: "Nothing happened, no damage was done, the class proved its trustworthiness and its appreciation of the great privileges it enjoyed, and convinced everyone (but the Janitor) that it was to be trusted." This skeptical functionary, the "faithful, devoted, self-important Mr. Chapin, so invaluable and so exasperating," completely identified himself with the museum. His devotion to General Loring, the Curator, was so intense that a visitor, who asked Chapin if a large plant in the Egyptian Room belonged to the papyrus family, was sharply told: "No, it don't. It belongs to the Loring family."

Otto Grundmann, a Saxon by birth, whose long hair, very wide-brimmed hat, flowing tie, and marked foreignness, conformed to the current stereotype of a painter, continued as head of the school until his untimely death in 1890. The school was an object of popular interest and curiosity, for Winthrop Peirce recalled that "important looking people were constantly being shown through the class rooms. Among perfectly indifferent officials, the Postmaster of Boston, the President of the Boston and Maine Railroad, and the like, there were others who were obviously interested." In the latter group a favorite was Thomas G. Appleton, a unique specimen on the Boston scene. This dilettante son of the textile manufacturer and merchant, Nathan Appleton, made art, poetry, and collecting a substitute for a profession. Although his talk was so sparkling that Dr. Holmes alleged that he "has spilled more good things on the wasteful air in conversation than would carry a 'diner-out' through half a dozen London seasons," his advice, assistance, and contributions were eagerly sought by his neighbors when the serious business of founding a learned institution was considered. Tom Appleton had been one of the first trustees of the Boston Public Library in 1852; he was one of Harvard's first appointments to the board of the Museum of Fine Arts, and now he was a frequent visitor to the School of Drawing and Painting, always, as Winthrop Peirce recalled, "with the tallest of tall hats, and the smartest of topcoats and canes, looking like a Thackeray baronet, or the marquis in a French comedy, celebrated for his audacious wit and lavish buying of pictures, loved by young painters, to whom he was a generous patron and a joyous host. He was in Boston a solitary example of a type more the Medicean than the Bostonian, admired but not quite approved of."

In the second year, when the more advanced pupils drew or painted from models posing for the head, the idea of a life class arose. While this was under discussion, William R. Ware told the students that "the horror of some of the Trustees at the idea of a nude model in their chaste Museum of Fine Arts was too great to be overcome." The project was postponed, though not for long, for Ernest Wadsworth Longfellow, son of the poet, who was just home from Italy and was painting in Cambridge, obtained permission to use one of the schoolrooms that was empty in the afternoon. Ernest Longfellow, according to Peirce,

> asked the men of the drawing class to join him in drawing from the nude, his permission being, he told us, strictly limited to the male nude. The cost of the model was shared by the class. Those who availed themselves of this chance to study the figure met on certain afternoons with a carefully locked door, to enjoy the sense of being in opposition to their elders, always so dear to youth.

With this entering wedge, the first formal life class was opened during the third year of the school. There was, of course, a letter to the *Transcript*, considering the function and history of the nude in art, with comment on the serious, respectable, hard-working occupation of the male model. The writer described the life-class room, which he was surprised to find so bare, with an utter lack of the "velvet hangings, tapestry, and carved furniture associated with studios"; he further noted how, during the rest period, "the shapely young model" could be seen looking at the various drawings of himself, "like Adam wandering through the art galleries of Eden."

The third-floor room given the school in 1879 was, in Winthrop Peirce's recollection, so "wide, high, and beautifully lighted, it was abandoned with regret" when the school and the museum left Copley Square thirty years later. When Dr. William Rimmer died in the summer of 1879, the painter Frederic Crowninshield, recently returned from a decade of study in Europe, took over the instruction in anatomy, and, until he removed to New York in 1886, assisted Otto Grundmann in the drawing and painting classes. Crowninshield built himself a studio, which proved a genial gathering place for students out of hours, for it was beyond the domain of the redoubtable janitor, Mr. Chapin.

The students behaved well and maintained a high *esprit de corps.* In 1879 they formed the Boston Art Students' Association, with H. Winthrop Peirce as its President. Originally restricted to members and ex-members of the School of Drawing and Painting, when it was later enlarged to include persons interested in art not connected with the school, it changed its name to the Copley Society. But while still in its restricted form it began in June 1882 the publication of an occasional short-lived periodical called *The Art Student.* Students' work was reproduced, including sketches made during an 1882 summer outing to Richmond in the Berkshires. One of the students, having just read Lalanne's treatise on etching, tried his hand at the medium to provide a frontispiece for the December 1882 issue. Thus Frank W. Benson's first print, *Salem Harbor,* appeared in the second number of *The Art Student,* although thirty years were to pass before he etched another plate.

An early group photograph of students, posed before the Copley Square museum, shows Benson — immensely tall and jaunty in a

SALEM HARBOR. Etching by Frank
W. Benson, 1882

boater — as well as Edmund C. Tarbell, and Holker Abbott, who, according to Peirce, "elected to be a worker for art rather than a producer which, in view of what he has accomplished, one should not regret." They worked hard in class, and out of hours enjoyed creating a *vie de Bohème* with like-minded elders. During an Artists' Festival in the museum, William R. Ware came disguised as Sophocles, proving to Winthrop Peirce that "there was at least one middle-aged Yankee who could come as a Greek statue, and look the part." Francis D. Millet, who lectured on Greek and Roman dress at the school and had done the stage setting and costumes for the Harvard production of Sophocles' *Oedipus Tyrannus* in 1881, was seized by the dramatic possibilities of the museum's new picture gallery, which at the east end had a few white marble stairs, leading to the adjacent Allston Room. By hanging a curtain in the arch, above them, he created a stage on which pupils of the school and young male models could be posed in *tableaux vivants* before a select audience who gladly paid the then high price of $2.00 a ticket for the benefit of some worthy cause. On 21 and 22 April 1885, when money was being raised for the eventual purchase by subscription of Henri Regnault's *Automedon with the Horses of Achilles*, the cast included Otto Grundmann as Zeus, and Holker Abbott as a Greek soldier, supported by thirty or more pretty girls.

C. Howard Walker had in the year 1884–85 established a department of decorative design in the school. When Frederic Crowninshield migrated to New York two years later, Joseph R. De Camp and Miss Lillian Greene took over his classes. In 1889, the former students Edmund C. Tarbell and Frank W. Benson, now becoming established as painters, took charge respectively of the Painting and Antique classes. Otto Grundmann, whose health had become precarious, took a year's leave and sailed for Europe in 1890. As he died at Dresden on 27 August, Benson and Tarbell added his work to theirs, and settled down for a period of continuous and productive teaching that lasted for almost a quarter of a century. When Philip L. Hale joined them in the nineties, he took over the classes drawing from the cast, while Tarbell continued to teach painting and Benson directed students drawing and painting from the nude model. They were subsequently joined by the sculptor Bela L. Pratt, who taught modeling, and, at various times, by Dr. George H. Monks, and Dr. Edward W. Emerson, who gave courses in artistic anatomy.

The Museum of Fine Arts and its school had one great moment on the nation's artistic stage when in 1908, through the personal interest of President Theodore Roosevelt, Dr. William Sturgis Bigelow and Bela L. Pratt collaborated in the designs for the $5 and $2 ½ gold coins, using the incised effects of Egyptian reliefs in the museum to achieve their revolutionary designs.

A student's-eye view of the school in the late nineties is recorded in the diaries of Marian Lawrence, a daughter of the Right Reverend William Lawrence, Bishop of Massachusetts, who was one of its students on and off from the time she was eighteen until her marriage to Harold Peabody in 1906, despite interruptions caused by her considerable American and European travels. She began with Philip L. Hale, who was then teaching drawing from the cast, whom she described as "an excellent teacher, but alas, nobody wanted his pictures." When in 1897 he criticized unfavorably her drawing of *David*'s hair, she said, "I didn't know you meant me to copy each curl, it takes so much time." He turned to face her and said in his serious but gentle way, "If Michelangelo took the time to sculpt them I think you could take the time to copy them more carefully." As a result of this kind of gentle correction, she set seriously to work, and a few weeks later in May 1897 won the Concours for the Antique with her drawing of the Apoxyomenos. She was greatly cheered by the award, although at her father's suggestion she let the $50 prize money go to the runner-up. While Hale's own paintings never enjoyed the success of Tarbell's and Benson's, he had great gifts as a teacher, which incidentally very probably enhanced the talents of his wife, Lillian C. Westcott, whom he married in 1902, and who became an abler painter than he.

Marian Lawrence in February 1898 moved on to the life class, then held in Frederic Crowinshield's old studio, which had been moved to the lot behind the Copley Square museum. This she described as "a most unhealthy place, heated by a big stove, near which one roasted and far from which one froze." There she had useful criticism from Benson, which trained her to progress to Tarbell's portrait class, in which an unexpected crisis arose when she discovered her esteemed skating teacher posing on the model stand.

It *was* embarrassing; and ridiculous too. I didn't know whether to bow or not to bow and I hastily arranged my things to do his back thinking this would be the more tactful place to take. But I soon found that in order to get off the stand for rest periods he had practically to jump over me so it was the worst place I could have chosen. After two days of struggling not to catch his eye I decided that it was more sensible to bow, which I did and he said "Good morning, Miss Lawrence," with great dignity.

The School of Drawing and Painting operated under the direction of its own Permanent Committee, which raised modest funds for equipment and prizes. As the museum charged no rent for the use of rooms and collections, the expenses of the school were normally met from the fees paid by students. Although relations were friendly, there was long a tentative air of impermanence about the whole undertaking. The Permanent Committee, in its 1882 report, observed: "At present it occupies its quarters in the Museum somewhat on the footing of a poor relation. The Trustees of the Museum cannot venture to adopt it into their family and assure it a permanent home with them till it has funds of its own enough to assure them that it will not become a burden." This relationship was made more explicit in a memorandum printed in the museum's 1883 annual report concerning the position of the trustees in regard to education in the fine arts. Prepared by Professor William R. Ware, Secretary of the school's Permanent Committee, and approved by the museum trustees on 15 August 1881, this document pointed out the trustees' policy of allowing various schools to occupy rooms in the museum rent free, charging only for heating and cleaning. As the classes were temporary and tentative, without permanent endowments, the trustees, having satisfied themselves that the direction of the classes was in good hands, had asserted no further control or right of visitation. But if such instruction were to receive permanent endowment, the trustees would feel it obligatory upon them to assume care of the funds and take responsibility for the general direction of the instruction. They would insist that such endowments be ample, so that the museum should in no case be forced for its own credit to supplement those funds from its own resources. The trustees declared themselves prepared to receive and expend any sufficient funds that might be placed in their hands to promote education in the fine arts as well as in the industrial and decorative arts, erecting the necessary building, purchasing the necessary collections, and directing the necessary instruction. This memorandum seems to have been a wise *caveat* against permitting the extensive educational tail, created in the first flush of enthusiasm in 1876, from wagging the museum's dog, which was having a hard enough time keeping its four feet balanced on the ground.

More than a decade and a half was to pass before the School of Drawing and Painting received any permanent funds of a magnitude that would warrant a closer tie with the museum. During the academic year 1897–98, the twenty-second of the school's operation, J. William Paige bequeathed $30,000 to the trustees of the Museum of Fine Arts, provided $10,000 should be added to it by 16 July 1899, to create a fund whose income should be used to send a pupil of the school abroad every year for a two-year term, with a stipend of $800 a year. The contingent sum was secured by the appointed time, and the scholarship inaugurated. Robert Charles Billings at his death in 1899 left the school the sum of $100,000 as a permanent fund. As the school was not incorporated, this fund was placed by the Supreme Court in the hands of the museum's trustees, to be held by them for the benefit of the school. As Edward W. Hooper, Treasurer of the Permanent Committee, had died at the end of the school's twenty-fifth year, the survivors of the committee petitioned the trustees in October 1901 asking

(1) That this School be now recognized by your Board as belonging to the Museum, and intrusted with the responsibility of doing a part of its educational work;
(2) That your Board assume control of the School;
(3) That the School be known officially as the "School of the Museum of Fine Arts," be entitled to use the seal of the Museum, with the words "Museum School" attached.

As favorable action was taken on 30 October 1901, the twenty-sixth annual report bore for the first time the title "School of the Museum of Fine Arts." The poor relation had, at last, been taken into the family, but only because rich relatives had made bequests!

Returning to earlier years, the Library, as a separate department of the museum, was established with its own basement room in 1880, in charge of Edward H. Greenleaf, who had been Secretary of the Museum from 1878. At this point, Greenleaf became the first full-time professional member of the staff other than the Curator, acting not only as Librarian but as Curator of the Gray engravings, and as an assistant to the Curator, General Loring.

During 1878, before the completion of the new wing, two special exhibitions were held in the Gray Room, one of woodcuts in the spring, and a second of etchings, chiefly by American artists, in the autumn. With the additional freedom made possible by enlarged galleries, temporary exhibitions multiplied in size and number. The death of William Morris Hunt on 8 September 1879 inspired a large memorial exhibition of his work later in the autumn. Two hundred and two of Hunt's oils and over a hundred charcoal drawings and pastels were shown, beginning 11 November 1879. A sixty-page catalogue, containing an essay by John C. Dalton, prepared for the occasion, went through four editions. The exhibition aroused such interest that, although scheduled to close on 15 December, it was extended through January 1880. Indeed, on one Sunday afternoon, no less than 4,400 persons crowded in to see it. This was in sharp contrast to an exhibition of Contemporary Art, held the previous spring in conjunction with the Boston Art Club, which opened on 22 April 1879 and closed on 24 May. Although more than eight hundred pictures, water colors, drawings, marbles, and bronzes were sent by contributors from all parts of the United States, the show failed to attract the wide attention that it merited.

The Hunt exhibition was followed by the showing of 112 portraits by Gilbert Stuart, which included many brought from a distance, from 3 May to 15 October 1880. There followed a display of works of living American artists, which was more enthusiastically received than its predecessor in 1879; a memorial exhibition of 124 drawings, paintings, and sculpture by Dr. William Rimmer, who had died on 20 August 1879; the showing of 160 drawings and paintings by, and engravings after, William Blake, brought to this country by Mrs. Alexander Gilchrist, the widow of Blake's biographer; and finally the exhibition of 160 drawings and water colors by John Ruskin, lent by

Professor Charles Eliot Norton, a trustee of the museum. In 1881 there were large exhibitions of American etchers, of the works of Washington Allston, and of American wood engravings, all with published catalogues, as well as smaller showings of Christmas cards designed for Messrs. Prang and Co. and of colored glass, designed and executed by John La Farge.

The variety and quality of objects exhibited in the years 1879–1881 attracted wide attention; in 1882 attendance reached a new high of 183,155, but as always less than 10 percent of these paid admission. The figure, like many statistics, is not strictly trustworthy, for in 1882 for the first time the pupils of the school were passed through the registry gate on their way to classes. Nevertheless, even the enlarged building was getting crowded, for the Committee on the Museum reported:

> We feel bound to repeat our annual complaint of want of space to exhibit what we have fitly, and our want of means to increase the collections already made. Any one who enters the so-called Loan Room, for instance, when it is comparatively empty of visitors, must perceive its overcrowded state, and he who goes there on a free day, will be uncomfortably impressed with the fact. This want of room is not only to be regretted because it makes all convenient study of the many valuable objects there difficult at any time, and impossible on free days, but also because it is a source of danger. Again, it is certain that nothing contributes so much to the real enjoyment of, and the good to be derived from a work of art as freedom from oppressive interruption in the process of examining it. Some inconvenience is unavoidable at times in a Museum, but we submit that in our case much could be done towards reducing it to a minimum by increasing our accommodations. This should be done as soon as possible, either by adding another side to the present edifice, or by putting up a temporary building on the vacant lot, to which the casts could be removed, leaving the halls, which they now fill to overflowing, to be used for the placing of many objects now crowded together in the rooms of the second story.

During 1883 the trustees instructed the Executive Committee to propose plans for an enlargement of the building. The solution favored was to build, at the same time, sections of wings extending south along both Dartmouth Street and Trinity Place, which would give an opportunity for the symmetrical growth and development of all departments. The plans prepared by Sturgis and Brigham provided for an additional floor space of some 6,780 square feet on each of the principal stories. On the first story the greater part of the new space would be given to casts of sculpture, and the remainder to antiquities. On the second story the extension of the west wing would be used for decorative arts. The new east wing would provide for additional pictures and engravings, as well as a large room for temporary exhibitions, which would avoid the present dilemma of displacing pictures in the main gallery whenever a temporary showing of new material was scheduled. There were, however, no funds clearly in sight for these improvements; moreover the annual deficit of $7,870 from operating expenses, paid from unrestricted funds, had reduced such funds to about $34,000. "It is plain," Martin Brimmer pointed out, "that this state of affairs cannot last long." Charles C. Perkins in the same 1882 report observed: "While the Museum exists it must either increase or decrease; for, like all other things in this world, it cannot stand still. Give it room for growth, and there need be no apprehension as to the result; cramp it and leave it to struggle with insufficient resources, and the fair promise of its early years will never be fulfilled." There was also the urgent need of providing increased assistance for General Loring:

> For want of helping hands, much which should be done is left undone, and the chief officer is overwhelmed with work which he should not be called upon to do. Ever active, in season and out of season, he has made the interests of the Museum his own ever since they were first confided to him; and it is incumbent upon us to show our appreciation of his unflagging zeal by relieving him as far as possible from doing personally what others can do equally well under his direction, in order to leave him time to do what no one can do so well as himself.

Thus in the autumn of 1883 the Committee on the Museum prepared a special report on the increase of the collections, which amounted to a reassessment of policies for the future. To accomplish the broad purposes stated in the museum's charter requires "careful economy of our narrow space and our limited funds." The committee proposed:

> In using our space, the first object should be to give it to those things which have the greatest interest and beauty; the second, to secure the proportionate growth of all the departments of the museum.
>
> In using our funds, we must be governed by substantially the same considerations; with this distinction, that while we can have no more room for the collections than we can afford to build, we can fortunately exhibit many more works of art than we can pay for. As a rule, original work is beyond our means. Sculpture of the best periods is absolutely out of our reach. Of pictures, drawings, and engravings by good masters, and of the finest examples of decorative art, we could buy but a small number. The whole value of our collections depends substantially upon two resources: the one, that costly original works are collected by many persons who generously lend or give them to the Museum for the public benefit; the other, that, in sculpture and some of the other arts in which the best examples are not procurable either by the Museum or by individuals, reproductions of almost equal value for study can be had at a reasonable cost.
>
> It seems, then, too plain for argument that we must rely principally upon the liberality of others for original works of art, and that we should spend the greater part of the money available for purchases in buying reproductions. Upon what plan these should be bought is the important point to determine.

After detailed consideration of the types of reproductions that are most appropriate, the committee addressed itself to the circumstances that should justify the exceptional instances in which original works of art should be purchased. These were:

> *First.* When the Museum, by joining in or supplementing a subscription, can make a desirable acquisition by a comparatively small outlay.
>
> *Second.* When there is an opportunity to obtain a work of decora-

tive art which would be of value as a study for designers. In regard
to this, it is to be remembered that the Museum has always received
a generous support from gentlemen who were partly moved by the
conviction that many manufactures could be benefitted by free
access to well selected examples of design.

Third. When a good representative work of a Boston artist, especially of the older school, can be bought, it being one of the functions of every museum to put on its walls a fair exhibition of the
progress of local art; and

Fourth. When an exceptional chance is offered to secure a work
of permanent value at small cost.

It was then pointed out that up to 1 January 1883 the trustees had
spent $18,005 for reproductions, chiefly casts of sculpture, and
$7,756 for original works, of which $1,912 was for painting and
sculpture of American artists, and $4,824 for works of decorative art.

The general conclusion of this somewhat Scottish sounding document was that to frame a scheme for the purchase of original works
of art was practicable only in the most general way. To make the
ideal a reality, "we shall have to do exactly what other collectors do,
— watch opportunities and seize them, try to fill the important gaps
first, and keep the growth of the Museum proportionate in all its
parts."

In 1884 there were still no funds for building in sight, while a
deficit of $10,293 had reduced the unrestricted funds of the museum
to about $25,000. However there was a cheering bequest of $100,000
from Harvey D. Parker, a farm boy from Maine who had prospered
in Boston as proprietor of the Parker House. This sum on receipt was
to be invested as a permanent fund, of which the income would be
used for the support of the museum. This would clearly help reduce
future deficits, although it would by no means eliminate them, even
if no major projects were added. And it was unfortunately true, as
C. C. Perkins pointed out in the report of the Committee on the Museum, that "the collections are as ill at ease within bounds long since
too narrow for their disposal, as a growing boy who, for want of
means to purchase a new suit of clothes, must crowd himself into the
old one which he had even last year outgrown."

Although through limitations of space there was but one special exhibition in 1884 — a memorial to George Fuller (1822–1884) held from 24 April to 13 May — this attracted more interest than anything since the tribute to William Morris Hunt. And the year was marked also by the gift by the Archaeological Institute of America of a large collection of antiquities excavated at Assos in Asia Minor under the Institute's auspices. The 156 sculptured or inscribed fragments of marble and stone, 344 pieces of pottery, 27 of glass, 3 of gold, 57 of metal, and 851 coins constituted, with the single exception of the Way collection, the most important single gift made to the museum since its foundation. The gift also suggested the possibility of acquiring original objects of classical antiquity through ties with archaeological expeditions, and showed that the plaster cast was not necessarily the only means of representing Greek sculpture in the museum's collection. Here, after all, was an archaic architrave from the temple at Assos, with a relief showing *Herakles pursuing centaurs*, as well as a pair of recumbent sphinxes, heraldically facing

HERAKLES PURSUING CENTAURS. Relief from the temple at Assos, 6th century B.C. *Gift of the Archaeological Institute of America. 84.67*

each other, on another fragment of the architrave, and one of the four lion's heads which decorated the corners of the gable sima of the temple. In 1885 a similar addition of original antiquities was received when the Egypt Exploration Fund gave the museum a collection of objects recently excavated by Mr. (later Sir) Flinders Petrie, in acknowledgment of American contributions toward the expense of the expedition. A further gift from the same source was received in 1886. Two great Etruscan sarcophagi, brought to Boston for an

ETRUSCAN SARCOPHAGUS. About 330 to 300 B.C. 86.145

International Exhibition at the Mechanics' Building in 1883, were lent to the museum in 1884 by their owners, Messrs. J. J. Jarvis and George Maquay of Florence. Two years later the museum succeeded in buying one through the help of Mrs. Gardner Brewer, while the Boston Athenæum purchased the other, and has lent it to the museum ever since.

In October 1885, when E. H. Greenleaf was given several months' leave of absence to visit museums in Europe, Sylvester R. Koehler, who had (with Charles C. Perkins and William C. Prime) started in

1879 the *American Art Review*, became temporary curator of the Gray engravings during Greenleaf's absence, while Edward Robinson accepted a year's appointment as assistant curator of classical archaeology. The sorrows of overcrowding continued, for in order to show a collection of 453 English water colors, brought to this country by Henry Blackburn, it was necessary to use the rooms of the Gray collection, thus temporarily removing prints from exhibition.

Early in 1886 Henry P. Kidder, Treasurer of the museum from the beginning, died and was succeeded by John Lowell Gardner. Another tie with the foundation of the institution was broken with the death on 25 August 1886 of Charles C. Perkins, Honorary Director and Chairman of the Committee on the Museum. General Loring spent several months of the year in Europe, his first absence since the establishment of the museum. While he was abroad, Messrs. Robinson and Greenleaf filled in for him most acceptably. After a decade of operation, the museum had lost two of its most stalwart supporters. It was still pretty insolvent, but the receipt of a bequest of $50,000 from Richard Perkins, to be held like the Parker bequest as a fund of which only the income could be used, was a hopeful straw in the wind. The trustees were, moreover, making an appeal for a subscription that it was hoped would achieve at least $250,000.

The 1886 report is distinguished by the first appearance of a detailed report of the Department of Classical Archaeology, submitted by Edward Robinson. The Committee on the Museum, in noting Mr. Robinson's preparation of a new catalogue of the Greek and Roman sculpture, reaffirmed that it is in casts and other reproductions that "we can make the most assured progress." Nevertheless, Edward Robinson's report is chiefly devoted to original objects. He mentions the two great Etruscan sarcophagi, and discusses the antiquities from Naukratis, excavated in 1885 by Flinders Petrie, that have been given by the Egypt Exploration Fund. Perhaps the most significant sentence is one whose importance will only become apparent in later chapters: "Since the beginning of the new year [1887], but fortunately in time for acknowledgment in the present report, Mr. S. D. Warren has enriched the Museum by the gift of a figurine of the best type of Greek terra-cottas, purchased by Mr. Edward P. Warren, in Athens, representing a nude youth descend-

ATHENA. Bronze, Greco-Roman. *Gift of Samuel Dennis Warren.* 87.7

HELIOS. Terra-cotta, Greek. *Gift of Samuel Dennis Warren.* 87.1

ing through the air." Eventually this nude youth, presumably Helios, the sun-god, was to be followed by companions who routed the plaster casts that had seemed so all-important in the museum's first decade. But that is a later story. Here it need only be noted that Samuel Dennis Warren gave later in 1887 a bronze statuette of Athena that he had purchased from Josef Zervas, by whom it had been discovered in 1871 on a mountain known as the Ettringer Bellerberg, between Coblenz and Bonn, on the Rhine.

CHAPTER III

The Lean Years

Deficits and overcrowding characterized the Museum of Fine Arts in the late eighties and early nineties. Although only the most microscopic sums were available for the purchase of works of art, generous lenders and donors were pouring in extraordinary objects from Japan in quantities that raised serious problems. Charles G. Loring, summarizing in 1901 the first twenty-five years of the museum's growth, wrote:

> The administration was conducted with the most rigid economy, yet the Treasurer's books showed a yearly deficit. For some twenty years its history was a long wearisome struggle against poverty. Purchases were out of the question. Starting with but a few objects it could call its own, the policy of seeking loans was adopted. It needed but a nucleus to be deposited in each department to have it draw other objects to itself. For fifteen years the exhibits were chiefly borrowed. The record of the loans fills eighteen volumes.
>
> Gradually the tide turned. Gifts began to come in of paintings, prints, jades, porcelains, metal work, textiles, books. It would be impossible to select any for special mention; the walls and cases bear eloquent testimony to their number, their value, their beauty.
>
> This growth and the offer by Dr. William Sturgis Bigelow and Dr. Charles G. Weld to lend their unrivalled collections of Japanese art, and the prospective acquisition of the Japanese pottery collected by Mr. Edward S. Morse, led the Trustees in 1886, to solicit means to again extend their building.

Their goal was $300,000 which would provide not only additional galleries but assure some protection against annual deficits from operating expenses, which were slowly but surely melting away the museum's modest unrestricted funds. By May 1887, $218,000 had been received from fifty-eight donors, in sums ranging from $500 to $24,000. Mrs. Gardner Brewer had given the largest sum, while Dr. Charles G. Weld (1857–1911), a young Boston physician who was already applying an ample China Trade inheritance to collecting Japanese art, contributed $15,000. His father, William F. Weld, gave $10,000, as did nine other men, among whom were five trustees, Martin Brimmer, John L. Gardner, Henry L. Pierce, Nathaniel Thayer, and Samuel D. Warren. Although $240,711 had been subscribed by the end of 1887, and only another $10,000 came in during the winter, it was clear that the addition had to be built, even though this effort had not solved the problem of current operating expenses. The 1887 deficit was $7,111; that of 1888, $8,841.

The plans prepared by John H. Sturgis called for parallel wings, 60 feet long, on Dartmouth Street and Trinity Place, connected by a corridor, 24 feet wide and 210 in length, that would enclose the northernmost of the two open interior courts projected in the original plan. With this addition the museum building would cover a half of the total lot. The original plan of a main entrance in the center of the Dartmouth Street façade was, however, abandoned, because of unexpected changes in the development of this southernmost portion of the Back Bay.

When filling of the area was undertaken, the Back Bay had been designed with Beacon and Marlborough streets, Commonwealth Avenue, and Newbury and Boylston streets paralleling each other, intersected by eight cross streets, mnemonically provided with alphabetical names running from Arlington to Hereford. South of Boylston Street the continuation of this orderly pattern was confused by the tracks of the Boston and Providence and the Boston and Worcester railroads, which intersected, in the form of a great St. Andrew's cross, at the site of today's Back Bay Station, just south of the Museum of Fine Arts building. To avoid grade crossings, Huntington Avenue was laid out diagonally, running parallel to the Boston and Providence tracks, leading southwest from the intersection of Boylston and Clarendon streets. This thoroughfare crossed St. James Avenue (the next major street parallel to Boylston on the south) at Dartmouth Street. Thus the land between Clarendon, Boylston, and Dartmouth streets and St. James Avenue consisted of two areas, one an irregular quadrangle occupied by Trinity Church, the other a triangle, separated from each other by Huntington Avenue. In the apex of the triangle, M.I.T. had built in 1875 a corrugated iron drill hall and gymnasium, to the west of which were four vacant house-lots. South of these lots, a back alley ran from Dartmouth Street to Huntington Avenue, and south of this was a tiny triangular plot of land, which the Museum of Fine Arts bought in 1879 for $2,630 to keep open. In the 1879 report Martin Brimmer remarked, "it is to be hoped that the city will find it for the public interest to secure the unoccupied land in front of the Museum between St. James Avenue and Boylston Street, and to lay it out as a public square."

This hope was encouraged when the Massachusetts Legislature, on 22 April 1880, granted the city land on the southerly corner of Dartmouth and Boylston streets, extending south to St. James Avenue, as a site for the construction of a new Boston Public Library. Thus in 1883 the city took title to the Boylston and Dartmouth streets and Huntington Avenue triangle; M.I.T. removed its drill hall to the site of the Hotel Lenox, and Copley Square — which had never been contemplated in the original planning of the Back Bay — stumbled into being. The most energetic proponent of the square was Stanton Blake (Harvard A.B. 1857), a banker with business interests in Amsterdam and London and a collector of Dutch painting, who was elected a trustee of the museum in 1882. To name this new open space for the painter John Singleton Copley was logical in view of the presence of the Museum of Fine Arts. With the museum on the south side, the projected Boston Public Library on the west, the Second Church and private houses on the north, and Trinity Church on the east, the new square was clearly to be the chief focal point of the Back Bay. Dartmouth Street, which ran, across railway bridges, into the already seedy South End, was equally clearly not to become the important thoroughfare that Sturgis and Brigham had anticipated in their original designs for the Museum of Fine Arts. Thus the idea of an imposing entrance in that street was abandoned, and the exist-

MUSEUM OF FINE ARTS AS ENLARGED IN 1888–89. The photograph is later than 1898 for it shows to the left a part of the Hotel Westminster, the construction of which in that year raised doubts about the wisdom of remaining in Copley Square.

ing St. James Avenue façade, looking onto the new Copley Square, continued to be the principal approach to the Museum.

Although John H. Sturgis died early in 1888, the construction of the addition was carried on by his successors, Messrs. Sturgis and Cabot. Construction began in 1888, and the building was completed the following year, although it was only opened to public view on 18 March 1890. The 60-foot wings, extending along Dartmouth Street and Trinity Place, were of simpler design, with less decorative work, than the St. James Avenue façade. The first thought had been to build only these, at an estimated cost of $150,000, and retain $100,000 of the funds that it was hoped would be subscribed to provide income to reduce the annual operating deficit. But, as William Endicott, chairman of the fundraising committee, noted in a report of 13 February 1888,

A study of the plans soon convinced the Building Committee that it would be very desirable at once to connect these two wings by a

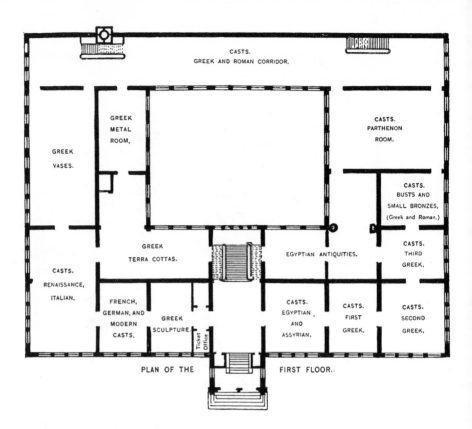

CASTS.
GREEK AND ROMAN CORRIDOR.

GREEK
METAL
ROOM.

CASTS.
PARTHENON
ROOM.

GREEK
VASES.

CASTS.
BUSTS AND
SMALL BRONZES,
(Greek and Roman.)

CASTS.
RENAISSANCE,
ITALIAN.

GREEK
TERRA COTTAS.

EGYPTIAN ANTIQUITIES.

CASTS.
THIRD
GREEK.

FRENCH,
GERMAN, AND
MODERN
CASTS.

GREEK
SCULPTURE.

Ticket
Office

CASTS.
EGYPTIAN.
AND
ASSYRIAN.

CASTS.
FIRST
GREEK.

CASTS.
SECOND
GREEK.

PLAN OF THE   FIRST FLOOR.

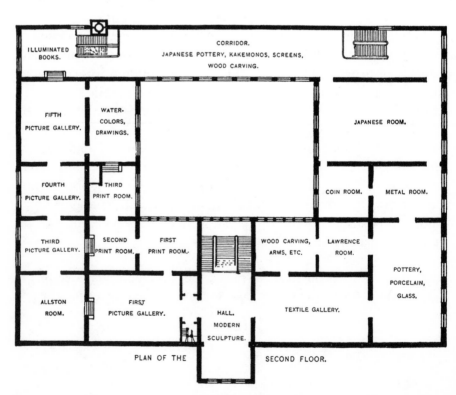

ILLUMINATED
BOOKS.

CORRIDOR.
JAPANESE POTTERY, KAKEMONOS, SCREENS,
WOOD CARVING.

FIFTH
PICTURE GALLERY.

WATER-
COLORS,
DRAWINGS.

JAPANESE ROOM.

FOURTH
PICTURE GALLERY.

THIRD
PRINT ROOM.

COIN ROOM.

METAL ROOM.

THIRD
PICTURE GALLERY.

SECOND
PRINT ROOM.

FIRST
PRINT ROOM.

WOOD CARVING,
ARMS, ETC.

LAWRENCE
ROOM.

POTTERY,
PORCELAIN,
GLASS,

ALLSTON
ROOM.

FIRST
PICTURE GALLERY.

HALL.
MODERN
SCULPTURE.

TEXTILE GALLERY.

PLAN OF THE   SECOND FLOOR.

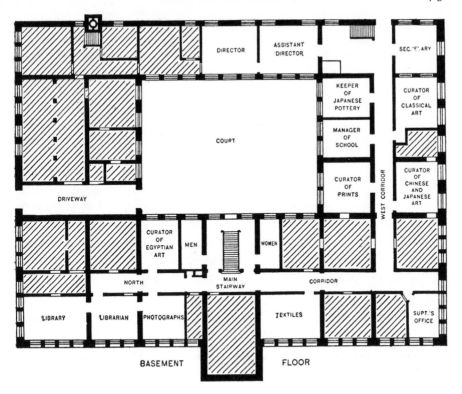

FLOOR PLANS OF MUSEUM OF FINE ARTS AS ENLARGED IN 1888-89.

corridor, twenty-four feet in width and two hundred and ten feet in length, rather than to leave such connection for the future. The advantage of having a continuous passage around the building, so that a crowd of visitors could be accommodated without confusion, the greater safety in case of panic, and the requirement of more space than would be furnished by the two wings, were so manifest, that the only hesitation possible was on account of the additional cost, estimated to be about $75,000.

But when proposals were received from two gentlemen of this city [Doctors Bigelow and Weld], each a large contributor to the Building Fund, to deposit in the Museum their valuable collections brought from Japan, thus making an exhibit of Japanese curios probably equal to any in the world, it was evident that the question was decided, and that the extension must be made, cost what it might.

The new building, therefore, will probably cover about twelve thousand square feet, doubling the present capacity of the Museum. But so crowded has it become that all of this space will find immediate use.

When the museum reopened in 1890 with its vastly increased space, major rearrangements had been made in the placing of the collections. The casts, for example, had to be completely rearranged, for their original locations had been made with the expectation of a future main entrance in Dartmouth Street. When this was abandoned, it became necessary to achieve a chronological sequence related to the St. James Avenue entrance, a matter of considerable labor and concern to Edward Robinson, Curator of Classical Antiquities. The first room at the right of the entrance, formerly called the Fourth Greek Room, became devoted to casts from Egyptian and Assyrian sculpture; the room opening from that to casts from archaic Greek art, followed by two rooms of casts illustrating the transitional period.

EGYPTIAN AND ASSYRIAN CAST ROOM AFTER 1890. This was the first gallery to the right of the main entrance.

AN EXTENDED PROSPECT OF PLASTER CASTS AFTER 1890. The photograph was taken from the Renaissance Cast Room at the northeast corner of the building, looking toward the Greek Cast Rooms at the northwest corner.

Entering the new wing along Dartmouth Street, there followed a room containing busts and small bronzes, Greek and Roman, which led into the very large Parthenon Room, entirely filled by casts of the Parthenon and from the Temple of Apollo at Bassae, The new Greek and Roman Corridor, along the south of the building, led to the Trinity Place Wing, and the large Hall of the Maidens, where, somewhat to Robinson's distress, the casts from the Porch of the Maidens of the Erechtheum and of reliefs from the Great Altar at Pergamon, had for reasons of space to be placed in defiance of chronology. Continuing along the outer galleries, the visitor passed through the room of Italian Renaissance casts (formerly devoted to architectural casts), and regained the main entrance by way of two rooms occupied by French and German Renaissance casts, and by those of modern sculpture. Gothic and Moorish casts were in a new room lighted from the interior court, leading out of the Greek and Roman Corridor before

the entrance to the Hall of the Maidens. It will be seen that strict
pedagogical chronology had had to bow to the considerable size of the
collection, and to the dimensions of individual replicas. Robinson
noted, not without pride, the relative size of the Boston collection of
casts and of those of various European museums, in the following
figures:

Royal Museum, Berlin	2,271
University Museum, Strasburg	819
Museum of Fine Arts, Boston	777
Academic Museum, Bonn	723
Museum of Plaster Casts, Dresden	613
Fitzwilliam Museum, Cambridge	529
Museum of Plaster Casts, Vienna	453
Museum of Plaster Casts, Munich	418
South Kensington Museum	338

Back of the cast galleries and parallel to them on the courtyard
were, on the west side, three rooms of Egyptian antiquities that con-

EGYPTIAN ANTIQUITIES ROOM AFTER 1890. This gallery containing original
material was lighted from the interior court.

tained the Way collection, John Lowell's sculpture from Karnak, and the considerable number of objects, including large sculptures, that had been given in recent years by the Egypt Exploration Fund. In the corresponding rooms on the east side of the entrance hall were the Classical vases, Roman terracottas, figures from Tanagra and Myrina, the objects from Assos given by the Archaeological Institute of America, the two Etruscan sarcophagi, and other original material.

The east side of the second floor was assigned to paintings, water colors, drawings, and prints, with five picture galleries running along the St. James Avenue and Trinity Place façades. The First Picture Gallery contained Italian paintings of the fourteenth to seventeenth centuries, and French pictures of the eighteenth. Two still lifes by Jean Baptiste Siméon Chardin, *The Kitchen Table*, given by Mrs. Peter Chardon Brooks in 1880, and *Teapot with Fruit*, given by Martin Brimmer in 1883, hung here. The Allston Room beyond contained twenty pictures by that artist, fifteen by Copley, as well as works of Smibert, Trumbull, Blackburn, the two Peales, and others. In the Dutch Room were pictures bought by the late Stanton Blake in

THE KITCHEN TABLE. Jean Baptiste Siméon Chardin. *Gift of Mrs. Peter Chardon Brooks. 80.512*

THE TEAPOT WITH FRUIT. Jean Baptiste Siméon
Chardin. *Gift of Martin Brimmer. 83.177*

1880 from the Prince Demidoff collection at the San Donato Palace
in Florence, and deposited by him in the Museum of Fine Arts the
following year. When Blake died in 1889, he left the Museum $5,000
and the option of buying these pictures for $22,500. His Harvard
classmate Francis Bartlett promptly gave $10,000 from a fund left
by his father, Sidney Bartlett, to be applied toward this purchase,
while $7,200 was subscribed by various friends. Thus, by adding
$300 from its own meager purchase funds, the museum became the
owner of a collection that included Jan van Huysum's *Vase of
Flowers*, Gabriel Metsu's *The Usurer*, Nicolas Maes's considerably
overpainted *The Jealous Husband*, Ruisdael's *The Ruined Cottage,*
and a Simon Verelst *Still Life*. A few German pictures also hung in
the Dutch Room. The adjacent French Room was hung with paintings by Corot, Millet, Rousseau, Troyon, Diaz, and their contemporaries, while the Fifth Picture Gallery showed some modern French
works by Couture, Courbet, and Meissonier, but mainly the paintings
of Boston artists of the preceding forty years. In this last room hung
the immense *Automedon with the Horses of Achilles* by Alexandre
Georges Henri Regnault (1843–1871), which had been acquired by
subscription in 1890. This picture, much admired by art students of
the time, had been painted in 1868 as the artist's first *envoi* from the
French Academy in Rome, only three years before he was killed at
the battle of Buzenval during the siege of Paris.

THE USURER. Gabriel Metsu. *Purchased from Sidney Bartlett Bequest.* 89.501
THE JEALOUS HUSBAND. Nicolas Maes. *Gift by subscription.* 89.504

Contrary to the normal practice of submitting the study of a nude figure rather than a complete picture for the first *envoi*, Regnault added a rearing bay and a restive sorrel horse to the muscular figure that dominates a canvas over 10 feet square. Of this version of Achilles' charioteer, the driver of the immortal horses Balius and Xanthus, he wrote: "J'ai fait du grec à ma manière; c'est une traduction libre." A decade after the young artist's death, the picture was owned by Levi P. Morton, United States Minister to France, at whose sale in New York in 1882 it passed to Samuel A. Coale, Jr., of St. Louis. The new owner, finding his prize unmanageable for domestic hanging, sent it first to the Boston gallery of Williams and Everett, and in 1884 lent it to the Museum of Fine Arts. The huge canvas so excited the art students of the School of Drawing and Painting that a public subscription for its purchase was opened. The middle-aged were less thrilled, for Sylvester R. Koehler, the future first Curator of the Print Department, wrote a letter on 15 February 1884 to the *Boston Daily Advertiser* in which he denounced the painting as a "piece of bravado, or if you will, bravoura and nothing more. Do

AUTOMEDON WITH THE HORSES OF ACHILLES. Alexandre Georges Henri Regnault. *Gift by subscription. 90.152*

you feel the classical spirit in it? It is only a very French circus."

Frederic Crowninshield of the school faculty leaped to the defense
of his students' taste, only to be rebutted by Charles Herbert Moore,
Harvard teacher of drawing and design, who informed readers of the
Advertiser that he regarded the picture as "about the most pernicious
thing that could be placed before young students of painting." As
the newspaper had suggested that the museum purchase the picture
while it was still on display at Williams and Everett's gallery, a letter
in its defense from Ralph Wormeley Curtis (Harvard A.B. 1876)
was welcomed. Writing from Tangier on 18 March 1884, this thirty-
year-old son of the Daniel Sargent Curtises — Bostonians who long

lived in the Palazzo Barbaro in Venice — concluded his remarks with the lively counterattack: "As to diet, we firmly believe that juicy (underdone, if you will) porterhouse steak, broiled on red-hot coals, by Henri Regnault, is more 'healthful pabulum' than mushy *tête de veau* art boiled in Preraphaelite tepid water."

The students persevered in their campaign; the museum applied $285 contributed in 1878 by French residents of Boston and $715 from the Everett Fund, but it was 17 July 1890 before the purchase price was obtained and *Automedon with the Horses of Achilles* finally became the property of the Museum of Fine Arts. Forty years ago it still held a dignified place in the painting galleries; today it is skyed above bookcases in the library. It is at least visible, which is more than one can say for the even larger (9' 8 ½" by 16' 5 ⅝") oil of the *Pearl Mosque in the Palace, Delhi*, by the Russian artist Vassili Verestchagin (1842–1904), which was given in 1892 through another public subscription. Both these gifts were so huge that, like many products of contemporary art, they could only be housed in a public institution; both were the works of artists who died in war, although at very different ages. Henri Regnault was killed at twenty-eight in the Franco-Prussian War; although Vassili Verestchagin lived to be sixty-two, he was a casualty of the Russo-Japanese War, for he died when *Petropavlovsk* was sunk in the harbor of Port Arthur by the Japanese. One wonders where some of the equally vast and currently admired abstractions of "action painters" of the third quarter of the twentieth century will wind up seventy-five years hence.

From the Fifth Picture Gallery entrances led to the Japanese Corridor and to the new room facing the courtyard, which was assigned to water colors and drawings. Here were shown drawings and charcoals by Copley, Allston, Hunt, and Rimmer; water colors by living artists, foreign and American; 22 drawings by Millet, and 26 by William Blake. The Print Department had gained a Third Print Room in the new wing, looking on the courtyard. Thus, there were three rooms available for showing portions of the Gray Collection (6,000 prints) as well as the 7,000 examples of print-making that the museum had acquired on its own, chiefly by gift.

In the old west wing the Textile Gallery, the Wood Carving and Lawrence rooms, and the West Room (pottery, porcelain, and glass) were much as they had been, but in the new wing were a Coin Room and a Metal Room. The remainder of the new wing contained a large Japanese Room, while the Japanese Corridor, at the south of the building, contained pottery, *kakemonos*, and screens. The Committee on the Museum, in its 1890 report, proudly and justly stated:

No public museum offers so extraordinary a display of Japanese art as is found in the Japanese room and the corridor adjoining, for which we are indebted to Dr. Wm. Sturgis Bigelow and Dr. Chas. G. Weld. The sword guards, the ornaments of gold, and other metal work of exhaustless fertility of design, and remarkable delicacy of workmanship, the carved ivories, netsukes, and bronzes, panels of wood-carving illustrating the legends of Buddha and the fairy tales of old Japan, the textiles, the superb lacquers, will be a perpetual delight to all interested in the creation of that most artistic of modern nations.

In the corridor is hung a small portion of the Fenollosa Collection of Japanese paintings, lent to the Museum by Dr. Weld; it combines a complete historical series of original works, illustrating all the schools, and nearly all the leading masters of Japanese pictorial art, from its origin in the VIIth century to the present day. It includes also a considerable number of Chinese originals, and a few Corean, sufficient to illustrate the continental origin of much in Japanese art. A large collection of copies of famous works in Japanese public and private collections, made under Mr. Fenollosa's supervision during the last ten years, forms an important adjunct.

Here, too, is the Morse Collection of Japanese pottery. In bringing the collection together, Mr. Morse has endeavored to secure specimens of every province in which pottery has been made, including work of every age; also the work of every maker and every variety of mark; and, further, to secure every kind of object made in pottery. The collection thus far embraces over four thousand five hundred specimens, nearly six hundred kinds of wares, over a thousand different marks. It is arranged in provinces, of which there are fifty-six represented. Most of the original specimens, figured in the famous work of Ninagawa, belong to the collection.

The workings of serendipity, by which the Museum of Fine Arts so early found itself possessed of the most remarkable Japanese collection in the Western world, will be the subject of a later chapter.

Here it suffices to say that it was chiefly the advent of this collection which led to the enlargement of the museum, which in its turn made the financial structure of the institution more precarious than ever. As the decision to build the Japanese Corridor almost eliminated any relief that the 1886–1888 subscription of $250,000 might have afforded the deficit in operating expenses, the trustees in 1889 proposed a plan for annual subscriptions of ten dollars each, which, it was hoped would not only make ends meet, but give the museum a wider support than it had previously received. As an inducement, each subscriber would receive a ticket admitting four persons at all times when the museum was open. More than 1,000 persons became annual subscribers the first year, while in 1890 the number rose to 1,510. In the latter year the names of annual subscribers filled some seventeen pages in the annual report.

This new source of revenue did not balance the budget, for in 1890 the trustees had, to complete the furniture and fixtures in the new building, to borrow $10,000 from the Merchants' National Bank and $17,000 from Lee, Higginson and Company, with no clear vision of how this debt was to be repaid. The subscriptions provided a helpful source of income, but deficits continued. In 1893 the difference between income and outgo was $5,847, while the debt had been increased to $35,000 chiefly because of the installation of electric lighting. From 1891 Martin Brimmer had annually pointed out the need of still another addition, that would provide on the first floor a lecture hall and on the second more exhibition space for the growing Japanese collection. On the second repetition he gloomily observed: "In consequence of the depression in business in 1893, it was not thought best to appeal to the liberality of the public for means to enlarge the Museum; but this cannot be deferred much longer."

With the enlargement of the Museum, attendance increased by leaps and bounds. In 1890 it had been 186,677; in 1891 it rose to 217,643, and continued to increase until the figure of 301,315 was reached in 1895. However gratifying such statistics, they solved no financial problems, for, as had always been the case, nine-tenths or more of the visitors swarmed in on free days. In 1895 the Sunday average was 2,187, the Saturday 1,509, while that of paying days was 94. Thus only $6,053 was received in admissions during that record year. In 1896 even the freeloaders proved fickle, for the attendance dropped to 194,975. The explanation offered by the Executive Committee is worthy of quotation. "This may be accounted for in part by the fact that owing to the absence of the director in Europe during a part of the summer, there have been fewer special exhibitions than usual, and possibly by the prevalence of bicycle riding, attracting to that out-door recreation many persons who would otherwise have spent some leisure hours at the Museum." The figure rose in 1897 to 228,458, but when it dropped in 1898 to 202,205, the decline was once more blamed, at least in part, to "the very prevalent use of the bicycle leading many to out-of-door amusement," especially on Sundays.

A hope of eventual solvency began to dawn in the nineties, not from increased attendance or annual subscriptions, but from a growing number of bequests from former trustees and friends who understood the dilemma of an institution that tried to give everything possible to thousands of people, without receiving a penny of city or state assistance. In January 1889 the museum's seven trust funds totaled only $197,500. Later in that year $5,000 was received as an anonymous gift through George W. Wales, while in 1890 legacies of $5,000 each were received from Mrs. Turner Sargent and Miss Sara Greene Timmins. In 1893 a bequest of $48,945 was received under the will of Mrs. Martha Ann Edwards, while Catharine Page Perkins, the widow of Richard Perkins, an earlier benefactor, left $87,775, a sum subsequently increased to $102,000. So many similar bequests followed that in January 1899, the total of trust funds was not $197,500, but $1,706,453. The specific amounts listed are worth noting.

I. *Principal and Income restricted to certain uses:*

Sylvanus A. Denio Fund	$50,000	
William W. Warren Fund	50,000	
		$100,000

II. *Income restricted to certain uses:*

B. P. Cheney Fund	$5,000	
John L. Gardner Fund	20,000	
Otis Norcross Fund	6,500	
Abbott Lawrence Fund	10,000	
Julia B. H. James Fund	146,500	
		$188,000

III. *Income unrestricted:*

Everett Fund	$7,500	
Richard Perkins Fund	50,000	
"R.W." Fund	5,000	
Samuel E. Sawyer Fund	2,000	
George B. Hyde Fund	93,000	
Ann White Vose Fund	60,500	
Ann White Dickinson Fund	40,000	
Henry L. Pierce Fund	50,000	
		$308,000

IV. *Wholly unrestricted:*

N. C. Nash Fund	$10,000	
Harvey D. Parker Fund	100,000	
Turner Sargent Fund	5,000	
Sara G. Timmins Fund	5,000	
Martha A. Edwards Fund	49,000	
Catharine P. Perkins Fund	102,000	
Henry P. Kidder Fund	10,000	
Isaac Sweetser Fund	47,000	
Arthur Rotch Fund	25,000	
Moses Kimball Fund	5,000	
B. P. Cheney Bequest Fund	5,000	
Cornelia V. R. Thayer Fund	10,000	
Henry L. Pierce Residuary Fund	730,000	
		1,103,000
Profit and loss on trust investment:		7,453
		$1,706,453

Henry Lillie Pierce (1825–1896), a trustee from 1883 until his death, bequeathed $50,000 and a fifth of the residue of his estate to the museum. As the residuary fund raised the total of his bequest to $780,000, he was, beyond question, the most generous benefactor of the museum in the nineteenth century, so far as funds were concerned. He was a native of Stoughton, who left school at seventeen, farmed for a bit, and in 1849 went to work in the cocoa factory of his uncle, Walter Baker, at Milton Lower Mills, of which he eventually became the owner. He opposed the Know-Nothing movement when it was at its height. Of his two years as Mayor of Boston (1872, 1877), Wendell Phillips remarked that if Diogenes came to Boston, he would find his honest man in the mayor's chair. He gave generously to struggling colored schools in the South and to small Western colleges. As he never married, much of his very large estate, derived entirely from cocoa and chocolate, went to institutions, including the Museum of Fine Arts, and Catholic and Unitarian churches alike.

These bequests considerably relieved the financial plight of the museum. Indeed, thanks to them, the treasurer's report for 1899 — when operating expenses had risen to $60,838 — actually showed a surplus of $8,906, which was credited to the temporary loan account to repay in part the deficits of former years. Unfortunately, for reasons that will appear later in this chapter, this was a unique phenomenon that was not to recur in the immediate future. But the hopeful increase of unrestricted funds led the trustees in 1894 to adopt a policy that would permit some part of such gifts or bequests to be used for the purchase of a work of art, or a collection of high and permanent value, to which the name of the donor would be attached. Thus the names of major benefactors would be visible in the galleries of the museum, rather than being hidden away in the small type of treasurers' reports. So the decade of the eighteen nineties saw major additions to the museum's collections, not only from living donors but from the generous dead.

The immense Edward S. Morse Collection of Japanese Pottery was purchased in 1892 by a subscription fund raised by General Loring. The following year Major and Mrs. Henry L. Higginson gave Roger van der Weyden's painting St. Luke drawing the portrait of the Virgin — after three-quarters of a century still one of the museum's greatest treasures — which they had purchased at the Duc de Durcal sale. Also in 1893 Mrs. Frederick Lothrop Ames gave, in the name of her late husband, two Rembrandt portraits, as well as the great Indian Mughal carpet that is described and illustrated in Chapter XI. Soon after the death in January 1896 of Martin Brimmer, president of the museum from its foundation, Delacroix's Entombment was given in his memory by the subscription of friends.

Prior to 1894 purchases of consequence could only be made through the subscriptions of friends. By this means an important collection of watercolor drawings of William Blake was acquired in 1890. An enthusiasm for this artist had been aroused in Boston by the loan exhibition of 1880, which took place only four years after the

ST. LUKE DRAWING THE PORTRAIT OF THE VIRGIN. Roger
van der Weyden. *Gift of Mr. and Mrs. Henry Lee Higginson.*
93.153

first important display of his work in London. Consequently, when
nine drawings for *Paradise Lost*, seven for Shakespeare's plays, nine
of scriptural and prophetic subjects, and eight for *Comus* — all formerly in the collections of Thomas Butts and C. J. Strange — came
on the market, they were greatly desired by the museum. Mrs. John
L. Gardner and George Nixon Black provided funds for the *Comus*
drawings. The others were purchased by the subscriptions of Mr. and
Mrs. Martin Brimmer, Edward W. Hooper, the Misses Ellen and
Ida Mason, Mrs. Henry L. Higginson, Mr. and Mrs. Samuel D.
Warren, Miss Annette P. Rogers, and Mrs. Daniel Merriman of
Worcester. Such funds were informally raised among friends, with no
reference to the subscription figuring in the Treasurer's report.

THE ENTOMBMENT. Eugène Delacroix. *Gift by contribution
in memory of Martin Brimmer. 96.21*

Even more extensive acquisitions resulted from the use of portions
of unrestricted funds for purchases. The remarkable additions to the
Classical Department that were bought largely from the bequest of
Mrs. Catharine P. Perkins will be described in the next chapter, but
paintings were acquired from a number of funds. From the William
Wilkins Warren Fund were purchased in 1895 the portrait of Mrs.
Palk, 1761, by Sir Joshua Reynolds, Eugène Delacroix's *The Lion
Hunt*, John Constable's study for *The White Horse*, Gilbert Stuart
Newton's *A Spanish Girl*, and George de Forest Brush's *Mother and
Child*. A *Madonna and Child with St. John*, formerly in the Beckford
and Alexander Barker collections, believed at the time to have been
the work of Botticelli was bought in the name of the Sara Greene

THE CREATION OF EVE. William Blake, from his nine illustrations
to Milton's *Paradise Lost. Purchased by subscription.* 90.95

THE MAGIC BANQUET. William Blake, from his eight illustrations
*to Milton's Comus. Gift of Mrs. John L. Gardner and
George Nixon Black.* 90.123

THE PHILOSOPHER (OR GEOGRAPHER). Purchased as a Ribera, later attributed
to Luca Giordano. *James Fund.* 99.315
COUNT ALBORGHETTI AND HIS SON, OF BERGAMO. Giovanni Battista Moroni.
Turner Sargent Fund. 95.1371

THE LITTLE ROSE OF LYME REGIS and THE BLACKSMITH OF LYME REGIS. James Abbott McNeill Whistler. *William Wilkins Warren Fund. 96.950 and 96.951*

Timmins Fund; Giovanni Battista Moroni's portrait of *Count Alborghetti and son, of Bergamo,* from the Turner Sargent Fund. In the next year the Warren Fund was used to acquire Gilbert Stuart's portrait of Mrs. Richard Yates, Whistler's *The Blacksmith of Lyme Regis* and *Little Rose of Lyme Regis,* and a self-portrait of William Morris Hunt, while Sir Henry Raeburn's portrait of T. P. Baillie was purchased from the Abbott Lawrence Fund. Abbott H. Thayer's *Caritas* was bought in 1897 from the Warren Fund, aided by a subscription. The Abbott Lawrence Fund was used to acquire John Opie's portrait of Charles Dibdin, and the Otis Norcross Fund for a Malbone miniature of Washington Allston. In 1899 the Warren Fund was charged with four Winslow Homer's water colors, of which *Leaping Trout* is here reproduced. From the Julia D. H. James Fund, Ribera's *The Philosopher* was purchased, while the Henry L. Pierce

Fund provided J. M. W. Turner's *The Slave Ship* — long lent to the museum — as well as highly important Classical antiquities that will be described in Chapter V. These purchases of the nineties offer a marked contrast to the conviction of previous decades that only plaster casts could be afforded.

The largest and most varied loan exhibition of tapestries ever held in the United States was shown at the Museum of Fine Arts from 26 January to 28 February 1893. The pieces included, which ranged from Coptic work of the second or third centuries to contemporary French products of the Gobelins manufactory, were described in a catalogue prepared by Frank Gair Macomber, a local insurance man and collector. Among the examples exhibited was a large (nearly 14 by 19 feet) early sixteenth-century Flemish tapestry of *The Destruction of the Egyptians in the Red Sea*, lent by Thomas R. Plummer of South Dartmouth, Massachusetts, in which a highly complacent Moses, garbed as a medieval king, points with satisfaction to equally medieval Egyptian knights who are foundering in the sea through the weight of their armor. When the trustees in 1894 adopted the policy of applying portions of gifts and bequests for the purchase of works of art, negotiations began for this great medieval tapestry, which is recorded as the first acquisition of the year 1895.

Sylvester Rosa Koehler, who was appointed Curator of the Print Department on its establishment in 1887, was a learned and energetic addition to the museum staff. Born in Leipzig in 1837, he was

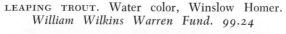

LEAPING TROUT. Water color, Winslow Homer. *William Wilkins Warren Fund.* 99.24

THE DESTRUCTION OF THE EGYPTIANS IN THE RED SEA. Flemish tapestry, 16th century. *Otis Norcross Fund. 95.1*

brought to the United States as a boy of twelve, where he followed his father in embracing an artistic career. Ten years' experience as technical manager of the lithographic firm of L. Prang and Company in Boston gave him mastery of the details of technical processes. Although the scholarly periodical, the *American Art Review*, that he launched in 1879 with Charles C. Perkins and William C. Prime of New York, only survived for two years, Koehler constantly contributed articles on the graphic arts to American, English, and German journals. When he came to the Museum of Fine Arts in 1885, he had already been curator of the graphic arts section in the United States National Museum at Washington.

In the spring of 1887 Koehler published an 84-page catalogue, *Exhibition of the Etched Work of Rembrandt, and of artists of his circle . . . principally from the collection of Mr. Henry F. Sewall of New York*, to accompany a special display of nearly 500 prints. In the introduction he described the Sewall Collection as "the richest in Rembrandts and the most complete, historically, of all the private collections in the United States." For a special exhibition of Dürer's work in the winter of 1888–89, also accompanied by a detailed catalogue, he drew upon both the Sewall and Gray prints. Almost as soon as Koehler became Curator, he began urging increased acquisitions by the Print Department, against the possible withdrawal of the Gray Collection, which he described as "certain to occur some day." He spoke with particular feeling about the Sewall Collection, "the result of the labors of nearly half a century, brought together at prices now totally past recurrence," which he believed could be bought for far less than would be needed to reconstruct it again by buying, piece by piece, in the market. Again in 1888 and 1889 Koehler made urgent pleas for the acquisition of this collection of some 23,000 prints, that was rich in the works of the early Italians, of Rembrandt, and of Dürer. In 1890 the President and Fellows of Harvard College renewed their agreement to lend the Gray Collection of Engravings for a further period of seven years, and Koehler temporarily ceased to speak of the Sewall prints.

S. R. Koehler was not a mousy curator, content to be ignored by committees. The memory of his outstanding proficiency in New England profanity, delivered with a marked German accent, has

SYLVESTER ROSA KOEHLER.
Drawing by Emil Richter, his
successor as Curator of the Print
Department.

survived for three-quarters of a century among the oral traditions of
the museum. In his annual report of the Print Department for 1894,
he wrote, with a certain asperity:

> Although the recommendations which I ventured to make in my
> earlier reports led to no results, I am tempted to repeat them here.
> If the Print Department had had any funds at disposal at the time
> of the Peoli sale, the acquisitions for the Museum might have been
> still more important. As it was, so much time was lost in the attempt
> to raise a small amount of money, that the first day of the sale had
> passed before your representative was able to be present. The
> matter is still worse when occasion offers to secure some special
> bargain through a dealer or otherwise. The necessity of obtaining
> the consent of a committee causes such a delay that this arrange-
> ment is almost equivalent to a safeguard against the securing of
> bargains. I would suggest, therefore, that a yearly appropriation
> for purchases for the Print Department, at the discretion of the
> curator, would be a wise provision.

The following year Koehler was in Europe, on leave of absence, but his 1895–96 report, submitted after his return, shows no indication that this suggestion was followed. Then in 1897 came the expected blow, when Harvard notified the Museum of Fine Arts of its intention to withdraw the Gray Collection. "The disaster, to the possible coming of which I had more than once called the attention of your honorable body," he wrote the Committee on the Museum, "but which, I was as often assured, would never come, did come at last." Thus, a combined collection of 41,986 prints was reduced by a stroke to 12,127. Koehler did not hesitate to say that only two courses were open: "Either to give up the Print Department entirely, or to strengthen it again by purchasing the Sewall Collection, to which I had called attention before, and which was still in the market."

The second course was happily followed, with the aid of the Harvey D. Parker Fund. Once again, the increase of unrestricted funds to a level where parts of them could be used for purchases saved the day. "What, therefore, appeared at first sight to be a disaster, has proved to be a blessing in disguise. The Print Department of the Museum now stands firmly upon its own feet, without the danger which heretofore always threatened it, of annihilation by an outside force over which it had no control." The Sewall purchase was promptly renamed the Harvey D. Parker Collection. Thus the name of an energetic Maine farm boy is preserved, not only through the Parker House roll but by means of the great assembly of prints that entered the Museum of Fine Arts as a result of his generosity.

As the Harvey D. Parker Collection was particularly rich in works of the fifteenth, sixteenth, seventeenth, and eighteenth centuries, Koehler applied funds obtained from the sale of duplicates for

prints of the most modern kind, of which the Museum had practically nothing, but which it is in duty bound to collect, while the authors of them are still living, so as to be able to show their work in its exhibitions. The question of like or dislike is not to be considered in this matter, nor can the Museum enter into the contest which is being waged between the partisans of the old and the new. Its aim must be to gather in its cases and to show to the public the work of the men and women, who now stand prominently before the world, leaving the public to judge of this work, without attempting to influence its opinions.

Thus work of Aubrey Beardsley and his contemporaries came early to Copley Square. Alas, Koehler had little time to enjoy his acquisitions, old and new, for he died suddenly on 15 September 1900, only nine months after Emil H. Richter had been appointed to assist him in the Print Department. Koehler's valuable library, and many of the prints that he had personally collected, remain in the department that he created.

The museum staff was of very modest size during the first twenty-five years. The Print Department and the Department of Classical Antiquities were only established in 1887, with Sylvester R. Koehler and Edward Robinson as their curators, respectively. A Department of Japanese Art was created on 15 March 1890, with Ernest F. Fenollosa as its first Curator. Two years later, after the purchase of the Morse Collection of Japanese Pottery, Edward S. Morse, Director of the Peabody Academy of Science (now Peabody Museum of Salem) was appointed the museum's Keeper of Japanese Pottery on a part-time basis. In 1890, after the strenuous exertions of rearranging the enlarged museum, the Director, General Loring, was given six months' leave for travel in Europe. During his absence from May to November, E. H. Greenleaf, the Senior Curator, acted on his behalf in administering the museum. Benjamin Ives Gilman joined the staff in April 1893 as Curator and Librarian, and in 1894, on Greenleaf's departure, also became Secretary. Fenollosa left Boston in 1895; although Arthur W. Dow was made Keeper of Japanese Paintings and Prints in September 1897, it was September 1899 before Walter M. Cabot was appointed the second Curator of the Department of Japanese Art. In the annual report for 1895, Samuel Eliot, on behalf of the Executive Committee, noted: "Fresh expenses are constantly proposed, and frequently incurred. The persons in the employment of the Museum are not slow in suggesting higher pay, and other drafts less easily avoidable are continually made upon our depleted treasury." The suggestion was acted upon, for the Director, whose salary had been $3,000, was increased to $4,000, while Edward Robinson was raised from $1,500 to $2,200.

Upon the death of Martin Brimmer in January 1896, William Endicott, one of the incorporating trustees of 1870, succeeded to the presidency. His gloomy report for 1897, which began with a reference to a reduction in the number of annual subscribers and continued with a deficit of $4,580 on an operating budget of $39,426, contains a rather plaintive reference to the annual grant of $90,000 from the city treasury for current expenses that the Metropolitan Museum of New York is reported to receive. Moreover, some of the terra-cotta pinnacles of the building had come loose and had had to be replaced! In 1898, although operating expenses had risen to $51,056, the deficit had, through increased unrestricted funds, shrunk to $2,321, while in 1899 there occurred the beatific, and almost unique, phenomenon of a surplus. On 10 December 1898 John L. Gardner, who had been the museum's Treasurer for thirteen years, died suddenly. He was succeeded by Charles Lowell.

To the ordinary worries about inadequate space were added in 1898 the fear of fire risk and the loss of light springing from the construction of the Hotel Westminster on St. James Avenue and Trinity Place. When the museum was first opened, its only dominating neighbor was Trinity Church. To the west, east, and south there were vacant lots of recently filled land. During the eighties a row of small private houses had been built on St. James Avenue, filling the western half of the block between Trinity Place and Clarendon Street. The eastern half of that block, which had been owned by Mathias Denman Ross, remained vacant until 1890, when his nephew, Denman W. Ross, built upon it, as an investment, an apartment hotel. The returns from this property, which he called The Ludlow, after his late father's middle name, Denman Ross regularly devoted to buying works of art for the museum. This eminently respectable establishment, much favored for half a century by the kind of Boston lady who would lend Henry James's latest novel to the local police constable, was a welcome neighbor.

In 1898, however, some less beneficent investors proposed to demolish the houses on St. James Avenue that separated The Ludlow from the Museum of Fine Arts and build upon the site a considerably taller Hotel Westminster. Faced with this prospect, the museum petitioned for legislation limiting the height of future buildings on

Copley Square to 90 feet. Although a bill to this effect was duly passed, the builders of the Westminster proceeded to go above that limit. The museum applied to the Attorney General for a restraining injunction, but hearings consumed much of the summer, during which the roof of the offending hotel was completed. In September an information in equity was signed by the Attorney General to compel the removal of any part of the Westminster above the 90-foot limit. Eventually this was enforced to such purpose that the Hotel Westminster for the next half-century and more had an oddly decapitated appearance. Although the trustees won this round, they still seemed considerably preoccupied by the likelihood of fire. Outside sprinklers were installed on the east windows, but not even these, and rolling iron shutters, eased their worries. By January 1899 they had come to have serious doubts about the wisdom of regarding Copley Square as a desirable location for the museum in the distant future. These concerns led them to look for some 400,000 square feet of land elsewhere, "while it was possible to obtain it within the limits of the city and at a reasonable price." Looking back from a distance of seventy years, the decision seems a wise and fortunate one, though it is also difficult to see why they had not envisioned the possibility of construction next to the museum, even though the lot in question had remained vacant for nearly three decades. If you do not own land, you cannot prevent other people from building upon it.

A new site was found, with a wide frontage on the Fenway and running through to Huntington Avenue, with a total area of 556,000 square feet, that could be bought for $703,000. Thus, in the year of the first surplus, the museum returned to precarious finances by the decision to move. A mortgage loan for $415,000 was secured at 3½ percent interest, the balance of the purchase price being obtained by temporary borrowing from unrestricted funds. The original grant of the Copley Square land from the city, made with the restriction that it should be used only as an open space or for the promotion of the Fine Arts, made it impossible for the museum to sell or mortgage the property, and practically impossible to remove to another location. Nevertheless, the city government, and the Boston Water Power Company, which had given the city the land in the first place, were understanding and cooperative in removing the restrictions, giving the museum a clear title to the Copley Square property.

As it would cost some $400,000 to complete the building on the present site, it seemed highly inexpedient to attempt any addition in Copley Square, if the museum were likely to wish to move within ten or fifteen years. Therefore the trustees had to decide whether to extend the existing building or to build upon the recently acquired Fenway land; whether, if they built in the Fenway, to make a complete removal, or move only one or two departments; how the money for a new building was to be found; and if by sale of the Copley Square property, "what is the most judicious course to be taken to that end?" In 1901 the problem was still unresolved, while the deficit had risen to $33,958. Some exchanges were made with the owners of adjoining property in the Fenway, which gave the museum 528,781 square feet of land between Huntington Avenue, Huntington Entrance, the Fenway, and a new street, subsequently laid out in 1907 as Museum Road.

At this point, with long decisions to be made for the distant future, there was a changing of the guard. William Endicott in January 1901 declined re-election as President, being then in his seventy-sixth year, and was succeeded by Samuel Dennis Warren (1892–1910). As the Director, General Loring, was also past seventy, Benjamin Ives Gilman was appointed to a newly created post of Assistant Director. On 27 February 1902, in the thirtieth year of his connection with the museum, Charles G. Loring wrote the trustees, resigning the directorship. Two days later he left the museum, never to return. He was appointed Director Emeritus with a pension, and it was hoped that he might return to special study in the Egyptian Department. Unfortunately his health failed rapidly, and on 18 August 1902 he died, widely lamented. On his death, Gilman fittingly applied to him Wren's epitaph, SI MONUMENTUM REQUIRIS, CIRCUMSPICE, remarking:

Hardly a room in our present building but shows some traces, and most show many of General Loring's hand; hardly a policy which the archives of the Corporation for twenty-six years record but has borne in conception, or received in execution, the impress of his

GENERAL CHARLES GREELY LORING AT HIS DESK. From the scrapbook of his
secretary, Miss Florence Virginia Paull (Mrs. Henri L. Berger).

personality. Compared with many similar institutions, there is a
friendly, almost homelike, atmosphere in our Museum, often
remarked upon by those who frequent it, that distinctly reflects the
character of its late head. Reticent and retiring by nature, he sought
no public recognition; but within the Museum no detail was too
small to escape his care . . . The record of this achievement can
never be fully written, but it is the dominant feature of the early
history of the Museum, and will materially modify its future.

CHAPTER IV

The Japanese Collection

The brachiopod, defined by the *Oxford English Dictionary* as "a bivalve mollusc, distinguished by having, on each side of the mouth, a long spiral arm, used in procuring food" is one of the least elegant or artistic works of creation. Charles Darwin's remark that certain of them "have been but slightly modified from an extremely remote geological epoch" suggests that it is one of the least imaginative or progressive forms of life. Yet, by the workings of serendipity, the brachiopod was directly responsible for the migration to the Museum of Fine Arts of immense quantities of great works of Japanese art and craftsmanship. This is the principle of "a little child shall lead them," or the Magi being guided by a star, reduced to a comic absurdity.

Brachiopods were the particular enthusiasm of Edward Sylvester Morse (1838–1925), a self-educated zoologist who had sat at the feet of Louis Agassiz in Cambridge before joining the staff of the newly endowed Peabody Academy of Science at Salem in 1867. One might note parenthetically that zoologists in the eighteen sixties were as responsive to the funds of new endowments as were behavioral scientists of the nineteen fifties. Once George Peabody of London had provided funds for the continuation, expansion, and renaming of the museum of the Salem East India Marine Society (established in 1799), aggressive and enthusiastic young zoologists were drawn to it like flies to honey. Although Frederick Ward Putnam, Alpheus Hyatt, and Alpheus Spring Packard, Jr., who came to Salem at the same moment as Morse, found their ways to greener pastures elsewhere within a few years, Morse stayed, and eventually made his career as director of the institution.

Having early become a convinced and enthusiastic Darwinian, which Louis Agassiz was not, Morse was fascinated to study the evolution of brachiopods from fossil remains to recent and living species. Although he had numerous fossils available, twenty years of searching the Atlantic coast from Eastport, Maine, to Beaufort, North Carolina, had produced fewer living varieties than he wished. In 1870 he published a monograph in which he argued that brachiopods were not shellfish but worms, which were more properly to be classified with the Annelida than the Mollusca. This had elicited a warm acknowledgment from Charles Darwin. Moreover, in 1871, when he was only thirty-five, Bowdoin College made Morse a Ph.D. *honoris causa*, a somewhat remarkable tribute to a state-of-Mainer without previous academic degrees. But as he longed to study the brachiopods of the Pacific, he took off in May 1877 for a three-month collecting expedition to Japan. Soon after his arrival in Tokyo, when he applied for permission to spend a month on the coast dredging, he was startled to receive as well the invitation to organize a department and found a museum of natural history at the new Imperial University. In the two decades that had passed since Commodore Perry's arrival, the Japanese, with startling rapidity, had begun to substitute for their traditional ideals the thoughts and habits of the Western world. It was not an easy transition, since many foreigners who came to Japan, especially merchants and missionaries, acted as if the Japanese were benighted heathen to be cheated or converted. As Morse's biographer, Dorothy G. Wayman, has written:

> Morse came into this atmosphere under unique circumstances. He arrived in Japan with no mission save to collect brachiopods. Having no professional preconceptions, he accepted the Japanese on a plane of equality. He included them with himself as seekers after scientific truth. He observed their civilization and culture factually, with a scientist's detachment, and accorded it validity in its own environment. This was the explanation of the instantaneous response of the Japanese, individually and officially, to his personality.

He soon found himself with a two-year contract, at a generous salary, on the faculty of the Imperial University of Tokyo. He dredged his brachiopods, excavated the shell mound at Omori, lectured on zoology and evolution, and, quite by accident, became fascinated by Japanese pottery.

This began when he chanced to find a pottery saucer in the shape of a shell. He looked for more, and, when he had assembled a certain number, proudly showed them to his Japanese friends. They were dismayed, although courteous, for these shell-saucers were neither old nor of creditable craftsmanship. This is not surprising, for, as Mrs. Wayman points out, Morse "had never read a book on history, or philosophy, or art. Architecture, music, and sculpture were terra incognita to him." At the time he went to Japan, "his idea of poetry was a good rollicking limerick. His favorite pictures were big bouncing horses by Rosa Bonheur. As for music, he doted on the 'Pilgrim's Chorus' performed by a brass band." But when his Japanese friends began to show him fine pottery, to cure him of his aberration for imitation shells, he learned that desirable examples could be recognized by an incised potter's mark. Although unable to read the written Japanese language, Morse had a memory so phenomenal that he could soon carry in his mind the visual appearance of hundreds of potter's signatures. He was an incurable pack-rat, with a passion for collecting anything within his reach. He also felt an equal compulsion to catalogue and classify whatever he collected. Japanese pottery began to compete with brachiopods during the hours when he was away from the lecture hall and the laboratory. Sunday afternoons he spent with Ninagawa Noritane, a learned antiquarian and student of ceramics, who would examine the pottery that Morse had bought during his walks of the previous week, instruct him in the "feel" of clays from different provinces, the methods of firing glazes, and sketch for him the signatures of famous potters. Such were the beginnings of the great Morse Collection of Japanese Pottery that was acquired by the Museum of Fine Arts in 1892.

By an equally unexpected turn of events, this rather tasteless scientist was responsible for initiating the career of a great student of oriental art, whose services both to the Museum of Fine Arts and to Japan were unique. As foreign applicants for teaching posts at the new Imperial University were frequently self-styled "authorities" of no competence, Morse was often asked to recommend qualified persons in various fields. Thus, when a teacher of philosophy was needed, Morse wrote to Charles Eliot Norton, asking for suggestions. As a result of this inquiry, Ernest Francisco Fenollosa (1853–1908), the Salem-born son of a Spanish musician, appeared in Tokyo in 1878 to become for two years Professor of Philosophy and Political Economy. Fenollosa had been the first scholar of the Harvard class of 1874 and class poet, receiving a fellowship that he used for study first in philosophy and then in the Harvard Divinity School. He brought with him to Japan a Salem bride, Lizzie Goodhue Millet, his boyhood sweetheart, whom he had married a few weeks before sailing. Ernest Fenollosa was a very different man from the energetic scientific-classifier Morse. Not only was he a poet, sensitive to music, he also was an incipient artist. Indeed when the School of Drawing and Painting at the Museum of Fine Arts opened in January 1877, he had been enrolled in the first class. While his formal role in Tokyo was to lecture on the history of Western philosophy from Descartes to Hegel, while he preached the gospel of Herbert Spencer to eager students, he was instantly receptive to the fast disappearing beauties of the old Japan. In Europe the transition from feudalism to an industrial world bemused by evolution had been spread over centuries; in Japan it was compressed into decades. As Van Wyck Brooks expressed it in his sketch of Fenollosa, "Japan, the hermit empire, that had thought itself the mightiest of nations, felt only a sudden humiliation as it confronted the wonders of the West; it went in for waltzing, mesmerism, planchette and cock-fighting, while everything Japanese seemed on the point of being swept away." At this moment in the course of the modernization of their country, many Japanese were so bemused by the marvels of progress that they became temporarily indifferent to their traditional arts and crafts. Artists skilled in the ancient ideals and techniques found themselves as little appreciated by the forward-looking as their Western counterparts do today among admirers of Jackson Pollock and Andy Warhol. Western novelties were in demand, but as the west had simultaneously acquired a taste for Japanese bric-a-brac, second-rate craftsmen were busy grinding out cheap products for export, while first-rate artists were neglected. Fenollosa found Kano Hōgai, whom he called "the greatest Japanese painter of recent times," selling brooms and baskets to support life. He set Hōgai to work again by taking lessons from him.

Although Morse returned to Salem at the expiration of his two-year contract with the Imperial University, and began in 1880 a thirty-six year tenure as Director of the Peabody Academy of Science, Fenollosa remained in Japan for many years. After the expiration of his original contract, he held the professorship of philosophy and logic from 1880 to 1886, although his interests turned increasingly to the arts. He became a passionate collector of paintings, acquiring everything that he could lay his hands upon and afford. At this moment opportunities were many, for private collections were broken up and objects were coming on the market from Buddhist monasteries no longer receiving government support. From his arrival Fenollosa was buying *kakemonos*. In 1879 he purchased one of two deer that was the masterpiece of the painter Ganku (1749–1838), the founder of the Kishi School. Furthermore, he undertook the systematic study of the history of Japan and China and of all schools of Japanese and Chinese art, molding his life to his studies to the extent of becoming a professing Buddhist and being baptized under the name of Tei-Shin. On 26 April 1884, he wrote to Morse:

> I don't know that I told you that I have received letters patent from Kano Yeitoku, the present head of the Kano house, adopting me (artistically, of course, not legally, though under Tokugawa it would have been legal) into the Kano family, and authorizing me to use the name Kano Yei (Yei being the first character of the artistic names of all past men of that line) and I have taken the name Kano Yeitan, the character Tan being that in the name Tanyu. My *nobu* name is Masanobu so that my full name is Kano Yeitan Masanobu. This I write in Chinese characters and have special seals.

He had by this time participated in forming an art club, called Kangwakwai, of which he and three artists, including the heads of the Kano and Tosa schools, formed the criticizing committee, empowered to judge and give certificates of authenticity to paintings.

When Edward S. Morse returned to New England late in 1879 he was more than a zoologist; he had become the principal source of knowledge about the traditional culture of Japan. As a careful observer of everything that fell under his glance, regardless of his previous experience, he could not resist noting, sketching, and classifying. Since he had personal charm of a sort, and a fervor for imparting what he knew, he became the local apostle of Japanese culture in Boston. Two series of Lowell Institute lectures that he gave in the winters of 1881–82 and 1883–84 not only created great local interest in Japan, but inspired various Bostonians to go there, especially young ones of ample means who were slightly bored by their native scene. Most significantly for the future of the Museum of Fine Arts, Morse caught the imagination of Dr. William Sturgis Bigelow (1850–1926) who eventually became as wholehearted a convert to Japanese art and religion as Ernest Fenollosa.

Being the son of Dr. Henry Jacob Bigelow and the grandson of Dr. Jacob Bigelow, who were ornaments of the Harvard Medical School for three-quarters of the nineteenth century, William Sturgis Bigelow inevitably passed through Harvard College with the class of 1871, received an M.D. in 1874, and went to Europe for five years' further medical study in Vienna, Paris, and Strasbourg. Although he acquired an enthusiasm for bacteriology from his association with Pasteur and Ranvier, his temperament was too sensitive to make surgery or the care of patients attractive to him. On returning home he set up a private bacteriological laboratory in Boston, but his father, who thought little of this, pressed him into taking the post of surgeon to out-patients at the Massachusetts General Hospital. As this uncongenial work left him little leisure for his laboratory, he soon lost interest in the practice of his profession. Having been attracted by the Lowell Institute series on Japan, Dr. Bigelow asked Edward S. Morse to spend a month with him in the summer of 1881 at Tuckernuck Island, off Nantucket, where he indulged in the taste for luxurious discomfort (or primitive conditions at disproportionate expense) that has long been typical of Bostonians on islands and in other remote family summer enclaves.

In the eighteen seventies when William Sturgis Bigelow was studying abroad he had had a foretaste of Japan through the objects of

DR. WILLIAM STURGIS BIGELOW. Charcoal drawing, John Singer
Sargent, 1917. 17.3174

Japanese craftsmanship that were coming to the attention of French
painters and smart Parisians, in large part through the importations
of the Paris dealer Samuel Bing. Dr. Bigelow's cousin, Mrs. Henry
Adams, in writing her father from Paris on 28 September 1879 about
her first Worth gown, "which not only fills my small soul but seals it
hermetically," and other delights, included this message. "Tell Bil
Bigelow we went to his 'Bing' and were interested in his Japanese
things. I succumbed to a small piece of Japanese silver, a matchbox,
which I wear as a pendant from my chatelaine. Tiffany's are good,
but this is better. It's so nice in travelling to have tapers always under
one's fingers. You see, it's a seed vessel of some kind, and the calix

opens on a hinge as a cover." Cousin "Bil" had obviously contributed more to Bing's profits than Clover Adams, if one recalls the hundreds of Japanese objects (mentioned in Chapter II) that he had lent to the Museum of Fine Arts in 1880 and 1881. Already from his Paris days a substantial collector of Japanese lacquer, bronzes, swords, and *netsukes*, he was a willing victim of Morse's enthusiasm for the country that produced such treasures. Daily association with Morse at Tuckernuck increased Bigelow's desire to get out of Boston and go to Japan. There was no reason why he should not, for, being a grandson of the China Trade merchant William Sturgis, he had ample means to follow his inclinations. Morse hankered to return to Japan, not only to seek more specimens of pottery, but to gather an ethnological collection for his Salem museum that would fully illustrate the fast-vanishing traditional culture of that country.

So in May 1882 William Sturgis Bigelow and Edward S. Morse set out together for Japan. When they arrived in Tokyo, Ernest Fenollosa and his young Japanese friend, ally, and former student, Okakura-Kakuzo (1862–1913), joined them for a journey through the principal centers of art and antiquities. During this journey Fenollosa was on the lookout for paintings, Morse was scooping up pottery and thousands of ethnological objects for Salem, while Dr. Bigelow, who did not have to count his pennies in the manner of his companions, was eagerly searching for anything of high quality that came within his reach. The journey also was significant for the future attitude of the Japanese toward their own treasures, if one may credit an anecdote told Mrs. Wayman (while collecting material for her biography of Morse) in 1939 by the eighty-two-year-old artist Atomi Gyokushi.

> At night, by candlelight in the inns, shut behind the seclusion of the translucent paper *shoji*, sprawled on the soft straw mats, they would show each other the treasures found that day, and Okakura, their interpreter, eager to perfect his English, would sit quietly listening. Bigelow would have a rare old pair of swords, perhaps; Fenollosa a *kakemono*, Morse a tea jar or bowl. One night Morse suddenly fell silent. It was unprecedented, and the others asked him what was wrong.

"Many fine things of Japanese art are now on the market, like those we are buying. It is like the lifeblood of Japan seeping from a hidden wound. They do not know how sad it is to let their beautiful treasures leave their country," answered Morse.

His words went like a sword into the heart of the young Japanese sitting in the shadows. In that moment Okakura conceived a mission. On his return to Tokyo he went to officials and important citizens and never rested until they, too, recognized the situation. Morse's words were the seed, flowering in the mind of Okakura, that produced the law of *Kokuhō* (National Treasures) by which, in 1884, all remaining objects of ancient art were registered and restricted from export.

But before this took place, multitudes of works of Japanese art of the highest quality had passed into the hands of Bostonians, through whom they eventually came to enrich the Museum of Fine Arts. The Asiatic Department of the Museum has today some 5,000 Japanese paintings, 60,000 prints, 7,700 ceramics, 2,500 tsuba, 600 swords, 200 Nō masks, 800 Nō costumes, and 1,000 *netsukes*, many of which are the result of the pre-1884 collecting by Morse, Fenollosa, and Bigelow.

Although Edward S. Morse left Japan late in 1882 to return around the world to Salem, William Sturgis Bigelow spent seven unbroken years in the country, collecting in many areas. Like Fenollosa, he embraced the Buddhist faith, and was its practitioner in as high a rank as was possible for a layman. He had, indeed, gone through the preliminary stages of induction into the priesthood and had received his "name in religion." When he returned to Boston, his religious convictions were not flaunted, or even visible to the casual observer, but Japanese art and Buddhism remained his guiding lights for the rest of his life. He never resumed the practice of medicine. After his father's death he was appointed in 1891 by Harvard College to fill the vacancy thus created on the board of trustees of the Museum of Fine Arts, being annually reappointed until his own death in 1926.

In all external appearances he was a conservative Bostonian, appropriately housed at 56 Beacon Street, overlooking the Common, who was kind to his friends in a whimsical manner. Thus in March 1893 he wrote to Mrs. John L. Gardner:

Now I come to a very delicate matter to communicate — so much so that I hardly know how to approach it — I have taken a great step — a great liberty — there is a lady involved — you are directly concerned — I tried to act for the best — the fact is that she was *so* beautiful and *so* intelligent and had *such* grey eyes and *such* perfect ears and *such* a disposition that I have ventured to christen her Mrs. John L. Gardner and to call her Belle for short, as I could not really use the whole name and then whistle.

She is a Chesapeake puppy.

Mugs are in order.

Yours sincerely,
W.S.B.

P.S. She is *very* attractive.

But she was not long-lived, for, in August, Mrs. Gardner received a lugubrious parody of a French *faire part* by which the dogs "Mmes. Rose et Minnie et MM. Grover Cleveland, Rough et Marengo II (dit Ring)" announced the death of "Mrs. John L. Gardner II (dite La Belle) leur soeur, belle-soeur, nièce, cousine, et fiancée, décedée à la suite d'une convulsion de dentition."

In a similar vein in 1903 Dr. Bigelow casually remarked to the enchanting Mrs. Joseph Lindon Smith, who had recently had her second child, that he had forgotten to give her a wedding present. He offered a unique della Robbia mantel for the house that the Smiths were then building in Dublin, New Hampshire, *provided* "Joe must locate it personally in one of the endless rooms, in endless warehouses, containing Bigelow's oriental and Italian possessions, 'mostly unlabelled,' he warned." The stipulation caused no trouble, for, Mrs. Smith reports, "the very next evening, Joe returned from a trip to Boston in a truck, bringing back far more in antiquities than the mantel."

This perceptive collector, namer-of-dogs, and giver-of-mantels, who, in Henry Adams' phrase, "lounged about Christie's like a dilettante of Hogarth's time," also delivered the 1908 Ingersoll Lecture at Harvard, published as *Buddhism and Immortality*, which concludes with this superlatively phrased passage:

There is a Japanese proverb that says, "There are many roads up the mountain, but it is always the same moon that is seen from the top." The Japanese themselves, with a liberality worthy of imitation, apply this saying to different forms of religious belief. The mountain may well typify matter, and the summit the highest accessible point on which a climber can stand and maintain his separate individual existence in terms of consciousness drawn from the material world. This peak may be accessible by any religion, or without any religion; but Buddhism and its genetically associated systems look beyond. The mountain top is the apotheosis of personal existence, the highest form of consciousness that can be expressed in terms of separate individuality, — a sublime elevation, where many a pilgrim is content to pause. Below him are the kingdoms; above him are the stars; and kingdoms and stars alike are his. But it is not the end. Deeper than the kingdoms, and higher than the stars, is the sky that holds them all. And there alone is peace, — that peace that the material world cannot give, — the peace that passeth understanding trained on material things, — infinite and eternal peace, — the peace of limitless consciousness unified with limitless will.

That peace is NIRVANA.

Dr. Bigelow in 1920 deposited in the Massachusetts Historical Society a series of diplomas issued to him in Japan in 1888 in the name of Gesshin, as a Buddhist disciple, bearing the seals of the Hieizen monastery and a list of various teachers through whom knowledge of the faith (according to the Tendai sect) was transmitted until it reached the student receiving the diploma. When he died six years later, Bishop Lawrence buried him from Trinity Church, but, following instructions, his body was clothed (by John Ellerton Lodge, the museum's curator of Chinese and Japanese art) in the cloak that Buddhist priests of the Shingon sect commonly wear when engaged in ritual practice. The rosary which he was accustomed to use in prayer was looped over his left hand. Half of his ashes, together with objects that he used in prayer, were sent to Japan to be cared for by the priests of the Hōmyōin-Miidera temple to which he was attached. This was indeed a surprising sequel to Edward S. Morse's search for brachiopods half a century earlier. That search had equally unexpected consequences for the Museum of Fine Arts, for the rich fruits of Dr. Bigelow's collecting were the decisive element in leading the trustees in 1886 to seek to enlarge their building. To an institution whose purchases had been chiefly confined to plaster casts, William Sturgis Bigelow was the first provider of original works of art in magnificent quantity. Moreover, his gifts opened to Boston a new world of aesthetic experience that in the end prevailed over the pedagogical neatness of the plaster cast.

A fascinating footnote to the Japan that Dr. Bigelow knew during his seven years' residence is preserved in Edward S. Morse's book *Japanese Homes and Their Surroundings*, published in 1885 and dedicated to Dr. Bigelow. Morse kept an extremely informative illustrated 3,500-page journal of his years in Japan that only appeared in print in 1917, under the title *Japan Day by Day*. It might not have appeared even then had not Dr. Bigelow exerted pressure, for when Morse jubilantly told his friend that he had obtained a long leave of absence from Salem to finish a number of studies on mollusks and brachiopods, Dr. Bigelow snapped back:

> The only thing I don't like in your letter is the confession that you are still frittering away your valuable time on the lower forms of animal life, which anybody can attend to, instead of devoting it to the highest, about the manners and customs of which no one is so well qualified to speak as you. Honestly, now, isn't a Japanese a higher organism than a worm? Drop your damned Brachiopods. They'll always be there and will inevitably be taken care of by somebody or other as the years go by, and remember that the Japanese organisms which you and I knew familiarly forty years ago are vanishing types, many of which have already disappeared completely from the face of the earth, and that men of our age are literally the last people who have seen these organisms alive. For the next generation the Japanese we knew will be as extinct as Belemnites.

Happily Morse obeyed, although in reducing his vast journal to two volumes of approximately 450 pages each he chose chiefly material that concerned the life of Japan rather than the artistic and collecting enthusiasms of himself and his cronies.

In the autumn of 1884 Ernest Fenollosa wrote from Tokyo to Morse in Salem that he had had a hell of a time this summer.

Been off 2 months and a half, with the Doctor [William Sturgis Bigelow] and an officer of Mombusho, who was sent on a special commission to travel with me and study art. We have been through all the principal temples on Yamashiro and Yamato armed with government letters and orders, have ransacked godowns, and brought to light pieces of statues from the lowest stratum of debris in the top stories of pagodas 1300 years old. We may say in brief that we have made the first accurate list of the great art treasures kept in the central temples of Japan, we have overturned the traditional criticism attached to these individual specimens for ages, the Dr. has taken 200 photographs and I innumerable sketches of art objects (painting and statues); and more than all, I have recovered the history of Japanese art from the 6th to the 9th centuries A.D. which has been completely lost . . . I am proving that some of their supposed treasures are relatively worthless and bringing forth the real gems from unknown holes. But it is significant that the Mombusho, hearing that I was to travel this summer for this purpose, should have appropriated money for a special commissioner to travel with me, to study according to my methods and to find out for the government where the really good things are.

Fenollosa's personal collection had, by this time, grown to such dimensions that, becoming concerned about its future, he sought Morse's advice.

Already people here are saying that my collection must be kept here in Japan for the Japanese. I have bought a number of the very greatest treasures secretly. The Japanese as yet don't know that I have them. I wish I could see them all safely housed forever in the Boston Art Museum. And yet, if the Emperor or the Mombusho should want to buy my collections, wouldn't it be my duty to humanity, all things considered, to let them have it? What do you think?

There is no record of what Morse thought, but Fenollosa's collection *did* achieve permanent safe housing in the Museum of Fine Arts, thanks to a second Boston physician who preferred travel in the Far East to the practice of his profession. Dr. Charles Goddard Weld

THE BURNING OF THE SANJO PALACE (detail). Full color on paper, 22 feet 10 inches long. Japanese, Kamakura period, 13th century. *Fenollosa-Weld Collection.* 11.4000

(1857–1911) was seven years Dr. Bigelow's junior, but he too was possessed of a China Trade fortune which gave him freedom of movement. Having received his M.D. from the Harvard Medical School, he became a surgeon, attached first to the Massachusetts General and Carney hospitals in Boston and then to the Chambers Street Hospital in New York. Retiring after a few years from active surgical practice, he traveled widely. Like other Bostonians who had fallen under the spell of Edward S. Morse, he too went off to Japan, where he became an active collector of swords and sword ornaments and other examples of Japanese crafts. Dr. Weld's most decisive act was to buy in 1886 Ernest Fenollosa's great collection of paintings, most of which he promptly deposited in the Museum of Fine Arts. A stipulation of the sale was the paintings be known officially as the

Fenollosa-Weld Collection, and that they be placed in Boston. Out of friendship for Morse, Dr. Weld added to the Peabody Museum in 1906–7 a large exhibition hall to house the great collection of Japanese ethnology which had been assembled as a complement to the works of art that were destined for Boston.

Upon Weld's death on 18 June 1911, he bequeathed to the Museum of Fine Arts the objects that he had earlier deposited there. Their extent will be appreciated from the preliminary inventory included in the 1911 museum report.

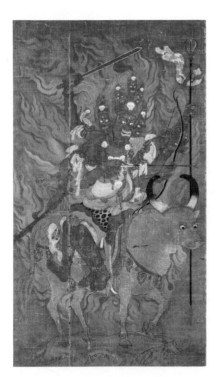

DAI-ITOKU MYO-O (CONQUEROR OF DEATH). Japanese painting, Kamakura period, 13th century. *Fenollosa-Weld Collection.* 11.4037

JITTOKU LAUGHING AT THE MOON. Japanese painting, Ashikaga Idealistic period, late 15th century. *Fenollosa-Weld Collection.* 11.4123

Japanese swords	165
Sword guards	151
Other sword furniture	286
Suits of armor	15
Pouch ornaments	142
Mounted tobacco pouches	21
Pipes	29
Vessels of metal, ornaments, etc.	22
Objects of lacquer, and inro	35
Netsuke and ondome	98
Pipe cases, fans, etc.	9
	973
Chinese and Japanese paintings	1,099
Total	2,072

The same report gave the following condensed accounting of Dr. William Sturgis Bigelow's gifts to the museum in the same field:

Japanese swords	493
Sword guards	1,041
Metal work	579
Silver	116
Glass	356
Pottery	172
Embroidery	196
Fans	125
Lacquer	1,207
Ivory	147
Inro and netsuke	797
Books	4,000
Carved wood	397
Masks	246
Sculpture	133
Other objects	1,200
Chinese and Japanese paintings	3,634
Total (not including prints and sketches)	14,839

MONKEYS. Japanese six-fold screen, by Sesshū, dated 1491. *Fenollosa-Weld Collection. 11.4141*

LANDSCAPE, SCENES ON A LAKE. Japanese six-fold screen, by Oguri Sotan, Ashikaga Idealistic period, late 15th century. *Fenollosa-Weld Collection. 11.4149*

THE ISLANDS OF MATSUSHIMA. Japanese six-fold screen by Kōrin (1658–1716). *Fenollosa-Weld Collection. 11.4584*

MOUNT FUJI SEEN BY WOODCUTTERS. Japanese
print from the series 36 *Views of Fuji* by Hokusai
(1760–1849). *Bigelow Collection.* 11.19717

It was remarked as noteworthy that of the 4,733 paintings in the
Fenollosa-Weld and the Bigelow collections, less than 700 proved
to be copies or forgeries.

Although Dr. Bigelow and Dr. Weld were the greatest benefactors
of the Museum of Fine Arts that can be chalked up to brachiopods,
Edward S. Morse's lectures on Japan led a considerable number of
other Bostonians to that country. Mr. and Mrs. John Lowell Gardner, who had had Morse lecturing in their music room at 152
Beacon Street, went there in 1883. From Yokohama on 30 June 1883
Mrs. Gardner wrote: "we are still here, dear friend, and it is so
fascinating that I well understand Sturgis Bigelow who cannot tear
himself away." She continued:

> Sturgis Bigelow never seems to have us off his mind for one
> moment and is constantly turning up here for tiffin or dinner, or
> else telegraphing to us that we must go up to Tokyo for this or that
> or the other, and consequently we have tiffined and dined together
> in every conceivable place and style; and I should say we have
> drunk gallons of the canary-colored tea out of their dear little cups
> and have eaten pounds of sweets as we three have sprawled about
> on the soft, clean mats, in the funny little shops, looking at curios
> . . . Bigelow wears the Japanese garment always when in his
> house, and shoes are such an unheard-of thing on the pretty mats
> that I kick mine off on every occasion.

The Gardners visited both temples and wrestling matches before moving on to China in the autumn. Their nephew John Gardner Coolidge (1863–1936), a member of the Harvard class of 1884, spent the years 1887–1889 in Japan and Korea, although his subsequent collecting, which now enriches the Museum of Fine Arts, was in the field of Chinese porcelains.

Percival Lowell (1855–1916), of the Harvard class of 1876, spent the decade 1883–1893 in the Far East, chiefly in Japan. The chief products of his *Wanderjahre* were several charming books on Japan, rather than the collecting of works of art; in later years he turned to astronomy, building his observatory above Flagstaff, Arizona.

After the death of his wife, Henry Adams came briefly to Japan with John La Farge. While on the way, he wrote John Hay from San Francisco on 11 June 1886: "At Omaha a young reporter got the better of us; for when in reply to his inquiry as to our purpose in visiting Japan, La Farge beamed through his spectacles that we were in search of Nirvana, the youth looked up like a meteor, and rejoined: 'It's out of season!' " For Sturgis Bigelow it certainly was not, for he was still there seeking Nirvana, after his fashion, in collecting as well as in Buddhism. On 8 April 1883 Mrs. Henry Adams had written her father: "Am glad Bil Bigelow is so happy in Japan; Boston is so depressing to him that I doubt if he ever can live there; and why should he?" Three years and a quarter later, Mrs. Adams was dead and Bil Bigelow had appointed himself "master of ceremonies" for her desolated husband's visit to Japan. From Yokohama on 9 July 1886 Adams wrote again to Hay, remarking, "Fenollosa and Bigelow are stern with us. Fenollosa is a tyrant who says we shall not like any work done under the Tokugawa Shoguns. As these gentlemen lived two hundred and fifty years or thereabouts, to 1860, and as there is nothing at Tokyo except their work, La Farge and I are at a loss to understand why we came; but it seems we are to be taken to Nikko shortly and permitted to admire some temples there." After ten days of heat and smells in Yokohama and Tokyo, Adams and La Farge were translated to the cool heights of Nikko, where Sturgis Bigelow lived in the summer with Mr. and Mrs. Fenollosa. Restfully installed near them in "a little Japanese toy-house" looking onto a waterfall, Adams wrote on 17 July 1886 to Theodore F. Dwight: "As yet we have found little to buy, and nothing very well worth getting; but we are doing our best to spend our money. Here at Nikko are no shops to speak of. Kioto is the place for purchases and we do not feel confident of getting there. Fenollosa and Bigelow are the highest authorities on lacquers and kakemonos; but they can only pick up a good thing now and then." With their aid Adams spent considerable time in a frustrating effort to secure handsome works of art for himself and John Hay to adorn the twin houses that H. H. Richardson had designed for them in Lafayette Square in Washington, but the picking was poor. From Yokohama, Adams had complained to Hay, "I am trying to spend your money. It is hard work, but I will do it, or succumb." Already by 1886 opportunities had so shriveled that *kakemonos* were not to be got and porcelain worth buying was rare. A great deal of superlative material had already gone to Boston, but, what was even more significant, the Japanese were returning to their senses and once again showing a proper concern for their artistic tradition.

As we have seen, Ernest Fenollosa was already making artistic inventories for the government in 1884. Two years later he and Okakura-Kakuzo were made members of the Imperial Art Commission sent abroad by the Japanese government to study methods of art education in Europe and the United States. When Fenollosa sailed for San Francisco in October 1886, in company with Adams and La Farge, he did so in the capacity of a Japanese official, traveling under Japanese orders and credentials. For a member of the Harvard class of 1874, he had gone a long way in a dozen years!

Upon their return from the West in 1887, the commissioners began planning the curriculum of a new Fine Arts Academy in Tokyo, which would link the traditional past of Japan with new systems of art instruction. Fenollosa and Okakura were made managers of the new institution. The painters from Fenollosa's club of artists acted as instructors, while he himself taught aesthetics and art history. When an art department was established in the Imperial Museum both men were on its board, while Okakura was as well made director of the New Art School of Ueno, Tokyo. Thanks to Fenollosa and his younger disciple, the traditions and techniques of Japanese painting and drawing had been reinstituted in the schools. In July 1889, when things were going swimmingly in Tokyo, Ernest Fenollosa was asked to return to Boston to establish a Japanese department in the Museum of Fine Arts. With the new art movement under way in Tokyo but still not fully accepted, the invitation posed problems. On the other hand, the indiscriminate enthusiasm for everything Western that had prevailed at the time of his arrival in Japan a dozen years earlier was giving way to a conservative nationalism. Moreover, his own collection of paintings, thanks to Dr. Weld, was already in Copley Square. In April 1890 he accepted the Boston offer, and, having been decorated with the Order of the Sacred Mirror, reserved for those who had performed distinguished personal service to the Emperor, sailed from Yokohama the following July.

While returning around the world from Japan in 1883, Edward S. Morse had studied pottery wherever he could find it. In London he had entered in his journal: "The more I see of these various collections, the more I think of the wonderful character of mine. All the collections here and in Paris will not equal mine in value and hardly in number." Others shared this view, for he received tempting offers from collectors for single specimens. However, these he refused, for he wished to have the collection in Boston as a unit. As a scholar living on an institutional salary, who had gone into debt to acquire objects, he could not give his collection to the Museum of Fine Arts with any more readiness than that institution, granted its infinitesimal purchase funds, could offer to buy it. To the consternation of family and friends, he borrowed money to add a wing to his Linden Street house in Salem to provide for the proper display of the collection, nearly losing the house through the burden of debt. In 1887, as President of the American Association for the Advancement of Science, he enjoyed the perquisite of a trip to Europe as delegate to the meeting of the British association of the same name. He made good use of his time. Not only did he visit a German palaeontologist at Kiel specializing in brachiopods, but through Louis Gonse, editor of the *Gazette des Beaux-Arts*, in Paris he found at Bing's "the greatest addition yet to the collection."

Various friends were making vigorous efforts to procure funds that would keep Morse's pottery in Boston. Dr. Denman W. Ross urged its acquisition, saying in an 1889 letter,

> The collection illustrates, better than any collection of works of art which I have ever seen, the principle which underlies all true artistic activity, — the principle that it is not enough to invent new types of things, but each type must be improved and perfected according to the ideal which it suggests to the imagination . . . You remember what the old philosopher said: A little thing makes perfection, perfection which is not a little thing. This is the lesson which Prof. Morse's pots and jars teach us. The differences between one example of a type and another are slight; but every example represents a distinct effort to realize the ideal.

As General Charles G. Loring's efforts to raise funds were nearing the goal, Morse made a last journey to Europe in 1889 in an attempt to make the collection as complete as possible. While this plunged him even more deeply into debt, he spent happy weeks in Paris and London with collectors and dealers.

In 1890, when the new wings of the Museum of Fine Arts were completed, Morse deposited his great collection there. It had been valued by appraisers at $100,000. By the spring of 1891 over $50,000 had been raised for its purchase, although oddly enough this does not appear in the printed treasurer's reports of the time. Apparently General Loring was unofficially securing funds from friends, who doubtless included Dr. Bigelow, Dr. Weld, and, very probably, Dr. Ross. In 1892, when the subscription seemed to have stalled at $76,000, Morse accepted that sum, and happily paid off his mortgages and loans. On 5 March 1892 he noted: "my pottery is squared up and after paying my bills I shall have something left to invest." In consideration of his willingness to accept a smaller sum than the appraised value, he was appointed Keeper of Japanese Pottery at the Museum at a small stipend. For a decade he worked at the task of writing a monumental *Catalogue of the Morse Collection of Japanese Pottery*, which was published in 1901. This large quarto of 384 pages printed at the Riverside Press, with 68 photogravure plates and 1,545 cuts of potters' marks, sold for $20.00, with

a large-paper edition at $50.00. It was the first monumental cata-
logue to be published by the Museum of Fine Arts. Seven years later
R. L. Hobson wrote Morse that in cataloguing the Japanese pottery
in the British Museum, it had been his mainstay.

For five years Ernest Fenollosa stayed as Curator of the Japanese
Department at the Museum of Fine Arts. Although the Curators of
the Print Department and of Classical Antiquities regularly printed
accounts of their activities in the museum's annual report, no
similarly detailed record of his ever appeared there. There was much
work to be done in unpacking, studying, cataloguing, and arranging
the vast collection of objects that had come to Boston through
Bigelow and Weld. In spite of limited space, Fenollosa arranged
varied exhibitions, first of the work of Hokusai, then of early nineteenth-century *kakemonos* by Kaibun and Hoyen, of sixteenth-century screens with gold backgrounds from the museum's collections,
as well as loan exhibitions of color prints owned by S. Bing, pre-
seventeenth-century Japanese paintings and metalwork lent by Mr.
Shirasu of Tokyo, and forty-four Chinese Buddhist paintings of
the eleventh and twelfth centuries, lent by the Temple Daitokuji of
Kyoto. Before the latter exhibition returned to Japan, ten of the
pictures were purchased (five by the museum and five by Denman
W. Ross) in order to provide the temple with funds for much needed
repairs.

In the autumn of 1893 Fenollosa took as part-time assistant in the
department Arthur Wesley Dow, an Ipswich-born, Paris-trained
painter, who had for some months been informally reveling in the
riches of the museum's Japanese collections. Together they worked
to develop a system of art instruction for American schools that
would translate Fenollosa's Japanese theories into terms that would
make sense to students whose earlier training, if any, had been along
conventional Western lines. The most tangible theoretical evidence
of the system was Dow's monograph *Composition*, first published
in 1899, which went through a number of editions. Dow turned to
making wood-block prints in which, with considerable skill, he
applied Japanese techniques to New England expression. Soon after
an 1895 exhibition of these color prints at the Museum of Fine Arts,
Arthur Dow received the offer of an instructorship in composition

A LOHAN FEEDING A HUNGRY SPIRIT. Chinese painting on silk by Lin T'ing-kuei, Sung dynasty, dated 1178. *Ross Collection.* 06.292 From the Temple Daitokuji of Kyoto.

AHRATS AND GIFT BEARERS IN BAMBOO GROVE. Chinese painting on silk by Chou Chi-chang, Sung dynasty, dated 1180. 95.5 From the Temple Daitokuji of Kyoto.

at the Pratt Institute, so went off to Brooklyn to put his and Fenollosa's theories of art education into practice.

The acquisition of another assistant in the Japanese Department in the autumn of 1894 led, a year later, to Fenollosa's departure from Boston. Mary McNeil Scott, a handsome Alabaman in her late twenties with two children by previous marriages, had lived for several years in Japan when married to her second husband, Ledyard

Scott, a consul at Kobe. After divorcing Scott, she began writing; as she knew some Japanese and was enthusiastic about the country, Fenollosa engaged her to work at the museum. On 2 October 1895 Mrs. Fenollosa was granted a divorce in Minneapolis, and on 28 December he married Mary McNeil Scott in New York City. In the autumn of 1895 Fenollosa had applied for a leave of absence; in April 1896 his resignation was accepted. Thus his connection with the Museum of Fine Arts ended abruptly and unexpectedly. He simply left Boston, without apparent regrets, with the intention of supporting himself by lecturing.

While Fenollosa's second marriage was a happy one, for Mary keenly shared his intellectual interests, their return to Japan in July 1896 proved a disappointment. The government was less disposed to employ foreigners than it had been in earlier years. Although he plunged into the study of Noh drama, and for two years taught English at the Tokyo Higher Normal School, Fenollosa and his wife returned to New York for good in 1900. The remaining years of his life were devoted to writing, lecturing, and assisting Charles L. Freer in the formation of the collection that is now in the Freer Gallery of Art, Smithsonian Institution. Although Ernest Fenollosa died of a heart attack in London on 21 September 1908, the results of his studies were not lost, for Mary completed from notes his *Epochs of Chinese and Japanese Art,* which was published in two volumes in 1912, while Ezra Pound found his notes a rich bed of poetic imagery. 'Noh'; *or Accomplishment: a Study of the Classical Stage of Japan* appeared in London in 1916 as the joint work of Fenollosa and Pound. On the first anniversary of his death, Fenollosa's ashes were reburied in Japan in the gardens of the Miidera Temple, where the site was marked with an open pagoda with five stone memorials, dedicated to his memory by the Japanese government, by Arthur Wesley Dow and Charles L. Freer, by Gaston Migeon of France, and by Laurence Binyon of the British Museum. On the slope below Fenollosa's pagoda, half the ashes of William Sturgis Bigelow were placed after his death in 1926. Although Ernest F. Fenollosa had no further ties with Boston after his abrupt departure in 1895, his name is one that should always be remembered with gratitude in the Museum of Fine Arts.

In September 1897 Arthur Wesley Dow returned from Brooklyn to the museum as Keeper of Japanese Paintings and Prints. He arranged an exhibition of screens by artists of the Sesshu, Kano, and Tosa schools during the winter of 1897–98. In the following summer he placed on display screens and *kakemonos* by Kano Tanyu and his brothers Naonobu and Yasunobu, which were followed in the fall of 1898 by a selection from the works of the Kose, Kasuga, Takuma, and Tosa schools. Among these were paintings lent by Denman W. Ross. After two years at the museum, Dow returned finally to teaching; for the twenty years following 1903, as head of the Fine Arts Department at Teachers College, Columbia University, he had a major influence upon art instruction in American schools.

The second Curator of the Japanese Department at the museum, Walter Mason Cabot, appointed in 1899, served only until 1902. Unlike Fenollosa, he regularly noted the activities of his department in the published annual report, giving accounts of special exhibitions of paintings and prints arranged, chiefly, from the collections of William Sturgis Bigelow and Denman W. Ross. Paul Chalfin, a painter, then succeeded, first as Curator pro tem, and then as Curator. Although in 1903 the name was altered to Department of Chinese and Japanese Art, the staff consisted of the curator and two secretaries, one of whom was Japanese. In March 1904 Okakura-Kakuzo came to Boston to study and catalogue paintings and drawings in the department.

After a decade as Director of the New Art School at Ueno, Okakura resigned in 1897 when political pressure had brought fresh waves of Europeanism to bear. At this moment, when Fenollosa had returned and found himself unwelcome, it was demanded that European methods should become increasingly prominent in the instruction in Okakura's school. Six months later, thirty-nine young artists grouped themselves around Okakura and opened the Nippon Bijitsuin, or Hall of Fine Arts, at Yanaka, in the suburbs of Tokyo, based on the assumption that "the old art of Asia is more valid than that of any modern school, inasmuch as the process of idealism, and not of imitation, is the *raison d'être* of the art-impulse." The words are Okakura's, from his *The Ideals of the East with special reference to the Art Of Japan*, published in London by John Murray in 1903. In an introduction to this book, Sister Nivedita of Ramakrishna-Vivekânanda had written: "If we may say that Mr. Okakura is in some sense the William Morris of his country, we may also be permitted to explain that the Nippon Bijitsuin is a sort of Japanese Merton Abbey." Through his work with the Imperial Archaeological Commission, Okakura knew the art of his own country more thoroughly than any other man. Furthermore, during several visits to China he had become familiar with nearly every place noted in its religious, artistic, or political history. From two years spent in India he became equally acquainted with its religion, art, and philosophy. Thus when he opened *The Ideals of the East* with the sentence "Asia is one," he knew whereof he spoke. Okakura's grasp of Western art and literature was likewise extraordinary. Through his books, which included *The Awakening of Japan* (1904) and *The Book of Tea* (1906), he interpreted East to West with subtlety.

Shortly before Okakura came to Boston, John La Farge wrote Mrs. John Lowell Gardner about him in these terms: "I should like to add to any knowledge you may have of him my statement that he is the most intelligent critic of art, and I might also say of everything, that I know of. His very great learning in certain ways is balanced by his perception of the uselessness of much that he knows. I think that he is one of the very few persons whom you should not miss enjoying." Although, until his death in 1898, John L. Gardner had been the ever-helpful Treasurer of the Museum of Fine Arts, his wife, clearly the most imaginative and inspired art collector in Boston, took little interest in the museum's affairs. In this, as in other matters, she resembled "The Cat that Walked by Himself," for her mind worked faster and more divertingly than those of most of her well-upholstered relatives and neighbors. So, soon after her husband's death, she began the construction of Fenway Court, the great palace that was to house her collection and become the Isabella Stewart Gardner Museum. Her paintings far outshone those owned by the Museum of Fine Arts at the time, for the young Bernard Berenson, who had gone to Europe with her assistance soon after his graduation from Harvard in 1887, was alert to inform her of significant opportunities. While her pictures would then have been a godsend in Copley Square, there never seems to have been any question of their going in that direction. For, let us admit it, the Museum of Fine Arts in its first thirty years was too solemn, too pedagogical, too given to the unprovoked doing of artistic and intellectual good, to appeal to a mind like Mrs. Gardner's.

A small incident of family comedy may illustrate the situation. In 1887 J. Randolph Coolidge (1828–1925) the husband of John L. Gardner's sister Julia, wished to give a painting to the Museum of Fine Arts. When he applied to his sister-in-law for advice, Mrs. Gardner suggested that he buy John Singer Sargent's *El Jaleo*, originally exhibited at the Paris Salon of 1882, which the artist had recently brought to Boston. Feeling that the subject of a Spanish gypsy dancer, however admirably painted, was unsuitable for his purpose, J. R. Coolidge did not buy the picture, which his brother Thomas Jefferson Coolidge (1831–1921) promptly snapped up for his own house. It took Randolph Coolidge, whose own Beacon Street

EL JALEO. John Singer Sargent, 1882. *Isabella Stewart Gardner Museum, Boston.*

L'AMI DES HUMBLES. Léon Augustin Lhermitte, 1892. *Gift of J. Randolph Coolidge. 92.2657*

house was liberally adorned by naked ladies in marble, bronze, and oil, including a vast Bouguereau, some five years to find a picture that seemed to him appropriate as a gift to the Museum of Fine Arts. This finally proved to be Léon Augustin Lhermitte's *L'ami des Humbles*, exhibited in the 1892 Salon, which depicts the supper of Christ at Emmaus in the setting of a French peasant's cottage. Although the Lhermitte canvas has long since disappeared into storage at the museum, Sargent's *El Jaleo* occupies a distinguished position at Fenway Court. In 1914, when Mrs. Gardner was demolishing her music room to make way for the present tapestry gallery, T. Jefferson Coolidge lent her the picture for the summer while his house was closed. She designed the Spanish Cloister for its dramatic exhibition so skillfully that when Coolidge saw it in this superb setting he promptly gave it to her!

Whatever Mrs. Gardner may have thought of the Museum of Fine Arts, she and its new Japanese adviser understood each other at once. Okakura-Kakuzo came to Fenway Court on Sunday, 27 March 1904, for the first time. From then on, whenever he was in Boston, they enjoyed each other's company as John La Farge had predicted. Moonlight on the walls of the flower-filled courtyard at Fenway Court inspired him to the following poem:

THE STAIRWAY OF JADE

The One
Alone and White.

Shadows but wander
In the lights that were;
Lights but linger
In the shadows to be.

The Moon
White and alone.

The stars have dissolved
To make a crystal night;
Fragrance floats
Unseen by flowers;
Echoes waft,
Half answered by darkness.

A shadow glides
On the stairway of jade —
Is it a moonbeam?
It is the One?
In the Abode of Solitary Shadow?

Although the crowded galleries and basement storerooms of the Museum of Fine Arts in Copley Square were a sad contrast to the inspired beauty of Fenway Court, Okakura rejoiced in the objects that they contained, for in the January 1905 *Bulletin* he wrote:

The importance of the collection of Japanese and Chinese paintings in the Museum has been recognized for many years by students of Oriental art. Personally I have had opportunities in the past to know certain of its great treasures, but it is only upon examining it since last March that I began to realize its preeminent place among the Oriental collections in the world. I do not now hesitate to say that in point of size it is unique, and that in quality it can only be inferior to the Imperial Museums of Nara and Kioto; while for the schools of the Tokugawa painting it is unrivalled anywhere.

Before he returned to Japan at the end of February 1905, Okakura had examined some 5,000 examples of graphic art and had written critical notes of 3,642 of them as the basis of a future catalogue. He also studied the Japanese sculpture in Dr. Bigelow's collection and the great reference library that he had assembled, which was stored, for want of space, in the Copley Square building.

When Paul Chalfin left the curatorship in 1905 to accept the Jacob H. Lazarus Scholarship for the Study of Mural Painting in Italy, Okakura-Kakuzo was appointed Adviser to the Department. He returned to Boston in October 1905, having made a number of purchases for the museum during his absence, and bringing with him a collection of photographs of objects in the Imperial Museum at Tokyo, sent as a gift from that institution. In November 1905 the trustees appointed Okakura, Curator of the Department; although he felt obliged to decline because of obligations in Japan, he willingly agreed to continue as Adviser, spending what time he could here.

When Visiting Committees were first instituted, Edward Jackson Holmes (Harvard A.B. 1895, LL.B. 1899) was appointed in 1907 chairman of the committee for the Department of Chinese and Japanese Art. He had some firsthand acquaintance with the Far East, for he had traveled around the world for a year between college and entering the Law School. He had met his wife, Mary Stacy Beaman, while both were exploring Upper Burma. He was a grandson of Dr. Oliver Wendell Holmes; although his father, Edward Jackson Holmes of the class of 1867, had died when he was only eleven years old, he had inherited many interests from him. In the fiftieth anniversary report of the Harvard class of 1895, Ned Holmes wrote, sixty-one years after his father's death:

I inherited an interest in art from my father. He was obliged to give up the practice of law on account of asthma, but refused to

become an invalid and devoted himself with unrelenting energy
to his original life interest — art and archaeology. He had an
extraordinary gift for making history live. He took me to Athens
and Rome when I was ten years old [1883] and made the ancient
Greeks and Romans more real to me than my own living friends. He
made me feel the fire of the spirit in temples, cathedrals, statues,
paintings, and the importance of museums as preservers of our
world inheritance. So, when circumstances permitted me to do
what I wanted, I gave my whole life and thought to the Boston
Museum of Fine Arts.

Moreover, after his father's premature death in 1884, his mother,
Henrietta Goddard Wigglesworth, had married Walter Scott Fitz,
who had gone to China in 1860 as agent of Wetmore, Cryder, and
Company in Tientsin, and had been a partner in the great China
Trade of Russell and Company from 1870 until his retirement in
1878. Although Ned Holmes was officially a Boston lawyer and
private trustee, his chief interest throughout his life was in the arts.
Whenever his own resources proved inadequate for any generous
assistance to the Museum of Fine Arts, his mother could invariably
be counted upon to help. Thus, when Okakura returned to Japan he
took with him a special subscription fund for the purchase of works
of art to which Mrs. W. Scott Fitz had been the most substantial
contributor.

To carry on curatorial work in Okakura's absence, Francis Gardner
Curtis (1868–1915) was appointed Associate of the Department of
Chinese and Japanese Art, and J. Arthur MacLean, Assistant in
Charge of Collections. Curtis, who was a cousin of the late John
Lowell Gardner, promptly devised in the Copley Square building a
"Japanese Cabinet," which he described in the 1906 report as

an attempt to furnish for the objects there exhibited a background
somewhat similar in tone to that which would be found in some
old temple in Japan. It does not in any way try to reproduce the
interior of a temple, but merely aims to render an atmosphere of
dignified simplicity suitable to the proper exhibition of its contents.
The dais and the moulding half-way up the wall are of cypress,
treated by an "age" stain to a silvery brown, while the walls up to

the moulding are covered by an undyed burlap, above which is plain white plaster. No labels are placed upon any of the objects in the cabinet, but upon the seat in the centre of the room are kept several printed or typewritten descriptions of the various exhibits together with a plan of the room showing their location.

In 1907 Curtis was appointed Associate Curator. He was largely responsible for the design of the main floor Japanese galleries of the new Huntington Avenue building, where by the use of architectural elements and rice-paper screens an appropriate atmosphere was evoked.

In the spring of 1908, Francis Stewart Kershaw was added as Keeper of the Chinese and Japanese Collections exclusive of Pottery, which remained Professor Morse's semi-autonomous bailiwick, while Langdon Warner (Harvard A.B. 1903), who had studied with Okakura in Japan the previous year, became a second Assistant. The following year Warner, who to his dying day looked more like the oarsman that he had been as an undergraduate than an Oriental scholar, was promoted to Assistant Curator. Various Japanese were brought to the department for special curatorial work. In 1906 Shisui Rokkaku and Kakuya Okabe were engaged in cataloguing the collections of lacquer and metalwork, cleaning and repairing objects where necessary, and building special boxes for the preservation of pieces that had heretofore lacked them. The next year they were joined by Motokichi Tamura, who repaired and remounted many screens and *kakemono*. The distinguished sculptor Chunosuke Niiro helped repair sculpture. Although these appointments were temporary, Kojiro Tomita, who joined the department in 1908, is still in Boston more than sixty years later.

Finally in 1910 it was at last possible to persuade Okakura-Kakuzo to accept a one-year appointment as Curator. This post he was induced to hold until his premature and greatly lamented death, at the age of fifty, in September 1913. The trustees of the museum passed the kind of resolutions that trustees always pass under such circumstances, while William Sturgis Bigelow and John Ellerton Lodge (who was soon to become curator of the department) wrote for the December 1913 *Bulletin* a feeling memoir, the conclusion of which is quoted here.

It was a pleasure to go to see pictures or hear music with him. His appreciation was keen and his judgment sound and extremely discriminating. After a Beethoven symphony he said to his companion, "This is perhaps the only art in which the West has gone farther than the East." On the other hand, when taken, in spite of his misgivings, to hear a modern, comic opera, with its loud orchestra and chorus and its stage crowded with color and tinsel, he said, smilingly, next day, "It was like an iridescent nightmare." He liked Raphael and disliked Rubens. Of the Cubist pictures he said: "I stretch out my mind toward them; I touch nothing." He was a past master in those refinements of Japanese civilization which are part of the education of a gentleman, such as writing poetry and arranging flowers, in music, in the formal tea ceremony, fencing, and jujitsu. He was an "Admirable Crichton" in his way, with a grasp of the best intellectual products of the highest civilizations on both sides of the world, which completely invalidated Kipling's famous line:

"Oh, East is East, and West is West, and never the twain shall meet."

They met in Okakura-Kakuzo.

In his memory Dr. Denman W. Ross gave the museum a large Chinese stone figure of the *Bodhisattva Maitreya*, of the sixth century A.D., perhaps the finest sculpture that had until then come out of China. It is characteristic too that Langdon Warner's *The Craft of the Japanese Sculptor*, published thirty-three years later, bears the dedication:

OKAKURA KAKUZO
IN PIAM MEMORIAM

No account of the beginnings of the Oriental collection of the Museum of Fine Arts would be complete without mention of the imaginative help of Denman W. Ross. It would be invidious to classify him as an Orientalist, for there were few departments of the museum that did not benefit by his omnivorous collecting and generosity, but no reader is likely to fall into that error, for his name is bound to recur throughout this book. He has already been mentioned earlier as the nephew of Mathias Denman Ross, who secured the land for the building of the museum in Copley Square, but he

THE BODHISATTVA MAITREYA (MI-LO). Limestone, Chinese, Northern Wei dynasty. *Gift of Denman W. Ross in memory of Okakura-Kakuzo. 13.2804*

now reappears as one of the remarkable little group from Harvard classes of the seventies, whose early and unexpected interest in the arts proved to be of lasting benefit to the Museum of Fine Arts.

Bigelow was of the class of 1871, Fenollosa of 1874, Weld of 1879, and Ross was a member of 1875. As he lived longer than the others, only dying in 1935, he is the first of the great protagonists of

DR. DENMAN WALDO ROSS. Charcoal drawing, John Singer
Sargent, 1917. *17.3175*

this history that I knew, for he was still teaching at Harvard in the
nineteen twenties when I was a student. By then he was in his seventies — massive, rubicund, somewhat dogmatic in his theories of
design, and occasionally short of breath, but still eager to collect, to
teach, and to enjoy beauty. Fortunately arbitrary retirement ages had
not then been invented. I never dared to penetrate his courses, for
I had no proficiency in drawing, but I went occasionally to his high-
ceilinged house at the junction of Brattle, Sparks, and Craigie streets,
where Cambodian Buddhas, prehistoric Chinese roofing tiles, and
many other unexpected works of art were to be seen. I have never
forgotten the summer evening in 1925 when Dr. Ross and I had
dined at Elmwood with Kingsley and Lucy Porter. We left together.

Pausing at the corner of Elmwood Avenue and Brattle Street, Dr. Ross sniffed the fragrant air and, with great deliberation and dignity, pronounced: "You know — a friend of mine once said — that no *gentleman* [expressed with great emphasis] in Cambridge WALKS — *except* upon Brattle Street —— unless he has business elsewhere." We then sedately walked down Brattle Street to our respective abodes.

Although Ross was born in Cincinnati in 1853, his parents came to Cambridge and acquired the large house at 24 Craigie Street that was his home for the rest of his life. After being graduated in 1875 with highest honors in history, Denman Ross returned to Harvard in the autumn for graduate work in history with Henry Adams. He also at that moment attended the first lecture that Charles Eliot Norton gave, after his appointment as Professor of the History of Art. Although Henry Adams flew the academic coop in 1877, Ross persevered with a subject that Adams had suggested. In 1880 he received the degrees of A.M. and Ph.D., his thesis being published in 1883 under the title of *The Early History of Land-Holding among the Germans.* Such investigations were so little to his taste, however, that, after the death in 1884 of his father, who had opposed his messing with art, Ross abandoned history for good.

The fruits of Denman Ross's collecting appear in annual reports of the Museum of Fine Arts from 1883 onward, the objects that he lent or gave being of the most catholic variety. Drawings by Du Maurier, an Etruscan bronze handle, a pair of Venetian wrought-iron doors, a Persian tile, 53 water colors by Joseph Lindon Smith, Chinese porcelains, a John Constable water color, 1,010 pieces of Coptic, Turkish, Persian, and Italian textiles — the lists are staggering and confusing. The laconic listing of his gifts in 1896 is a case in point.

Two hundred and fifty-eight pieces of Coptic tapestry-weaving and other Egyptian mummy cloths, dating from the 1st to the 7th century, A.D.; also about three hundred and fifty pieces of embroidery, lace, priest's robes and altar hangings, velvets, brocades, 17th centuries; and an embroidered bed cover, Mexican, of about etc., mostly Spanish, French, and Italian, of the 15th, 16th and the middle of the 17th century; a book of samples of Japanese weaving, 2,013 in number; a relief in plaster, painted, Florentine, of the 15th century, "The Madonna and Child"; a double gate of wrought iron, Venetian, of the 14th century; a wrought iron window guard of the 15th or 16th centuries; three pieces of carved wood, Venetian, and a carved stone shield and crest, late florid Gothic Venetian; a wrought iron knocker, Venetian, 14th century; three pieces of leather work, Spanish, and five pieces of Japanese pottery to the Morse collection; two bowls, Hispano-Moresque; one bowl, Moorish, and one of Spanish make.

Such varied lists, read without personal knowledge of the collector and his standards, would suggest the wholesale and indiscriminate accumulations of a William Randolph Hearst or a Henry Ford. Nothing could be further from the truth. Denman Ross's entire life was spent in a search for beauty, for high artistic achievement, wherever and in whatever form it could be found. Whether an object were Eastern or Western, exotic or commonplace in its use, popularly esteemed or ignored, made not the slightest difference. If it met his standards of design and if it were for sale, he bought it, with a high probability that it would eventually reach the Museum of Fine Arts, either as a gift or loan. His comment on Morse's Japanese pottery, quoted earlier in this chapter, gives a clear indication of his guiding principle.

Early in 1906, Dr. Ross gave the museum all the objects that he had previously lent. This single act transferred the title of more than 1,800 Japanese prints of exceptional quality, nearly 100 Chinese, Japanese, and Tibetan paintings, and numerous Japanese sword-guards, bronze vessels, and examples of woodwork. Five European paintings included in the gift show the catholicity of his taste, for these were three Monets, a Tiepolo sketch of the *Apotheosis of a Poet*, and a remarkable portrait of Arnauld d'Andilly by Phillippe de Champaigne (1602–1674). Such great gifts simply cleared the decks for more collecting. In the autumn of 1913, when he gave the great Bodhisattva Maitreya, he filled the Renaissance Court (now destroyed) of the present museum with some of the purchases that he had made during the previous year, in Asia, Egypt, and Europe.

Here again the variety was overwhelming, for there were sculptures, paintings, porcelains, pottery, and textiles from Japan and China; sculptures in stone and bronze from Cambodia, Siam, Java, and India; a series of drawings and paintings from Persia and India; a great variety of Coptic and Arabic textiles, as well as those from China and Japan, manuscripts, early printed books and bookbindings, representing the art of Europe.

The explanatory comment on the exhibition that Dr. Ross contributed to the December 1913 *Bulletin* is worthy of note as a confession of faith. Although freely stating that "the exhibition has no unity of character," he sets forth the unity of vision that inspired his collecting.

The appeal of any object to the sense of vision, disregarding the effect of environment, depends upon the materials which have been used, the tones of it, its lights and colors, and its measures and shapes. The beauty and value of the object are discovered by comparing it with other objects of the same kind. It is the eye, of course, that tells us what is better and what is best. To know the best of its kind we must have seen it. The best is then our standard of judgment. As a rule we should avoid discriminating in kinds. Things are comparable only when they resemble one another. To be comparable things must have at least something in common. We can compare the red of a painting with the red of a piece of porcelain, but to prefer pictures to porcelains is absurd. To speak of certain arts — Sculpture, Architecture, and Painting — as superior or major arts, and of others as inferior or minor arts, is misleading. It is a proposition which suggests that a second-rate picture may be preferred to a first-rate cup or vase. The same principles of design which are followed in painting a picture are followed in making the cup or the vase, and the only important question is, To what extent has the sense of beauty been expressed? It may be fully expressed in the cup and not at all expressed in the picture. We shall do well, therefore, to compare only those things that are comparable, seeking the beautiful always in the best of its kind.

It has not been intended in gathering this collection to illustrate the history of art or the ways of craftsmanship, though that is done incidentally. The history of art is indiscriminate. It chronicles both decadence and development. Our real interest lies in art itself as the expression of life. We want to know what life has been when it has been stirred and moved by the sense of beauty and the appreciation of what is best in the relativity of things, when it has risen above the struggle for existence and the sordid ways of business into the world of ideals, when it is concerned not so much with what it is as with what it ought to be. The value of art does not lie in its own history, but in the higher life which it expresses and reveals to us. We see in the masterpieces of art what life has been at its finest moments and what it ought to be again and again. It is for this reason that the study of art is one of the most important of all studies for everybody.

In the course of his collecting Denman Ross was to enlarge the Oriental collections of the museum to include India and the Near East; thus, although he is remembered in many departments, he takes a place in this chapter with Dr. Bigelow and Dr. Weld. Perhaps the greatest piece of good fortune of the Museum of Fine Arts in the nineteenth century was that in its first decade it attracted three such men, still in their thirties, with the ability to collect and the imagination to do so in directions that were then still uncharted. Other Bostonians might buy paintings of ephemeral interest at Paris salons; these three gave thousands of objects that are among the incomparable treasures of the Museum of Fine Arts.

On the basis of the man who knew the man who shook the hand of George Washington, the museum still has a living tie with the beginning of its Japanese collection, for Kojiro Tomita, who was brought from Japan by Okakura in 1908 as a boy of seventeen, only retired in 1963 from the curatorship to which he had been appointed in 1931. Fortunately he is still with us, as a link with Okakura-Kakuzo, who was the friend and ally of Fenollosa, Morse, Bigelow, Weld, and Ross.

From Mr. Tomita's perceptive and capacious memory I learned only recently of a moving incident concerning the monumental statue that Denman Ross gave the museum in 1913 in memory of Okakura. Okakura himself had seen this sculpture in China in 1906 when it had just been uncovered after many years of partial concealment in the Pai-ma ssu Temple in Lo-yang. Having been greatly moved by it, he returned four years later to the White Horse Temple, only to find that it had disappeared. During the interval between these visits, the sculpture had been taken by a dealer to Paris, where Ross saw and bought it. So in the end, through Denman Ross's unfailing instincts, the statue came to the museum as a memorial to the man who had greatly loved it.

CHAPTER V

The Classical Collection

"I have always said and believed that it was hate of Boston that made me work for Boston. The collection was my plea against that in Boston which contradicted my (pagan) love." This autobiographical remark by Edward Perry Warren (1860–1928), a Bostonian expatriate who lived the greater part of his life in England, is reinforced by another reported by his biographers, Osbert Burdett and E. H. Goddard. "When asked whether he gave Greek antiquities to American museums for the sake of the hundredth person who might appreciate them, or whether the ideas for which these antiquities stood were a fundamental challenge to American conceptions, he replied: 'For both reasons, but especially for the latter.'"

This man's distaste for the city of his birth and for "American conceptions" had as beneficent an effect upon the growth of the classical collections of the Museum of Fine Arts as Dr. Bigelow's and Dr. Weld's love affairs with Japan had upon the formation of the Japanese department. On the opposite side of the world, and in a very different field, Edward Warren similarly proved to be the right collector, in the right place, at the right time.

Warren was born in Boston on 8 June 1860; and grew up at 67 Mount Vernon Street. While a Harvard undergraduate, he agonized his way from the Calvinistic Congregationalism of his grandfather through the Episcopal church to a state of active disbelief in everything except classical Greece. After receiving an A.B. cum laude with the Harvard class of 1883, he went to New College, Oxford, to read classics. In the summer of 1885, when his eyes were too weak to permit reading, he went to Greece with William Amory Gardner (Harvard 1884), a master at the recently opened Groton School. While in Athens he bought the terra-cotta figurine of a nude youth descending through the air (mentioned at the end of Chapter II) that his brother gave to the Museum of Fine Arts the following year.

The family had been involved with the museum from its beginning. Edward Warren's mother had given a large blue and green Chinese jar soon after the Copley Square building was opened in 1876. His father, Samuel Dennis Warren, a highly successful paper manufacturer who was a trustee from 1883 until his death in 1888, gave a large Millet canvas of a *Shepherdess* in 1877, and lent a number of paintings at other times. His older brother, named for their father, was a trustee from 1892 until his death in 1910, and for six of these years President of the museum. On the death of his father in 1888, Ned Warren inherited property more than adequate to relieve him from the necessity of returning to New England, where he would have been a misfit in every possible sense. Fortunately his older brother Sam managed the affairs of the S. D. Warren Paper Company with competence, enthusiasm, and profit.

Within two years of his father's death, Edward P. Warren established himself in a spacious eighteenth-century house on the High Street of Lewes in Sussex, where he created a rarefied and sumptuous retreat in which bachelor scholars who shared his classical enthusiasms might devise a world of their own remote from the scene around them. Although full of artistic treasures, Lewes House had little nineteenth-century comfort about it. Candles provided the only lights and quills were the only pens, although there were good wine and food, good horses in the stables, and numerous Saint Bernard dogs roaming about the premises. It was a scene created to foster the good life as described by Aristotle and Plato, in which the owner was soon joined by like-minded friends made at Oxford. Warren was a born collector, whose scholarship ran not so much to books as to objects of Classical antiquity. When he settled in Lewes House, he induced a Lancashireman John Marshall, an Oxford friend, to join him in the role of resident secretary. Although Marshall had come from Liverpool to Oxford in 1881 with a Classical Scholarship at New College, he only met Warren in 1884. As he took a first in both Mods and Greats he was advised to apply for a fellowship at Merton, but declined to do so. He went up to Oxford intending to enter the Church, but having abandoned that conviction, he wished to see no more of the university. As Classical studies remained his only certain light, Warren's invitation to join him provided a solution of sorts for his problems.

EDWARD PERRY WARREN.   JOHN MARSHALL.

The search for antiquities led Warren and Marshall to follow auction sales, visit private collections from which objects might conceivably be purchased, and travel widely over the Continent and the Mediterranean. At the great Van Branteghem sale of Greek vases in Paris in May 1892 their serious collecting began, after which Marshall went off to Italy to explore such possibilities as Count Tyszkiewicz's collection of vases, glass, gems, and small bronzes in Rome. As purchases increased in quantity, a Roman apartment became necessary as a secondary base of operations, and additional secretary-companions were needed at Lewes to keep up with correspondence and accounts. Richard Fisher came to Lewes House in 1891, and for a decade ran the household and stable and practiced photography. G. V. Harding came from a solicitor's office about 1894, at approximately the same time that Matthew Stewart Prichard, also from New College, more recently a barrister, joined the group. Prichard, perhaps the keenest and most capable of the company was then, like Warren, in his early thirties. He made sense out of papers and accounts, experimented with photography and vase-cleaning, studying chemistry in order to find methods of cleaning the deposits from antique marbles. As the occupants of Lewes House kept very much to themselves, only emerging on horseback or in canoes, or appearing at the local swimming baths which were their equivalent of the classical palaestra, they enjoyed a considerable reputation for eccentricity.

A later secretary recalled Matthew Prichard as

a kind, rather grave and studious man ever with a book of some kind, who while shaving taught himself Turkish or Arabic by means of lists of words on slips of paper stuck in the frame of his mirror. Prichard was always courteous, fair and just in all his dealings with the workpeople and tradesmen who came to the house and very liberal with tips when work was done. He taught many of the Lewes lads to swim, and even the burly George Justice, a local cabinet-maker who made many things for Lewes House, including the big oak gates that dignified the entrance from the lane to the stables, and later became the chief dealer in antique furniture in the town. George would never have attempted to swim had it not been for Prichard's interest in the local swimming baths. Prichard never wore a costume (nor did anyone from Lewes House). He loved to get the fellows to pose for photographs, but plates and films being much slower in those days his photographs of diving were rarely successful.

After one of his trips to the Mediterranean, Prichard developed a fad for Orientalism. "In the streets of Lewes he wore a Turkish fez, walked in the middle of the road with an abstracted air, impervious to the jibes and jeers of the locals, salaamed on entering a room, used Turkish or Arabic phrases on greeting and departure, and gave the impression that he had a private working-arrangement with Allah."

In spite of the benevolent confusion of individual interests that went on under the roof of Lewes House, Warren and his friends developed a remarkable system for finding and buying Classical antiquities of high quality. Although John Marshall did much of the traveling and exploration, Warren once noted: "Prichard at least was the foundation of sane collecting. With his help our finances were made clear." This last was necessary, for Warren's enthusiasm for buying often strained even his ample income, leading to raids on his capital, which invariably produced anguished cries from his brother Sam in Boston.

It became apparent to Samuel D. Warren soon after he became a trustee in 1892 that his brother's personal knowledge and enthusiasms might be turned to the benefit of the Museum of Fine Arts, which prior to that time had largely confined its Classical aspirations to the assembly of plaster casts. The museum's curator, however, was a competent and experienced Classical scholar. Edward Robinson (1858–1931) of the Harvard class of 1878 had, after one year at the Harvard Law School, begun the study of Greek art and archaeology. In 1881 he took part in the excavations at Assos in Asia Minor conducted under the auspices of the Archaeological Institute of America, and for the greater part of the next four years he was in Europe, traveling in Greece and Italy, and studying at the University of Berlin. He came to the Museum of Fine Arts in the autumn of 1885 with a one-year appointment as "assistant curator in classical archaeology." He remained, however, for twenty years. In the spring of 1887, during the general reorganization that followed the death of Charles C. Perkins, the Department of Classical Antiquities was formally established, and Robinson named as its first Curator.

With the help and advice of Professor Rodolfo Lanciani, who had recently visited Boston, Robinson purchased in 1888 fourteen Roman marble busts, including portraits of Tiberius and Balbinus, some terracottas, vases, Arretine pottery, and bronzes. The following year he bought a few more marbles and terracottas, as well as two black-figure hydrias. These purchases were necessarily inexpensive for they were made from the income of the Everett and Cheney funds, whose combined principal only amounted to $12,500. A great deal more money was spent buying casts, which were paid for from general funds, and which, moreover, appealed to the didactic tendencies of some of the trustees. In the 1886 report of the Committee on the Museum, J. Elliot Cabot had observed:

> Original works will generally be beyond our reach, or else of doubt-
> ful or inferior value; but, through casts, we can acquaint ourselves

with the best, the standard examples, in their most essential qualities. A collection of casts such as we have, at a very moderate cost, and without any danger of wasting our money through mistakes of judgment, would be in some respects of more value for study than any existing collection of originals; since there is none that affords the means of comparison which the student needs.

This cautious and prudent principle, which reminds me of the illiterate motto LUXURIA CUM ECONOMIA used by a chain of Ginter restaurants in Boston during my childhood, led to the purchase of plaster casts in great numbers. Although Robinson had enthusiastically prepared a descriptive *Catalogue of Casts from Greek and Roman Sculpture* in 1887 that subsequently went through several editions, had assisted the Metropolitan Museum in enlarging its collection of casts, and had a firm belief in their usefulness for instruction, he still longed for more originals in Boston. In his 1888 report he had written:

> So far as sculpture alone is concerned, we can hardly hope for any considerable collection of really fine Greek originals; and yet I need hardly remind you of the value which even one first-rate specimen, if it were only a head or a torso, would have for our Museum. It would fill a place which an entire collection of casts fills but imperfectly, both in attracting, interesting, and instructing the public, and as an inspiration for artists and students of art of our community.

This aspiration became more reasonable in the nineties as substantial bequests began to be received. The actions of the trustees in 1894 in adopting a policy of using some part of unrestricted bequests for the purchase of works of art brought its fulfillment nearer. The Warren brothers had already been helpful to the Museum of Fine Arts. Samuel D. Warren had given in 1887 a Greco-Roman bronze statuette of Athena, found in 1871 on the Rhine. Edward P. Warren in the late eighties and early nineties had given anonymously various vases and other objects. Although his gift of a "wonderfully fine set" of Dürer's *Apocalypse* in the Latin edition of 1498 was reported by S. R. Koehler among the Print Department's most important acquisitions of 1893, this deviation from custom occurred only at the special

request of the Director. On 15 August 1893 Ned Warren had written General Loring: "I usually do not wish to have my name associated with any gift, but in this case, since you suggest it, we will make
an exception."

On 2 January 1893 Edward Warren wrote Martin Brimmer a long
letter, full of significance for the future of the Classical collections.

> I have written to Mr. Robinson about a bronze for the museum
> and toward which I am willing to subscribe. At the same time it is
> a cart-before-the-horse sort of business to secure a bronze for the
> Museum now when it is unprovided with ancient subjects for study
> in cheaper materials. My policy is always to decide on a purchase
> from the point of view of its ultimate worth, not of present needs.
> I keep in mind the student of, say fifty years hence, who, if I could
> do what I wanted, would then find ready to hand a small but
> valuable collection. By that time other American museums would
> be in the field, and, unless they bought collections ready made, it
> would take some time to do what has already been done in Boston,
> not to speak of the expense which might even have been increased
> by American competition. On this the foreign dealers are, I suppose,
> only just beginning to count. But to do what I want I should need
> to be able to count on a larger and more certain supply of funds
> than can, I fear, be expected at present from the friends of the
> museum, already overtaxed.

While it is not easy to reconstruct in detail the evolution of the arrangement by which Edward P. Warren came to act as collector of
Classical objects for the Museum of Fine Arts, one draft proposal
suggested that the Warren family provide £1,000 annually for five
years, to be matched by a similar sum found in Boston, with which
Warren would purchase antiquities, on behalf of the contributors, to
a sum not exceeding £2,000 in each year. While his purchases would
be considered the property of the museum as soon as approved by the
Committee on the Museum, any not approved would be withdrawn
and retained by him without charge.

In the summer of 1894 Samuel D. Warren came to Lewes. The
brothers discussed Ned's collecting, the expenditure for which was
causing them both anxiety. Later in the summer, when Ned Warren

met Martin Brimmer at Innsbruck, they considered the idea of applying some of the museum's unrestricted funds to Classical purchases, in accordance with the recently developed new policy. The following autumn, Edward Robinson, who had first encountered Edward Warren in Munich in 1891, paid his first visit to Lewes House. What he saw there caused him to write to Martin Brimmer from London on 15 September 1894 thus:

> This visit has for the first time made Warren's position perfectly clear to me, and I am therefore prepared to act more intelligently in regard to it than I have hitherto. His knowledge and experience as a collector have developed greatly during the last three years, and from the fact that he has been trying to secure only first rate things, he has had opportunities placed at his disposal, the existence of which I had not even suspected . . . In his search for fine vases he has come across remarkable pieces of sculpture, and finding that the chances of getting these — I mean even original Greek works — is by no means as remote as we have hitherto supposed, he now proposes to devote all his energies to securing these, taking vases by the way as he finds them. But the undertaking is far too expensive for one man alone. As a preliminary, he must dispose of the vases, which represent an investment of more than $15,000, and he must be able to count on strong financial support. The nature of these purchases is such that it would be impossible to spare the time to consult a committee in America in every case. He must have the money ready, else the impatient discoverer or owner will carry his treasure elsewhere . . .
>
> For here, instead of a dealer, we have a man who is doing everything he can to help the museum, who is fixing his prices as low as he can afford to, not reckoning the incidental expenses he has been to in securing the opportunities for purchase, in no case putting the price higher than he actually paid for the specimen in question.

With such unanimity of opinion developing between Warren and the museum, arrangements were completed before the end of the year for a shipment from Lewes House to Boston that included fifty-nine vases (chiefly from the Van Branteghem collection), eighty coins, ten gems, and various objects in gold, bronze, and marble.

These were purchased from the Catharine P. Perkins Fund. Thus Edward Robinson's report for 1895 contained a description of the first substantial group of original Classical antiquities to be deliberately bought by the museum.

In 1895 Warren returned to Boston for the first time since 1890, bringing John Marshall with him for a visit, to work out detailed arrangements for future purchases. He was already casting covetous eyes on the Ludovisi collection in Rome, which contained the great fifth-century relief of the Birth of Aphrodite, known as the Ludovisi Throne, and wanted in the worst way to secure it for Boston. With this in mind, it was (unsuccessfully) suggested that Martin Brimmer form a syndicate to guarantee $125,000 for purchases, in five equal installments of $25,000 a year. Brimmer never completely understood Warren's principles of operation, for he wrote him on 24 July 1895 saying that the museum did not want more Greek vases, giving this insipid excuse: "We cannot be wholly collectors, i.e. we cannot be governed in our purchases by artistic merit alone, even with archaeological interest and rarity as subordinate considerations. We must also be controlled by the needs of those who use the museum." This reasoning recalls a tale of the French Revolution in which a man drinking in a wineshop saw a mob rush past. He left hastily, observing: "There go the people. I must follow them. I am their leader!" It was also in diametric opposition to Ned Warren's principle of deciding on a purchase "from the point of view of its ultimate worth, not of present needs."

Warren pondered over this letter during his return voyage to England. Finally on 4 September 1895 he sent Martin Brimmer a nine-page reply in which he summed up the guiding principles of his collecting. In this he wrote:

> I appreciate the difficulties in the way of the Museum; its many needs, and the natural desire that its acquisitions should be not only ultimately valuable, but well-timed and, as far as may be, immediately popular; but I want to make my own position distinct.
>
> My object is that the Museum should in time possess one of the fine Greek collections in the world, and so make the study of Greek art possible in Boston. Every acquisition should be a step to that end. This collection, to be intelligible, should contain, not sculpture

only, but gems, vases, coins and good examples of all the minor arts. It does not provide exclusively for the demands of existing laymen; it rather supplies a field for thorough students of art, not at present as numerous as they may be later on.

There is no doubt that in the space of one or two generations such a collection could be formed as need not fear comparison with European museums, but to form it, the Museum must look ahead, seize occasions as they arise, and take into consideration the present opportunities and those likely to occur, adapting itself, in short, to the inevitable conditions of the situation. In my opinion a policy of CHOICE, which guided by *a priori* principles disregards these conditions, can only result in obtaining an inferior collection at a larger price. To be successful one must needs be an opportunist. One must not impose a preconceived order of purchase when things come on the market so erratically. Every variation from the opportunist rule implies an ultimate loss to the Museum, either in money or in the importance of the collection.

Warren then turned to the views of the Committee on the Museum, as transmitted by Brimmer, that "it would decline to purchase the Bourgignon or any other large collection of vases now or in the future on the ground that the present collection increased, it may be, by the occasional purchase of a fine specimen suffices for the needs of those who use the Museum" and that "collections of coins are interesting historically rather than artistically and can be represented by reproductions, while gems are difficult to exhibit." Warren considered these pointless views in turn.

First, a general exclusion of vases seems to me neither practicable nor desirable: not practicable, because they constitute the chief means whereby a connexion with dealers and archaeologists is opened and maintained; not desirable, since they satisfy the needs of students, the Museum must eventually have a good sized collection. This kind of purchase could be more or less held in check; but not, I think to the extent which the Committee desires.

After expressing his views about coins and gems, he continued:

Let the Committee exclude nothing of excellence from its net. Let it not impose an artificial scheme on the varying opportunities.

> If in each purchase we are guided by what the British Museum, or the Louvre, or Berlin, thinks worthy of exhibition in its prominent cases, or of illustration in its handbooks, we cannot go far wrong; whereas if we neglect a good chance, because it does not tally with immediate needs, and take instead a less favourable opportunity to secure other things, our record will not please those who come as well as it pleases ourselves. They might prefer what we have abandoned.

Warren expressed his readiness to do what he could with the money that might be available, provided all opportunities were to be measured "by an ultimate, and not by a temporary, standard."

> Any collection thus made might be small, but it would be final as far as it went, and the money would be bestowed to the best advantage.
>
> For this object I am ready to do what I can. In any case you should know my views clearly before you collect money (if you so intend) on my behalf. The committee, if it pleases, shall choose between its method and its man, but I could not act heartily on a narrower basis. So far as I can I am willing to defer to conditions of temporary expediency, but this implies my buying and holding in reserve, rather than the refusal of important opportunities, and I had rather close my collection than give up the method which seems on the whole not to have failed of what was intended.

The committee's decision to forego "its method" to keep "its man" was doubtless influenced by the opinion of Warren formed by Professor Charles Eliot Norton, the Harvard arbiter of taste, who had been a trustee of the Museum of Fine Arts since 1877. Warren and John Marshall went to Ashfield late in July to stay with him. After they had spent thirty-six hours in his country retreat in western Massachusetts, Norton wrote Martin Brimmer on 26 July:

> Could he act freely as agent for the Museum, I have no doubt that he would before long make it one of the important museums of the world. But, as I said to him, he needs for this not less than a million dollars. It is a pity he cannot have free disposal of such a sum. The marbles which he now proposes — the Ludovisi bas-

reliefs and their mate, which I hope the Trustees consented to buy, would help the Museum, I believe, to obtain the desired million. They will not indeed, be of much interest to the general public, but they are of such a character, and of such importance in the history of Greek art, that the possession of them will make the Museum famous in the eyes of students of Greek art, and this will help to confirm the public pride in it.

In the autumn of 1895, Matthew S. Prichard was writing to General Loring from Lewes House about the details of a second shipment, to be purchased from the Catharine P. Perkins Fund. This included a Greco-Roman marble statue of Hermes, the Broadlands Aphrodite, and a colossal bust of Alexander the Great, as well as an enchanting bronze portrait head of Arsinoë II, wife of Ptolemy II Philadelphus of Egypt, that was probably made before 281 B.C. while she was still the wife of Lysimachus, King of Thrace.

As half a dozen vases were included, face was saved on both sides of the Atlantic. The plan agreed upon was that Warren should charge the cost price, plus 25 percent — later raised to 30 — for overhead expenses. Although this system frequently left him well out of pocket because of the extensive organization that he had built up

PORTRAIT OF ARSINOË II. Greek bronze, early 3rd century B.C. *Perkins Collection.* 96.712

THE BOSTON THRONE (front). Greek marble three-sided relief, ca. 470–460
B.C. *Pierce Fund.* 08.205 Counterpart of the so-called Ludovisi Throne in Museo
delle Terme, Rome.

and because of the traveling involved, it was satisfactory to him on
account of his conviction that the United States especially needed
what Greek art could give. "We are doing," he wrote, "the work most
needed of all works, supplying eventually the terrible gap that exists
on this new continent, the absence of that which delights the eye and
rests the soul."

Even with its improved finances the Museum of Fine Arts could
not afford to buy everything that Warren found. When the opportunity arose to purchase something of the first magnitude, like the
fifth-century relief that is a companion to the Ludovisi Throne, Warren would do so, at considerable financial inconvenience to himself,
even though there was no immediate likelihood of the museum's considering its purchase. This sculpture, which he bought in 1896, remained at Lewes House until 1908. He did everything within his
power to acquire the even more beautiful companion piece, depicting
the Birth of Aphrodite, until the Ludovisi sculptures in 1901 passed

permanently out of reach into the Museo delle Terme in Rome. The singularly beautiful Praxitelean head of a girl from Chios that Warren bought in 1900 only got to Boston ten years later. But this caused him little concern, for the museum during the next four or five years cooperated generously and trustingly with him. In his words, "It entrusted large sums of money to its agent without ever being sure of anything but repayment in money; and what is still more unusual, accepted his decision with regard to all purchases as final. In short it abdicated the control of a good portion of its inheritance — a daring move, but one which proved to be wise."

This was indeed an abrogation of normal practice, for all purchases of works of art had remained from the beginning entirely in the hands of the Committee on the Museum, rather than with the Director or Curators. The original by-laws had provided that the officers shall be "a President, a Treasurer, and an Honorary Director, who shall be chosen from the Trustees; a Curator and a Secretary." Article 4 provided that "The Curator shall, under the Trustees, have the general charge and management of the Museum," but "the preservation of the collections" was only one of a series of responsibilities that involved appointing the Janitor, "the observance of proper order and quiet," and keeping the records. It was the Committee on the Museum, of which the Honorary Director was chairman

THE BOSTON THRONE (end reliefs).

ex officio, that was given "supervision and control of all collections belonging to the Museum, and of the arrangement and exhibition thereof," and "charge of all purchases of works of art which may be authorized by the Trustees." The Curator was to act as executive officer and secretary of this committee, but was to be a member only if he were a trustee. Charles G. Loring, the first Curator, was in fact a trustee, although he had been elected in 1873 on a personal basis rather than because of his professional tie with the museum. Following the death of Charles C. Perkins in 1886, the by-laws had been revised to eliminate the office of Honorary Director and to transfer to the new office of Director — General Loring wearing a new hat — the functions previously assigned to the Curator. Although a new article provided for "one or more Curators," "who shall render such assistance to the Director, and perform such special duties as may from time to time be determined by concurrent vote of the Executive Committee and the Committee on the Museum," the powers of the Committee on the Museum remained unchanged.

The thoughts of the trustee members of the committee on acquisitions were not always profound or inspired. When he visited Lewes House in 1894, Edward Robinson wryly told Ned Warren of one suggestion he had received: "I have something here which will help you in your selection, if not give you your selection ready-made; a list of the casts made for the Louvre of which the greatest number of copies is sold." He reported how Dr. Henry J. Bigelow had caused the rejection of a fine terracotta on the ground that "no healthy woman could be formed at the hips like that," and of another member of the Committee on the Museum who had asked, "I want to ask you for my own information — and I'll take your word for it — whether an original statue is in any way more valuable than a cast." It is therefore in no way surprising that the committee's reaction to Warren's shipments was often acquiescent rather than enthusiastic. When the first group had been unpacked, Robinson wrote Warren:

> My expectation of the enthusiasm these would excite in the Committee's breast has completely miscarried. Their attitude is that of supposing that "these are the best we can expect to do in the way of sculpture," and to that extent they are not disappointed in

the purchase. They do not think it a mistake — and this ought to satisfy you. I had hoped for more, but what is the use? The artists who have seen the pieces are enthusiastic about them, and delighted to have them here.

This was a situation where the absence of positive complaint had to be regarded as an accolade.

In 1896, when Warren sent fewer vases and more sculpture in marble, limestone, and bronze, the reception was more exuberant. "The Committee came, saw, and were vanquished." Arthur Astor Carey, "being the newest member, had not trained himself to suppress his enthusiasm, and expressed himself accordingly, but Mr. ——'s effort to contain himself caused his face to change from crimson to purple, and his symptoms grew dangerous." This shipment and that of the following year, which included the highly sympathetic archaic stone lion found near Perachora on the isthmus of Corinth, were credited as the gift of the Catharine P. Perkins Fund. In 1898, when 299 classical purchases were made from the Henry L. Pierce Fund, Robinson's account of acquisitions filled 75 of the 132 pages in the annual report. Among these were various gems from the collection of Count Tyszkiewicz, while the next years Warren sent a considerable number of gems from the Marlborough Collection, which proved to be extremely popular. The fourth-century gold earring depicting Nike driving a chariot, which is still one of the most remarkable known specimens of Greek jewelry, came in 1898; the archaic bronze statuette of Hermes holding a ram was included in the shipment of the following year.

For the first five years Warren's arrangement with the Museum of Fine Arts proved generally harmonious. When he came to Boston in 1900 his brother Sam gave a dinner for him, at which Charles Eliot Norton, always a faithful admirer, said: "There is not and never has been in America or in Europe a man with such capacities, will and circumstances for collecting, and the Museum must be entirely dependent upon him; if Mr. Warren's life were shortened, the hopes of this Museum would die with him." After this occasion, which brought him in personal touch with many people interested in the museum, Ned Warren wrote:

LIMESTONE LION FROM PERACHORA. Archaic Greek, about
550 B.C. *Perkins Collection. 97.289*

Someone must die and leave lots of money to the Museum. We
shall get our 100,000 [dollars], but this only sees us for a very
small period, say a year. There we knock against a wall again. The
death is much to be wished of some prominent citizen whose loss
will be keenly felt by all, and most of all by the Museum. The
President says that the trouble with the Museum is that people
(meaning himself?) don't die fast enough.

GOLD CLASP FOR A NECKLACE. Greek, 4th century B.C. *Henry Lillie Pierce Fund. 99.375*
WEDDING OF CUPID AND PSYCHE. Roman sardonyx cameo, signed by Tryphon. *Henry Lillie Pierce Fund 99.101* Known as the "Marlborough gem."

NIKE DRIVING HER CHARIOT. Greek gold earring, early 4th century B.C. *Henry Lillie Pierce Fund. 98.788*

The last remark is one that has often been felt, and sometimes expressed in the last seventy years that have passed since that evening. Although William Endicott who made it at the dinner survived until 1914, he declined re-election as President in January 1901, and in 1907, after thirty-seven continuous years of service, resigned as a

HERMES HOLDING A RAM. Greek bronze
statuette, 5th century B.C. *Henry Lillie
Pierce Fund. 99.489*

trustee. He was succeeded in the presidency by Samuel Dennis Warren.

In spite of the growing enthusiasm for the increase of the Classical collection, the purchase late in 1899 of the Fenway land for a new building hobbled the museum's finances. For a decade the planning and construction of this building became the chief preoccupation of nearly everyone. Edward P. Warren felt that the concern with construction at the expense of collecting was mistaken and shortsighted. Sir John Beazley in his essay "Warren as Collector" thus summarized his subject's views.

> He thought that the trustees would have been wise to defer building and to spend their money on increasing the classical collection while they had the opportunity. As the result of many years' effort, he had obtained complete control of the market in classical antiquities. Almost everything that was good, whether a

new find or an old, came to him for the first refusal. Competition
had all but ceased. The chief private collectors in Europe were
dead, or had withdrawn from the field. The museums were comparatively sluggish. The British Museum could do nothing; Berlin
could do nothing; the Louvre did nothing. Building could be done
at any time; but his organization, allowed to decline, could not be
reconstructed, and the market, once lost, could never be recovered.

This was, indeed, a bitter disappointment to Edward Warren. In
the past decade he and John Marshall had exercised "a sort of
duumvirate over the traffic in antiquities, Berlin, Copenhagen, and
London being glad to get their leavings," as his biographers well put
it.

They had done good work together and the ten years' collaboration
bore in many ways the finished stamp. Not often are two men
found with genius so complementary, possessing between them
qualities so well adapted to a great undertaking — Johnny's con-

HEAD OF HOMER. Greek marble, Hellenistic period. *Henry Lillie Pierce Fund.*
04.13
HEAD OF A MAN. Roman terracotta, late 1st century B.C. *By contribution. 01.8008*

summate knowledge of his subject and his eagle's eye for detail, Ned's ability to handle men. In a trade so full of tricks and tricksters, when any day they might have blundered to the tune of hundreds of thousands, they had fallen into no serious error. Ned had shown himself in activity and enterprise, in spite of severe illness, a true American, in every way equal to a decade's involved and successful dealing.

Now at the moment when they were able to buy pieces of first-rate importance at prices that were not prohibitive, the Museum of Fine Arts chose to invest its efforts in bricks and mortar! For this change Ned Warren substantially blamed his brother Sam. "And the justification of it all is not holy, not even commercial; it is traditional," he wrote. In a similar mood John Marshall wrote:

> There is no place for me in Boston: I am more or less *Museummensch*. Under Sam's management the Boston Museum will flourish, perhaps as New York, with finances in magnificent order and all gentlemen and businessmen at the helm . . . no harsh words, never a suspicion of the truth to disturb their self-satisfaction. Good dinners, over-dressed women, and fine society.

Although the skies resembled a Scandinavian winter afternoon, an occasional ray of sun broke through the clouds. Robinson had written Edward Warren in January 1900,

> Mr. Frank Bartlett walked into my office the other day — January 2, to be exact, — and announced his intention of giving to the Museum one hundred thousand dollars, the entire sum, principal and interest, to be devoted to the purchase of original objects for the Department of Classical Antiquities!!! He asked me to draw up a form of letter, announcing his gift to the President in such terms as should leave it as free from restrictions as possible — and in short to arrange the whole matter for him in the way that should be most satisfactory to you and myself . . . Mr. Bartlett does this instead of leaving the money as a bequest to the Museum . . . He has no wish to be consulted as to the things to be bought, and when I ask him, says only, "You must treat me in this matter as though I were dead." All I have been able to learn from him definitely, is

that he would rather the money did not go for gems, if other good things were to be had, but even here he says he will not make any condition or restriction. The whole sum may even be put into one thing if that seems wise. He wishes to leave it absolutely in our hands.

This opportune and generous benefaction of Francis Bartlett (Harvard A.B. 1857, A.M. 1870), a Boston lawyer who had been a trustee since 1890, was at the time cloaked in complete anonymity. The only reference to it in the 1900 report is the otherwise unexplained appearance in the Treasurer's report for a Special Fund of $100,000 among those qualified as "Principal and Income restricted to certain uses." Only in 1902 was Bartlett's name added to it; in the 1903 report the entire sum had been "expended for collections." Thus Robinson's 1903 report records the gift by Bartlett of 20 marbles, 66 vases, 60 fragments of vases, 39 terracottas, 20 bronzes, 62 coins, 13 gems, 8 objects of gold and silver, 2 miscellaneous — a total of 290 items. Among these was the fourth-century Praxitelean marble head, now known as the Bartlett Aphrodite, which is one of the most beautiful examples of Greek sculpture in existence.

THE BARTLETT APHRODITE. Greek marble, 4th century B.C. *Bartlett Collection.*
03.743
HEAD FROM CHIOS. Greek marble, 4th century B.C. *Gift of Nathaniel Thayer.*
10.70

The influx of original works of classical art had by 1903 caused a major rearrangement of the first-floor galleries to the east of the main entrance from Copley Square. The first room in the front, which had at the 1890 opening contained casts of modern sculpture, was now given over to original Greek marbles; in the second the recently arrived Bartlett Collection had displaced French and German Renaissance casts. Italian Renaissance casts still held their ground in the corner gallery, but in the long room beyond it (on the Trinity Place façade) Greek vases had supplanted the "Hall of the Maidens" sequence of Greek casts. The adjacent gallery, lighted from the courtyard, that had once contained Gothic and Moorish casts, was in 1903 given over to Greek bronzes, coins, and gems. Before the Copley Square building was finally abandoned in 1909, casts had been ejected from a part of the Greek and Roman Corridor, and one portion of it partitioned off to create still another exhibition room for Greek sculpture.

AMPHORA SIGNED BY AMASIS. Greek black-figured vase, 6th century B.C. *Henry Lillie Pierce Fund.* 01.8026

MEN WITH GIRL PLAYING FLUTES. Greek red-figured stamnos, 5th century B.C.

HERAKLES DRAGGING CERBERUS FROM HADES. Greek red-figured plate, attributed to the Cerberus Painter. *Henry Lillie Pierce Fund.* 01.8025
INTERIOR OF A KYLIX. Greek red-figured vase, 5th century B.C. *James Fund.*
10.211

Presumably because of the Bartlett gift, the trustees had made no
appropriation in 1900 for the purchase of Classical antiquities. As a
result, early in 1901 Edward Warren undertook to raise a purchase
fund of $50,000 by private subscription, the trustees having agreed
to add a matching sum, to be expended for two years' purchases.
According to Sir John Beazley,

> The figure was reached, but with difficulty, and Robinson thought
> the appeal ill-timed. It had put a strain on the Trustees personally
> which none of them liked, and a strain on the friends of the
> Museum to which only a few had responded cheerfully; everyone
> agreed it to be a measure that could never be resorted to again; and
> the general feeling was that it would not do to ask the Trustees for
> a further appropriation for a long time to come. Robinson advised
> Warren not to be deceived by the fact that the money had been
> raised: he must see the matter in its true light; consider its bearing
> on the future; and nurse his resources accordingly.

So, in spite of the sunshine of Francis Bartlett's generous interven-
tion, the skies clouded again.

The difficulties of the situation led Edward Warren in 1902 to
approach the Committee on the Museum with a new proposal. He

was ready to accept a reduction of the pace, for the museum's collection had already reached the stage where it was not easy to add to it if its high standards of excellence were to be maintained. He made three stipulations if the collecting were to continue: first, he must have liberty to revalue the antiquities then at Lewes House according to his conscience in accordance with current market values, as the costs-plus-30-percent system was inadequate in view of the expenses of his organization; second, he must be assured of an annual grant of a certain sum for the next three years; and, third, a lump sum of $100,000 for one particular group of antiquities. This Sir John Beazley described as "a very peculiar sending, not in the least popular, but such as would suit him, could he be the donor, better than many they had had in late years; it would consist chiefly of a choice collection of small bronzes, and a collection of coins — 'on a table and a few pedestals you would have the whole. They would afford no ground for popular effect; but the connoisseur would be satisfied.' " Without such assistance, Warren warned that it would be impossible for him to continue collecting for the museum along the old lines. His first request was the only one that was completely granted. Edward Robinson had warned him against the tripartite application. Only a third of the money that Warren requested was promised. It became clear that the great period of Classical collecting for Boston was drawing to a close, pushed aside, as Warren had feared it would be, by the demands of the new building. Although funds for a further purchase were voted in August 1904, this was the last regular appropriation for Classical antiquities for some years.

Several administrative matters that are dealt with more fully in other chapters must be briefly mentioned here to elucidate their effect upon the development of the Classical Department. When General Loring resigned as Director in 1902, Edward Robinson became his successor, continuing, however, as Curator of what was now called the Department of Classical Art, with the help of a new Assistant Curator, Oliver Samuel Tonks. Later in the year Matthew Stewart Prichard came to Boston from Lewes House to fill a new post of Secretary to the Director. This move, in view of Ned Warren's feelings about his brother and the museum at the moment, was regarded as tantamount to "joining the opposition." Of this episode Warren's biographer has written:

This action, of which only Warren's account survives, caused a breach, which for all Warren's efforts was never healed. Warren kept in touch through a common friend, but Prichard would never forgive him for certain opinions which he thought had been expressed about himself. The appointment was happy neither for Prichard himself — he felt compelled to resign within a few years — nor for the Warren family: Sam was President of the Museum Trustees at the time and insisted on the appointment, though he had been warned well in advance that it would be regarded as an unfriendly act.

In the course of 1905 there developed a brouhaha at the Museum of Fine Arts, to be considered in Chapter VI, which led to Edward Robinson's resignation as Director. It was accepted on 9 December, and on the 18th he was appointed Assistant Director of the Metropolitan Museum in New York. There followed a sequel, best described in the words of Sir John Beazley.

John Marshall was invited to become agent, at a fixed salary, for the collection of classical antiquities on behalf of New York; and Robinson could claim that he had "been able to transfer to the Metropolitan Museum the men and methods by which the collection of Greek and Roman antiquities in the Boston Museum of Fine Arts had been so successfully built up since 1895," New York now stepped into the place that had been occupied by Boston, and the steady policy of the Museum, the co-operation of the authorities, and assured and ever-increasing funds, enabled Marshall, in the twenty-three years between 1905 and his death, to build up those magnificent collections which now place New York in the forefront of classical museums.

As John Marshall married in 1906, the old ties of Lewes House were broken in other ways than the end of the Warren-Marshall agency for the Museum of Fine Arts.

Edward P. Warren liked and respected Professor Arthur Fairbanks, who in 1907 succeeded Edward Robinson as Director and Classical Curator in Boston. Soon after his appointment Fairbanks wrote Warren to explain that, although no money was immediately available for purchases, the Committee on the Museum was deeply interested in securing the balance of his collections, sooner or later. Robinson and Marshall in New York had an equally keen interest in the antiquities that were still at Lewes House. It was amicably decided that the greater part of them should be free for purchase by the Metropolitan, if wanted there, although Warren would be free to reserve the few that seemed to him most necessary to round out the Boston collection. He explained to Arthur Fairbanks that he could not reserve everything for Boston, partly because Marshall had had so close a partnership in the collecting, and partly because indefinite reservation froze funds that he needed for other purchases and projects. It has earlier been noted that the companion relief to the Ludovisi Throne, which Warren had had at Lewes House since 1896, only became the Boston Throne in 1908 when it was finally purchased from the Henry L. Pierce Fund.

The Chios head of a girl, which Rodin extravagantly admired, was another of the late arrivals. Early in the century it had been suggested that Warren might offer the head to Thomas W. Lawson for $150,000 to be given to the Museum of Fine Arts. By energetic stock speculations, Lawson had accumulated a fortune estimated at $50,000,000. As he was reputed to have spent some $6,000,000 on his estate "Dreamwold" at Egypt on the South Shore; had paid a florist $30,000 for a carnation bearing his wife's name; and had built the yacht *Independence* to defend the America's Cup in 1901, Lawson clearly had the means to assist the museum if he chose. It would obviously be no use to ask him for a gift for general purposes, or for the purchase of undetermined antiquities, but there was a hope that if confronted with one of the most attractive ancient masterpieces, which might henceforth be called the Lawson Head, he might succumb. As is usually the case in such seemingly logical but improbable attempts, he did not. It was only in 1910 that the *Chios Head* came to Boston, as an (at first anonymous) gift of Nathaniel Thayer. The head had been carved lifesized for insertion in a draped statue. The generous donor later confessed to the architect Herbert W. C. Browne that when he first saw the sculpture he was startled to discover that he had provided so substantial a sum of money to buy a head without a top or back!

Other objects eventually came from Lewes House through the continued magnanimity of Francis Bartlett, who in 1912 gave the museum a building in the heart of Chicago that was carried at a value of $1,350,000. In conveying the deed to this property, which brought in an annual rental of over $50,000, Bartlett expressed the wish that for three years the income be used "to purchase works of art selected, approved, and recommended by the Curators of the respective departments, or other experts employed by the Museum, which will add distinction to the collections of classical antiquities and paintings." He expressed the hope, but did not impose the obligation, that the income should thereafter be used in the same way. He thus became the largest single benefactor of the museum down to that time, as well as one of the most considerate, wise, and understanding of trustees. It was with the income of Francis Bartlett's gift of 1912 that the museum eventually completed in February 1927, the year before Warren's death, the purchase of the great collection of classical gems that had been his particular enthusiasm in collecting after the end of the Warren-Marshall duumvirate. Even though association with the museum thus continued throughout Ned Warren's life, it was the decade 1895–1905, and more especially the first half thereof, that saw the most fruitful collaboration, and that transformed the Classical Department from a great assembly of casts to a first-rate and highly varied collection of original works of art.

Under the pseudonym of Arthur Lyon Raile, Edward P. Warren published two volumes of verse — Itamos (1903) and The Wild Rose (1913) — the first of which excited the admiration of Robert Bridges. A prose retelling of Greek legends, called Alcmaeon, Hypermestra, Caeneus, was published under his own name by Blackwell at Oxford in 1919. But for many years he labored over a magnum opus in three small volumes entitled A Defence of Uranian Love, which was privately printed in a very limited edition at the end of his life.

In addition to the Boston collecting, Warren longed to do something to strengthen Greek studies at Oxford. The ideas that he most favored were the establishment of a Classical Lectureship at Corpus Christi College and the "fortification" of one college as a specially Greek College. Although the latter idea proved impracticable, he did provide in his will for the endowment of a Praelectorship at Corpus.

In April 1915 he was elected an Honorary Fellow of Corpus, which proved a congenial refuge from the wartime loneliness of Lewes. From his election until the end of the war, Warren had rooms in Corpus, in whose Senior Common Room he found himself very much in his element.

In later years Warren lived so quietly that little was heard of him. John Marshall died in February 1928, and on the following 28 December, Ned Warren followed him. To the moment of his death he was attempting, by the sale of objects, stocks, and mortgages, to raise the £30,000 that he provided in his will for the Corpus Praelectorship, but without success. At his death it was found that the bequest would have to accumulate for at least fifteen years before it reached a sum that would permit the college to carry out Warren's hopes. In one of the last letters that he wrote Sir John Beazley, a few months before his death, Warren remarked retrospectively: "I have had much happiness in the thought of three things done: the Bostonian Collection, *The Wild Rose*, the *Defence*."

After the deaths of Marshall and Warren, Professor Ludwig Curtius published a joint tribute to them in the *Mitteilungen des Deutschen Archäologischen Instituts, Römische Abteiling*, which concluded:

> The lives of the two men are only properly understood by bearing in mind their thorough grounding in the Classics at Oxford; and their collections for the Museums at Boston and New York, the splendid antique Classical departments of which they established. They were the last of the great antique art collectors of the previous century. But the enthusiasm, which with Tyszkiewicz and Stroganoff, was that of the grand cavaliers, and with Karl Jacobsen was an admitted imitation of Ludwig I of Bavaria, was with them the call to serve an ideal. As they understood it, life revealed itself in its truest meaning in Greek Art, and Warren wished to enrich neo-American culture through it. He was a man of means, although not rich according to modern standards and he husbanded his resources. Neither whim nor opportunity governed them in their collecting, but their choice was the outcome of a systematic, artistic, and wide knowledge of the antique, such as was not possessed by any of their predecessors. They had as much humour and com-

mercial instinct in their dealings with the quaint fraternity of Art dealers as they had energy and persistence; and in spite of all their "detective cunning," they remained "gentlemen" because to them the Cause meant more than the Individual.

CHAPTER VI

The Battle of the Casts

Denman W. Ross, whose combination of taste, generosity, and good feeling caused him to do more thoughtful things than occur to most New Englanders, gave the museum in 1902 a portrait of William Locke by Sir Thomas Lawrence in memory of General

PORTRAIT OF WILLIAM LOCKE. Sir Thomas Lawrence. *Gift of Denman Waldo Ross in memory of Charles Greely Loring. 02.514*

Charles Greely Loring. Loring's retirement from the directorship earlier in that year, followed so soon by his death, closed the first act in the history of the Museum of Fine Arts. In thirty-two years a building had been achieved, enlarged, and finally rejected as inadequate for the future. Loan exhibits were being crowded out by permanent collections, while in the field of Japanese art the museum's possessions were unique in the Western world. Greek marbles and vases of high quality were encroaching upon the pedagogically inspired sequence of plaster casts. The generous bequests of recent years proved that at least some Bostonians valued the museum so highly that they wished to enlarge its usefulness and insure its future. The *dramatis personae* also had changed almost completely, for of the 1870 incorporators only two — Charles William Eliot and William Endicott — were still on the board in 1902. Martin Brimmer, the first President, had died in 1896 at the age of sixty-six; his successor William Endicott had voluntarily resigned the office at seventy-five. Samuel Dennis Warren, who became the third President on 17 January 1901, although only forty-eight at the time, was fully conversant with the problems of the museum, for he had been elected a trustee in 1892 just before his fortieth birthday. Age levels were fast dropping, for Edward Waldo Forbes (Harvard 1895) was still in his twenties when chosen to fill General Loring's place on the board. He died only on 11 March 1969 as Trustee Emeritus, having served the museum longer than Queen Victoria reigned. Such a record has only once been approached by President Eliot's fifty-six years as a trustee. One could wish that all choices of young men were as inspired and fruitful as this one, for Edward Forbes proved to be a remarkable collector and a generous benefactor not only of this institution but of the Fogg Art Museum at Harvard which he directed for three decades.

Edward Robinson was appointed Director on 27 May 1902, retaining for the time being his old post of Curator of Classical Antiquities. Here again was an important change. General Loring was a Boston gentleman who had greatly assisted his fellow trustees by turning an interest in Egyptology developed through travel to the task of administering an art museum. Robinson's entire adult life had been devoted to the professional pursuit of classical art and archaeology.

CHARLES GREELY LORING and EDWARD ROBINSON. *Portraits by Edmund Charles Tarbell commissioned by the trustees. 06.2455 and 06.1895*

In the fall term of 1893–94 he had given a Harvard course on the History of Greek Art to the completion of the Parthenon for, and in temporary place of, Charles Eliot Norton, and from 1898 until he became Director of the museum he held a regular Harvard appointment as Lecturer on Classical Archaeology. In choosing assistants in the Department of Classical Art, Robinson sought to maintain similar ties with the worlds of research and teaching. When Oliver Samuel Tonks (Harvard 1898 and a Ph.D. candidate in Classical Archaeology) left in 1903, after a year's service as Assistant Curator, to teach Greek at the University of Vermont, he was replaced by Burt Hodge Hill, fresh from three years at the American School of Classical Studies, Athens.

While Benjamin Ives Gilman continued as Assistant Director, Secretary of the board, and Librarian, Matthew Stewart Prichard came from Lewes House to the new post of Secretary to the Director, presumably at Samuel D. Warren's behest. A Department of Egyptian Art was created in 1902. Albert Morton Lythgoe, who was appointed its first Curator, soon went to Egypt, not only to purchase some

Egyptian antiquities but to gain experience in excavation by collaborating with Dr. George A. Reisner, who was then heading a University of California expedition. Although the 639 oils and panel pictures, 216 water colors, and 38 miniatures that the museum owned did not seem to warrant the creation of a Department of Paintings, they needed care and rearrangement; thus John Briggs Potter was appointed Keeper of Paintings. Everything to do with the physical care of the building and its custodians and night watchman was delegated to William W. McLean, a newly appointed Superintendent of the Building. This extensive reorganization sprang from a conviction — possibly Warren's — that the museum had reached a state of complexity where no single man could cope not only with the administrative management of the whole but with the detailed demands for expert knowledge in various branches of learning. After a decade of operation, departments of Prints and of Classical Antiquities, headed by separate curators, had been organized in 1887. Now fifteen years later, when the collections had immeasurably increased, further subdivision became necessary, although it moved slowly both because of limited funds and the difficulty of securing fully qualified people.

The purchase late in 1899 of the Fenway land for a future building had put a considerable strain on the museum's finances. While the treasurer's report for 1899 had shown a surplus of $8,906.33 — the first in the museum's history and one of the very few at any time — diminished income because of the sale of securities, mortgage interest, and $8,000 taxes on the new land produced a deficit of $38,686.83 in 1900 and $33,958.86 in 1901. Some financial relief was achieved by the sale of the Copley Square building and land appurtenant for $1,800,000 to a syndicate known as the Copley Square Trust. By a contract signed on 22 April 1902 the purchase price was payable in three installments of $500,000 on 20 June 1902, 1904, and 1906, and the balance of $300,000 on delivery of the deed and possession, which, in the option of the museum, could take place either on 20 June 1907, 1908, or 1909. The museum was to pay 4¼ percent interest on the installments as paid until delivery of possession. This first payment of $500,000 was used to repay the draft on general funds, in excess of the amount borrowed, for the purchase of the land. The sum to be received for the Copley Square land, less the cost of the Fenway land, plus a small fund earlier raised for projected additions to the old building, was expected to provide some $975,000 toward the cost of the new museum. The keys to this solution had been the willingness of the City government and the Boston Water Power Company to remove the original restrictions that would have prevented the sale of the Copley Square property, and the good fortune of the museum's trustees in finding a purchaser willing to pay a substantial sum for it even though delivery could not be made until several years in the future.

The agreement gave the museum some leeway for planning, but, as every moment was needed, a Building Committee consisting of Dr. Williams Sturgis Bigelow, Morris Gray, Francis Lee Higginson, Henry S. Hunnewell, and Samuel D. Warren was appointed on 27 May 1902 with full powers to procure plans, specifications, and estimates. The President served as Chairman and the Director as Secretary, with Thornton K. Lothrop acting as Dr. Bigelow's substitute during the latter's absence abroad. This committee then employed the architect R. Clipston Sturgis, nephew of the designer of the Copley Square building, to study present and prospective needs of the museum in relation to the Fenway site, with the understanding that such employment would cease on completion of the study, leaving the museum entirely free to proceed in any direction that it chose. Clipston Sturgis associated with himself for this investigation Edmund M. Wheelwright as consulting architect.

As the Isabella Stewart Gardner Museum, a few hundred yards away from the Fenway site, was nearing completion, Samuel D. Warren wrote Mrs. Gardner thus on 14 August 1902: "Mr. Prichard leads me to hope that the Museum Building Committee can obtain the benefit of your views as to the best mode of procedure. This is in line with a hope I had previously entertained — and I can assure you the Committee will be very glad to give careful consideration to any suggestions you may be willing to make." Matthew Prichard met Mrs. Gardner almost as soon as he arrived in Boston. As with Okakura-Kakuzo soon after, they immediately understood each other and became fast friends and close allies. After a first visit to the still-unfinished Fenway Court, he wrote her on 23 February 1902 the first of a series of 285 letters, that only ended with her death in 1924.

The morning after you showed me your house, I came across a story in the course of my work so apposite to your undertaking, and expressing so exactly my appreciation of it, that I venture to send it to you.

It concerns a picture painted by Protogenes the Caunian who lived at Rhodes.

"It is said to have taken Protogenes seven years to paint, and they tell us that Apelles, when he first saw it, was struck dumb with wonder, and called it, on recovering his speech 'a great labor and a wonderful success.' " Μέγας ὁ πόνος καὶ θαυμαστὸν τὸ ἔργον.

(You must not think that there exists any pretense in me to call myself Apelles!)

It will interest you to know that the great Greek king, Demetrios Poliorketes, when besieging Rhodes, refrained from attacking the most vulnerable point of the city, for fear of injuring this work of a famous artist. If ever it shall be the fate of Boston to suffer a siege, I hope that the adversary may be noble hearted enough to spare in like manner the noble result of your genius and energy.

MATTHEW STEWART PRICHARD. From the scrapbook of Miss Florence Virginia Paull (Mrs. Henri L. Berger).

Prichard could interest Mrs. Gardner in the affairs of the museum as few others could, for he had both taste and ideas, was learned, handsome, and whimsical. Moreover, he took the grave solemnities of Boston no more seriously than she did. A typical instance is his letter to her of 20 February 1905 in response to a teasing *mot* of Okakura's.

In my own case I regard it as a compliment to be told that I am
growing commonplace. Such has been my aim for the greater part
of my life; but I should doubt the reliability of the observation, did
it not come from so acute an observer as Mr. Okakura! You will see
me in a frock coat on Sundays now, passing along Beacon Street
and pounding regularly at the door knockers. The mornings I shall
pass in an automobile along the speedway — if I can find it. I shall
buy a dog, and hire a mistress, drink cocktails and join the Tavern
Club. I shall sail in a cat boat, get an introduction to Mrs. Stuyvesant
Fish, speak with bated breath of the Director, refer to Bigelow &
Morse as authorities on art, go to church (or become a Roman
Catholic), have an opinion of the negro question, the importation
of Jews, reciprocity and the tariff. I shall hunt, skate and go in for
mixed bathing; marry (in the end), grow fat and rich, endow a
school, rob the fatherless and widow, return to England and be
knighted. What experiences there remain for me to undergo!

Please remember to let me have Berenson's dicta about the
Velazquez.

During the summer of 1902, when Mrs. Gardner was at "Green
Hill" in Brookline, Prichard occupied a small flat on the ground floor
of Fenway Court. After the house was opened in 1903, while the
idly curious and dull visitors seeking to improve their minds were
witheringly discouraged, Prichard was always welcome to bring anyone who measured up to his standards. Paul Chalfin, Curator of the
Chinese and Japanese Department, and other young people came to
Fenway Court under Prichard's wing. The credentials that he
offered Mrs. Gardner for her forthcoming guests were often charm-
ingly simple, as in March 1904 when he described the future Beatrix
Farrand as "Miss Cadwallader Jones, of N.Y., a landscape gardener,
knows about art, bright and no trouble." A man of this kind, particularly with Isabella Gardner as an ally, was likely to have new and
original ideas about the future museum. As long as Matthew Prichard
was around there was little likelihood that traditionally minded
Bostonian "doers of good" would achieve in the Fenway an enlarged
duplicate of their Copley Square museum without a knockdown
fight.

Sam Warren and his Building Committee were equally determined to achieve an ideal solution if it were humanly possible. As there was no obvious precedent for the construction of an ideal art museum, they embarked on an extended experimental investigation. In 1903 they built a temporary Experimental Gallery on the Fenway land to try various methods of lighting paintings and sculpture. Professor Charles L. Norton of the Massachusetts Institute of Technology, Edward Atkinson of the Insurance Engineering Experiment Station, and W. R. McCornack, a recent graduate of M.I.T., worked closely with Clipston Sturgis and Edmund M. Wheelwright, the building committee, and members of the museum staff in testing the adaptability of both overhead and side lighting to the display of various types of works of art. Prichard was chairman of the committee concerned with the Experimental Gallery.

Early in 1904 Samuel D. Warren and Edward Robinson went to Europe in the company of Sturgis and Wheelwright to study European museums, and, hopefully, discover excellencies of detail that might be anthologized in the future Boston design. Before their return on 2 April they had visited some ninety-five museums in Italy, Germany, Switzerland, Holland, Belgium, and England. No one ideal model was found; some instances of how not to do it were seen, but the aggregate of suggestions derived proved to be helpful.

Seemingly in preparation for this three-month absence of both President and Director, Matthew S. Prichard was on 10 December 1903 made Assistant Director in place of Benjamin Ives Gilman. This seems to have been a rationalization of existing conditions, for Warren in announcing the appointment stated that "Mr. Prichard assumes duties which, for the most part, have been his for some time past." Gilman continued as Secretary of the Museum and Librarian, with added responsibility for publications, which were increasing in number. A bimonthly *Museum of Fine Arts Bulletin* began to appear in March 1903 as a means of taking to a wide public information that had hitherto been somewhat austerely presented in annual reports. *The Twenty-seventh Annual Report for the Year 1902* had appeared in improved typographical dress, provided by the University Press, Cambridge, with more complete information than in earlier years. Charles Lowell's treasurer's report for 1901 had occupied only four pages in a compressed and often enigmatic form that had changed little in a quarter-century. The document that he submitted for 1902 not only ran to ten pages, but gave detailed accounts of the dates of establishment and purposes of the various funds, together with sums expended for collections and unexpended balances. It thus presented a truer picture of financial reality by showing what money was actually within reach. From 1895 to 1901 the Sylvanus A. Denio Fund, for example, had appeared as $50,000 in the category "Principal and Income restricted to certain uses." In the 1902 report it became immediately clear that the restriction was "to the purchase of Modern Paintings" and that the entire $50,000 had already been expended for that purpose.

In addition to publications designed for a wide audience, Gilman had to see through the press a series of privately printed *Communications to the Trustees regarding the New Building*, in which the studies instigated by the Building Committee were presented to a limited audience. Moreover, he had himself written a *Manual of Italian Renaissance Sculpture*, published early in 1904 as a companion volume to Robinson's *Catalogue of Casts of Greek and Roman Sculpture*. An article in the March 1904 *Bulletin* described these as

> the only existing books treating of the great epochs of sculpture in the form of a commentary upon a collection of reproductions. Despite the manifest imperfections of casts, books like this greatly aid the student of the history of art in acquiring that familiarity with the works themselves, which is the indispensable foundation of his knowledge. To the much larger number of persons whose aim is purely that of intelligent enjoyment, they offer in narrow compass data, which if given at all in histories and monographs of art are often effectually concealed amid masses of material irrelevant to the inquiry into artistic intention.

So it came about that on 21 April 1904 Gilman resigned as Librarian to have adequate time for his other duties. He was succeeded in the library by Almy Morrill Carter (Harvard A.B. *summa cum laude* 1898, A.M. 1899) who had taught Latin in Robert College, Constantinople, before going to the Princeton Library. This new officer seems to have had some schizophrenic confusion about his own name. He appears in the rosters for 1905 and 1906 as "Almy M.

THE BASEMENT LIBRARY IN COPLEY SQUARE.

Carter"; in 1907 he turned into "A. Morris Carter," but by 1908 had emerged simply as our old friend Morris Carter, later to become the first director of the Isabella Stewart Gardner Museum. Heaven knows what he thought he was doing; presumably he changed his name legally, for the inflexible Harvard quinquennial catalogues, which disregard personal whims, list him as "Morris Carter [formerly Almy Morrill Carter]."

In a somewhat eccentric pamphlet entitled *Did you Know Mrs. Gardner? Morris Carter's Answer*, that he privately printed in 1964, he tells of being interviewed by Prichard and then being ushered into Edward Robinson's office, where, he recalled sixty years later,

> I can remember only one question that he asked me: Whom did I know in Boston? I feared that I would lose the job because I had to admit that I knew absolutely no one in the city, but perhaps that was my best recommendation to him and I did receive the appointment, to begin work on June 1, 1904. Not until long after, did I surmise that perhaps Mr. Robinson wanted to find out whether I knew Mrs. Gardner, because there was friction in the Museum.

When Warren, Robinson, and the architects had just set out for Europe on their fact-finding mission, Prichard wrote Mrs. Gardner on 3 January 1904:

My new duties, as Director pro tem., began yesterday, and I am still appalled at the amount, not of responsibility, but of work on my shoulders. It is not the loss of Robinson that counts so much as that of Warren who did an immense amount of work for us. It all comes back now on me.

Later in the month, on the 29th, he wrote again:

Robinson writes: "The Poldi-Pezzoli, to my great disappointment, has nothing to teach about either lighting or effectiveness of arrangement. With all its wonderful treasures it is a terribly overladen and overdone interior, more suggestive of Mr. Marquand's house than Mrs. Gardner's, with which it is not worthy to be compared."

You may like to hear this twitter from Italy.

The first of the *Communications to the Trustees regarding the New Building*, privately printed in March 1904 while the travelers were still in Europe, contained three papers by officers of the museum and the reprinting of various discussions published abroad. The first and longest article was M. S. Prichard's "Current Theories of the Arrangement of Museums of Art and their application to the Museum of Fine Arts." This essay, dated December 1903, is headed by a quotation:

Let thy mind still be bent, — still plotting where
And when and how the business may be done.
Slackness breeds worms; but the sure traveler,
Though he alight sometimes, still goeth on.

In the foreword he wrote:

The Museum has to consider a number of different interests: the public and the artist, each seeking inspiration for his life and work; the art student in a spirit of franker imitation; the specialist and the student who apply themselves to some special branch of the collections, regarding it critically, historically, or in relation to many branches of knowledge; the teacher for whom the exhibits are illustrations of his lectures. The balance between all these sometimes conflicting claimants must be held with a steady hand. The great division of the possessions of the Museum into the exhibition collections and the study collections is recommended especially to serve all interests fairly. In further favor of this method it may be said that it is not expensive. It demands much space for few objects. The remaining possessions of a museum may be stored economically, close together and without extravagant installation.

The first of the stated aims of a museum of art, Prichard defined thus:

A museum of art, ultimately and in its widest possible activity, illustrates one attitude toward life. It contains only objects which reflect, clearly or dimly, the beauty and magnificence to which life has attained in past times. The fruits of this exalted and transcendent life are gathered within its walls, and it is the standard of this life with the noble intellectual activity it presupposes that a museum of art offers for acceptance by its visitors. In a narrower sense, yet in part performance of its wider obligation, the aim of a museum of art is to establish and maintain in the community a high standard of aesthetic taste. In performing this task it is its function to collect objects important for their aesthetic quality and to exhibit them in a way most fitted to affect the mind of the beholder.

"This is the first and great commandment," to which all other aims, such as supplying information to the public about its possessions, encouraging art history, and similar investigations, are subsidiary.

Save for the passive encouragement of artists, the museum, so far as its exhibition is concerned, has nothing to do directly with the training of those who make art a profession. This is a separate function, and is fulfilled by schools of art. Our Museum extends to its School the support of a guardian to a ward, but the Museum's equipment is designed particularly to further the enjoyment of the public, and not to prepare artists for their calling.

Once upon a time museums tried to exhibit all that they possessed. Science museums first realized that collections should be divided into two series, one to be shown to the public, the other reserved for students. As an art museum exists primarily for the general public, the objects shown should be so arranged that the ordinary visitor has his powers aroused and his emotions stimulated. Therefore there must be enough space to secure the individual effect of each object shown, and the visitor should not be fatigued by being offered too much, even of beautiful objects. "That curator," Prichard states unequivocally, "will best attain his aim who recognizes among his exhibits what is superfluous and eliminates it." So only a portion of the possessions of a museum can be exhibited; the rest must be cared for out of sight "in such manner that they are readily available for educational purposes or purposes of research." Note the clear distinction that places the use of objects "for educational purposes" out of sight, in the storerooms or classrooms, *not* in the galleries.

Consequently, Prichard required not only large enough exhibition space to house all the exhibition collection, but adequate quarters for each curator near the materials reserved for study. "Such rooms will serve as laboratories wherein problems relating to art may be considered with befitting ease and comfort," while "the addition of a class-room will complete for each department the equipment of a small university dedicated to a special branch of aesthetic enlightenment."

With equal forthrightness Prichard stated that the historical classification of objects is preferable to the technical; that they should be arranged by the cultures and periods that produced them rather than by the materials of which they are made. This was in sharp contradistinction to the South Kensington theory, carried over into Copley Square, whereby separate rooms were devoted to ceramics, wood carving, metals, textiles, and coins. Moreover there should be no special rooms for "precious objects," "All objects in the Museum are precious, and all rooms strong."

Such a division implies the need of temporary exhibition rooms where from time to time materials from the study collections will be shown.

Naturally, the higher the standard of excellence it is wished to maintain, the larger will be the size of the study series, and the fewer the objects it is possible to show to the public. The air grows rarer the nearer you reach the summit of the mountain. But the public need not be confined to seeing a tithe only of the Museum's treasures. More embracing exhibitions should be presented to it occasionally.

Thus far, Prichard's essay has remained in abstract terms. At this point he comes specifically down to Copley Square and particularly the enthusiasms of his senior colleagues Edward Robinson and Edward S. Morse, when he writes:

> In considering the application of these principles to our collections it is necessary to be frank; our personal appreciation and devotion must not blind us to the facts.
>
> THE PUBLIC DOES NOT LOOK AT GREEK VASES.
>
> THE PUBLIC DOES NOT LOOK AT JAPANESE POTTERY.
>
> THE PUBLIC DOES NOT LOOK AT ANY LONG SERIES OF SMALL OBJECTS,
>
> save in the most perfunctory manner, at all. It is a waste of effort and space to show to the public what the public does not regard. Put these collections, therefore, excepting a few of their very choicest examples — changing these from time to time if the collection is very rich, — into the study series, where they can be seen and well seen by every one who cares to see them; and on occasion let them be brought forth and exhibited for a limited time in the temporary exhibition galleries.

Prichard looking ahead suggested that the rooms for the study series might prove the potential exhibition rooms of the future; that in the case of unanticipated expansion, they might be taken for exhibition, and a compensatory study area provided according to circumstances, alongside, above, or below. He weighed in against artificial reconstruction of environment to provide settings for objects. "A work of art, it has been said, does not need the help of a background, but only to be unhindered by it." In local terms, however, he could contemplate the use of some actual room or rooms to illustrate the art of Colonial New England.

We should be on safe ground, and could perpetuate in this way some record of the local genius. It is known that there are collections of this nature in Boston, and persons might be found eager and able to forward the scheme. The Colonial room imagined would be authentic and not the achievement of an imitator. The sacrifice of one or two contemporary paintings from the Museum collection to devote to such an interior would not be great; their individual value would be lost, it is true, in enhancing the effect of the room, but this would be a small drain on our resources.

Such an experiment he preferred to "attempting to give one of the picture galleries, with all its particular limitations, the air of the period of Copley. The impression on a number of paintings submitted to this artifice and elaboration might not certainly be favorable," and the risk might be incurred "of swamping the contents in the decoration," as in the Henri II room in the Louvre.

The last section of Prichard's essay deals with the library, where he strongly urged separate curatorial libraries and photograph collections for each department, in close proximity to the study collections and classrooms, with, however, all their contents entered in the catalogue of the central library. Thus any difficulty of deciding where to place the central library in the new museum disappears. "The interests of the general public alone remain to be considered, and in its location and conveniences the Library should conform to these."

The two other essays by officers of the museum were, although briefer than Prichard's, equally stimulating and rational. Paul Chalfin, Curator of Chinese and Japanese Art, in his personal capacity as a painter reported on the museum's paintings with reference to installment, storage, and administration. He proposed that the Committee on the Museum consider keeping the number of paintings fixed at about 750 for a term of years. There were at the time 1,101 paintings in the museum, of which he considered only 730 worth having by a lenient standard of grading. Of the 730 sheep, 419 were owned by the museum and 311 were lent. If his limit were accepted, he proposed that some 500 paintings be kept on permanent exhibition, the first 250 "displayed so as to 'impose' and to 'inspire,' in rooms of as reticent a character and as beautiful an appointment as the Museum could devise or afford"; the next 250 shown less splendidly as a "study series," where copyists and other serious students could work with easels, tables, and chairs; and the lower 230 be stored awaiting repair, classification, special study, or (in most cases) ejection.

In a three-page essay, "The Monument and the Shelter," Benjamin Ives Gilman began by pointing out that these types of buildings differed "in that external appearance determines the design of the former and internal purpose that of the latter," that "it is possible to plan a shelter only when we know what it is that is to be sheltered." In the absence of facts about internal needs, "we must perforce base our design on fancies of these needs, and strive first of all to incorporate these fancies in a structure which shall be successful externally." This had been the situation when the Copley Square museum was built.

> When the designs for it were made there were no collections to house, or only the smallest, and no exacter knowledge of the requirements of their administration. A building was therefore demanded and supplied, first of all to make a dignified and appropriate appearance; and in the second place to contain a number of spacious galleries, some toplighted and some sidelighted, besides a basement capable of use for general office and service purposes. All other museums built since in America and most of those erected during this period abroad have been obliged to follow the same hypothetical and theoretical course.

So the Museum of Fine Arts, "having no past and being in ignorance of the future," had thirty years earlier necessarily fallen back upon "a creditable specimen of the monumental plan."

In 1904, having acquired a past and large collections, the museum could, with professional aid, settle in detail the requirements for sheltering its possessions, and for their administration, present and prospective, before considering a design.

> It is sought to plan a house for known things — allowance being made for change and addition — and no longer a casket for hoped-for jewels, to be represented meanwhile by a monumental exterior. This is the mark of an adult institution, living no longer mainly in dreams of the future, but shaping its course chiefly by facts of the present. In the form in which the architectural problem of a home

for the Museum now presents itself, it is that of giving to a content approximately known a form both apposite and attractive — that of designing a Shelter to rival a Monument in beauty.

All three papers in the first *Communications to the Trustees* were notable for their thoughtful good sense and applicability to the business in hand. Prichard's essay in particular is not only brief and admirably expressed; it is practically a blueprint for the planning of the new building and a foretaste of principles that were to become general in museums elsewhere some years or decades in the future. Here is a mind nourished by the classics successfully at work upon a practical problem. Yet his proposals were running counter to the tobacconist's window theory of museum installation — "all my goods on display" — that was current at the beginning of this century. The rich profusion of the Copley Square galleries doubtless seemed to some trustees a visible testimony of accomplishment, while it can have given Robinson and Morse little pleasure to be told that THE PUBLIC DOES NOT LOOK AT their hard-sought Greek vases and Japanese pots. Prichard had said the right thing, at the right time, but to some of the wrong people; doubtless his words made sense to the President, who had imported him for just such purposes.

There were, in the course of 1904, more tugs-of-war going on in the basement offices of the Museum of Fine Arts than were apparent

TETRADRACHMS OF HIERON, 478–467 B.C. Syracusan coins in the Greenwell Collection purchased in 1904.

to the 295,416 persons — only 31,523 of whom had paid admission — that passed through the galleries above. In fact Morris Carter's little pamphlet of reminiscences suggests a somewhat conspiratorial air below stairs, in which trustees, staff, and friends were plotting, as if they were disguised as yew-trees in the moonlit garden scene of a Mozart opera. Morris Carter tells, for example, a tale of Mrs. Gardner keeping Dr. Bigelow — a supporter of Edward Robinson — away from a Building Committee meeting by the bait of luncheon at Fenway Court with Okakura. Something of this masked ball atmosphere is reflected in Prichard's letter of 27 August 1904 to Mrs. Gardner, which refers to the 1,313 Greek coins, largely from the famous collection of Canon Greenwell, that were included in Edward P. Warren's last shipment from Lewes House.

> The meeting of the Trustees was a great success, and the coins were purchased *nemine contradicente*. Frank Higginson was enthusiastic, while Morris Gray was prevented from attending owing to a fall. He had called on Mr. Warren who told me he thinks he would have supported the motion to purchase! There is no doubt in my mind that the Museum acted wisely, though had it not been for you heaven only knows what would have happened. The Director is quite surprised at the ease with which the matter went, and little knows how it all came about.
>
> The good that people do lives after them, and your influence in this matter will be just another of the good things you have done for America.

So it is worth remembering that by some Isabelline tactic otherwise unrecorded the number of Greek coins in the Museum of Fine Arts was nearly trebled, and the average quality of the collection heightened, while adding a number of rare as well as beautiful specimens.

The year 1904 proved to be the last, for some time, of major purchases from unrestricted funds, not only of Classical antiquities but of any works of art. As Edward P. Warren had foreseen, the demands of the building program were about to push collecting off to the wings of the stage. But before unrestricted funds became frozen because of this situation a number of important paintings had been purchased. The sum of $80,000 from the Henry L. Pierce

DON BALTAZAR CARLOS AND HIS DWARF. Diego Rodriguez de Silva y Velázquez.
Henry Lillie Pierce Fund. 01.104
PIETÀ. Carlo Crivelli. *Anonymous gift supplemented by James Fund. 02.4*

Fund was allocated in 1901 for the purchase of Velázquez's portrait of *Don Baltazar Carlos and his Dwarf* from the Castle Howard collection; in the same year a portrait of a lady by Franz Hals was bought from the Pierce Fund. In 1902 there was acquired (partly by anonymous gift and partly by purchase from the income of the James Fund) the 1485 *Pietà* by Carlo Crivelli that Bernard Berenson considered the most original of all that painter's treatments of this sublime subject. John Marshall had two years earlier succeeded in buying this picture from the Panciatichi-Ximenes Collection in Florence, although paying rather more for it than had been intended. On receiving this word from Marshall, Edward Warren had written: "The Crivelli is a satisfaction. It is not for the M.F.A. yet." As it appeared there so soon after, one suspects a Warren source for the anonymous gift that supplemented the James Fund.

When Samuel and Edward Warren's mother, who had been an enthusiastic collector of paintings, died in the autumn of 1901, she bequeathed the museum a sum of money which permitted the purchase from her estate of a number of her pictures. Thus in 1903 Sir Thomas Lawrence's portraits of Lord and Lady Lyndhurst, Richard Wilson's *Tivoli and the Roman Campagna*, Jean Léon Gérôme's *L'Eminence Grise*, Jules Dupré's *On the Cliff*, and several other paintings came to the museum through the Susan Cornelia Warren Collection Fund. In her memory her children gave *The Death of the Virgin* by the Nuremberg painter Michael Wohlgemut (1434–1519), who had been one of the teachers of Albrecht Dürer. John Singleton Copley's great conversation piece of Mr. and Mrs. Ralph Izard of Charleston, South Carolina, painted at Rome in 1775 against a background of Classical antiquities, was bought with the help of the Edward Ingersoll Browne Fund. In the same year was also purchased Rembrandt's portrait of his father (Arthur Rotch Fund) and *Danaë and the Shower of Gold* (Martha Ann Edwards Fund), Van Dyck's portrait of Anna Maria Schodt (one-half Isaac Sweetser Fund, one-half anonymous gift), and Goya's delightful portrait of his son (Julia Bradford Huntington James Fund).

While Samuel D. Warren and Edward Robinson were in Europe visiting museums early in 1904, John Singer Sargent told them of a portrait of Fray Feliz Hortensio Palavicino, which he described as

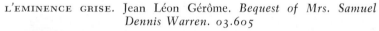

L'EMINENCE GRISE. Jean Léon Gérôme. *Bequest of Mrs. Samuel Dennis Warren. 03.605*

THE DEATH OF THE VIRGIN. Michael Wohlgemut. *Gift of the children of Mrs. Samuel Dennis Warren in memory of their mother.* 03.610

MR. AND MRS. RALPH IZARD. John Singleton Copley. *Edward Ingersoll Browne Fund. 03.1033*

"one of the best El Grecos I ever saw," that was offered for sale in Madrid. Although the price was £4,000, Sargent remarked: "There seems to be a considerable awakening of interest in El Greco's pictures, the Louvre has lately bought two, I hear — that may account for the big price." Warren authorized Robinson to offer $15,000; the deal was soon closed at $17,000, which showed the advantage of buying slightly ahead of the general taste of the time. It is significant that Sargent, who idolized Velázquez, was responsible for Boston's acquiring the first El Greco to enter the permanent collection of an American museum. The picture was promptly exhibited, for the young Royall Tyler (1883–1953), future Byzantine scholar but then enamored of Spain, wrote on 29 August 1904 to Mildred Barnes (later Mrs. Robert Woods Bliss):

I went to the Museum to see the El Greco which is well hung, and a beautiful picture. For a small collection they have some good

things, but a lot of truck too. Some of the Japanese things are good.
I like Boston architecturally far better than New York, and think
Beacon Street has a nice line, save for the tall Bachelors apartment
[48 Beacon Street] which ruins it. Copley Square I don't like.

The El Greco was purchased from the new Sarah Wyman Whitman Fund, as was also a Velázquez portrait of Philip IV that had
been discovered by Dr. Denman W. Ross in Madrid. Soon after the
arrival of the Velázquez, an anonymous letter casting doubts on its
genuineness was received; as a lively hubbub in the press and art
journals ensued, the June 1905 *Bulletin* was devoted to printing
favorable opinions from Bernard Berenson, Roger Fry, and a great

FRAY FELIZ HORTENSIO PALAVICINO. El Greco. *Isaac Sweetser Fund.* 04.234
PHILIP IV. Studio of Velázquez. *Sarah Wyman Whitman Fund.* 04.1606

TWO MIRACLES OF THE EUCHARIST. French tapestry, early 16th century. *James Fund. 04.76*

battery of artists and critics. Further favorable testimony from two Velázquez specialists, Professor Carl Justi of Bonn and Sir Walter Armstrong, Director of the National Gallery of Ireland, which was printed in the October 1905 *Bulletin*, reinforced the reputation of the portrait. Later opinion attributes the portrait to the studio of the painter.

An old favorite of my childhood, also bought in 1904 from the James Fund, is the early sixteenth-century French tapestry *Two Miracles of the Eucharist*, one section of which bears the legend:

> Ung payen sans honneur passa
> Par le devant le sainct Sacrament
> Mais son cheval se humilia
> Puys crut le payen fermement.

The pious horse, kneeling before the Host carried in a ciborium by a well-satisfied cleric, conveyed to me a vision of the later Middle

Ages that was pleasingly reinforced by Wohlgemut's *Death of the Virgin* and Van der Weyden's great *St. Luke drawing the portrait of the Virgin*.

During the summer of 1903 the Fifth Picture Gallery was cleared for a temporary loan exhibition of the portraits executed by John Singer Sargent during his recent visit to the United States. Here were the portraits of Brigadier General Leonard Wood, James Whitcomb Riley, Edward Robinson, Mrs. Fiske Warren and her daughter Rachel, Major Henry Lee Higginson, Mrs. William C. Endicott, Jr., Judge William C. Loring, and thirteen other subjects. Indeed everything that Sargent had done during this trip was exhibited save for the portraits of President Theodore Roosevelt and of John Hay. Clearing the walls for this exhibition led to considerable rearrangement of the galleries. This reshuffle involved a more conspicuous place in the First Gallery for the great Van der Weyden, which had recently been cleaned in order to remove patches of subsequent repainting.

The July 1904 *Bulletin* contained an article "The New Museum within the Present," which described the changes that had been made with the aim of "so installing each individual object that it may produce its full effect upon the spectator." Many things were withdrawn entirely from exhibition; the rearrangement of those that remained had been attempted as an experiment toward better installation in the new building.

> This rehanging of the pictures will, it is expected, bring many of them for the first time to adequate view. At a recent rehanging of the Rubens Gallery in the Louvre, a French critic remarked, "Although we have looked at these pictures daily, we have never seen them before." It is hoped that all visitors to the Museum will similarly recognize, in these attempts to approximate in our present building towards the conditions of the new one, a virtual enrichment of the contents of our galleries.

Although Edouard Manet's early masterpiece *The Street Singer*, exhibited as a loan in 1905, was bequeathed to the museum by Mrs. J. Montgomery Sears, it only returned for good in 1966 upon the

THE STREET SINGER. Edouard Manet. *Bequest of Mrs. J. Montgomery Sears. 66.304*

termination of a life interest in the picture by Mrs. Sears's daughter.

In the 1904 President's report, Samuel D. Warren proudly pointed out that $269,589.28 — the largest amount in the history of the museum — had been spent for works of art during the year. He summarized further the investment of $1,324,683.62 in purchases during the years 1895–1904, beginning with the bald statement:

"The purchases of classical antiquities, begun in the year 1895, have come to an end. Further acquisitions from the Museum's late source of supply are not at present contemplated." In that area $676,904.18 had been spent during the decade; $525,809.35 had been devoted to buying paintings, $57,561.71 to prints, $27,996.51 to Chinese and Japanese art, $15,622.87 to Egyptian art, and $20,789.00 to miscellaneous collections. Of this $1,324,683.62, $886,885.79 had come from unrestricted trust funds and $67,467.60 from general funds. Only $370,330.23 had come from trust funds that by their terms could only be used for certain purchases. Warren spoke with feeling of the collection, "which serves worthily to illustrate the expression of the Hellenic genius"; of the notable additions of paintings; of the manner in which the Print Department had, when the Gray Collection was recalled to Harvard, been saved from extinction by the acquisition of the equally valuable Harvey D. Parker (formerly Sewall) Collection; of Albert M. Lythgoe's recent purchases in Egypt for the new Egyptian Department. He paid tribute to the way in which generous collectors had built the Department of Chinese and Japanese Art, and Dr. Denman W. Ross the textile collection.

As for the future, the needs of the painting collection of the Chinese, Japanese, and Egyptian collections were well defined. The most pressing gaps to be filled were in the field of European or Western art other than paintings — early Christian, medieval and Renaissance — and in Persian and Arabic art. He pointed out, however, that the greatest factor in acquisitions had been the Henry Lillie Pierce Residuary Fund, of which $615,220.65 had already been spent, and only $182,779.35 remained invested. "The Trustees must recognize the fact," Warren cautioned, "that the safe limit of the expenditure of unrestricted funds has been reached, and that, in the absence of new benefactions, the work of collecting must now be confined within narrow limits of special funds." They were indeed narrow, for, under the new austerity program, only $16,414.70 was spent in 1905 for purchases.

As the studies for the new building progressed, the future of the huge collection of plaster casts raised many problems. When the enlarged Copley Square museum had been opened in 1890, casts filled the entire first floor, occupying half the exhibition space in the

A SAMPLE OF THE PROBLEM POSED BY CASTS. A gallery in Copley Square
filled to overflowing.

whole building. In the dozen succeeding years many had been
trundled off to storage as galleries were required for recently arrived
original works of Classical art. Now the question of space to be
assigned to such reproductions in the future building assumed major
importance. There were two diametrically opposed views. Edward
Robinson and Benjamin Ives Gilman had written books that used the
Classical and Renaissance casts as the basis for studying the history
of art. Matthew S. Prichard despised casts, which he likened to the
player piano, the squawky cylinder-disk phonograph, and other
mechanical vulgarities that substituted for music at the time. Prichard's hopes for the new building centered around liberal space for
the exhibition of the finest objects, with the remaining possessions of
the museum "stored economically, close together and without extravagant installation." Now plaster casts if stored close together could
not be seen. As they were often large and always breakable, they
could not be trucked in and out of storage for temporary showing.
There were so many of them that, if given any kind of adequate

exhibition space in the new building, the tail would be wagging the dog.

Edward Robinson, on 12 September 1904, wrote an immensely long letter about casts to the members of the Committee on the Museum and the Building Committee. He began by stating that it had been assumed until recently that all the casts would be brought together in one section of the new building in a single large area. In the early summer, however, a suggestion was made to the Committee on the Museum — one suspects by Prichard — that the casts be distributed among the different departments. According to this theory casts of Egyptian sculpture would be in the Department of Egyptian Art, not in the rooms with original objects but in spaces easily reached from them. One possibility would be to put casts in basement rooms, connected by stairways with the appropriate exhibition rooms above. Robinson devoted several pages to pointing out the practical problems involved in such decentralization, for he clearly favored bringing all the casts together in one section or wing of the building "constituting a museum in themselves." He then counterattacked vigorously with a proposal to expand and enlarge the cast collection. He piously invoked its increasing use by school classes, adding that "many classes of adults have been formed during the last fifteen years for the especial purpose of studying this one collection." He further suggested that if the casts were augmented, the museum could exert influence "as a national factor in artistic education, if it were to offer to the country a standard collection which could be followed more or less completely in other places." The example of Boston had stimulated the formation of cast collections in other cities as well as colleges; shall we now let the museum "sink into a secondary position, and let others perform the work which it began?"

This rather wordy communication did not settle the matter, even though Robinson invoked the sacred name of "education" in much the way that some Americans in a tight spot fall back on the unassailable virtues of motherhood and respect for the flag, for President Warren asked the Secretary and the Assistant Director for their comments on it. Benjamin Ives Gilman in a brief letter of 8 November 1904 replied that three considerations inclined him against "making the collections of casts a prominent feature in the new Museum, and in favor of their subordinate and provisional treatment." First he denied that devoting an important section of the new building to collections chiefly useful in teaching the history of art would be "an act of leadership in artistic education." This would in no way demonstrate two fundamental truths about art and its study, that "in an exhibition of fine art instruction becomes a mean, the end being appreciation" and that "the knowledge of art history is not the same thing as the comprehension of art works, but a very different and immeasurably less important thing." These two ideas — that "instruction was made for art and not art for instruction" and that "the friendship of the individual work is far more valuable than any knowledge of the sequence of one upon the other" — would both be left out in the new museum "were educational material to appear there on a par with works of art." Gilman's second point was even more telling: "To emphasize casts anew in a second building would be to perpetuate a feature of the collections originally incorporated under stress of necessity." He recalled the 1883 statement of the trustees: "As a rule original work is beyond our means." In third place to make the cast galleries an unchangeable part of its plan "would oppose a tendency to specialization of function, which is the general law of growth among institutions as elsewhere."

Again in response to a request from the President, Matthew S. Prichard set forth his views in a letter of 1 November 1904. With Gilman he recognized the aesthetic aim of a museum of the fine arts.

> The Museum is for the public and not for any caste or section of it, whether student, teacher, artist or artisan, but is dedicated chiefly to those who come, not to be educated, but to make its treasures their friends for life and their standards of beauty. Joy, not knowledge, is the aim of contemplating a painting by Turner or Dupré's *On the Cliff*, nor need we look at a statue or a coin for aught else than inspiration and the pleasure of exercising our faculties of perception. It is in this sense, furthermore, that they are accepted by those who visit our galleries, in accordance with the teaching of Aristotle, who recognized that the direct aim of art is the pleasure derived from a contemplation of the perfect.

Casts assist a secondary aim, that of teaching. "We should not exhibit them, therefore, for they belong in the reserved series, and to exhibit them would be to put them frankly on a level with works of art."

Prichard continued: "Let me be clear: I do not say, 'Do not teach'; what I say is, 'Do not exhibit the machinery.' "

As he enumerated objections to the exhibition of casts, Prichard warmed to his work with a fervor reminiscent of John Adams. Casts are "engines of education and should not be shown near objects of inspiration. They are data mechanically produced; our originals are works of art." The museum has reached a point in its development that warrants the attention of strangers; they come for what we have collected ourselves, "not for a conventional collection of trite reproductions such as is the stock in trade of every ready-made museum of art." By encouraging haste and discouraging leisure we at last "even destroy that contemplation which Mr. Gilman calls the 'consummation of a work of art.' The visitor, anxious to move on, passes the casts scarcely deigning to glance at them; in this semi-conscious state he not only omits to notice them, but by the same token misses many of the finest originals in the world as well, seeing nothing till he reaches the paintings, where he may rest and be thankful." If casts have uses, they belong in another institution altogether, such as a university or a school.

Having disposed of the chief claim for casts, namely their usefulness as educational material, and having found it irrelevant to the museum's primary aims, Prichard considers the artistic claims of casts, and finds them wanting. Although the physical shape is retained, it does not reproduce the emotional force of the original at a weaker rate. "So true is this that the one thing possible to predicate of every cast, which might indeed be inscribed under each in a museum, is THE ORIGINAL DOES NOT LOOK LIKE THIS." After dismissing casts as "the Pianola of the Arts," Prichard stated: "The exhibition halls of our Museum have the same right to be free of mechanical sculpture as the programmes of the Symphony Concerts, which set the standard of musical taste in Boston, have of exemption from mechanical music." In conclusion he observes that "in our hands is the touchstone of appreciation for the community," and asks whether we may not "leave to those more richly endowed with means than we, attracted rather by the ideals of education than those subtler ones of beauty, the task of constructing the great educational museum of reproductions?"

The light of the sun is not exhausted; the direct message may still be heard. Originals are yet to be obtained. It will be time to collect reproductions when the fountain heads of inspiration and beauty have run dry. Till then let us stand watchful and let us direct our enthusiasm into deeper channels, leaving the cast to others. We do not seek the original of this time or that time, but the message of beauty whatever its language, its age or its source. The world is open to us, and for the cost of establishing and maintaining a collection of casts, will yield treasures of real significance. Do not our youth and vigor impel us along the path of discovery, or is the reward to be the portion of others?

My plea, then, is that in the new building our galleries should be freed of casts, and that the Museum should become — a gem in fair setting — a museum of works of art.

The forces were now aligned and battle was imminent. On 3 November, two days after he had written this letter to Warren, Prichard wrote to Mrs. Gardner:

The fight is on for Tuesday, when the building committee and the committee on the museum have been asked to meet for the decision of questions of great moment. *Nos morituri te salutamus.* I shall lose; but I shall have lit a great lamp — the lamp of real appreciation, of the first rate, of aesthetic conviction. Here are the forces:

For me	*Against me*
S. D. Warren, probably	Robinson
D. W. Ross,	W. P. P. Longfellow
Templeman Coolidge?	Cummings
Edward Forbes?	Bigelow, *probably*

Uncertain
Henry Hunnewell,
Morris Gray,
Lothrop,
Arthur Cabot,
Frank Higginson.

I wish I could regard it, like an Okakura, with grim humor and indifference. I suppose I must be content to have brought the matter to some sort of issue.

On the 10th, he wrote again to Mrs. Gardner:

> Another afternoon fighting about casts. The parties define them-
> selves in this way — on the Committee of the Museum: Longfellow,
> Cummings, Bigelow in favor of casts; Ross, Templeman Coolidge,
> Cabot, S. D. Warren against casts. The blessing is that the strong
> men stand pat — But you know my feeling of the weak.

The architect William Pitt Preble Longfellow, who having been
a trustee since 1883 had grown up with the casts, moved (in the
spirit of Neville Chamberlain at Munich) "that the Building Committee be informed that it is not the desire of the Committee on the
Museum to provide in the present plans for a material increase in
the collection of casts." Although this was duly voted by the Committee on the Museum, it in no way resolved the fundamental conflict. The second of the *Communications to the Trustees*, printed in
December 1904, contained a section "The Collection of Casts in
the New Museum." Here were reprinted Robinson's, Gilman's, and
Prichard's letters, together with the vote and the section of a letter
on the subject addressed to Warren by Longfellow. His rather unin-
spired communication, which tried to agree in part with both camps,
cannot have greatly pleased either. Briefly there was "peace in our
time." But it was hardly a healthy situation to have the Assistant
Director and the Secretary firmly aligned in print, through action
of the President, against the Director, even though *Communications
II* was intended only for the use of the Board of Trustees.

Communications III, entitled "The Museum Commission in Europe," which was printed in January 1905, contained a seventy-three-
page report of observations by R. Clipston Sturgis, a thirty-one-page
supplementary report by Edmund M. Wheelwright, a descriptive
index of the many museums visited, and eighty-seven plates. As the
Experimental Gallery on the Fenway land was only removed in
November 1905 after two years of tests, it was January 1906 before
the report of findings was issued as *Communications IV*. Before his
and Wheelwright's employment concluded on 31 May 1905, R.
Clipston Sturgis submitted in printed form a *Report on Plans Presented to the Building Committee*. This very sensible document was

based on the ideals of concentrating the exhibitions on one main floor, of disposing the various departments in separate portions of the building, of observing the principle of selected exhibits, and still having convenient communication between the departments. Only after this exposition did Clipston Sturgis reach the thorny question of casts. He pointed out that to exhibit them, top-lit, even in the most compact manner would require nearly 50,000 square feet, and that, although such an area was considered a necessary element in every plan made for well over a year, the size of the block hampered seriously every design made.

> The collection is so large that its mere bulk will attract attention, which I believe to be out of proportion to its value, and my own feeling is that the casts should occupy no place where they are liable to detract from the value and interest of the originals. My ideal would be a separate museum connected with that part of the group which is educational in character, the school and the lecture room. But this is a wide question and one of which there may be differences of opinion.

The preliminary plans that Sturgis suggested were of a one-story museum, although this story was raised sufficiently above the outside grade to give an amply lighted ground floor, which would contain offices, study rooms, the Print Department, and other exhibitions, like the Greek vases and the Morse collection of pottery, where very high ceilings were not required.

The uneasy peace of divided counsels continued until the summer of 1905. In the spring Edward Robinson was in Europe, representing Harvard University and the Museum of Fine Arts at the reopening of the enlarged Art Gallery at Aberdeen, Scotland, and receiving an honorary doctorate of laws from Aberdeen University. The truce ended abruptly on 12 August when Edward Robinson handed the trustees his resignation as Director and Curator of Classical Antiquities. His letter, sent to every member of the board and printed in the *Transcript* of 22 August, stated simply that he was "not in sympathy with the policy of administration of the Museum, especially in matters affecting the position of the Director but not within his control." On the 28th, when the trustees met to consider the resignation, Prichard wrote Mrs. Gardner: "The question of Robinson's resignation was at once referred to a committee. I do not care very much for the look of things, since committees are unsatisfactory things, but it will all end one way or another, and that is good. In the meantime, our progress is stopped, but, maybe, it will be stopped more effectually later." The committee was a dignified and venerable one — Charles Eliot Norton, Charles W. Eliot, John Chipman Gray, Charles Sprague Sargent, and William Endicott — none of whom had been closely associated with the in-fighting that had been going on. These gentlemen interviewed the Director, the President, the Secretary, the Assistant Director, the Librarian, the Keeper of Japanese Pottery, past and present members of the Executive and Museum committees, and even the Superintendent of Buildings.

"It became evident," the committee reported to the trustees, "early in the investigation that the limits of the authority of the Museum Committee and of the Director and the Assistant Director were so ill-defined as to deprive the Director of the independence and the authority without which no Director could hope to discharge the functions of his office satisfactorily to himself." This had "created strained relations between officers of the Museum and confusion in the minds of subordinates," a situation fully reflected in Morris Carter's little volume of 1964 reminiscences. The source of this confusion sprang from the character of the by-laws. One hears the voice of John Chipman Gray in the sentence: "Had the By-Laws defining the functions of the Committee on the Museum and of the Director been intended to bring about a conflict of authority, their first clauses could hardly have been more effectively framed." The committee had hoped that by radical changes in the by-laws and other measures which they were prepared to recommend, Robinson might be induced to withdraw his resignation. As they were disappointed in this hope, they regretfully recommended to the trustees that it be accepted. They considered it essential that the by-laws be radically amended before any negotiations to secure a new Director were opened.

Accordingly, the trustees on 9 December 1905 accepted Robinson's resignation "with extreme regret." On 18 December, he was appointed Assistant Director of the Metropolitan Museum in New

York, where within a few years he succeeded to the directorship and spent the remainder of his life. It was noted in the previous chapter how this translation moved the current center of gravity in Classical collecting from Boston to New York. The February 1906 *Bulletin*, which reported Robinson's resignation, also stated that the trustees had on 18 January 1906 adopted amendments to the by-laws,

> aimed at giving to the Director a large share of responsibility as administrative head of the Museum, to the Curators larger powers in respect to the management of their respective departments, and to the whole staff a voice advisory in regard to the general welfare of the Museum, thus relieving, in considerable degree, the Trustees, through their committees, of the more detailed supervision of the administration with which they have charged themselves since the foundation of the Museum.

It was high time too, and past, had the trustees considered the example of the neighboring Boston Public Library, which had slatted about in the doldrums from 1877 to 1895 while a similarly over-industrious board of trustees solemnly tinkered with the details and minutiae of library administration. At the same annual meeting of 18 January 1906 the trustees authorized the Building Committee to proceed to obtain detailed plans, specifications, and bids for the new museum, in accordance with the studies carried on during the previous two and a half years. Furthermore they appointed J. Randolph Coolidge, Jr., Temporary Director of the Museum.

Coolidge had qualifications for the post other than being the eldest son of the 1892 donor of Lhermitte's *L'Ami des Humbles*. After being graduated *magna cum laude* from Harvard in 1883, he had studied architecture at the Ecole des Beaux-Arts in Paris, and had practiced his profession in Boston, becoming President of the Boston Society of Architects in 1905. In 1899 he was elected a trustee of the Boston Athenæum, which designated him as a trustee of the Museum of Fine Arts in the same year; he served on the museum board until two years before his death in 1928. He was a kindly, lovable man with an inquiring mind, who was deeply concerned about the people and institutions of Boston. Thus at a time of frayed tempers, he was a valuable peacemaker and a man well able to keep the institution on course. At the 1906 annual meeting, the President had been empowered to appoint Visiting Committees of five members each to the various departments of the museum. Coolidge's reply to an inquiry from one of their members concerning their functions could not be bettered after more than sixty years.

I would have the Committee become intimate with the department and befriend it. Each committee should therefore aim at the completest possible knowledge of the collections in its Department and of the officers in charge of these collections. Intimate friends may be trusted not to interfere except in real emergencies, but to be ever ready to give sympathy and help according to their resources. They will understand the Curator's aspirations for his department, the necessary limitations of expenditure by the Trustees, and will discern an opportunity when it exists to do for the Museum what the Museum cannot do for itself. With a familiar knowledge of the officials, the resources, the needs and possibilities of the Department, the Visiting Committee may be trusted to decide when and how to give valuable assistance, whether by suggestion to the Curator, conference with the Director, or report to the Trustees. They are not inspectors, not directors, not even a body of experts, although there may be experts among them, — merely wise and kind friends.

Although J. Randolph Coolidge, Jr., only served as Temporary Director for 1906, during that year his initiative achieved two things repeatedly requested but never accomplished in the past: the creation of a Lecture Room, opened in March, and the publication in August of the first edition of the *Handbook of the Museum of Fine Arts.* This bound volume of some three hundred pages contained a wealth of illustrations of the finest objects from all departments, with brief but excellent text, floor plans, and a succinct history of the museum, all compressed into a size that would fit in the pocket. Although constantly revised and reprinted, as the museum moved and enlarged its collections, the *Handbook*'s format was so satisfactory that it persisted without change until 1964.

The search for a new director was protracted, for the internecine warfare of 1905 hardly made Boston seem an attractive spot for the peaceloving, particularly when the complications of building and installing a new museum were taken into account. Although on 12 January 1906 Matthew Steward Prichard was demoted from Assistant Director to the odd post of Bursar, he continued his activities without diminution. His colleague Morris Carter recalled that

> during the next few months he originated and set in operation a method of recording and cataloguing objects of art in the Museum, similar to the card cataloguing system used in libraries, except that every museum card bears a small photograph of the subject it represents. Some modification of this system, which is Prichard's most valuable contribution to museum administrative methods, is now used by all the larger museums in the United States.

Morris Carter, who was around at the time with open eyes and ears, recalled the enthusiasm with which Edward Robinson's friends had received the news of his prompt call to the Metropolitan Museum.

> Here was a vindication stronger than any committee could devise, and great was the indignation against the foreigner which had resulted in this loss to Boston. This indignation was also directed in less degree to Mr. Warren, who would have gladly resigned at once, but he was committed to a great task and he would not withdraw until that task was completed. He was determined to secure the best possible plans for the new Museum building.

The following July, Prichard left the museum entirely to become Secretary of a Committee on the Utilization of Museums of Art by Schools and Colleges, which was based at Simmons College. Although this suggests the feeling that peace could be most quickly restored by the elimination of the second of the two principal combatants, Samuel D. Warren paid Prichard this tribute in the 1906 President's report.

> A man of unusual capacity for work, a student and a thinker, a master of administrative detail, and a resourceful organizer, he combines with these qualifications an appreciation and natural discrimination in matters of art, with special knowledge of its develop-

ments in Greece. In the organisation and administration of the present Museum, and in the planning for the new one, he has rendered the Museum service of a very high order.

Prichard went to Europe in the summer of 1906. After his return to Boston in the autumn, he wrestled for a year with the somewhat inconclusive labors of his new committee. In June 1907 he went back to Europe for good. Although he never returned to Boston, most of his principles were eventually embraced by the Museum of Fine Arts, where today there is not a plaster cast to be seen. He continued to be the close friend and constant correspondent of Isabella Stewart Gardner for the remaining seventeen years of her life.

The membership of the Building Committee, which was authorized on 18 January 1906 to proceed with plans for the new museum, was revised to consist of Samuel D. Warren, J. Randolph Coolidge, Jr., Henry S. Hunnewell, Morris Gray, and Gardiner M. Lane. Through the spring of 1906, they, working closely with members of the museum staff, evolved what was known as the "Staff Plan" for requirements that would best serve the institution's aims and purposes. The production of final plans was entrusted to Guy Lowell, with R. Clipston Sturgis, Edmund M. Wheelwright, and Professor D. Despradelle of M.I.T. retained as advisory architects. The design achieved was accepted by a unanimous vote of the trustees on 19 July 1906 and adopted as the plan for the new building. At the same time a committee to consider ways and means of the construction of the new building was appointed, consisting of Warren, F. L. Higginson, John C. Gray, Charles S. Sargent, and Nathaniel Thayer. Plans and specifications were submitted to contractors on 28 November, and bids received and opened on 19 December 1906.

The contract for the new museum was signed on 4 February 1907 and ground broken on 11 April, in expectation of completion by 23 February 1909. The estimated cost was $1,573,000, which left, after sums already given or promised to the Building Fund, $623,650 to be raised. Although construction was under way in 1907, the administration of the museum was still in a state of flux. Once the plans were approved by the trustees on 19 July 1906, Samuel D. Warren let it be known that he would not be a candidate for re-election to the presidency the following January. He had successfully carried through the planning of the building, and wished to take his leave. Thus on 17 January 1907 the trustees elected as President Gardiner Martin Lane (1859–1914). Although he had been graduated from Harvard *summa cum laude* in classics in 1881 and was offered a post in the Latin Department, Lane went instead to Lee, Higginson Company to spend his life in business. As he always retained his love of the classics, and developed a keen interest in Egyptology, he was a useful choice. He was still in his forties, and having only been elected to the museum board the previous year, was free of preconceptions derived from earlier squabbles. At the same time J. Randolph Coolidge, Jr., relinquished his post, as he had warned his colleagues he would have to do after a year's service. Consequently, Benjamin Ives Gilman was appointed Temporary Director, while Morris Carter became Secretary to the Director and Registrar although retaining charge of the Library.

With this temporary crew the museum continued until 1 August 1907, when Arthur Fairbanks, Professor of Greek and Greek Archaeology at the University of Michigan, entered upon his duties as the third Director. He too was in his forties, having been born at Hanover, New Hampshire, on 13 November 1864. He was a member of the Dartmouth class of 1886, had studied at the Yale Divinity School, the Union Theological Seminary, and the University of Berlin before receiving a Ph.D. from Freiburg-im-Breisgau in 1890. He had taught Greek at Dartmouth and sociology and comparative religion at the Yale Divinity School before becoming Professor of Greek at the University of Iowa in 1900, a post he relinquished to take the Michigan professorship which he left on coming to Boston.

Although Samuel Dennis Warren remained a member of the Building Committee until the completion of the new museum in 1909, his retirement from the presidency in 1907 marked the end of his active participation in museum affairs. He died on 19 February 1910, less than a month after his fifty-eighth birthday. When Matthew Prichard returned to Paris from Burgundy early in April he wrote Mrs. John L. Gardner an extraordinary tribute to Warren, compounded of affection, grief, and prejudice. Frederick Jackson Turner, after reading *The Education of Henry Adams*, wrote his

MATTHEW STEWART PRICHARD. Etching
by Henri Matisse. *Isabella Stewart Gardner
Museum.*

colleague Edmond S. Meany: "Don't take his account of Harvard as a historically accurate portrait: it is rather a cartoon by a brilliant critic of Harvard's imperfections, and, in that respect truthful and helpful." Prichard's account, taken on the same terms, is a useful contribution to a cloudy era in the history of the Museum of Fine Arts.

Returned from the south I found your letter written a fortnight ago speaking of Sam Warren. Let me put on paper for you in a few words the direction of his activity in the Museum as it seems to me at a distance of time and space and without details, completeness or competence.

You know as I do not, for I was not there, what the Museum was when Sam Warren became its president. It was despicable and despised. A few families had a special cult for it, regarded it as their appanage, practised their influence on it, discussed together their activity in its past, their aspirations for its future; on Sundays it was visited by loquacious Italians, but on week days the temple was closed to all save the initiated who appeared to bully the director and oversee their family tombs. For it was recognized that one room belonged to this family and another to that. They had a prescriptive right to arrange and contribute what they would and exclude the rest, by right of birth they were experts in their corner or corridor and would hesitate to visit another lot in the cemetery unaccompanied by the representative of its tribal chief. To understand the Museum of the moment it would be necessary to study savage customs, for it was the last sanctuary (unless the Athenæum was another) of the Boston aborigines, and totem and taboo, animism and magic, custom, rite, precedent and mystery were imprinted all over it. An unseen wall of sanctification defended it from the impure and profane. It had its House of Levi, its inherited priesthood; and frightened tradesmen endowed it with their millions that their descendants might be smiled upon by its popes and hierarchs. I can only imagine that Sam Warren was chosen its president because it was thought that he would be strong to guard the sanctuary and extend its occult influence.

Perhaps it would all have ended for the best had not he been faced at once with the problem of moving the collections to some other and freer site. The movement hinged on that contingency. In the course of preparing for the transference of the shrine, its holiness was wrecked, its altars torn down, its ritual abolished, for Sam Warren opened its windows and ventilated it with the air of the world's experience. There is no doubt in my mind that he was opposed almost from the start because of his attitude of liberalism and his indifference to aristocratic prejudice and tenure. For he was opposed by his trustees, by Boston society, by Boston artists. Had he appealed to the public through its papers he would have been supported, but he had a curious indifference to obstacles and loved to reach the next corner walking quietly across the street even though warned that there were people out for him with shotgun and stiletto.

He effected, or was in the course of effecting when he resigned the presidency, three fundamental changes in the Museum with the intention of dragging it up from its position of picturesque barbarism to be the foremost of museums, the type for the museum of the future. He destroyed its character as a private, tribal, family institution, to make it a public matter. He transformed, that is, its aim from *cult to cultivation*, from aristocracy to democracy, from privilege to people. This was the whole basis of his action. The other two changes of which I speak are really but examples of his guiding principle. The second change which I find entirely in accord with the whole trend of modern life in its most advanced thought was that from science to art, from knowledge to feeling, from investigation to enjoyment. He was convinced of the reality of this innovation. For him the important thing was not to know the date of an object, the name of its author, the causes of which it was the effect, but to respond to its influence and throb with it, to live more powerfully in consequence of its impulse. He accepted at once the proposal to consider the public and its sentiment before the professor and his facts, to live forward instead of existing backwards. You know how bitterly he was attacked for inaugurating so dangerous a principle. He was supposed to be overthrowing and under-rating all the monuments of knowledge. But for the third change he was profoundly odious to the initiated, although it established that the charges brought against him of indifference to science were unfounded. It consisted in this. Hitherto the trustees were regarded, owing to the accident of their birth or their success in money making to be very wise. They were *ex officio* infallible or as nearly infallible as people in a community may be. If they voted a curiosity to be a work of art, it became a work of art *ipso facto*; if they determined to buy a picture, it became a masterpiece; no question of connoisseurship was too difficult to be solved by their solemn vote. Well, that was changed. Sam Warren wished to have men of knowledge as well as people of feeling in the different departments of the Museum and there was a gradual devolution of authority from the Trustees to the staff, from prejudice to knowledge, from the *a priori* to experience.

These changes involved an organization of a museum staff, not a reorganization for there was none before, but an organization of every department, of every office, the preparation of a frame into which in the future the activities of the Museum could fit without friction. This work was unfinished when he left affairs in the hands of others. It would have enabled the Museum to extend its influence easily and far, but I don't dwell on the details which are complicated and uninteresting and which were known to no one as intimately as to him. Nor do I repeat to you the story you know so well of the preparation for the new building and its execution: you know in fact its later chapters in which I no longer appeared. I have said enough to suggest to you the enormous flow of thought in his mind during the years he was responsible for the Museum's activity. I have said too, that Boston did not stand by him, in fact, outside a handful of people and the Museum staff he was completely isolated. More extraordinary still, only a portion of the staff upheld him. The staff was the most ragged body of waifs and strays ever disciplined into an army by the most desperate of captains. It was recruited from everywhere except from Massachusetts. (If I except Dr. Robinson and Professor Morse who were true to their New England influence and did not understand him.) Who would ever have thought that with the aid of people that chance rained into the place, — German blood, Japanese blood, Jewish blood, English blood as well as Yankee — with no ties in the community, he could have produced the changes he brought about?

For Sam Warren had no knowledge about museums to start with and no developed feeling for art: these subjects were foreign to him. But he had vitality. Life made a demand upon him and he arose and responded to it. His infinite love, modesty, patience and confidence carried him through, and with himself he bore his little band. Never, indeed, did he seem to work more efficaciously and calmly than in a shower of bullets. He was a man, in short, — and you will realize the meaning of the appreciation — who did not stop short of being great. There was no hesitation, no search for security, no self-seeking, but during those years when there were demands made upon him by his family, by his business and by his other interests, demands which time has shown to have been mortal, he was able to conceive a great principle, effect it and inspire with faith and devotion those whom he associated with him in his task. He was a great liberator, those for whom he introduced liberty did not know him, for they were the American public, the trammels from which he freed them were inherent and immanent in inchoate society. He was one of nature's elect who fulfil the exactions of life and for reward fall dead as they drag her car to the door of the temple. It is for us who saw and know to render thanks.

The next day Prichard sent off another letter that contained this paragraph:

I hear all that is horrible, as we all do, and the rumour that there was ill-feeling and disappointment that Sam Warren did not leave a large legacy to the Museum. Do you remember the prose poem of Turgenev where the peasants ask for pieces of the rope which has served to hang the noble who has sacrificed his life for them, the tradition being that fragments of the criminal's noose is

CORONATION OF THE VIRGIN. School of Valencia, 15th century. *Gift of Denman Waldo Ross in memory of Samuel Dennis Warren. 10.36*

a powerful talisman? Little things, they do not see that he has endowed them with life which enables them even to thirst for dollars; they should seek elsewhere for their pelf.

When the customary resolutions concerning Warren's death were printed in the April 1910 *Bulletin*, Prichard exploded from Paris to Mrs. Gardner.

My dear Mrs. Gardner, I have read the Bulletin note on dear Sam Warren, and have found a use for the Trustees. They can all go to Hell — and sit as a committee to assist Rhadamanthus and company in judging the souls of the righteous! Their very hearts must be made of compressed broad-cloth. There is no sign, in deed, that salvation shall spring from their loins.

He should, in fairness, have excluded Denman W. Ross, whose gift to the museum in memory of Samuel Dennis Warren of a Spanish fifteenth-century panel painting of the *Coronation of the Virgin* was illustrated on the cover of the April *Bulletin*. There was deep feeling on the cover although there were dry words on the next page.

CHAPTER VII

The Huntington Avenue
Museum

For six months after his retirement as President, Samuel D. Warren retained the chairmanship of the Building Committee. This too he resigned on 18 July 1907, being succeeded by Henry S. Hunnewell, but not until he had published in the June 1907 *Bulletin* an illuminating account of the new museum then under construction.

BIRD'S-EYE VIEW OF THE COMPLETED MUSEUM OF FINE ARTS. Guy Lowell's drawing of 1907.

The illustrations included Guy Lowell's plan for the completed scheme that would fill the entire property at some point in the future, as well as floor plans of the first third then being built. Obviously a great amount of space was to be gained even by the construction of only the first stage. The Copley Square museum contained 26,930 square feet of space and occupied a rectangle of 154 by 212 feet; the building under way would provide 73,000 square feet within a rectangle of 240 by 501 feet. The main entrance fronted on Huntington Avenue for the convenience of visitors arriving by streetcar, but there was ample open space for future development along the Fenway and Museum Road, for of the 518,714 square feet owned, 445,714 were unoccupied. Even Guy Lowell's plan for the completed scheme, with a museum building of 182,500 square feet, a school of 16,650, a separate building for casts of 26,680, and open courtyards of 79,130, would still leave 213,754 square feet available for a generous perimeter of lawn and approaches. The parking lot had not then entered into anyone's thoughts, for even a decade later those Bostonians who owned automobiles were able to leave them outside houses and shops during visits without unduly encumbering the public highways.

In describing the completed scheme, Warren noted that it called for three distinct but connected buildings:

(1) The large central group of departments, intended for the exhibition and study of works of art and for the administration of the museum.
(2) A large and well-lighted structure for casts from sculpture in the northwest corner of the lot.
(3) A building for the School in the irregular triangle formed by the first-mentioned buildings and the public highway on the west.

Only the first third of the first of these was being built at the time. The second represented a theoretical agreement that, if casts were necessary, they should be under a separate roof, well isolated from the main collections. Thus, although Matthew S. Prichard had left the museum, he had won at least a partial victory in the battle that had embittered the years just past. This cast building never was built,

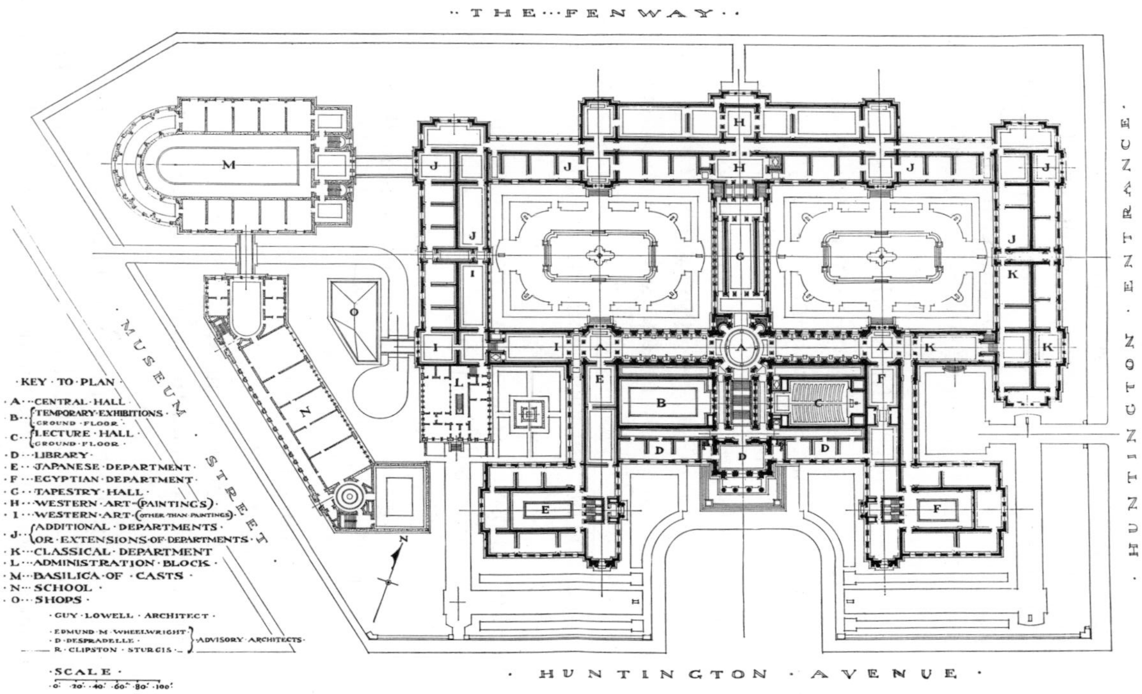

PLAN OF THE COMPLETED MUSEUM OF FINE ARTS. Guy Lowell's drawing of 1907.

· HUNTINGTON · ENTRANCE ·

· THE···FENWAY··

· MUSEUM · STREET ·

· HUNTINGTON · AVENUE ·

KEY·TO·PLAN

· A···CENTRAL·HALL
· B···TEMPORARY·EXHIBITIONS. (SECOND·FLOOR)
· C···LECTURE·HALL. (GROUND·FLOOR)
· D···LIBRARY
· E···JAPANESE·DEPARTMENT
· F···EGYPTIAN·DEPARTMENT
· G···TAPESTRY·HALL.
· H···WESTERN·ART·(PAINTINGS)
· I···WESTERN·ART·(OTHER·THAN·PAINTINGS)
· J···{ADDITIONAL·DEPARTMENTS. (OR·EXTENSIONS·OF·DEPARTMENTS)
· K···CLASSICAL·DEPARTMENT
· L···ADMINISTRATION·BLOCK
· M···BASILICA·OF·CASTS
· N···SCHOOL.
· O···SHOPS.

· GUY·LOWELL·ARCHITECT·
· EDMUND·M·WHEELWRIGHT ·
· D·DESPRADELLE · } ADVISORY·ARCHITECTS·
· R·CLIPSTON·STURGIS·

· SCALE ·
0 20 40 60 80 100

for, by the time of Prichard's death, he had won an unconditional victory; the casts had disappeared. Nor was the Museum School ever permanently housed according to this plan. To continue with Warren's description,

The underlying principles of arrangement and lighting observed in the main building are:

First, a division in plan into segments to contain departments structurally separate, each constituting a museum complete in itself, with a well-defined circuit for the visitor.

Second, a division in elevation into a main floor for general exhibition purposes, with the opportunity for overhead illumination, and a lower floor less in height devoted to objects compactly exhibited and accessibly stored, and to curators' offices, special libraries and classrooms.

Third, the provision, in every room on both floors, of ample light, free of disturbing reflections, and arranged to fall in the direction which will show to the best advantage the objects therein to be displayed.

The building may be described as a group of museums under one roof, the space in each devoted to collections compactly arranged and to rooms for study being approximately equal to the gallery space, and the design of each being determined by the need of good lighting.

The plan of the first section somewhat resembled a letter H with the ends enclosed, placed on its side, with wings projecting toward Huntington Avenue that created a large forecourt leading to the main entrance. Two-storied glass-roofed courtyards occupied the center of each wing and the open spaces of the H. The completed scheme called for a very much larger H with closed ends toward the Fenway, in which galleries were ranged around two very large open garden courts.

On entering the building from Huntington Avenue, a monumental stairway leading to a Rotunda on the main exhibition floor invited the visitor to proceed directly to the principal galleries. Formidable as this stairway was, it nevertheless involved less climbing than in Copley Square, for here there were only forty steps from the street to the main floor — nine to the ground floor and thirty-one more to

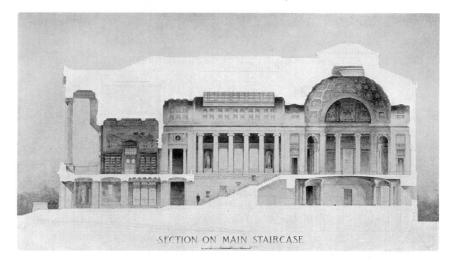

SECTION ON MAIN STAIRCASE

SECTION OF THE BUILDING ON THE MAIN STAIRCASE. Guy Lowell's drawing of
1907.

the main floor — against the fifty-two — sixteen from the street and
thirty-six between floors of the old building. The great domed
Rotunda, located at a point nearly equidistant from the center of
each of the departments, was the point where the visitor was enabled
to make his first choice.

In the building as completed, he may pass forward toward the north
through a large top-lighted gallery of tapestries, or through the
flanking colonnades, to the Department of Paintings, lying east and
west upon the Fenway. Instead, he may turn either to the right or
to the left, through a wide exhibition corridor, side-lighted through
long windows with low sills having an outlook on the two large
open spaces, to be treated as formal gardens. This corridor — the
main artery of the completed whole — will terminate in two minor
lobbies, from each of which the visitor may enter one of two of the
main departments, — namely from the eastern lobby, the southeasterly wing devoted to the art of Egypt or the easterly block
assigned to Classical art: from the western lobby, the southerly
wing assigned to the Department of Chinese and Japanese Art or
the westerly block of Western Art. Again, from the central rotunda
he may pass forward southward, through either of the corridors
flanking the central staircase, and find himself in the Library over
the portal.

Having reached the main floor, the visitor may go to the principal exhibition galleries of all departments without change of level. One or all are accessible from the Rotunda without even going up or down a single step. He may after his visit descend the central staircase and leave the museum as he came in. If, however, he wishes to pursue some investigation further than the material exhibited on the main floor permits, he may descend to the ground floor by one of several subsidiary staircases, where the other collections of the department are either exhibited or in easily accessible storage, with curatorial offices, specialized libraries, and study rooms near at hand. Since the ground floor has communicating corridors throughout, he may pass to another department or leave the building without returning to the main floor. Conversely, a serious and specialized visitor may reach the offices and reserved collections of any department from the ground-floor entrance without ascending to the main floor.

This was the grand design for the future, but how was the total plan to be reduced to a size suitable for the present collections — that is, the first stage then being built — without sacrificing the underlying principles of arrangement and lighting? Warren explained the solution:

> The proposed building is complete in itself, with little sacrifice of the ordered arrangement of the completed whole, while the completed whole will incorporate the part first erected with but slight structural changes. The main factor in the result was the device of the auxiliary exhibition corridor twelve feet in width and top-lighted, which runs east and west from the central lobby, parallel with, and a temporary substitute for, the larger transverse corridor described above as the main artery of the Museum. The latter is thereby free in the proposed building for the Department of Paintings, for which its width of thirty feet well adapts it. The width of the top-lighted picture galleries of the ultimate scheme, determined by careful experiment and observation, is but thirty-four feet . . . With extensions east and west, this space is divided in accordance with the needs of the collection into four top-lighted galleries and four side-lighted rooms . . . When the larger corridor is released by the pictures, the smaller one, ceasing to exist

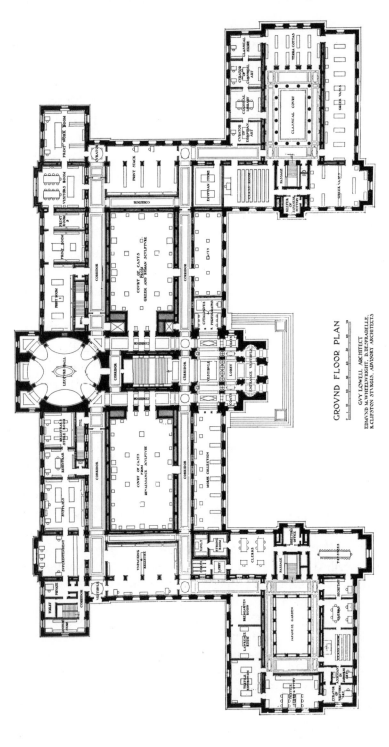

GROVND FLOOR PLAN

GVY LOWELL ARCHITECT
EDMVND M.WHEELWRIGHT, D.DESPRADELLE,
R.CLIPSTON STVRGIS, ADVISORY ARCHITECTS

GROUND FLOOR PLAN OF FIRST SECTION COMPLETED IN 1909.

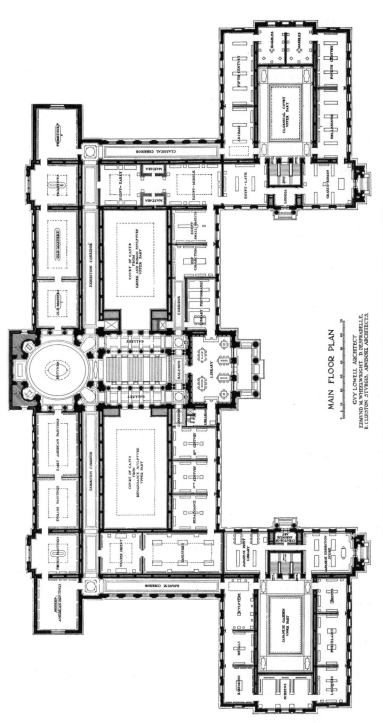

MAIN FLOOR PLAN OF FIRST SECTION COMPLETED IN 1909.

as a thoroughfare, may be needed for exhibition, or will afford valuable space for service.

In the first stage the Egyptian Department shares its future space in the southeasterly wing with the Classical Department. Similarly the Department of Chinese and Japanese Art shares its southwesterly wing with the Department of Western Art. Both Egypt and Western Art exercise squatter's rights in five rooms looking on the forecourt that are eventually destined for the extension of the Library. The departments of Paintings, and of Western and of Classical Art are temporarily, although adequately, housed for the time being. Those of Chinese and Japanese Art and of Egyptian Art are permanently installed, so far as they go, but will later need the space assigned them in the completed scheme. The two top-lighted courts flanking the entrance stairway, although planned for eventual use as special exhibition and lecture halls, are for the present to accommodate the cast collection, while a smaller temporary lecture room is provided in the ground-floor crypt, under the Rotunda. The Print rooms and the textile collections are in temporary but agreeable ground-floor space that will eventually be turned to other permanent uses.

An account of the architectural scheme, written by J. Randolph Coolidge, Jr., to accompany Warren's article, begins with the sentence: "The new building was not deliberately planned as an architectural monument, but inevitably became one from the dignity of its purpose and the necessary amplitude of its extent." Although planned from the inside out, a building with a total front elevation of 501 feet, comprised of two 94-by-128-foot wings flanking a forecourt 232 feet wide and 110 deep, cannot escape a certain monumentality, particularly when cut granite has been used. While a four-column Ionic portico rose above the main entrance, and each of the wings had two modest Ionic pavilions, the exterior was, as Coolidge pointed out,

decorous and reasonable, shows restraint and good taste, and illustrates to architects at least a number of serious difficulties successfully overcome. With two stories of very moderate height, the main exhibition story averaging but twenty feet, it required no little ingenuity to counteract the effect of lowness of the mass due to the great extent of the building. This is accomplished by offsetting the long horizontal lines of the belt courses and of the cornice with the verticals of the numerous windows, high and not too broad, in each story.

The forecourt was, after all, big enough to contain within it the façade of the Boston Public Library; with its salient entrance and advancing wings it was intended "to impress, invite and gather in all comers."

Matthew Prichard, who was as likely to be critical as anyone, wrote to Mrs. Gardner on 19 November 1906:

> Imagine, the plans all finished, and, save for a great slice of "architecture" in the middle, consisting of the entrance, they correspond with our principles, as I understand them. My wicked feeling is that, had I been in the Museum in the summer, even that rather dismal feature would have been eliminated. I think dismal, for I do not see how it can correspond with any true feeling save of the most conventional kind.

The grand staircase and Rotunda did, indeed, warrant description as a "slice of 'architecture,' " but they were almost the only concession to pure grandeur in the building; they at least served the purpose of steering visitors straight up to the main exhibition galleries without crowding and confusion. When one thinks back to the Copley Square museum, and considers some of the people involved, it is a tribute to Warren's support of Prichard and Gilman that there was only one such "slice."

Construction began first upon the two wings, in order to provide the most prompt shelter for the Egyptian, Classical, and Oriental collections, whose transportation and installation was thought to present the greatest difficulty, and upon the powerhouse that was to provide heat. By mid-September 1907 the powerhouse and its chimney were all but completed, while the foundations of the wings were finished and those of the main block were advancing to a junction. As December and January were mild months, the walls of the wings had risen substantially by 25 January 1908.

SOUTHWEST WING ON I JUNE 1908.

Arthur Fairbanks, soon after taking over as Director on 1 August 1907, began consultations with the staff about the probable costs of operating the new building when completed. He estimated that the care of the building and collections, including salaries, heating and lighting would reach about $115,000 a year. As the only income available for such purposes consisted of annual subscriptions of about $17,500, paid admissions of about $5,000, and income from unrestricted funds (if not reduced to help pay for construction) of roughly $60,000, which totaled $82,500, another $32,500 was annually needed from some other source. In consequence, he suggested that the museum needed additional endowment of at least $750,000 simply to exist in its new quarters. Such an increase would do nothing to provide for new works of art, which would have to come by gift or through the small income of $19,000 a year from funds restricted to purchases.

By the end of 1908 gifts to the Building Fund, without any

SOUTHEAST WING ON 1 MAY 1908.

organized effort, had reduced the estimated $623,650 needed to complete the building to $518,925, while the annual subscriptions had risen from 1,097 persons giving $17,432 in 1907 to 1,432 contributing $20,985. But, as there was still no sign of the $750,000 endowment for operating expenses that Arthur Fairbanks had indicated as a minimum, the museum needed $1,268,925 — and that right soon. In the President's report for 1908 Gardiner M. Lane contrasted the situation of the Museum of Fine Arts, which received no help whatsoever from city or state, with the assistance provided museums elsewhere. The Metropolitan Museum of Art in 1907 received from the City of New York $160,000 toward the cost of operating buildings that had been built and equipped by the city and leased in perpetuity, rent-free. Examples of similar although smaller grants from the cities of Chicago, St. Louis, and Philadelphia were cited. But wishful thinking, inspired by such generous precedents elsewhere, produced no solution in Boston. Although President Lane recommended in 1909 that the Finance Committee be authorized to apply to the City of Boston, or to the cities of the Metropolitan District, for an annual grant sufficient to pay expenses of administration and maintenance, in return for free opening to the public for five days in the week, nothing came out of such efforts. Mayor John F. Fitzgerald petitioned the Legislature in February 1911 for legislation authorizing the city of Boston to appropriate not over $50,000 in any single year toward the maintenance of the Museum of Fine Arts. The bill was referred to the Joint Standing Committee on Cities, which returned it to the Senate and House with an adverse report. After the Mayor had tried again in 1912 with similar result, no further efforts were made in that direction. Save for the gift of the Copley Square land, everything achieved in the past forty-two years had been from the gifts of private individuals, and so it was to continue for an even longer time.

By September 1908 the new museum was walled and roofed in with the exception of the central "slice" which contained the entrance hall, library, and main staircase, while internally the galleries were plastered, provided with windows, and ready for finished floors. In the Egyptian Department the two Mastabas, or tomb chambers, which had been in storage since their acquisition, had been set into their permanent location in one of the galleries. Nearby foundations were being laid for a temporary building to house the Museum School. As the permanent structure called for as the third element in Guy Lowell's completed scheme would have cost $75,000, its construction would have reduced the school's capital to only $35,000.

HUNTINGTON AVENUE FAÇADE ON 3 SEPTEMBER 1908.

THE FENWAY FAÇADE ON 3 SEPTEMBER 1908.

It was consequently determined to put up a fireproof temporary one-story structure of iron, brick, and cement on the same site at a cost of about $19,000. In a series of studios around two courts William M. Paxton, Philip L. Hale, Edmund C. Tarbell, Frank W. Benson, and Bela L. Pratt could, without frills, teach their students quite as satisfactorily as in the basement and backyard at Copley Square. Moreover, the building would be good for at least thirty years, by which time the school might have attracted larger funds. On 8 February 1909 the school opened its spring term in the new structure, for the first time under its own roof, although occupying land furnished rent-free by the museum. It had, however, cost $38,000, exclusive of equipment, rather than the anticipated $19,000. In the end it had been built of plaster stucco, with a slate roof.

The estimated cost of $1,573,000 for the new museum fell less wide of the anticipated mark than had that of the school. On 31 December 1909 the actual cost of the building proved to be $1,589,487.79. With $1,214,492.73 spent for land and improvements and $83,988.23 for moving and installation, the grand total proved to be $2,887,968.75. During the year 1909, $162,800 was subscribed toward building costs and $174,226 to the much needed maintenance fund. This had not been enough for the need, for in spite of $1,756,000 proceeds from the sale of the old building and lot and $611,118.68 contributed by private individuals, the trustees still had to draw upon $520,850.07 of unrestricted funds.

At the beginning of 1909 objects began to be moved into the basement storerooms of the new building, work continuing as rapidly as rooms were ready to receive any part of the collections. Nevertheless, only four exhibition rooms in the old building had to be closed before 2 May 1909 when the entire building was permanently closed to the public. The William Hayes Fogg Art Museum of Harvard University generously provided some of its limited space for the temporary exhibition during the closed months of thirteen pieces of Greek sculpture, three Renaissance sculptures, and twenty-three paintings from the Museum of Fine Arts. Thus paintings like the Van der Weyden, the Crivelli, the El Greco portrait, Velázquez's *Don Baltazar Carlos*, and other particular treasures were available to summer visitors in Cambridge.

Plans for moving had been so ably made by the curators that the old building was empty and ready to be delivered to its new owners on 20 June 1909, the date agreed upon seven years earlier. William Wallace MacLean, Superintendent of Buildings and Grounds, organized a force of men to assist with the regular porters and custodians, who worked with such care that nothing of value was broken or damaged, and with such efficiency that outside help was required only for a few of the heaviest pieces of stone. Edward J. Moore, museum photographer for more than half a century, took advantage of the move to photograph out-of-doors a number of large objects to complete the registration cards for the system devised by Matthew Prichard in the spring of 1906. Mr. Moore recalled that only two horse-drawn vehicles, constantly traveling back and forth between the buildings, were required for the job. One group of men stationed in Copley Square collected and loaded objects, another in Huntington Avenue accomplished the unloading. Such was the state of public order in 1909 that no guards accompanied the vehicles. There were merits in the pre-Brink's life of Boston! So a few days short of thirty-three years after the opening of the museum in Copley Square, the land passed to its new owners, and eventually became the site of

another Boston institution, the Copley Plaza Hotel, which today
operates under the alias of Sheraton-Plaza.

The new building was formally opened on 9 November 1909 by
the first of a series of receptions to annual subscribers, donors, public
officials, teachers, and others. Following these dedicatory receptions,
the museum became regularly accessible to visitors from 15 November. During the first week, when the admission fee was waived on
all days, 37,500 persons appeared. Most of them began, as they were
intended to, by going up the great stairway (with its barrel-vaulted
ceiling pierced by skylights) to the Rotunda, where light came from

THE ROTUNDA AS COMPLETED IN 1909. Through the doorway may be seen one of the temporary painting galleries that
served until the construction of the Evans Wing.

the top of a coffered dome, as in the Pantheon. Once on the first stair landing, the extent and spaciousness of the building broke upon the visitor, for the Ionic colonnades that flanked the stairway on the main floor opened onto corridors from which one could look down into the huge glass-roofed east and west courts.

From the Rotunda, painting galleries opened to left and to right, but a visitor bent upon a methodical investigation of the museum would defer entering them in favor of the minor transverse corridor on the right, where the circuit of the picture galleries theoretically began. This long skylighted corridor was hung with pictures with little obvious relation to one another: the two Bouchers, the Athenæum's pair of Roman Panninis, and other oils, followed by watercolors of Burne-Jones, Troyon, Barye, Millet, and others, as well as several Egyptian subjects by Joseph Lindon Smith. The latter were not only attractive pictures but suggested that a right turn near the end of the corridor would bring one into the Egyptian Department. Although at the extreme end another corridor ran, at a right angle, into the Classical Department, a doorway at the left led into the First French Room, where Dupré's *On the Cliff*, Diaz's *Gypsies*, and various works of Courbet, Millet, Daubigny, and Delacroix were hung. The December 1909 *Bulletin* stated, "A little canvas by Constable presents a piquant contrast to the French work about it" in this room, though it is not clear at this distance of time why that should have been desired. The Second French Room, a cul-de-sac to the east, showed such large canvases as Regnault's *The Horses of Achilles*, Lerolle's *By the Riverside*, the Lhermitte version of Emmaus, and Corot's *Dante and Virgil*. The circuit then returned through the First French Room to the Gallery of Old Masters, where Italian, Spanish, and Flemish paintings were hung.

Across the Rotunda was the Early American Room with canvases by Copley, Stuart, West, and Trumbull, including the unfinished Stuart Athenæum portraits of George and Martha Washington, as well as portraits of Samuel Adams, John Hancock, and General Henry Knox, permanently deposited by the City of Boston. From this local portrait gallery one entered the Second American Room, dominated by Abbott H. Thayer's *Caritas*, where were hung examples of the then-contemporary and just-past generation of American artists

— Hunt, Fuller, Inness, Picknell, Homer, La Farge, Brush, Chase, Tarbell, and others. In the Third American Room canvases by Twachtman, Taber, Benson, Paxton, Metcalf, and De Camp were shown, in company with the two Monets (given by Denman W. Ross in 1906) and other Impressionist paintings. Here too were a pair of household gods in the shape of Thomas Gold Appleton, an original trustee and early benefactor, painted by Frederick P. Vinton, and Edmund C. Tarbell's memorial posthumous portrait of General Charles Greely Loring, commissioned by the trustees in 1906. The last of the seven picture galleries, although designated in the *Bulletin* plan as Late French, showed Washington Allston's *Uriel* and *Elijah in the Desert*, canvases by Trumbull, Sully, Page, and Healy, as well as a portrait in relief of Dr. George Bartol by the sculptor Bela L. Pratt. Although the use of temporary space had caused some illogicalities of arrangement, the new picture galleries gave a pleasing effect, for they were well lighted and tastefully hung.

The Department of Egyptian Art, whose creation will be described in Chapter VIII, presented a wholly new countenance in the new museum, for some of its most massive possessions were there properly shown for the first time. Its first room, entered from the east transverse corridor of paintings, was the impressive Gallery of the Mastabas, in the center of which were installed the two Fifth Dynasty chambers from tombs at Saqqara. The walls of these chambers were covered with hieroglyphics and with exquisite carvings in low relief representing scenes from daily life which retained some of their original coloring. Between the entrance and the mastabas, objects from the prehistoric and Old Empire periods were exhibited; beyond them were monumental sculptures from the Middle and Early New Empires. The Way Collection was installed in a room opening to the right, while directly beyond the Gallery of the Mastabas were the New Empire and Ptolemaic rooms, between which was a tiny room containing chiefly a ceremonial loincloth of cut gazelle skin from the reign of Tuthmosis IV. These galleries, unlike those for paintings, were part of the permanent provision for Egyptian art in the completed scheme of the museum, for sculptures of such dimensions and weight were not idly to be trucked about. The Gallery of the Mastabas had required special structural provi-

EGYPTIAN GALLERY OF THE MASTABAS. The two 5th Dynasty chambers from tombs at Saqqara, installed in the center of the gallery in 1909, bisected the room for more than half a century.

sions to bear its load; indeed nearly sixty years were to pass before any major changes were made in its arrangement.

The Department of Classical Art's joint tenancy with Egypt of the southeast wing, once considered to be temporary, has become permanent, for Egypt, instead of ousting Greece and Rome, has, over the decades, expanded in other directions. At the end of the east transverse corridor of paintings sat a colossal headless Hellenistic statue of Cybele as an indication to the visitor of the location of the Classical collection. At this point another corridor (containing cases of iridescent glass and some sculptured heads) ran to the right (leading parallel to but independent of the Gallery of the Mastabas) to the southeast wing; here six Classical galleries surrounded a two-story glass-roofed central courtyard. Facing the entrance from the corridor of the Archaic Room was the monumental lion from Perachora; here too were fine early bronzes, two marble stelae, and a restricted selection of early vases and terra-cotta figurines. The Fifth Century Room was arranged to lead up to the great Boston Throne, which had only the previous year finally come from Lewes House, and which was shown for the first time in the new museum. As companions were other marbles, a few of the finest fifth-century vases, coins, and gems, and the gold Nike earring. Most of the finer marbles were installed in the two next rooms; here were the Bartlett Aphrodite, the Perkins Hermes, a Hellenistic head of Homer, and the recently arrived Chios head. In the Fourth Century Room were marbles of that period, bronze mirror covers, and a splendid series of terra-cotta figurines from Tanagra. Figurines from Attica, Corinth, and other localities were shown in the Late Greek Room, with large bronzes, coins, jewelry, and gems, including the famous Marlborough cameo.

Roman portrait heads surrounded the gallery of the central court, from which a staircase led down to the subsidiary Classical exhibition

CLASSICAL COURT AS COMPLETED IN 1909.

FIFTH CENTURY GREEK ROOM IN DECEMBER 1909. The recently acquired Boston Throne stands before the east wall.

FIFTH CENTURY GREEK ROOM IN DECEMBER 1909.

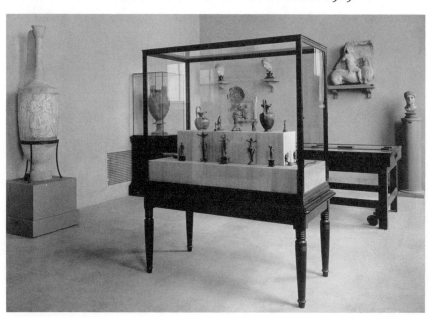

GREEK VASE ROOM IN DECEMBER 1909. Although a selection of the finest examples were shown in the main floor galleries, as in the Fifth Century Room, the bulk of the vases were segregated in this ground floor gallery in accordance with Prichard's principles.

rooms and offices of the department. Here were the very large series of Greek vases, Arretine pottery, and terra-cotta subjects that would attract chiefly the serious student. Here too was the office of the Egyptian Department, equally accessible from its galleries, as both the New Empire and Ptolemaic rooms on the main floor connected with the Classical court on either side of the stairway.

The Division of Western Art in 1909 had no curator but was administered by the triumvirate of John Briggs Potter, Keeper of Paintings, Miss Sarah G. Flint, Assistant in charge of Textiles, and Miss Florence V. Paull, Assistant in charge of other Collections. It was a kind of catch-all, for it included not only the arts of Europe and of European influence elsewhere but of the Near East, as well as primitive America and Africa. The minor transverse corridor from the Rotunda — to the left at the head of the stairway, opposite the one that led to the painting galleries — was lined by groups of cases containing Peruvian, Coptic, and Persian textiles, with rugs and large framed textiles hung above. It will be remembered that the extent, variety, and high artistic quality of the textile collection had been in great part due to the acquisitiveness and generosity of the ubiquitous Dr. Denman W. Ross. Toward the end of the corridor a door on the left led into the Nearer Orient Room. In Copley Square examples of the decorative arts had been separated into rooms by materials, as at South Kensington, iron with iron, glass with glass, regardless of country or century. Now in Huntington Avenue a historical classification had been substituted, by which objects of all kinds, except paintings, were brought together by regions and periods. Thus, the Nearer Orient Room showed on its walls Persian and Turkish rugs and velvets, and in its cases Hispano-Moresque, Persian, Rhodian, Damascus, Arabic, and Syrian faience, Arabic pottery, Persian lustered tiles, as well as Persian, Indian, and Saracenic metalwork. This was the museum's first venture in the separate showing of Mohammedan art. Next came the Tapestry Gallery where were hung large Flemish and Brussels tapestries, some owned by the museum and others lent by friends. Along the front of the building were the Sixteenth, Seventeenth, and Eighteenth Century rooms, with windows lighted from the forecourt, which contained tapestries, textiles, furniture, glass, metalwork, and all kinds of decorative arts of those centuries. Although the exhibits were chiefly European, two cases in the Eighteenth Century Room were filled with seventeenth- and eighteenth-century American silver, deposited by various local churches and private collectors.

As Western Art was temporarily housed in rooms destined eventually for the expansion of the Department of Chinese and Japanese Art and the Library, it was obliged to spill over into Oriental country for the accommodation of its two "period rooms." The Lawrence Room had been transported from Copley Square and fitted into this new location in the ground floor of the southwestern wing. Here its dark oak panels made a suitable background for the extensive collection of amber bequeathed to the museum in 1901 by William Arnold Buffum, an energetic collector and author of *The Tears of the Heliades, or Amber as a Gem* (London, 1898). Next to the Lawrence Room was installed a somber little paneled Swiss sixteenth-century interior, with tile floor, lighted by painted Swiss glass, known as the Bremgarten Room. At the age of seven or eight, this apartment delighted me beyond measure, partly because it was (both temporarily and inappropriately) adjacent to the Japanese Garden, in whose pool goldfish were swimming.

Although the administrative offices of the museum, Miss Flint's textile study and office, and the Lawrence and Bremgarten rooms pre-empted the ground floor of the southwest wing, the main floor was the province of the Department of Chinese and Japanese Art, both for the time being and the future. From the end of the Corridor of Western Art, a long Japanese Corridor led south to these galleries which, as in the opposite wing, made a continuous circuit around the central court. As this was conceived as a permanent installation, more architectural effort was devoted to the treatment of this court than had been possible in its Classical counterpart. Around a pool in the center of the court a Japanese garden was created in the semiformal style of a temple forecourt, with neatly raked sand, carefully chosen rocks, stone lanterns, and fu-dogs that guarded the approach to a recess where gilded Buddhas sat. Without attempting to reproduce Chinese or Japanese interior decoration, the department used natural wood and plaster in a structural relation that has always pleased the sensibilities of the Japanese. By masking the windows with *shoji*, or sliding screens of paper, a soft, diffused, and exceptionally pleasing light was achieved, while in the Buddhist room the wooden columns and brackets followed in general style those used during the Nara Period (eighth century, A.D.), when Japanese temple architecture reached its noblest development. These rooms after sixty years still bear the imprint of Okakura-Kakuzo's stay in Boston.

Just as Cybele, at the end of the east transverse corridor, guided the visitor to the Department of Classical Art, so a large carved wooden figure of Amida Dai Butsu (of the Fujiwara Period), placed at the end of its Western counterpart, indicated the entrance to the Oriental galleries. The Porcelain Corridor, at the door to which this carving was placed, was devoted to an exhibition of Chinese and Korean ceramic art, chronologically arranged. The first fourteen centuries were illustrated by the Macomber Collection of Chinese Pottery, supplemented by museum pieces; the last five were represented by the porcelains that were among the most brilliant manifestations of the Chinese genius. The first two galleries showed Tibetan and Chinese Buddhist paintings, a seventh-century stone bas-relief of Kwannon, early bronze ceremonial vessels and mirrors, and jade, while on the walls hung examples of poetic and lay schools of Chinese painting.

Next came the First Japanese Room, where in the *tokonoma*, or raised recess of honor, hung the eighth-century Hokei Mandara, that was one of the chief treasures of the Fenollosa-Weld Collection of Japanese paintings. Most of the floor space was given to the smaller examples of Japanese Buddhist sculpture. The more monumental pieces were in the adjacent Buddhist Room, where they were shown in a setting suggestive of temple architecture, devised by Francis Gardner Curtis. The central figure was a ninth-century Shaka from

JAPANESE TEMPLE ROOM IN MAY 1910.

the Ross Collection, while the other figures ranged in date from that time to the fifteenth century. The cases in the Second Japanese Room contained lacquers from the Bigelow and Weld gifts, while suits of armor and three swords of especial quality occupied the *tokonoma*; above them hung ink paintings of the fifteenth and sixteenth centuries. The *tokonoma* of the Third Japanese Room was reserved for the rotating exhibition of screens and *kakemonos* of the Momoyama and early Tokugawa periods, while in a case under the window was the thirteenth-century Heiji Monogatari, generally known as the Keion Roll; this representation of the burning of the Sanjo Palace during the twelfth-century wars was one of the greatest treasures of the Bigelow Collection. Korin's great wave screen and paintings by masters of the Ukioye School hung on the walls of the Fifth Japanese Room, while in its cases were sword-guards from the Bigelow, Weld, and Ross collections that showed the skill of the Japanese metal-worker at its highest point. The two other rooms on the main floor of the wing contained the exhibition-storage and print library of the department. Other works of art were shown in the gallery of the Japanese Court, while on the walls of the staircase leading down to the garden various wood-carvings and carved beam-ends were decoratively displayed.

The Morse Collection of Japanese Pottery, in order to be installed as a unit, was placed in a long gallery on the ground floor to the left of the main entrance. Although it was then at some distance from the other Oriental collections, this location was chosen with an eye to the future, when the Chinese and Japanese department would have retrieved from administration and Western Art the ground floor of the adjacent southwest wing. While Prichard's capitalized THE PUBLIC DOES NOT LOOK AT GREEK GASES. THE PUBLIC DOES NOT LOOK AT JAPANESE POTTERY had doubtless given offense to Edward Robinson and Edward S. Morse in 1904, they had had their effect, for these, and other long series, were properly placed on the ground floor of the new museum, close to other study materials and well separated from the main floor galleries where a more rigid selection of fewer examples of a very high quality was exhibited.

The 1909 provisional placing of the much disputed cast collection in the large east and west courts flanking the main stairway, pending the construction of a separate building for them, was a satisfactory compromise. Although visible from the main floor corridors leading from the Rotunda to the Library, the casts could only be reached from the ground floor. Thus, not even the most thoughtless visitor could wander from great originals to plaster copies without consciously going downstairs to a floor deliberately designed for work and study rather than pure appreciation. There was not space for all the casts by any means, but most of the earliest Greek ones were placed in the east court, while Renaissance casts were in the west court. Here it was possible to exhibit for the first time reproductions of the equestrian statues of Gattamelata by Donatello and of Bartolomeo Colleoni by Verrochio and Leopardi, which had remained in storage ever since Francis Bartlett had given them. Here too there was space for the cast of Niccolo Pisano's pulpit from Pisa and the eastern doors of the Baptistery at Florence. Indeed it is not entirely clear what else could have been shown to advantage in such tremen-

WILLIAM MORRIS HUNT MEMORIAL LIBRARY IN AUGUST 1920.

dously tall galleries as these courts. In later years, when casts had gone to the boneyard, floors and stairways were inserted to transform the courts into thirteen special exhibition rooms on two levels.

The Print Department was temporarily, although commodiously installed in two galleries and an adjacent study room at the back of the central block on the ground floor. This was a vast improvement over Copley Square, where the exhibition rooms were on the second floor and the office of the department in the basement. The William Morris Hunt Memorial Library, so named because of the generosity of his daughter Mrs. Horatio Nelson Slater, had a spacious reading room on the main floor, directly above the main entrance. Tapestries and large paintings were hung above the bookshelves and wainscotting that lined the lower reaches of its walls. It had been placed in this conspicuous position, easily accessible from the Rotunda, to invite use by visitors to the chief galleries. An adjacent front room commodiously housed the collection of photographs. For the time being, which has stretched to more than sixty years, the library stacks were inconveniently tucked overhead in the attic, for Western Art and the Way Collection were temporarily installed in rooms designed for the eventual use of the Library.

So, only a few weeks short of forty years after the incorporation of the Museum of Fine Arts, it was installed in a workable new building, so thoughtfully planned as a shelter for its collections as to be superior to any other museum in the United States in suitability for its function. All this had been the work of private individuals without official governmental assistance or encouragement. This new museum was now the responsibility of a new generation of Bostonians, for when it opened in November 1909 Charles William Eliot, who had resigned the presidency of Harvard University earlier in the year at the age of seventy-five, was the only active trustee who had been one of the incorporators in 1870.

CHAPTER VIII

The Egyptian Department

Egyptian antiquities entered into the plans and aspirations of the Museum of Fine Arts almost from the beginning, for the gift of the Way Collection in 1872 and the need of installing it in one of the Boston Athenæum galleries had drawn Charles Greely Loring into the service of the museum. When the Copley Square building was opened in 1876, the Egyptian pieces that John Lowell had purchased at Luxor forty years earlier were the only original works of ancient sculpture owned by the young museum. In the next decade a number of gifts were received of Egyptian scarabs, amulets, small funerary figures and bronzes, purchased by Bostonians during Mediterranean travel; as they lacked documentation as to source, they were of relatively minor value. The phenomenal growth of the museum's Egyptian collection during the years between 1885 and the Second World War was, however, chiefly the result of the support of meticulously scholarly excavation.

A French archaeologist, Mariette Bey, who served as Director-general of Antiquities for the Egyptian government from 1851 to 1881 had greatly aided the preservation of art and history by protecting the sites of tombs and by building a government museum in Cairo. When the British occupied Egypt in 1882, an agreement was made between the British and French governments that a Frenchman should always head the Antiquities Service in Egypt, with English inspectors working under him; in consequence, Gaston Maspero, who had succeeded Mariette Bey in 1881, continued in the post of

Director-general. To achieve excavation without bearing the cost, and to satisfy the interest of foreign scholars and institutions in Egyptian antiquities, the government granted concessions for excavation under certain conditions. A responsible excavator, who agreed to keep proper records, report all finds to the Egyptian government, and publish scientific reports within a reasonable time, might be granted the right to dig in a specified area, put up necessary buildings on government land, and obtain a share of the objects he discovered for the foreign institution that sponsored his work, provided he paid his own expenses. An English research group, the Egypt Exploration Fund (later called the Egypt Exploration Society), carried on digs financed by private donors and by English museums and universities, who received, in return for their assistance, a share of the objects found. Such a cooperative arrangement offered great advantage to its subscribers, for any objects received had a known source which was recorded in the society's published reports; moreover, as the society worked economically at cost, without consideration of profit, it was a considerably cheaper way of acquiring objects than buying in a clandestine commercial market. As the Reverend William C. Winslow maintained American headquarters in Boston for the Egypt Exploration Fund, the trustees of the Museum of Fine Arts began in 1885 to subscribe regularly in support of that group's excavations. This practice being continued until 1905, a respectable number of Egyptian objects would arrive annually in Boston, nominally as gifts from the Egypt Exploration Fund. Among these were a black granite seated statue of Ramesses II and a winning limestone relief portrait of an unidentified monarch of the New Kingdom, both excavated at Nebesheh in the Delta, a tiny marble head of King Amenhotep II from Hu in Middle Egypt, and a painted mummy portrait of the second century A.D. from the Fayum.

As General Loring had first become ensnared by the arts through travel in Egypt, such acquisitions received his enthusiastic attention and study during the quarter-century he was in charge of the Boston museum. With his retirement and death in 1902, and with considerable growth of the collection, it became desirable to add an Egyptologist to the staff of the museum. Thus, on 15 September 1902 a separate Department of Egyptian Art was established, with

Albert M. Lythgoe as the first Curator of Egyptian Antiquities. A Harvard graduate of the class of 1892 (A.M. 1897), for a time attached to the American School of Classical Studies at Athens where he worked under Dr. Waldstein in the excavations at Argos, Lythgoe had turned to Egyptology, in which he began his studies under Professor Wiedemann at Bonn. After serving as an instructor in Egyptology at Harvard in 1898–99, Lythgoe went to Egypt to assist in excavations directed by his slightly senior fellow-alumnus, George Andrew Reisner (Harvard A.B. *summa cum laude* 1889, A.M. 1891, Ph.D. 1893). Originally an Assyriologist, Reisner went to Germany after taking his doctorate and continued his early interest at Göttingen, but as a second subject studied Egyptology with Adolf Erman at Berlin. Under Erman's aegis he was appointed an Assistant in the Egyptian Department of the Berlin Museum, and in that capacity went to Egypt in 1897 to catalogue the amulets and models of ships and boats in the Cairo Museum.

While he was engaged in that occupation, Mrs. Phoebe Apperson Hearst, a regent of the University of California and mother of William Randolph Hearst, who had just made the conventional trip up the Nile, became fascinated by the activity in the Cairo Museum. Seeing an opportunity to enhance the prestige of her state university by excavation, she engaged Reisner as director of an expedition that she financed under the auspices of the University of California. Work began in 1898 at Quft in Upper Egypt, moving the next year to the cemetery at Nag-ed-Dêr, where Albert Lythgoe joined Reisner. It was after three years of field work with the Hearst Egyptian Expedition that Lythgoe was chosen as the first Curator of Egyptian Antiquities in Boston. He was well qualified to head the new department.

Although Lythgoe took over his new post in the autumn of 1902, he was obliged by previous commitments to Reisner to return to Egypt for the winter of 1902–3. But this could be turned to the advantage of the Museum of Fine Arts, for, as Edward Robinson reported to the trustees,

an arrangement has been made by which a considerable proportion of his time there will be spent in our interest; and the Museum will therefore be benefited by the studies which he will be able to make with especial reference to our collection, by the establishment of friendly relations in our behalf with the Egyptian authorities, and by the acquisition of additions for our collection, for which you have granted him an appropriation.

Lythgoe's first report as Curator, written at Girga, Upper Egypt, on 2 January 1903, summarized the objects that had come to the Museum of Fine Arts through the Way gift and the Egypt Exploration Fund, and pointed out that "while, as a matter of fact, it does include at least a few examples from nearly every dynasty in Egyptian history, yet in many cases these are by no means adequate for illustrating all phases of the art of the period." He hoped to fill in as many *lacunae* as possible by purchases in Egypt, for, he observed,

It is a fact well known to those living and working in Egypt that the systematic plundering of the tombs and cemeteries by the natives, which has gone on continuously since the middle of the past century, and the scattering broadcast of the antiquities by the travellers to whom they are sold, has resulted in such a depletion of the antiquities of the country that the time is not far distant when it will be practically an impossibility to hope to add to our collection to any considerable extent; and it is at the present time that such additions must be made, if they are to be made at all. The work of collection which is now being pushed on in Egypt as systematically and completely as possible by representatives of the Berlin Museum, is a movement which we could wish to see followed not only by our own Museum, but by the other larger American museums as well.

Albert Lythgoe's time and appropriation were profitably spent in Egypt, for he was able to acquire for the museum from the Egyptian government, through the friendly interest and assistance of Gaston Maspero, two complete mastaba chambers of the Fifth Dynasty that had been excavated at Saqqara some years earlier by Maspero's predecessor, Mariette. These were approximately of the same size — about 12 feet long, 6 feet wide and 12 feet high inside; the finely worked limestone interiors of both were completely covered by painted low relief of delicate and beautiful quality, representing

MASTABA OF PTAH-SEKHEM-ANKH (detail). Egyptian Old Kingdom, 5th Dynasty, from Saqqara. *04.1760*

scenes from the life and customs of the Old Kingdom. The decorations from the tomb of Ptah-sekhem-ankh show the deceased seated before a table, with attendants bringing food and slaughtering oxen for his funerary meal. Other bands of relief depict the origin of the food: the cultivation of the land, the raising of cattle, the trapping of birds in marshes, and the like. The decoration of the tomb of Ka-em-nofret is similar in its depiction of the events of daily life. Both mastabas were examples of sculpture of singular charm as well as admirable documents of manners and customs that would have popular appeal. Although Lythgoe had suppressed casts of Egyptian and Assyrian objects to make room in his galleries for original objects, these tombs were too large and heavy to be installed in Copley Square with the prospect of a second move only a few years away. They were of necessity reserved for the new museum, where, as we have seen, they formed a conspicuous ornament of the largest Egyptian room.

MASTABA OF PTAH-SEKHEM-ANKH (detail). Egyptian Old Kingdom, 5th Dynasty, from Saqqara. *04.1760*

Another desirable purchase that filled a major gap was a group of wooden sculptures of the Middle Kingdom. The finest example was a three-quarter-lifesized statue of Wepwawet-em-hat, probably of the Tenth Dynasty, found at Assiut. This figure is represented standing in a characteristic Egyptian position, the left leg in advance, the right hand extended and grasping a staff as a support. The eyes are of enamel; the man wears only a massive black wig and a miniskirt. From the same site came five statuettes, and three groups of figures, one of which represents the slaughter of an ox for a sacrifice. Other wood carvings from Bersheh depicted characteristic pursuits of the time.

An admirable dividend from the new Curator's months in Egypt came in gifts from Theodore M. Davis of Newport, Rhode Island, a copper magnate who happily employed his years of retirement by excavating in the Valley of the Kings at Thebes on a concession that he had been granted by the Egyptian government. From his share of

WOODEN PANTHER. Egyptian, 18th Dynasty, from tomb of Tuthmosis IV. *Gift of Theodore M. Davis. 03.1137*

the objects uncovered in the Eighteenth-Dynasty tomb of King Tuthmosis IV, he gave to the Boston museum forty-five blue-glazed porcelains, each bearing the name of its royal owner, a wooden figure of a panther, a wooden panel carved in low relief from the arm of a chair, and two Canopic jars of limestone. Mr. Davis also gave one of the most extraordinary objects for workmanship that the museum possesses, a loincloth of intricately cut gazelle-skin of the finest and softest quality, which was once worn by the Eighteenth Dynasty royal fan-bearer Mai-her-peri. This he had unearthed just outside the tomb of its owner, who was one of the few private persons to be buried in the Valley of the Kings. From the Egypt Exploration Fund came objects from Professor Flinders Petrie's excavation at Abydos, which Lythgoe had visited during the winter.

The scientist and mine operator Alexander Agassiz noted incidentally in a letter that Theodore M. Davis' first interest in Egypt sprang from a little book by Martin Brimmer that Agassiz had lent him. Here again serendipity entered into the affairs of the Museum of Fine Arts. In 1892 Houghton, Mifflin and Company had published an 86-page suede-bound volume entitled *Egypt: Three Essays on the*

History, Religion and Art of Ancient Egypt, printed on handmade paper with a number of collotype illustrations. Although no author's name appears on the binding or title page, a preface by Martin Brimmer states:

> These essays were written during a recent journey in Egypt, with the constant assistance and able cooperation of my niece and fellow-traveller, Mrs. John Jay Chapman. They are indeed not less her work than mine. They were begun for the purpose of putting in order for our own instruction the results of our observation and of the best accessible knowledge of the whole subject. They are published in the hope that they may be useful as an introduction to works of higher authority.

Yet this reticent little volume, lent by the former superintendent of the Calumet and Hecla copper mines to another mining man, not only served "as an introduction to works of higher authority" but inspired the borrower himself to excavate in Egypt, and to give some of his finest discoveries to the museum that its author had nurtured during its first quarter-century.

In the following year, while clearing the tomb of Queen Hatshepsut in the Valley of the Kings, Theodore M. Davis discovered two royal sarcophagi, those of the Queen and of her father, King Tuthmosis I. Receiving the latter from the government, he presented it to the Museum of Fine Arts. This massive quartzite box, polished to mirrorlike surface and adorned with hieroglyphics and kneeling figures of the weeping sisters of Isiris, Isis and Nephthys, who attend the King as he assumes the form of that god, gave particular pleasure, for royal sarcophagi of this quality were seldom allowed to leave the country. Davis' gifts, supplemented by the purchases made by Lythgoe, "may fairly be said to have placed our Egyptian collection upon a footing where it now," he wrote in 1904, "represents the most characteristic phases, at least, of Egyptian art in the greater number of its branches." Moreover in 1905 Davis gave a group of alabaster and wooden models that had fallen to his share from the tomb of Queen Hatshepsut, as well as several examples of sculpture from his own collection.

SARCOPHAGUS OF TUTHMOSIS I. Egyptian, 18th Dynasty. *Gift of Theodore M. Davis. 04.278*   The photograph shows the piece as installed in Copley Square.

The quality and variety of Davis' gifts, as well as those of the Egypt Exploration Fund, clearly indicated that excavation was the best way to collect, even though a considerable portion of the discoveries had to remain for the share of the Cairo Museum. An unexpected opportunity soon permitted the Museum of Fine Arts to enter the field. The University of California Expedition, directed by George A. Reisner, had begun work in 1898 with a five-year contract, which had upon expiration been extended. In 1903, just as Reisner was beginning his second period, the Egyptian Department of Antiquities unexpectedly became amenable to granting concessions for the excavation of the valley temples and tombs near the great Pyramids at Giza. This area had been reserved by the government for half a century, until Gaston Maspero, despairing of protecting it from marauding thieves, unexpectedly opened it to excavation. Applications for concessions were submitted by Professor Steindorff of Leipzig, Professor Schiaparelli of Turin, and by Dr. Reisner on behalf of the Hearst Expedition. As Reisner told it,

THE THIRD PYRAMID AND FUNERARY TEMPLE OF KING MYCERINUS AT GIZA.

Our applications were granted with the request to divide the field amicably among ourselves. The division of the pyramids was easily arranged, as the Italians wanted the First Pyramid, the Germans wanted the Second, and I was willing to accept the Third. But we all wanted the great cemetery west of the First Pyramid. So that was divided into three strips running east and west, for which we drew lots. Professor Schiaparelli drew the southern strip, Professor Borchardt (acting for Professor Steindorff) drew the middle strip, and I drew the northern strip. As it turned out, the American or northern strip proved the most important. Here we found the great royal cemetery laid out on a regular plan, like a new town in our West, by Cheops and his architects, when the First Pyramid was built. In this royal city of the dead, nearly five thousand years ago, Prince Wep-em-nofrit, Prince Ka-em-aha, Prince Mer-ib, other sons and daughters of Cheops and his great courtiers, built their tombs.

Reisner had not long been exploring this magnificent site when Mrs. Hearst unexpectedly notified him in 1904 that she could no longer afford to continue to support the expedition. As it would have

WEST CEMETERY AT GIZA FROM TOP OF THE GREAT PYRAMID.

been heartbreaking to abandon this superlative concession and break up his efficient organization of native workmen, who had stayed with him since his first dig at Quft, Reisner obviously preferred to seek another sponsor if one could be found. Albert M. Lythgoe, who was in Egypt at the time of this crisis, saw it as a providential opportunity for the Museum of Fine Arts to sponsor excavations directly. As a result of negotiations that Lythgoe undertook on his return to Boston, George A. Reisner continued work without interruption in Egypt, but from 1905 under a new title, Director of the Harvard University – Boston Museum of Fine Arts Expedition.

Joint sponsorship between the museum and Harvard was natural, for Reisner was a Harvard graduate and Doctor of Philosophy while Lythgoe who had been reappointed Instructor of Egyptology for the academic year 1904–5 was to be promoted to Assistant Professor the following year. Such a collaboration would be mutually advantageous, for the University would be advancing learning in an important but difficult field while the museum would be adding to its galleries

authentic and thoroughly documented works of art. Gardiner Martin
Lane, a partner in Lee, Higginson and Company who was deeply
interested in the ancient world, raised among a few friends a fund of
$10,000 to defray the costs of such an expedition, with Reisner as
Director and Lythgoe as Field Director. The museum contributed
$1,000 additional and Lythgoe's services during the excavation sea-
son. An agreement which was readily reached between the two institutions gave to Harvard University the record and publication of
the results, and to the Museum of Fine Arts all objects alloted to the
expedition by the Egyptian government. A supervisory committee was
appointed, consisting of Lane as the representative of the subscribers,
Professor George Foot Moore on behalf of the University, and
Edward Robinson (soon to be replaced by Francis Bartlett) on behalf of the museum. Thus the Harvard University – Museum of Fine
Arts Expedition was organized in early May 1905, enabling Reisner
to keep his crew of competent Qufti digging at Giza.

Work began on 1 November 1905 and continued into February
1906 with highly gratifying results. Lythgoe's annual curator's report
for 1905, written at Giza on 1 February 1906, recounted the work
of clearing drift sand from the tombs in the shadow of the Great
Pyramid, photographing the area in detail, and of discovering important portrait statues, of which the museum would ultimately
receive a share. Some of the sculptures assigned to Boston were illustrated in the June 1907 issue of the *Bulletin*. These included a
superb limestone portrait head of the Fourth Dynasty, which Lythgoe
regarded as "probably the most important piece of Egyptian sculpture
in America," for he observed that, "the examples of these heads can
be numbered on the fingers of one hand," there being one or two in
Egypt and another that the Deutsche Orientalische Gesselschaft
excavated in 1903. Here too were Fifth-Dynasty statuettes of Ptah-
khenuwy and his wife, of Ikuw and his wife, and of a group of three
boys.

Although similarly profitable campaigns of the Harvard University – Museum of Fine Arts Expedition continued almost until
Reisner's death in 1942, Lythgoe participated only in the first, for on
19 July 1906 he resigned his curatorship to take effect 15 September.
His departure from the museum was a misfortune resulting from the

"battle of the casts," for Edward Robinson, having shaken the dust of Boston from his feet, not only engaged John Marshall to collect Classical art for the Metropolitan Museum but persuaded Albert M. Lythgoe to become that Museum's first Egyptian curator. His field work in Egypt from 1906 to 1926 was no longer with Reisner but as the director of a very productive Metropolitan Museum Expedition. In the future also Theodore M. Davis' gifts went to New York rather than Boston. But, even though the Metropolitan Museum, with the energetic personal enthusiasm of its president, J. Pierpont Morgan, became very active in Egypt, the Museum of Fine Arts was not likely to lose interest in its Department of Egyptian Art, for Gardiner M. Lane was elected a trustee on 18 January 1906, and, after Samuel D. Warren's resignation — still another sequel of the "battle" — President. George A. Riesner continued digging in Egypt, as he always had and always would to the end of his days, undisturbed by outside brouhahas; and when Reisner dug, he found. Thus, over the years the Egyptian collections in Boston grew and grew.

No second curator of Egyptian Antiquities was immediately appointed. For ten months after Lythgoe's resignation, the young and able Oric Bates (Harvard A.B. 1905) held the fort as Temporary Assistant in Charge. He then went off to study at Berlin and eventually to join Reisner's and other expeditions. In 1908 Louis Earle Rowe became Assistant in Charge of the department. Although Oric Bates helped in planning the installation of the galleries in Huntington Avenue while briefly back from Europe, he never returned permanently to the Museum, for in 1914 he became Curator of African Archaeology and Ethnology at the Peabody Museum, Harvard University, a post that he held until his premature death in an army camp during the 1918 influenza epidemic. On 21 April 1910 George A. Reisner was formally appointed the second Curator of Egyptian Art, although it was understood that his appearances in Boston would be few and far between.

In February 1911 Reisner returned to Boston for some months, during which he revised the exhibition in the galleries, superintended the restoration and registration of the many objects shipped by the expedition, and rewrote the Egyptian section of the museum *Handbook*. In his rather laconic report to the Director of the museum for

MYCERINUS AND HIS QUEEN KHA-MERER-NEBTY. Egyptian, 4th Dynasty, slate
schist pair statue. *Harvard-Boston Expedition. 11.1738*
THE ROYAL ARCHITECT MEHY. Egyptian, 5th Dynasty, wooden statue, from Giza.
Harvard-Boston Expedition. 13.3466

1911 he observed that the arrangement in the permanent collection
of the more important objects from the expedition had been "a very
difficult matter, owing to the importance of the objects and the lack
of space." This becomes a classic understatement when one recalls
that among the 1911 accessions were the slate group of King Mycerinus and his Queen; the slate triad of the seated Goddess Hathor, King
Mycerinus, and the personified Hare Nome; and fragments of a
colossal alabaster statue of Mycerinus — all Old Kingdom sculpture
of the highest quality and as large and heavy as they were superb.
Before Reisner returned to Egypt some two thousand objects had
been registered and $25,000 had been raised by subscription for the
coming campaign of excavation. On the Curator's departure, L. E.
Rowe resumed charge of the work of the department.

THE HARE NOME, THE GODDESS HATHOR, AND MYCERINUS. Egyptian, 4th
Dynasty, slate schist triad, from Giza. *Harvard-Boston Expedition. 09.200*
THE GODDESS HATHOR, MYCERINUS, AND MALE PERSONIFICATION OF A NOME.
Egyptian, 4th Dynasty, slate schist triad, from Giza. *Harvard-Boston Expedition.*
11.3147

Reisner was back in Boston again in 1912. When he returned to
the expedition in January 1913, Dr. Clarence S. Fisher came from
Egypt as Assistant Curator of the department for the first six months
of the year, so that Rowe might go out for some experience in excavation. Shortly after Rowe's return in July 1913 he resigned as Assistant
in order to become Director of the Rhode Island School of Design.
Fisher continued as Assistant Curator, alternating between field and
curatorial work, until September 1914 when he resigned to go to the
University of Pennsylvania Museum. At this point there appeared
on the scene Dows Dunham of the Harvard class of 1913, who, after
assisting Reisner in Egypt, was appointed Associate of the Department on 3 December 1914.

MYCERINUS, BUILDER OF THE GREAT PYRAMID AT GIZA. Egyptian, 4th Dynasty, colossal alabaster statue. *Harvard-Boston Expedition.* 09.204 As exhibited today, restored by William J. Young. A photograph of the Gallery of the Mastabas in 1909, reproduced on page 284, shows the fragmentary state in which the statue was first shown.

The prompt recruitment of two young Harvard graduates — Dows Dunham in 1914 and William Stevenson Smith in 1928 — both of whom assisted Reisner in Egypt and acted for him in Boston, becoming in due course the third and fourth Curators of Egyptian Art — made the history of the Egyptian department a seamless robe that cannot be divided in the ordinary chronology of chapters. The kind of continuity, almost apostolic succession, that has existed in the Egyptian Department for two-thirds of the museum's life, makes it necessary for this chapter to outrun its neighbors and reach the time of writing. This may be accomplished within acceptable limits of space because Dows Dunham's book *The Egyptian Department and Its Excavations*, published in 1958, provides an admirable and well illustrated account of the historical evolution. Unique among the museum's departments, the Egyptologists have not only done their own work but published their own history.

George A. Reisner did not return to Boston until September 1921. Although Dows Dunham went back to Egypt in October 1914, the museum's Registrar, Hanford Lyman Story, who had done some digging with the expedition in his time, became an informal *locum tenens*, unpacking and registering objects, preparing the annual departmental report, and generally tending store while the Curator and Associate were at work overseas. The painter Joseph Lindon Smith (1863–1950) also proved to be a useful and sympathetic link between Boston and Giza. A student of Otto Grundmann and Frederic Crowninshield in the Museum School, Smith, while an instructor there (1887–1891), had joined Edward Robinson in experiments in restoring the color of Greek sculpture. Although their efforts to color casts of the Hermes of Praxiteles and the Venus Genetrix — described in a joint museum publication of 1892 — had produced anguish rather than pleasure among visitors, this experiment made Joseph Lindon Smith, who was a very able watercolorist, aware of the assistance that a painter might render an archaeologist. When still in his twenties he became friendly with Mr. and Mrs. John L. Gardner, for she had caught him perched on a ladder in Venice, painting an oil of the head of the bronze equestrian statue of Bartolommeo Colleoni. In 1898, while on his way to Italy, Smith had yielded to a sudden impulse to explore the temples of the Nile Valley. Enchanted not only by the light, the landscape, and the temples, but especially by the sculptured reliefs, he began painting furiously. One day in December 1898, when he was painting a colossal head of Ramesses II at Abu Simbel, he met Mrs. Phoebe A. Hearst in much the way he had earlier encountered Isabella Stewart Gardner in Venice. She peered over his shoulder, and bought that painting and seven others, which she promptly showed to Reisner. In his delightful autobiography *Tombs, Temples, and Ancient Art*, Smith tells how Reisner,

> when he saw these paintings in Cairo, admitted with a blunt frankness which subsequently proved to be characteristic, that he had not been particularly keen to see any artist's attempt to reproduce temple bas-reliefs, because he thought it could not be done. He greatly encouraged me by saying my work made him feel differently, and that he hoped I would specialize in interpreting ancient art to students who came to museums. "You've accomplished the impossible," he told me. "Each painting is an archaeological record correct in details, but beautiful as a picture."

Indeed Smith's gifts proved eminently helpful to archaeology, for in many cases he was able to record color in newly discovered objects and reliefs which subsequently faded on exposure to the air. Yet later archaeologists could accept Smith's delightful paintings as an accurate record of what a piece looked like on discovery.

Joseph Lindon Smith, now accompanied by a beautiful and intelligent wife and two small daughters, returned to Egypt in the winter of 1904–5 to follow excavations and paint, as he was to do on so many occasions in subsequent decades. When finds from the Harvard University – Museum of Fine Arts Expedition were exhibited in Boston, they were often accompanied by a temporary showing of Smith's paintings of the excavations, which gave a vividness that brightened New England and interpreted the objects as well. His ties with the expedition and the museum were so intimate that from 1927 until his death he appropriately appeared on the museum roster of officers as Honorary Curator of Egyptian Art.

Although George A. Reisner maintained the headquarters of the Harvard – Boston Expedition on the Giza Pyramid Plateau west of

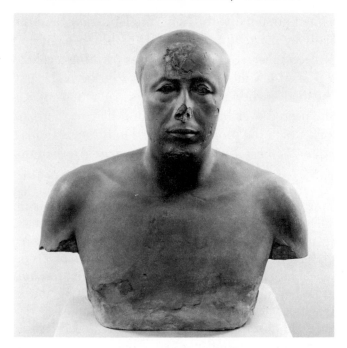

PRINCE ANKH-HAF. Egyptian, 4th Dynasty, painted limestone bust from the reign of Chephren, builder of the Second
Pyramid at Giza. *Harvard-Boston Expedition.* 27.442

Cairo and worked there almost continuously for nearly forty years,
the range of excavation work in Egypt and the Sudan extended well
south of the Fifth Cataract of the Nile. Close to his base he excavated
the majority of mastaba tombs in the great cemetery west of the Great
Pyramid, which were the burial place of nobles and officials from the
reign of Cheops into the Sixth Dynasty. He cleared the royal cemetery
east of the Great Pyramid, which contained the tombs of the mother
of Cheops, his queens, sons, and daughters, and their descendants;
excavated the Pyramid and Valley Temples of the builder of the
Third Pyramid, King Mycerinus, and the three small pyramids of his
queens. As Dows Dunham succinctly describes it,

> A little further south he excavated the Third Dynasty pyramid
> at Zawiyet-el-Aryan and adjacent tombs of that period and of the
> New Kingdom. Further south on the east bank of the Nile, he

found at Bersheh, the finest painted wooden coffin of the Middle
Period ever to have come out of Egypt, and still further up the river
in the cemeteries opposite the modern town of Girga, he dug a
whole series of sites ranging in date from Pre-Dynastic to Middle
Kingdom times. His work at Deir-el-Balas, north of Luxor, was
done in his early years of excavating for the University of California, and his Survey of Lower Nubia was undertaken for the Egyptian Government, not for us.

Then in 1913 he began his great pioneering campaign in the
Sudan which lasted until 1932, and which opened up a whole new
chapter by revealing much of the ancient history of the land of
Kush, Egypt's southern neighbor. As one continues up the Nile one
passes the five Egyptian forts which he examined in the Second
Cataract region and comes to the great Middle Kingdom site of
Kerma above the Third Cataract, which revealed to the archaeologists an entirely unsuspected culture. Still further upstream, below
the Fourth Cataract, are the great temples of Barkal which Reisner
excavated together with the neighboring Kushite royal cemeteries
of Kurru and Nuri, where he discovered the pyramid tombs of the
Kushite 25th Dynasty of Egypt and those of their successors. Finally,

PORTRAIT OF A NEGRO PRINCESS. Egyptian, 4th Dynasty, limestone, from Giza.
Harvard-Boston Expedition. 14.719
HEAD OF THE LADY SENNUWY. Egyptian, 12th Dynasty, granite statue (detail).
Harvard-Boston Expedition. 14.720

THE LADY SENNUWY. Egyptian, 12th Dynasty, granite statue of the wife of Hepzefa, the Egyptian Governor of Kerma in the Sudan. *Harvard-Boston Expedition. 14.720*

between the Fifth Cataract and Khartoum, the Expedition excavated the three great cemeteries at Meröe which range from the 25th Dynasty down to the end of the Meroitic period in the middle of the fourth century A.D.

Reisner accomplished these prodigious explorations because he was a single-minded man who would sacrifice his own comfort and convenience, and that of his family, to the advancement of learning. He cared nothing for money, save when it was needed to pay the

TUTHMOSIS III MAKING OFFERINGS TO THE RAM-HEADED KHNUM. Egyptian, 18th Dynasty, from Temple in Cataract fort at Kumma. *Harvard-Boston Expedition.* 25.1510

expenses of an expedition; these needs Gardiner M. Lane, Augustus Hemenway, and other friends in Boston gladly financed. His thorough training in Germany had led him to devise a uniquely complete system of recording evidence. He believed that the records of a well-conducted excavation should enable future scholars to re-construct in every detail the conditions found by the original ex-cavator; his records more nearly approached that ideal than most. By remaining almost constantly in Egypt he kept his crew of well-trained Quftis together, and was therefore sure that work would be accom-plished as rapidly, honestly, and accurately as was possible. In an article in the April 1911 *Bulletin* describing the excavation of the Pyramid Temple of Mycerinus in 1906–7, he told with pleasure how "Thirty trained workmen, having only iron bars and rollers, wooden beams, ropes and two improvised railway trucks, carried out in a few weeks over four hundred granite blocks ranging from one to seven tons in weight, and were so proud of their achievement that they boasted, 'We will build a pyramid if there is an order.'"

Dows Dunham observed that "Reisner always gave first place to archaeology as a means toward the advancement of our knowledge

OFFERING BEARERS FROM THE TOMB OF DJEHUTY-
NEKHT. *Egyptian, 12th Dynasty, painted wooden
figures, from El Bersheh in Upper Egypt. Harvard-
Boston Expedition. 21.326*

of ancient Egyptian civilization, and often said that the acquisition of Museum objects was a by-product of his work." The by-product of course was essential, for the flow of contributions toward his excavations was stimulated by the counterflow of superlative objects to the Museum of Fine Arts. Reisner's long uninterrupted stays in Egypt greatly increased the possibility of the museum's receiving unique pieces. The average excavator, going home at the end of a season's dig, had to divide his finds then and there with the Egyptian authorities. If they contained only one outstanding object, that single piece naturally went to the Cairo Museum. If Reisner found himself in such a situation, he could readily defer the division for another season or two until more had been uncovered. With a larger division there was greater assurance of Boston obtaining at least a part of the best pieces. Thus, Dunham recalls, Reisner held the polychromed portrait bust of Ankh-haf in his storeroom for several years until he found the tomb of Queen Hetep-heres.

> This unique group of royal tomb furniture of the Fourth Dynasty had to be kept in Cairo because it was from an undisturbed royal tomb which, by a special clause in the contract, must remain intact and in Egypt. The excavation of this sensational tomb occupied the entire time of the Expedition for nearly two years, and Reisner was

able to make a successful plea for the bust for Boston as a make-weight against this find.

So Ankh-haf came to Boston, as had the Old Kingdom wooden statue of Senezem-ib Mehy, the granite seated statue of the Middle Kingdom lady Sennuwy, and many other of the finest objects now exhibited in the galleries.

Just as the presence of Morse, Fenollosa, Bigelow, and Weld in Japan in the eighties, and of E. P. Warren and John Marshall in the nineties in Europe had assured Oriental and Classical objects of high quality for Boston that could not have been obtained (or afforded) at a later time, so George A. Reisner's years of excavation in the twentieth century enriched the Egyptian collection for remarkably modest sums. Again it was a matter of the right men at the right place at the right time. Dows Dunham expands upon this thought.

A good many years ago I made some calculations aimed at clarifying the monetary cost to the Museum of the collection — a calculation now much out of date. I took the total cost of running the Expedition from its first association with the Museum and placed against that the value for insurance in transit of the principal objects received during the same period, a valuation admittedly very low. The former was in round figures, about 10% of the latter. It is obvious, therefore, that from a purely dollars and cents point of view we have had a very good bargain. Clearly also, we have obtained through excavation masterpieces of Egyptian art which would simply not have been available for purchase at any price and on which it is really impossible to place any dollar valuation. Would anyone venture to name a price for the Hermes of Praxiteles? Then how arrive at the money value of such pieces as our Slate Pair of Mycerinus and his Queen, or the bust of Ankh-haf.

Although Dr. Reisner's excavations continued relentlessly through the First World War, it was impossible to ship across the ocean any of the objects assigned to the Museum of Fine Arts during those years. The staff of the department being overseas, H. Lyman Story and Joseph Lindon Smith kept things going in Huntington Avenue in their spare time, while Reisner's article "Known and Unknown Kings of Ethiopia" in the October 1918 *Bulletin* provided his supporters with a foretaste of the discoveries made during the seasons 1916–1918 in the royal cemetery at Nuri in the Sudan. At the end of the war it became apparent that there must be a full-time Egyptologist on hand in the department to cope with the wartime backlog of objects that would soon be arriving. Therefore Dows Dunham, who had rejoined the Harvard – Boston Expedition in 1919 after nearly four years' duty with the Motor Transport Service in France, was in October 1920 appointed Assistant Curator of Egyptian Art.

The first shipment of the museum's share of the Expedition's finds since 1914 left Egypt on 2 October 1919 and arrived safely in the spring of 1920. Although it consisted largely of gold utensils, jewelry, and other small objects, it included the large Twelfth Dynasty painted coffin of Prince Djehuty-nekht, found at Bersheh, that Reisner appraised as "the finest Middle Kingdom coffin in the world." As other shipments made in 1921 brought more than a hundred tons of material to Boston, a complete rearrangement of the exhibits became essential. Dr. Reisner returned to Boston in September 1921 after an absence of nearly ten years. During his stay, which lasted until February 1922, Dows Dunham carried on the Expedition's digging at Meröe in the Sudan. While both curators were in Egypt, Ashton Sanborn, the museum's Librarian, carried out Reisner's plans for the new installation of the galleries and put through the press the monumental report on the Expedition's excavations at Kerma, which appeared in 1923 as volumes V and VI of *Harvard African Studies*, published by the Peabody Museum of Archaeology and Ethnology, Harvard University.

A shipment of seventy-eight cases, containing objects from Reisner's excavations at Napata and Meröe, arrived in 1923. The colossal granite sarcophagus of King Aspelta (593–568 B.C.) was, because of its extraordinary size and weight, installed in the lower Crypt, where it emphasized the gloomy character of this monumental apartment, which served chiefly as a passageway between lecture room, administrative offices, and public toilets. The same shipment brought a granite statue of Tanutamon (666–653 B.C.) more than 12 feet in height, the gray granite altar dedicated in a temple at

Gebel Barkal by Atalanersa, King of Kush (653–643 B.C.), as well as a superb collection of Meroitic jewelry. Cecil Firth, working for the Egyptian Government at Saggara, asked Reisner in 1923 to lend him Dows Dunham to assist in the excavations there. Dunham had worked for Firth, paid by the Government for two seasons, when Reisner asked him to return. This led to his first and only quarrel with Reisner, who was difficult and inconsiderate to an assistant with a wife and two small children. Therefore, in October 1924 Dunham resigned as Assistant Curator of Egyptian Art, or was fired by Reisner, as one chose to look at the matter. After an absence of three years, Reisner spent the months of February to June 1925 in Boston. The large gallery opening on the right from the Rotunda, first used for paintings and later for the Nearer Orient collection, was at this time transferred to the Egyptian Department, for the exhibition of Old Kingdom sculpture. Blue stone floors, matching those in the original Egyptian rooms, were installed here and in the adjacent gallery by gift of Augustus Hemenway, who had been one of the constant supporters of the Harvard – Boston Expedition. On 2 April 1925 Thomas Richard Duncan Greenlees, who had worked with the Expedition, was appointed Assistant Curator of Egyptian Art, while the Registrar, Hanford Lyman Story, was given the additional title of Assistant in the Department in recognition of years of informal service. Rather than coming to Boston, however, Greenlees deserted the Expedition to join Annie Besant in India; consequently, when Reisner returned to Egypt, the departmental work was carried on by Story in such time as he could spare from other duties.

After some years of excavation in the Sudan, George A. Reisner resumed extensive work near his expedition's camp at Giza, where earlier campaigns had by no means exhausted the possibilities for work. During his absence in Boston in the spring of 1925, the Expedition photographer was taking pictures at the northern end of a street in the Royal Cemetery at Giza between the small pyramids of the queens of Cheops and the tombs of his sons and daughter. A leg of his tripod unexpectedly sank into a soft spot in the street. Investigation revealed a patch of plaster on the surface of the rock, which when removed disclosed a trench filled with dressed limestone

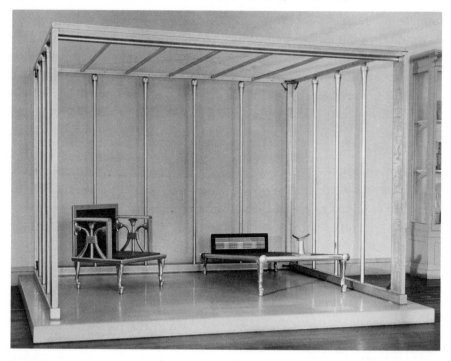

BED, BED-CANOPY, AND ARMCHAIR OF QUEEN HETEP-HERES. Replica of Egyptian, 4th Dynasty, wooden furniture overlaid with gold, from the original (discovered by Reisner) in the Cairo Museum. *29.1858, 38.873, and 38.957*

blocks that sealed a hitherto unexpected stairway. So an intact secret Old Kingdom tomb of some great personage who had lived at the time of King Sneferuw, the father of Cheops, became for the first time available for study. The excavation of this unexpected treasure occupied much of the next three years. It proved eventually to be the second burial place of Queen Hetep-heres, a wife of Sneferuw and the mother of Cheops, appropriately equipped with golden furniture and other accommodations for eternal convenience. Although this secret tomb had never been entered from the moment of burial until 1925, the Queen's sarcophagus proved to be empty! Reisner's solution of this mystery, summarized in the October 1928 *Bulletin*, suggests that his talents as a detective were on a par with those of Hercule Poirot, Lord Peter Wimsey, or the later James Bond. A sidelight on his proficiency in the "cops and robbers game" comes from his final bequest to Harvard of 1,300 volumes of detective stories! The Queen's magnificent furniture, described in the May 1927 and December 1929 *Bulletins*, obviously had to remain intact in the Cairo Museum, but skillfully made replicas of it have been displayed in Boston since 1938.

After the discovery of the tomb of Queen Hetep-heres, Dows Dunham made up his differences with Reisner, rejoined the Harvard – Boston Expedition and assisted in the excavation of that tomb. He was once more appointed Assistant Curator of the Egyptian Department as of 1 April 1926, although he did not return to Boston until June 1927. For the next twenty-seven years Dunham was chiefly responsible for the department's administration, although he frequently returned to the field during that time.

In the autumn of 1928, William Stevenson Smith, who had been graduated from Harvard College the previous June, came to the Egyptian Department as a student and volunteer worker, remaining save for the summer of 1929 until the end of the latter year, when he went to Egypt to join the Harvard – Boston Expedition. As with Dunham fourteen years earlier, he had come straight from Harvard. No two men have ever proved finer examples of the theory of "catch 'em young and train 'em on the job," for Bill Smith remained in the service of the museum and Harvard University until his death more than forty years later. Reisner returned to Boston for three months late in 1929, giving in that period three public lectures at the museum, a course of eight Lowell lectures, and three courses at Harvard, where he had been since 1914 Professor of Egyptology. He then vanished to Egypt for another decade, returning only in June 1939 for his fiftieth class reunion at Harvard, in the course of which he received the honorary degree of Doctor of Letters. During this period of continued excavation, the Harvard University Press in 1931 published his great folio *Mycerinus: The Temples of the Third Pyramid at Giza*, and the Oxford University Press his *The Development of the Egyptian Tomb down to the Accession of Cheops* in 1936. William Stevenson Smith, by then Chief Assistant on the Expedition, arrived at the museum in September 1937, bringing with him the manuscripts for the first volume of Dr. Reisner's *History of the Giza Necropolis* and of his own completed work, *A History of Egyptian Sculpture and Painting in the Old Kingdom*.

He returned to Egypt in December by way of London. Dunham, who had been named Associate Curator in 1934, remained on duty in Boston, assisted by Miss Elizabeth Eaton, who had come as a volunteer in 1932, and from 1937 by Miss Suzanne E. Chapman, whose talents as an artist were shared with the Department of Classical Art. Joseph Lindon Smith, Honorary Curator of Egyptian Art since 1927, was as always back and forth between Boston and Cairo, bringing news and his latest paintings of archaeological subjects, until the outbreak of war, when he went instead to Yucatan to make similar paintings for the Carnegie Institution of Washington.

William Stevenson Smith, who had been delayed in Europe by the outbreak of war, got back to Boston on 4 October 1939 to devote himself to work on Expedition publications. He received a Harvard Ph.D. in June 1940, and was on the following 17 October appointed Assistant Curator of Egyptian Art. An incident like the Second World War was far from budging George A. Reisner out of Giza, even though other armies than Napoleon's might soon be under the shadow of the Pyramids. He remained in his camp, working on excavation reports, even though he conceded to possible air raids by placing his records in one of the subterranean rock-cut tombs at Giza, and rigging offices and sleeping quarters for the staff in other underground chambers. Although his wife and daughter were persuaded to return to the United States in the summer of 1940, he stayed put, working as always, with the assistance of Francis O. Allen, formerly of the Oriental Institute in Chicago, who had joined the expedition staff in 1938. Reisner's eyesight had long been failing, but in July 1941 he was hurried to a Cairo hospital because of another serious illness. Although his life was despaired of for some days, he was able a few months later to return to the camp at Giza, where he died on 6 June 1942. Few men have ever served their institutions more devotedly or consistently through thirty-seven years. The Egyptologist Herbert E. Winlock, sometime Director of the Metropolitan Museum, wrote in an American Philosophical Society tribute: "George Andrew Reisner was without doubt the greatest excavator and archaeologist the United States has ever produced in any field."

Although Reisner's death marked the actual end of new work by the Harvard University – Museum of Fine Arts Expedition, the camp at Giza, with its priceless records and stores of objects not yet shipped to Boston, was kept in operation through the devotion of his secretary, Miss Evelyn Perkins, and of Francis O. Allen who was promptly named Acting Director of the Expedition. Allen was requisitioned for emergency work at the American Legation in Egypt and Miss Perkins was engaged in relief work in Cairo; nevertheless they succeeded by strenuous moonlighting in safeguarding the camp and looking after the welfare of the expedition's workmen. Fortunately the zone of combat operations, which had been uncomfortably close to Giza in the summer of 1942, moved westward. The museum could be of little assistance from Boston, for William Stevenson Smith and Miss Eaton had joined the Navy, and the department was manned only by Dows Dunham, now the third Curator of Egyptian Art, with the part-time help of Miss Chapman.

Although Huntington Avenue was several thousand miles further away from combat operations than Giza, air-raid precautions at the museum considerably hampered normal work. It had been determined that such pieces of major importance (or bulk) as could not be moved quickly in an emergency should be moved for safekeeping to space provided by Williams College in the western part of the state. To avoid the appearance of complete devastation in the galleries, William J. Young of the museum's Research Laboratory, who had already marvelously helped the department with the study, cleaning, and restoration of Egyptian objects, made casts of some of the sculptures removed, skillfully coloring them in imitation of the originals. So simulacra of Mycerinus and his queen, of the slate triad of Hathor, Mycerinus, and Nome, of the alabaster head of Sheksekaf, and of the red bust of Ankh-haf took the places for a few years of the hidden masterpieces. The removal of the El Bersheh painted coffin left room to install creditable but previously unexhibited objects from that site and from Assiut. Beads, necklaces, and faience horse-trappings replaced evacuated gold jewelry, while a series of Joseph Lindon Smith's paintings of Abydos brightened the walls. For a month following Dr. Reisner's death a small memorial exhibition was set up in the Rotunda, consisting of a photograph of him, two cases containing his major publications, and the alabaster head of Shepsekaf. In October 1942 the museum published William Stevenson Smith's *Ancient Egypt as represented in the Museum of Fine Arts, Boston*, a handbook to the collection in the form of a brief but admirable summary of Egyptian history and art, which is now in its fourth edition.

The evacuated objects returned home in May 1944, but it was June 1946 before William Stevenson Smith got back from naval service. That year saw the publication by Oxford of his *History of Egyptian Sculpture and Painting in the Old Kingdom*, and of the first volume of Reisner's *A History of the Giza Necropolis* by the Harvard University Press. (Although the latter work bears the date 1942, war conditions delayed its appearance for four years.) Bernard V. Bothmer, just returned from Army service overseas, was appointed Assistant in the Department. With five years of graduate training in Egyptology and six years of museum experience, he was well able to fit into the work.

In October 1946 Dunham and W. S. Smith went to Egypt to survey the scene and consider prospects for the future. It was necessary first of all to pack and ship to Boston the library, scientific records, and other property of the Harvard University – Museum of Fine Arts Expedition that would be necessary to complete such publications of Reisner's excavations as had remained unfinished at his death. Although for forty years all important finds had been divided with the Egyptian or Sudan governments, as the case might be, and shipped to Boston, Cairo, or Khartoum, there still remained a great amount of the debris of excavation, which, although of little exhibition value, had scientific importance. This had to be examined with care lest anything of future usefulness be discarded, and a division achieved with Boston and the respective governments. From this study five cases of antiquities, chiefly of archaeological value, were shipped to Boston, together with some 16,000 photograph negatives and twenty-eight cases of books and records. Both curators visited various sites previously excavated by the Expedition, making notes and studies needed for future publications.

The major decision of this extended visit was to discontinue the Expedition. The increased nationalism of postwar Egypt had diminished interest in foreign archaeological activity. It seemed unlikely that in any future contracts the old division of finds between the foreign excavators and the Egyptian Government would prevail. Thus some forty-two years after its creation the Harvard University – Museum of Fine Arts Expedition came to an end. The camp buildings and furnishings at Giza were turned over to the Egyptian Government, and the staff of Qufti workmen released with suitable compensation. As the majority of these men had worked with Reisner from the beginning, while the mean length of service of the entire staff was thirty years, Miss Perkins and the Foreman made exceptional efforts to find places for them elsewhere. It was a sad parting, as Dows Dunham noted in his 1947 report.

Nearly all the men were placed in suitable employment in addition to receiving generous compensation for long service, so that there is every prospect that no undue hardship will be suffered by them. Nevertheless the writer cannot refrain from recording that the task of bidding farewell to some twenty old and faithful servants of the Expedition on the day of his departure was one of considerable emotional stress. Finally he would wish here to make public acknowledgment of his sense of the deep obligation of the Expedition to Mohammed Said Ahmed, its faithful head Foreman. His intelligence, honesty, and utter devotion to the best interests of the Expedition as well as to the welfare of the men under his charge have been beyond praise. It was with genuine admiration and respect, and with the sense of parting from a real personal friend that the writer said goodbye to him on the first of May.

The ties with Harvard University and the Egyptian Department continued long after the Expedition ended, for (in the Reisner tradition) William Stevenson Smith for nearly twenty years as a Harvard Lecturer on the Fine Arts regularly gave a half-course on Egyptian art whenever he was in the country. It was of such quality that the Dean of the Graduate School of Arts and Sciences, Professor John Petersen Elder, a Classical scholar, attended it regularly a few years ago, and, at its conclusion, suggested that he would be glad to join the Visiting Committee of the Egyptian Department. And the members of the department are still at work completing the publication of the reports of the Harvard – Boston Expedition. The Harvard

University Press in 1950 published volume I, dealing with El Kurru, of Dows Dunham's *The Royal Cemeteries of Kush*. Other volumes of the series appeared in 1952, 1955, and 1963; volume III, concerning the decorated chapels of the Meroë pyramids was produced in collaboration with Miss Chapman, whose remarkable drawings have adorned and made intelligible many publications on Classical as well as Egyptian subjects.

On 18 February 1954 various promotions took place in the Egyptian Department, Smith becoming Associate Curator, Bothmer Assistant Curator, and Miss Chapman Special Assistant. In the summer of that year, Bothmer was given leave of absence to become Director of the American Research Center in Egypt, a post of which Smith had been the first incumbent for a year beginning February 1951. Bothmer, however, never returned to Boston, for after two years in Cairo he accepted a post at the Brooklyn Museum. In January 1956, in order to give his full time to the completion of excavation reports, Dows Dunham became Curator Emeritus, with William Stevenson Smith succeeding him as the fourth Curator. In that year Smith completed and revised Reisner's study of the tomb of Hetep-heres, which the Harvard University Press published as a second volume of *A History of the Giza Necropolis*. His own *The Arts and Architecture of Ancient Egypt* appeared in the Pelican History of Art in 1958, and in 1965 the Yale University Press published his *Interconnections in the Ancient Near East*. Dows Dunham not only brought out in 1960 (in collaboration with J. M. A. Janssen) the first of a series on *Second Cataract Forts*, published by the museum, but edited and prepared for the University of California Press a volume on the excavations of the pre-dynastic cemetery at Naga-ed-Der that Albert M. Lythgoe had conducted in 1900 before joining the staff of the Museum of Fine Arts. Three folio volumes of a *Papyrus Reisner* series have been prepared for museum publication by Professor William Kelly Simpson of Yale, a member of the department's Visiting Committee.

I have always been considerably moved by the meetings of that committee in the years since 1963 when I have been its chairman, for it has been composed of faithful friends who followed the precepts laid down by J. Randolph Coolidge, Jr., in 1906. Its meetings are held in the crowded workroom of the Egyptian Department, where the walls are lined with simple wooden shelves holding files of excavation notes. In a corner near the window is Suzanne Chapman's worktable, with the drawing of an Egyptian artifact or a Greek vase in progress. A few extraordinary works of art are sitting about for study; other objects have been brought up from storage. There is scarcely room for a dozen or so people to gather around a table. At the first meetings that I attended the company still included Mrs. Joseph Lindon Smith, the widow of the Honorary Curator of Egyptian Art, still beautiful past eighty, and Edward W. Forbes, looking as he approached ninety more and more like his grandfather, Ralph Waldo Emerson. Although long Director of the Fogg Museum, Edward Forbes had enriched the Boston collection by generous gifts. Until his death in 1968, Horace L. Mayer, who in the last fifteen years had given a great variety of remarkable objects to the department, was invariably present, although prevented by deafness from following much of the talk that went around the table. Among members who still attend there are close personal ties, for Mrs. F. Carrington Weems is the sculptress Katherine Lane and the daughter of Gardiner M. Lane who found the means of setting the Harvard University – Museum of Fine Arts Expedition in motion early in this century, and Mrs. Oric Bates, who worked constantly in the department as a volunteer from 1949 to 1967, is the widow of the scholar who held the fort in 1906 after Lythgoe's resignation. The Harvard Classicists J. P. Elder and Sterling Dow may well be there, with Kelly Simpson from Yale, the famous Egyptian philologist Richard Parker, the retired diplomat Donald P. Edgar, and the exuberant and useful Edmundo Lassalle from New York. I can think of few groups that have so consistently shared a benevolent and useful common interest in an institution, or of no setting that better represents the continuity of learning than this crowded, improvised, and shabby departmental office. I hope it is never "improved" by gray steel furniture and filing cases, and the theory of the tidy desk.

The postwar years have been filled not only with the steady publication of great volumes of excavation reports but with the study and appraisal of a mass of objects shipped from Egypt before 1940 that had not been exhibited. Some fine pieces have been placed in the galleries as a result of "re-excavation" from the department's store-rooms. Others of high quality, in periods already fully illustrated by exhibits, have been sold to other museums that had a specific use for such material. In 1964, for example, the department sold to the Metropolitan Museum three important Fifth Dynasty sculptures, excavated by the Harvard – Boston Expedition at Giza in 1920–21. The two three-quarter-lifesized limestone statues of an official and the granite portrait head that were then sold would never have left the storeroom in Boston because of the quantity of even finer Old Kingdom sculpture that was already on permanent display. As they would fill a useful purpose in the Metropolitan's collection, it seemed preferable to have them seen and appreciated there rather than hoarded away, unseen, here. Moreover the substantial sum received from the sale was added to the Egyptian Curator's Fund that is used for the purchase of objects that are especially needed.

During the life of the Harvard – Boston Expedition, the museum seldom if ever bought works of Egyptian art in the commercial market, in order to avoid any possibility of giving countenance to the clandestine trade by which Egyptian objects sometimes migrated to Europe. In the changed postwar world, where the opportunities of collecting by excavation have so greatly diminished, weak spots can only be strengthened through the gifts of generous private collectors

METHETHY. Egyptian, 6th Dynasty, painted wooden statue, said to be from Saqqara. *Arthur Tracy Cabot Fund.* *47.1455*

WOODEN STATUE OF A GIRL. Late Egyptian.
*Gift of the Class of the Museum and the
Egyptian Curator's Fund. 64.2178*

like the late Horace L. Mayer, a Benefactor of the Museum, or through purchase when especially remarkable pieces are offered for sale. The Egyptian Department has, unlike some others, only very limited funds that are specifically restricted for its use in this way, for its generous friends during the first half of this century made their gifts for the current support of its excavations. Therefore anything that it buys today must come from museum funds simply restricted to the purchase of works of art, which must be apportioned equitably among all departments; from the specific gifts of friends; or from turning to financial account objects not needed in Boston that would be highly useful in other institutions.

In the years since the war constant efforts were made through painting, lighting, and rearrangement to improve the effectiveness of exhibition. Although much was accomplished with modest expendi-

GALLERY E-2 AS RENOVATED IN 1963.

ture, the large room originally designated as the Gallery of the Mastabas (now E-3) remained much as it had been installed in 1909, for the massiveness of its objects defied change. In some fields an inspired curator with a good idea and a pot of paint, helped by a few willing hands, can transform an exhibition in a matter of days. Mastaba tombs and statues of Egyptian kings weighing some tons do not lend themselves readily to such flights of fancy. In 1963, however, when the last details of the renovation and reinstallation of the Old Kingdom galleries (E-1 and E-2) had been completed, this major problem was attacked. More than two years of solid work were required, for 69 tons of granite and 61 tons of limestone were moved and 180 white limestone blocks dismantled and reassembled before the new installation was completed.

Late in 1965 this and four adjacent Egyptian galleries were re-opened in new and dramatic form. The Old Kingdom mastaba chapels were moved from the center of E-3, where they had been placed when the museum was built, to the north end of the room. Rebuilt as they had once stood at Saqqara, they were in logical sequence with the two Old Kingdom galleries across the corridor. In the center of the room, colossal sculptures were newly set in places where they could be seen to advantage, while temple reliefs were let into the walls. Among these latter were two of great importance, picturing the Heb Sed of Orsokon II from his festival hall at Bubastis, which were exhibited for the first time in the present building. Since the move from Copley Square nearly sixty years earlier they had skulked in the basement because of the weight of useless granite at the back of the stones; with this sawed off they were built into the gallery walls where they could be seen to full advantage. Gallery E-4, which originally contained the Way Collection, was remodeled to exhibit the Bersheh coffins and other Middle Kingdom objects, while E-5 showed the New Kingdom in new fashion. The small adjacent room (E-6) was remodeled for the display of jewelry and amulets, while E-7 beyond became the Late Egyptian Gallery. Thus the series of seven rooms presented a chronological sequence of Egyptian art, in which sometimes recalcitrant objects were handsomely shown.

The field of the Egyptian Department was enlarged in 1958 to include responsibility for the Ancient Near East, an area that had hitherto been a stepchild of the Department of Asiatic Art. Although a number of fine pieces, like the Neo-Sumerian diorite portrait head of Gudea, priest-ruler of Lagash (ca. 2100 b.c.) had come into the possession of the museum, there was within existing departmental divisions little opportunity for their appropriate exhibition.

After their transfer to the Egyptian Department, a new gallery for them was skillfully and freshly designed by Carl F. Zahn in ground-floor space, in logical juxtaposition to the Egyptian and Classical galleries. This handsome new room has inspired numerous recent gifts and purchases, the most striking of which is the fifth-century b.c. Achaemenian silver bowl from Sinope on the Black Sea.

The year that the new gallery opened Edward Lee Bockman Terrace joined the department as an Assistant. Although still young, he had not, like Dunham and Smith before him, simply crossed the

GALLERY E-3 AS INSTALLED IN 1909.

GALLERY E-3 AS RENOVATED IN 1965.

GALLERY E-4 AS RENOVATED IN 1965.

ANCIENT NEAR EAST GALLERY. The head of Gudea stands on the pedestal; on the far wall are reliefs from the Palace of Ashurnasirpal II at Nimrud, 883–859 B.C.

ANCIENT NEAR EAST GALLERY.

Charles after graduation from Harvard, for he was a Dartmouth man who, after work there in classical archaeology, had studied Egyptology and Assyriology at Queen's College, Oxford. The latter interest made him especially useful for the new responsibilities of the department. In 1962 the museum published his handbook *The Art of the Ancient Near East*, which was written to elucidate the new gallery. In 1962 Edward Terrace was promoted to Assistant Curator; in 1968 he became Associate Curator and received the Harvard Ph.D. for which he had been working part-time for several years.

A chapter that records remarkable and consistent accomplishment by the Department of Egyptian Art over sixty-eight years ends on a note of sadness because of the sudden and premature death on 12 January 1969 of its fourth Curator, William Stevenson Smith. For over forty of his sixty-one years he had devoted himself without stint to the Harvard – Boston Expedition and the Museum of Fine Arts. As a student and assistant of his two immediate predecessors, he had acquired a continuity of knowledge of the museum's collections that can never be replaced; in his own right he was a highly productive scholar who interpreted the art and history of Egypt in terms respected by specialists yet attractive to any literate reader. He will be missed, for he was as amiable and unpretentious as he was able and learned. It is in keeping with his character that he left his entire estate — belongings, savings, and pension — to the Museum of Fine Arts, which had been his life.

CHAPTER IX

The Decent Docent

Description of the monolithic concerns of the Department of Egyptian Art brought the last chapter down to the time of writing. To understand the development of the Museum of Fine Arts as a whole, the reader must now turn back some sixty years to the opening of the Huntington Avenue museum. The building remained in the form described in Chapter VII for only five years and three months, for the opening of an extensive addition early in 1915 permitted major expansion of the exhibitions. Consequently, I now shall deal with the years 1910 through 1914 — the period of the first stage of the second museum. Its opening in November 1909 brought to a happy conclusion a decade of uncertainty and planning, for from the purchase of the Fenway land in 1899, problems of building and their relation to finances had never been far absent from the thoughts of anyone connected with the museum.

In this decade there had been extraordinary changes in trustees and staff. Samuel Dennis Warren had become President, pushed through the planning and construction of the new museum, resigned his office, and died on 19 February 1910, only three months after the building was opened. General Loring, the Boston gentleman whose concern with learning sprang from Egyptian travel and private study and whose able administration of the museum during its first quarter-century evolved from pragmatic experience on the spot, had been followed as Director by two academically trained Classical scholars, Edward Robinson and Arthur Fairbanks. Although a number of trustees had left the scene, the character and composition of the board had altered relatively little during this decade.

Of the sixteen elected trustees who had made the decision in 1899 to buy land in the Fenway, six had been scholars or men with some professional tie with the arts or learning, while the other ten were lawyers, bankers, professional trustees, manufacturers, or men concerned with some form of business; when the new museum opened the proportion was the same, although many of the individuals were different. The first group in 1899 consisted of President Eliot, General Loring, Professor Charles Eliot Norton (elected in 1877), Dr. Denman W. Ross (1895), and the architects William P. P. Longfellow (1883), and Charles A. Cummings (1897). A decade later Eliot, Ross, and Longfellow were still on deck, but with Professor Charles Sprague Sargent (1900), creator and Director of Harvard's Arnold Arboretum, Edward Waldo Forbes (1903), who filled the same joint role at Harvard's Fogg Art Museum, and the painter Thomas Allen (1909) as their colleagues. There was equal consistency on the financial side of the board. When Charles Lowell (elected a Trustee and Treasurer in 1898 on the death of John Lowell Gardner) died in 1906, he was succeeded as Treasurer by Francis Lee Higginson, who had been elected to the board in 1900 to fill a vacancy created by the resignation of Henry Lee Higginson. Gardiner M. Lane, President at the time of the 1909 opening, was also a partner in Lee, Higginson and Company. Following the death of Edward W. Hooper, sometime Treasurer of Harvard College, Morris Gray, lawyer and private trustee, was elected in 1902 in his place, while in 1907 the vacancies created by the death of Charles Lowell and the resignation of William Endicott were filled by A. Shuman and Robert Dawson Evans. The latter had been a generous subscriber to the Building Fund; the former was the proprietor of a men's clothing store at the corner of Washington and Summer streets, next door to C. F. Hovey's drygoods store of which William Endicott had long been a director.

Of the nine appointed trustees serving in 1899 all were men of taste or learning rather than of affairs; among them were some of remarkable energy and administrative experience, although not necessarily close to the arts. The three representatives of Harvard

College were Dr. William Sturgis Bigelow, Arthur Astor Carey (A.B. 1879), who defined his occupation as "the care of property and the furthering of various artistic interests," and Arthur Tracy Cabot (A.B. 1872, M.D. 1876), surgeon and Fellow of Harvard College from 1896. The Boston Athenæum was still represented by James Elliot Cabot (A.B. 1840, LL.B. 1845, LL.D. 1885), sometime lawyer, sometime architect, friend, literary executor, and biographer of Ralph Waldo Emerson, who had been appointed annually since 1870. The other Athenæum places were filled by Thornton Kirkland Lothrop (A.B. 1849, LL.B. 1853), friend and classmate of Martin Brimmer, and the architect J. Randolph Coolidge, Jr. (A.B. 1883, A.M. 1884). The Massachusetts Institute of Technology was represented by the meteorologist Abbott Lawrence Rotch, creator and director of the Blue Hill Observatory, the chemist James M. Crafts, then President of M.I.T., and the physicist-inventor Francis Blake who had patented the telephone transmitter. When Arthur Astor Carey resigned in 1902, Harvard appointed in his place the artist and collector John Templeman Coolidge, son-in-law of the historian Francis Parkman and a third cousin of J. Randolph Coolidge, Jr. Among the Athenæum appointments, J. Elliot Cabot was replaced in 1902 by Henry Francis Sears (A.B. 1883, M.D. 1887), who had left the practice of medicine in 1894 to devote himself to the affairs of the Athenæum and the Boston Symphony Orchestra. Dr. Sears was succeeded in 1904 by the architect Alexander Wadsworth Longfellow (A.B. 1876), and Thornton K. Lothrop in 1909 by Holker Abbott, a *peintre manqué* who founded the Copley Society. Under John Singer Sargent's portrait of Abbott in the library of the Tavern Club is carved Owen Wister's couplet:

> If one best Taverner could be
> Taverners, this was surely he.

This expressed a universal feeling for the man who was the mainspring of the club's activities in the decades 1902–1922 during which he was secretary. In the M.I.T. group, the astronomer President Henry S. Pritchett succeeded President Crafts in 1900. After

Pritchett left Boston to head the Carnegie Foundation for the Advancement of Teaching, the Institute in 1907 appointed in his place Augustus Hemenway, who was long a supporter of the Harvard University – Museum of Fine Arts Expedition.

Of the members of the board who served *ex officiis*, mayors, presidents of the Boston Public Library, superintendents of schools, and commissioners of education changed too frequently to play any significant role in the affairs of the museum. The exception was the Trustee of the Lowell Institute. The founder of the Institute, John Lowell, Jr., was posthumously an early contributor of Egyptian sculpture. His cousin and brother-in-law, John Amory Lowell, the first Trustee of the Lowell Institute, was a trustee of the museum from 1870 until his death in 1881. The second Trustee, Augustus Lowell, son of the first, served on the museum board from 1881, being succeeded in 1900 by his son, Abbott Lawrence Lowell, President of Harvard University 1909–1933, and in 1943 by the banker Ralph Lowell, the present incumbent. Thus the four Trustees of the Lowell Institute have been a significant element of judgment and continuity in the affairs of the museum throughout its first century.

In spite of the abilities of this varied and not insolvent board, and of the increased opportunities of the new museum, the years from 1910 through 1914 were financially lean and all too reminiscent of the eighteen eighties and early nineties. Beginning in 1904 the trustees had prudently ceased to spend unrestricted funds for purchases, and with reason, for, despite expressed hopes to the contrary, they had to pour more than half a million dollars of such funds into the completion of the building and the move. This depletion of capital upset the financial equilibrium very considerably, for unrestricted income from trust investments provided the major share of the annual operating expenses. Admission fees were only a drop in the bucket, for the crowds which ran up impressive figures of attendance came on Saturdays and Sundays when the gate was free. In 1908, the last full year in Copley Square, of 236,874 visitors only 18,849 paid a total of $4,731. In that year 1,432 persons made annual subscriptions amounting to $20,895, but it was the $86,060 of unrestricted income that carried the load.

As 1910 was the first full year in Huntington Avenue, everyone flocked in. Attendance soared to 279,820, of which the record number of 35,885 paid $8,971. But as the greater demands of the new building had increased operating expenses at least 25 percent, and as income from the depleted unrestricted funds had fallen to $46,237, it was only through the increase of annual subscriptions to $43,849 that the deficit for the year was as low as $1,535. Once general curiosity over the new building had been satisfied, attendance slid steadily downward until it reached 205,109 in 1914. In the same five years the number of annual subscribers rose from 1,498 to 1,710 but the total of their gifts declined until 1913 ($37,487); in 1914 the receipts rose slightly to $38,584. But, as operating expenses climbed steadily from $103,650 in 1910 to $161,061 in 1913, deficits of $30,000 to $40,000 a year were inevitable. In spite of special gifts made each year in an effort to balance the budget, unrestricted capital was being reduced every year from 1911 to 1914 by at least $21,500. Thus the first five years in Huntington Avenue, while aesthetically satisfying, were financially lamentable. Francis Bartlett's gift in 1912 of a building in Chicago valued at $1,350,000 was, it was true, the greatest single benefaction that the museum had received in its forty-two years of life. As this gift was restricted to the purchase of Classical art and paintings, the problem of paying salaries and the coal bill remained.

A missionary zeal to do good to others, to convert, to impart information, has long afflicted many New Englanders. To such people the reiteration of pious platitudes about education unconsciously becomes an acceptable substitute for thought. Fortunately for them, there have usually been willing victims at hand who would gladly listen to anything that was both free and "improving." The devotion with which audiences appeared for any series of Lowell Lectures, however abstruse the subject, until broadcast entertainment became available at home, is a case in point. The 1870 charter had defined the third responsibility of the Museum of Fine Arts as "affording instruction in the Fine Arts." Although it might have seemed that the prompt establishment of the School of Drawing and Painting in the basement of the Copley Square museum adequately fulfilled that obligation, the didactic urge remained unsatisfied. It will be recalled that Edward Robinson, defending his beloved plaster casts in 1904, had proudly stated that "many classes of adults have been formed during the last fifteen years for the especial purpose of studying this one collection." A drearier pastime can hardly be imagined.

As early as 1892 the architect J. Randolph Coolidge, Jr., while still studying at the Ecole des Beaux-Arts in Paris, had proposed in a letter to a friend that some system of expert guidance be provided in the museum's galleries. This he finally brought about, for, in addition to achieving a long-talked-about lecture room and *Handbook* during his year as Temporary Director, there appeared in the June 1906 *Bulletin* an article, "The Educational Work of the Museum. Retrospect and Prospect," which concluded:

> It has been proposed to the Trustees to consider the permanent appointment of one or more persons of intelligence and education who could act as intermediaries between Curators and the many who would be glad to avail themselves of trained instruction in our galleries. Through these *docents*, as it has been proposed to call them, the heads of departments could instruct many more persons than it would be possible for them to accompany through the galleries; and the illustrated lectures upon the collections prepared in the departments might be regularly given by these specially qualified aids both in the Museum and in the class rooms of neighboring schools and colleges.

The pretentious word "docent," at once advertising familiarity with an ancient language and vaguely suggesting a Trollopean church functionary, began to be used in the eighteen nineties by some American universities in obvious emulation of the German *privat-docent*, that is, a private teacher recognized by a university. I suspect its adaptation to museums to have been an inspiration of Benjamin Ives Gilman, Secretary of the Museum. At least in an essay reprinted in his *Museum Ideals of Purpose and Method*, published by the Museum of Fine Arts in 1918, he lapsed into seventeenth-century English to say that a museum fulfills its purpose "as it is *gardant* and *monstrant*; as it preserves and exhibits," but that a third adjective is necessary to express the full day of a museum. "Reserving the word *monstrant* for presentation to the bodily eye, we need another for the sharpening of the spiritual sight." That Gilman found in a phrase of Archbishop Laud: "The Church here is taken for the Church as it is docent and regent; as it teaches and governs," which permitted him to suggest that "a museum performs its complete office as it is at once *gardant, monstrant,* and *docent.*" Thus this third adjective happily entered the vocabulary of the Museum of Fine Arts in 1906, as it might not have done had the following quatrain by David McCord, entitled "History of Education," been written in time:

> The decent docent doesn't doze:
> He teaches standing on his toes.
> His student dassn't doze — and does,
> And that's what teaching is and was.

But as David McCord was only eight years old when Gilman sprang this invention, there was no one available to laugh it out of use.

The April 1907 *Bulletin,* which appeared while Gilman was Temporary Director, announced the creation of the office of Docent and the appointment thereto of Garrick M. Borden (B.S. Cornell University 1901, M.A. 1902) who had, after three years as an extension-course lecturer on the history of art at the University of California, become Assistant to the Secretary. It was stated that "The Docent will give any visitor what information he possesses about any or all of the collections. Visitors having special interests will be aided in pursuing them; those desiring to see the whole Museum at one visit will be guided to the principal objects without loss of time; for those interested in the newest accessions the Docent may have data not yet published." Arthur Rotch had jestingly observed in 1880 that we had not yet reached the height of civilization that included greeting at the museum entrance "by an obsequious and shabby individual who offers to explain the collections in one's native tongue," but in 1907 we were achieving the didactic utopia of personally conducted guidance without fee by a literate person appointed for the purpose. This was, according to Gilman, a Boston innovation, soon adopted by the American Museum of Natural History and the Metropolitan Museum, and in 1911 by the British Museum.

Appointments with the Docent were to be made by letter, or in person at the entrance for any hour not previously engaged, on Tuesday, Thursday, and Saturday mornings. Parties were limited to ten persons, and the Docent could be retained for only an hour, unless no one else were waiting for him. Gilman disclaimed any appropriate relation between the conventional methods of school instruction and the docent system. A museum of art, standing for absolute excellence and seeking to preserve only the best of the past, has the duty to aid its visitors "to assimilate certain of the highest achievements of minds at once mature and especially gifted." In consequence,

> The essential office of the docent is to get the object thoroughly perceived by the disciple. Hence, draw attention *to* the object first; talk *about* it afterwards, and only if occasion offers. In the words of François Coppée, "Voir d'abord; ensuite, savoir," else your auditor's attention will be divided between trying to decipher the object and trying to follow you. Again, the admiration of the docent is like the latent fire of a match, imprisoned in his head, and not effective without an interlocutor as igniting surface, and even an auditor beside as tinder. When these are seen to in advance, there will nearly always be an extended blaze. Hence, let the docent of a group provide himself at the start with a questioner (to be kept within bounds) and a hearer. Again, a formal talk upon a work of art may to advantage be repeated, but only up to the point at which further repetition does not improve it. This point will be reached after not very many repetitions.

G. M. Borden had as fellow-Docent L. Earle Rowe, Assistant in the Egyptian Department; in the last three months of 1907 they guided some 437 visitors. To drum up trade, placards announcing the museum's docent service were distributed in January 1908 among hotels, clubs, friendly and charitable societies, schools, libraries, "and other places of general resort in Boston and neighboring cities and towns," while C. H. Collester and Henry L. Seaver of the English Department at M.I.T. volunteered to act as Docents on Saturday and Sunday afternoons during the winter. Professor Seaver was an especially happy choice, for he was a learned and kindly man of wide interests; a student of Spanish Renaissance history and an amateur printer, among other things, he is still a much beloved honorary member of the Massachusetts Historical Society. In the February 1908 *Bulletin* a recent remark of Woodrow Wilson's about the preceptorial system at Princeton in relation to library work was quoted, with the observation that it applied *mutatis mutandis* to docent service in an art museum. President Wilson had written: "The chief and most characteristic object of library endeavor is to get men to read the best books and into the habit of reading . . . In the very process of doing this, they [the preceptors] guide to the best method of reading as well as to the best reading, and fulfill . . . the precise ideal after which librarians have been striving." This Benjamin Ives Gilman adapted to describe docent service: "The chief and most characteristic object of a museum endeavor is to get people to see the best art and into the habit of seeing it . . . In the very process of doing this they (the docents) guide to the best method of seeing as well as to the best sights, and fulfill . . . the precise ideal after which museums have been striving."

Another approach began in January 1908 with a winter series of Thursday afternoon conferences in the galleries, at which curators and visiting scholars discussed aspects of the collections. Subjects and speakers were announced in advance in the *Bulletin*; free tickets to the extent of seats available in limited space were to be had on application by letter or on the preceding Monday at the door. These conferences soon expanded beyond Thursdays. In March 1908 the new Director, Arthur Fairbanks, conducted a conference in the Bartlett Room on "Athenian White Lekythoi" on the 5th and 10th; Frank Gair Macomber spoke on Chinese pottery in the Textile Gallery on the 12th and 14th; Professor George Foot Moore of Harvard on "Egyptian Tombs and Burial Customs" in the First Egyptian Room on the 19th, 21st, and 24th, and Okakura-Kakuzo on "Chinese and Japanese Mirrors" in the Japanese Cabinet on the 26th and 28th. Furthermore the Committee on the Utilization of Museums of Art at Schools and Colleges, based at Simmons College, of which President Eliot was chairman and Matthew S. Prichard had become secretary for a year after leaving the museum, offered lecture courses for teachers beginning in 1906. When Simmons College withdrew financial support from this venture, the Museum of Fine Arts in

1908–9 offered two "Collegiate Courses," a half-course on the observation of pictures by Miss Alicia M. Keyes and a full course on the history of art given jointly by the Director and by Assistant Professor George H. Chase of Harvard University. Two colleges in the vicinity accepted these for credit by regularly matriculated students, while teachers in the Boston public schools were permitted to substitute such work for a regular promotional examination. The experiment was repeated in 1909–10, with a course on design by Dr. Denman W. Ross substituted for the history of ancient art. It will be recalled that Ross, in addition to being a trustee, collector, and immense benefactor of the museum, had been in his capacity as a painter, Lecturer on the Theory of Design at Harvard since 1899. In 1910 the Museum of Fine Arts joined with Harvard University and other institutions in the region to establish University Extension Courses that were generally accepted for academic credit. Thus in the year 1910–11 two quarter-courses were offered at the museum under the auspices of the Committee on Extension Courses: Garrick M. Borden's "Moslem Art and Civilization" and Arthur Fairbanks' "The Mythology of Greece and Rome."

Once the Huntington Avenue building was open all the educational activities begun in Copley Square were resumed with renewed zest. Each Sunday afternoon in certain departments docents were in attendance to give a gallery talk and guide visitors through the rooms. The areas dealt with varied from week to week so that there might always remain some departments in which visitors who did not take kindly to instruction might be left wholly to themselves. While some members of the staff occasionally acted as Sunday Docents, they could not be expected regularly to appear seven days a week. Thus these talks were chiefly by learned friends of the museum. Gilman as Secretary was theoretically responsible, but these arrangements were chiefly in charge of Professor Seaver, who was not only present every Sunday but himself gave more than twenty talks in different departments in the course of 1910. The Harvard faculty lent a hand too, for on 8 May 1910 President Eliot spoke in the East Court (among the Greek casts) on "The Training of the Senses and the Artistic Spirit"; on 17 July, Assistant Professor Arthur Pope considered "Dutch Interior Painting of the Seventeenth Century" in the Dutch-

Flemish Room; and on 6 November, Professor Ralph Barton Perry spoke in the Fourth Century Room on "The Relation of Greek Philosophy to Greek Art." Assistant Professor George H. Chase dealt with Greek painted vases on 10 July, while the Reverend Henry S. Nash of the Episcopal Theological School spoke on "Greek Art and the Gospel of Freedom" in the First Marble Room on 13 November. Charles Knowles Bolton, Librarian of the Boston Athenæum, described the paintings in the Early American Room on 3 July, and on 2 October spoke in the Library on "The Pictures of Rembrandt Illustrating His Home Life." Charles Hopkinson led visitors on a circuit through the picture galleries on 22 May and 10 July, while the woodcarver I. Kirchmayer on 27 November spoke in the Rotunda on the figures and ornaments that he had carved for the pulpit and reredos of Detroit Cathedral. The new Detroit reredos was also discussed on 6 November by the Byzantinist Professor Thomas Whittemore, who had on two Sundays earlier in the year given guidance in the Department of Egyptian Art. Eighteen gallery conferences were given on weekday afternoons in the course of 1910, mostly by staff members, although Francis Bullard, Chairman of the Visiting Committee and a distinguished print collector, conducted one in the Print Department.

Outside of the Sunday talks, some 237 lectures and other exercises, attended by 5,958 persons, were held at the museum during the course of 1910. Docent Service was provided to 3,611 persons, consisting of 119 school and college classes containing 2,221 persons, 67 parties from other organizations totaling 1,014, as well as 376 unorganized visitors. As the three regularly assigned Docents were outnumbered, most officers of the museum pitched in to help in emergencies, as became even more necessary in 1911 when 4,046 persons availed themselves of Docent service.

Although all these varied efforts had been aimed at serious instruction, one of the trustees, Theodore N. Vail, was seized with the desire to make the museum a place of recreation for slum children. Through funds that he supplied, a trained storyteller, Miss Dorothy Hopkins, was engaged. Each morning at 9:30 for two and a half months during the summer of 1911, fifty children, brought from settlement houses and school playgrounds, assembled in the lecture hall. In the course of an hour, slides of three or four paintings or pieces of sculpture were thrown on the screen; Miss Hopkins told a story inspired by each piece. The children were then taken to see the objects, given a postcard of one of them, and transported back from whence they had come. This practice was continued in succeeding summers until 1919. As Italians had been the mainstay of Sunday crowds in Copley Square, on November and December Sunday afternoons in 1911 the experiment of providing free cars and an Italian guide to bring selected groups from the North End to the new museum was tried. This benevolent effort was abandoned at the end of the year when funds ran out.

As Benjamin Ives Gilman, who had started the Docent service in 1907, was too occupied with other duties to continue it, the architect Huger Elliott, recently of the Rhode Island School of Design, was appointed in 1912 to the new post of Supervisor of Educational Work, as well as to new duties at the Museum School. Through the end of 1914, the period covered by this chapter, Elliott carried on along the lines inaugurated by Gilman. Docent service, conferences, University Extension courses continued. Henry L. Seaver carried the greatest share of the Sunday talks and guidance. While general museum attendance was falling once the novelty of the new building wore thin, the number of people coming to lectures and conferences rose. Docents accompanied only 2,334 persons in 1912, in contrast to 4,046 the previous year but in 1913 the figure went up to 3,368, and in 1914 to 3,385. In January 1914 Huger Elliott began the experiment of a course of twenty evening lectures on practical application of artistic principles for a group of twenty-five salesmen from Boston stores.

There are few efforts that the most "community minded" promoter of 1970 could devise that the Museum of Fine Arts did not try during its first five years in Huntington Avenue, yet virtue is not its own reward, at least immediately, for this was a period of decreasing income and mounting deficits. But the aims of this pioneering effort in gallery instruction were intellectual and disinterested, for, as Huger Elliott remarked in his first report as Supervisor of Educational Work, "Mr. Gilman's criterion that 'Docent service is not guidance, but companionship' has been faithfully upheld." I know this from personal experience, for I have remembered vividly for half a century a gallery conference given by Benjamin Ives Gilman on 31 December 1919 that I attended as a schoolboy of fourteen. The announced subject was "Thoughts for St. Sylvester's Day"; the scene the old Gothic Room, today's A-3 transformed out of all recognition for the exhibition of Indian sculpture. The medieval objects displayed there in 1919 were neither numerous nor very remarkable. Although electric lighting had been installed in the galleries in 1913, through the gift of a trustee who modestly concealed his identity, it was not turned on that afternoon — I suspect deliberately. A few people sat and listened attentively as the last snowy light of that bleak December afternoon glimmered on a few pieces of Gothic carving in gray stone. The lean, gentle, gray-bearded scholar said little about the objects, but somehow conveyed to me his conviction that the last day of the year — traditionally the feast of St. Sylvester, Pope from 314 to 355, during which the Roman Empire became Christian through the conversion of Constantine — was an appropriate time for reflective retrospection in such surroundings. So skillfully did he convey this that I have, whenever possible in the succeeding decades, returned to the Museum of Fine Arts on the last day of the year to recall that bleak but memorable afternoon. Gilman was not a "decent docent"; he was an inspired one, for neither I nor anyone else dozed. Any man who could convey so subtly to others this sense of companionship with the arts should be permitted the whimsy of borrowing an obsolete seventeenth-century adjective from William Laud. Henry P. Rossiter, who joined the museum staff in the year when I heard "Thoughts for St. Sylvester's Day," recently recalled how Gilman,

who often sent around little admonitory clichés about overcoming one's mistakes by doing better next time, etc., never tired of reminding us that the Museum was not a dead place, that most of its important objects were created from emotion at a boiling point, or from high spirits and affection, and could more properly be appreciated by dancing in front of them than by pondering them with solemnity or bewilderment; consequently, when in January or February, about 1921, it was proposed to open the Museum occasionally in the evening, he suggested a dance. But only the painting galleries were opened, with their dreary lighting, and instead of a dance, about twenty Back Bay ladies came in their best Queen Mary bibs and tuckers, with their men folk in tails and white ties, to promenade or chat for an hour. No music, no refreshments, no new paintings to look at. It was Art for Art's sake, and it didn't take.

The increase of activities in the new museum required a corresponding increase in staff. When Arthur Fairbanks became Director in 1907, he assumed also the duties of Curator of Classical Art, with an Assistant Curator, at first Sidney N. Deane and from 1908 Lacey D. Caskey, attending to the routine affairs of the department. In 1912 Caskey, who received a Yale Ph.D. that year, was appointed Curator, while in 1913 Morris Carter left the library to become Assistant Director, a post that had not been filled since Matthew S. Prichard's demotion seven years before. Foster Stearns (Amherst 1903) then became Librarian. In 1911 John Ellerton Lodge joined the Department of Chinese and Japanese Art, becoming in 1912 Assistant Curator. After the premature death of Okakura-Kakuzo, Lodge took temporary charge of the department, of which he was appointed Curator in 1915.

The major accessions of the Egyptian, Classical, and the Chinese and Japanese departments through 1914 have already been touched upon. It remains to consider the activities during this period of the Department of Prints and what were then called the Collections of Western Art. Emil H. Richter, who had been in actual charge of the Print Department since the illness of S. R. Koehler in 1899, continued as Curator *pro tempore* for several years. He had little of his predecessor's flair and flourish, and tended to get headaches or take to his bed when some trying piece of work had to be undertaken. It was characteristic that, as the cataloguing and mounting of the Harvey D. Parker Collection progressed, Richter had marked the mounts with a blind stamp from 1 to 20 in each print solander box, indicating that the work was finished and that the collection for all practical purposes would not be added to! On the credit side of the ledger, however, should be noted that Richter arranged the first important loan exhibition of early American engravings, held from 12 December 1904 to 5 February 1905. *A Descriptive Catalogue of an Exhibition of Early American Engraving* that he prepared at this time is still regarded with affection and respect by some collectors in the field. The prints shown were largely borrowed, Charles E. Goodspeed being the greatest lender, although George R. Barrett, Miss Alice F. Brooks, Dr. Charles E. Clark, Frederick L. Gay, Z. T. Hollingsworth, Frederick James Libbie, Henry S. Rowe, and D. McN. Stauffer each lent more than a score from their collections.

Possibly because of the interest aroused by this important exhibition, Emil H. Richter was appointed Curator of Prints, as of 1 January 1905, and given six months' leave with pay for study in Europe, through the generosity of Francis Bullard, a collector who had shown continuing interest in the museum. In many American cities self-made men have turned to collecting works of art as an appurtenance to their new place in the world; in Boston many of the great collectors have been men and women of inherited wealth, not necessarily enormous in terms of contemporary American fortunes, who have made collecting the major interest of their lives. The relation of three sons of the East India merchant William Story Bullard to the Department of Prints is a case in point. From their father's ships they had inherited the possibility of leisure; from their mother's brother, Charles Eliot Norton, a deep interest in the arts.

The oldest, William Norton Bullard (Harvard A.B. 1875, M.D. 1880), practiced medicine and became a great collector of medical incunabula. His books, which he gave to the Boston Medical Library, now have a distinguished place in the Francis A. Countway Library of Medicine at the Harvard Medical School. Stephen Bullard (Harvard A.B. 1878) entered the Harvard Law School, but withdrew because of illness in the middle of his second year. After two years of travel in Europe in search of health, he settled down to the quiet life of an invalid in Boston and Lenox. The youngest of the three, Francis Bullard (Harvard A.B. 1886, A.M. 1904), although more active than Stephen in travel, was never strong. Considering himself "essentially a student of philosophy and art," he wrote in 1911 in the twenty-fifth anniversary report of his Harvard class:

> My life in Boston is an uneventful one. My interests are my friends and the Museum of Fine Arts.

Inspired by my uncle, Charles Eliot Norton, I have been gathering together for the last ten years a number of fine prints, and my collection of Turner's Liber Studiorum is well known by collectors on both sides of the water.

When Visiting Committees were first appointed in 1906, Francis Bullard was named Chairman of that assigned to the Department of Prints.

At the beginning of 1907 Emil H. Richter attempted to arouse an interest in prints by giving a series of illustrated lectures on the development of the graphic arts first to the staff of the museum and then to the Visiting Committee. Accessions were relatively few and chiefly by gift, for there were no funds available for purchases. In 1908 he wrote rather plaintively:

> The Print Department stands greatly in need of two things: an annual allowance, be it ever so modest, and the privilege of sale of duplicates, and exchange of impressions by the Curator. With a fixed sum on hand every year, and with the possibility of weeding out inferior impressions or superfluous duplicate material and acquiring in their place prints of greater merit, the collection would be placed upon a basis of healthy growth which is at present entirely lacking. It is clear that even the slenderest means of purchase would bring the Department into communication with the market, with the commercial side of collecting, and would fit your Curator to answer inquiries and give advice in a sphere where the Museum is the one impartial adviser to whom the inexperienced can appeal.

As permission for the sale of duplicate prints was granted by the trustees, auction sales were held in Boston in November 1909 and in January and March 1910, the proceeds being set aside for new purchases, which would be recorded as the gifts of the donors of duplicates that had been sold. Thus in the spring of 1910 Richter was able to attend several important European auctions and acquire nearly fifty prints, among which were works of Holbein, Dürer, Altdorfer, Schongauer, Cranach, Rembrandt, and Nanteuil. Further help came following the death of Stephen Bullard in 1909, for he bequeathed a fund of $25,000 for the use of the Department of

Prints, the income of which, while primarily for purchases, might also be used to assist the Curator in his studies.

Francis Bullard in 1909 gave eleven Whistler lithographs and a series of woodcut illustrations of the Old Testament by Hans Holbein the younger. The following year he gave in memory of his uncle Charles Eliot Norton an extensive set of proofs and selected early impressions of the *Picturesque Views of England and Wales*, engraved after water colors by J. M. W. Turner. Many of the proofs showed Turner's corrections and directions to the engraver. In 1911 twenty-seven proofs of Turner's engravings to illustrate Lord Byron's works were purchased through the Stephen Bullard Fund, while Francis Bullard lent for exhibition his own collection of the Liber Studiorum and other Turner mezzotints.

Through funds raised by the Visiting Committee, additional help was obtained for the Department of Prints in 1911, while in 1912 the services were obtained of FitzRoy Carrington, a partner in the New York firm of print dealers, Messrs. Frederick Keppel and Company, and editor of *The Print Collectors' Quarterly*, which they published. As Richter wished to be relieved of administrative duties to devote more time to study, he took the title of Associate Curator. Carrington severed his business ties in New York, becoming Curator of the Department of Prints on 1 March 1913, and the following year a Lecturer on the History of Engraving at Harvard University. The Keppel firm having presented ownership of *The Print Collector's Quarterly* to the Museum of Fine Arts, Carrington continued to edit it, with Houghton Mifflin Company acting as distributors until 1920, when the periodical was transferred to an English publisher.

Francis Bullard died on 6 February 1913, in his early fifties, bequeathing the museum a substantial portion of his collection. Although the majority of the 1815 prints received from him were related to J. M. W. Turner, there were eleven proofs of Holbein's *Dance of Death*, thirty-four proof impressions of woodcuts by Albrecht Dürer, a magnificent example of Mantegna's *Battle of the Sea-Gods*, and sixty mezzotints by David Lucas after Constable, which were chiefly proofs of the *English Landscapes* series. Of the bulk of the collection, FitzRoy Carrington wrote:

BATTLE OF THE SEA-GODS (left half). Engraving by Andrea Mantegna.
Bequest of Francis Bullard in memory of Stephen Bullard, 1913.

The set of the "Liber Studiorum" is the finest and most comprehensive ever brought together, consisting, as it does, of 107 preliminary etchings, among them states hitherto unknown, 225 proofs, of which 41 are touched and annotated by Turner. Among these are a number of unique impressions. Moreover, there are 98 first states and almost as many later states; in all 535 prints. The wealth of this collection will appear from the fact that the "Liber Studiorum" was to have comprised 100 plates, but was abandoned when 71 had been published, the balance being left in all stages of incompletion; some were never carried further than the drawing.

A small, unpublished series of pure mezzotints by Turner himself, known as the "Little Liber," or "Sequel to the Liber," beautiful and exceedingly rare, are represented by 25 proofs, successive in many instances, and photographs of two unique prints not in the collection.

The remainder of the bequest, comprising 1,150 prints, covers Turner's illustrative activities from the *Copperplate Magazine* of 1794 to the plates by Lupton, Sir Frank Short, and others done long after his death.

THE CASTLE ABOVE THE MEADOWS. Etching by J. M. W. Turner
from the Liber Studiorum. *Bequest of Francis Bullard. 1913.*

The bequest was briefly described in the June 1913 *Bulletin*. A
*Catalogue of the Collection of Prints from the Liber Studiorum of
James Mallord William Turner Formed by the Late Francis Bullard
of Boston, Massachusetts, and Bequeathed by Him to the Museum
of Fine Arts in Boston* was handsomely printed in 1915 by the
Merrymount Press in an edition of three hundred copies for private
distribution by Grenville L. Winthrop as a memorial to the collector.

Following the death of Francis Bullard, his sister Miss Katherine
Eliot Bullard became a member of the department's Visiting Committee, while George Peabody Gardner (Harvard A.B. 1877), financier and director of many industrial corporations, who was a nephew
of John Lowell Gardner, became its chairman. Paul Joseph Sachs
(Harvard A.B. 1900) of New York, who was also appointed to the
committee, promptly helped remedy some of the department's defi-
ciencies by the gift of 216 prints, including some of the sixteenth
and seventeenth centuries, as well as lithographs by Raffet, Prout,
and Albert Sterner, and many American wood engravings. Also
through Carrington's ties, David Keppel of New York gave 374
prints of relatively recent French and English artists as a memorial
to his father, Frederick Keppel, who had come from the south of

JUNCTION OF SEVERN AND WYE. Drawn, etched, and engraved by J. M. W. Turner from the Liber Studiorum. *Bequest of Francis Bullard, 1913.*

Ireland and, after a period of farming in Canada and selling books in New York, had established the first major firm of print dealers in the United States.

Four months after his arrival, FitzRoy Carrington began work on an engraver's catalogue of the prints in the Museum of Fine Arts in connection with a similar effort at the Fogg Art Museum. This placed on cards the name of the engraver, the title of the print, its designer, its number in standard books of reference, and its museum registry number, process, and size. Each museum prepared duplicate cards for its holdings so that the catalogue of both collections would be easily accessible in Boston and Cambridge. By the end of 1913, 41,889 cards (including the duplicates) had been prepared, covering 9,030 prints in the Museum of Fine Arts, and 13,783 at the Fogg.

Carrington was full of life and activity. He began to raise money from many of his former clients at Keppel's not only for acquisitions, but for projects that would assist scholars. With funds supplied by Felix M. Warburg, he had Donald Macbeth of London photograph all fifteenth-century prints in European museums that had not already been published. These photographs, which were sold in sets at cost to other institutions, were a major contribution to the apparatus of print study. Arthur M. Hind of the British Museum, for example, found them invaluable when he came to rewrite his history of Italian engraving in the fifteenth century.

In 1914 David Keppel added 74 prints to the collection in memory of his father, while Miss Katherine Bullard gave 45 Goya aquatints of the *Caprichos* and *Proverbios* series. Although the Department of Prints was moving to new quarters, in which its possessions would be hung on the walls of rooms of suitable size, rather than "exhibited"

ASSUMPTION OF THE VIRGIN. Anonymous Florentine engraving, after Botticelli. *James Fund, 1915.*

LALVNA EPIANETA, FEMNINOPOSTO NEPRIMO CIELO FREDA HE VMIDA, ET FLIMATICHA M
EIANA TRALMONDO ZVPERIORE ET LOIMFENORE AMA LAGEOMETRIA ET CIO CHEAE2ZA
ZA PARTIENE DIFACCIA TONDA DIZTRA MEGANA METALLI ALARGIENTO BELLE CHONP
MFLE2EIONI LAFREA DETENPI ELVEFANO DEGLIELEMENTI LASVA ILLDI 2VO EILVEHERDI CH
ONLAHORA PRIMA 8 IFE2 Z ELA2VA NOTTE ERVELLA DELVENEREIA AMICO 2VO 8 GIOVE M
IMICO MARTEA VNA 2OLA ABITATIOILE ELCHANCHERO PRE2O A2OLE EME'M'RCHVRIO LAFEN
TASIONE EVA EILTAVRO LAMORTE OVEROVMILIATIONE EICONRIO VA M L2 EENGNI IN 2 8 COMICIANDO
DALOVANCHO IN2 E EI LAVIN EENCHRO ISGRADI FERN I Z MIN TH EECONDO FEMOENA MN 3 EE ADE2CO
EIE 2B I2 EENGNI CHONMVDAMEIFE EFIV BGFADM 26 MINVTH E2O 2ECHONDIE 4VE2TO 2IOIMOEFA
CHE FARTENDOEI LALVNA DAIOLE E TORNANDO AL LOFA2ZA FER F MIHV TIE 1M 2ECHONDI INE
DEE IFORE EGVEETO 2ICONDO EMOVIMENTO DIMAEO

PLANET LUNA. Anonymous
Florentine engraving. *Special
Print Fund, 1915.*

in museum cases, the Curator lectured at Harvard, edited *The Print
Collector's Quarterly*, and spent three months of summer study in
England. During his travels he was able to buy from the income of
the Stephen Bullard Fund a set of the Piranesi *Prisons* in the very
rare first state, and a Florentine engraving of about 1470 illustrating
Petrarch, entitled *The Triumph of Love.* The connection of the
Bullard family with the Department of Prints extended well beyond
the limits of this chapter, for in 1921, after the death of Miss
Katherine Bullard, her cousin Miss Ellen Bullard joined the Visiting
Committee. And in 1923 Dr. William Norton Bullard gave 376
prints and drawings that he had inherited a decade earlier from his
brother Francis, which were described in the October 1923 *Bulletin*
as "the most important gift of equal range which the Museum has
received since the acquisition of the Sewall-Parker prints in 1897."
Extending in time over many centuries, this gift included Dürers,
Mantegnas, and Rembrandts of conspicuous quality, Piranesis, an

BACCHANALIAN GROUP AT A WINE PRESS. Engraving by Andrea Mantegna.
Gift of William Norton Bullard, 1923.

early impression of William Blake's *Canterbury Pilgrims*, and works of Muirhead Bone, Whistler, Zorn, and other recent artists.

When the present museum opened late in 1909 the general catch-all known as the Collections of Western Art had never had a curator. It operated under the direction of John Briggs Potter, Keeper of Paintings, and two ladies, Miss Sarah Gore Flint, Assistant in Charge of Textiles, and Miss Florence Virginia Paull, Assistant in Charge of Other Collections. In 1910 Frank Gair Macomber was appointed Honorary Curator of the Department of Western Art (except Paintings and Textiles). (The museum long had in this area a passion for carefully descriptive titles of great length, which defied euphonious abbreviation in the manner of the New Deal and the Pentagon.) In the same year certain anonymous friends promised to contribute annually for three years a sum sufficient to provide the salary of a Curator of Paintings of established reputation. In 1911 the post was filled by Jean Guiffrey, Adjunct Curator of Paintings at the Louvre, to whom the French government had cooperatively given leave of absence for three years. As a condition of his coming, $100,000 a year was pledged for two years from private contributions and museum funds for the purchase of paintings. Guiffrey arrived in Boston in April 1911; early in May Mrs. Robert Dawson Evans offered to build that part of the proposed wing on the Fenway that was designed to contain the picture galleries, as a memorial to her husband who had been a trustee from 24 May 1907 until his death on 6 July 1909. Thus the second stage of building, which will be described in the following chapter, was to begin before the finances and operation of the first had been adequately stabilized. Nevertheless, the offer was gratefully accepted, and a Building Committee consisting of Henry S. Hunnewell, chairman, Alexander Wadsworth Longfellow, George Robert White, President Lane, and Mrs. Evans promptly appointed. Excavation began 21 December 1911.

The prospect of achieving the permanent galleries provided for in Guy Lowell's plan spurred interest in the new Curator's acquisitions. Guiffrey spent the early summer of 1911 in Europe, where he secured a portrait by Andrea Solario of Giovanni Bentivoglio from the Abdy Collection in London, landscapes by Francesco Guardi and Thomas Gainsborough, a 1549 Lucas Cranach portrait of a lady from the Thiem Collection of San Remo, and the 1829 portrait of the Marquis de Pastoret by Paul Delaroche, purchased in Paris at the sale of the Pierre Decourcelle Collection. For the American section Frederic Porter Vinton's *The River Loing near Grez* was purchased just before the artist's death, while Walter Gay's interior of the great salon of the Palazzo Barbaro was bought. In July 1911 a temporary exhibition of 45 paintings by Claude Monet, mostly owned by Boston friends and neighbors, was arranged to represent the several phases of the artist's career from 1876 to 1907. In November the Renaissance plaster casts of the west court were concealed by screens to provide space for a memorial exhibition of Vinton's work.

During two trips to Europe in 1912 Guiffrey succeeded in filling other gaps in the museum's collection. At the sale of the Weber Collection in Berlin a triptych by the early sixteenth-century Cologne painter known as the Master of St. Severin was acquired. A Florentine cassone panel by Jacopo del Sellaio of the story of Cupid and Psyche was the first Italian Renaissance picture of a secular subject,

MARQUIS DE PASTORET, CHANCELLOR OF FRANCE.
Hippolyte Delaroche, called Paul. *Picture Fund, 1911.*
11.1449

other than portraits, to enter the museum. A Claude Lorrain *Parnassus* was the most distinguished acquisition of this year, although Gainsborough's portrait of John Eld and John Singleton Copley's *A Triumph of Galatea* were purchased, as well as 22 water colors and drawings by John La Farge and 45 water colors by John Singer Sargent. The following year were purchased a Madonna by Bramantino and Turner's large *The Falls of the Rhine at Schaffhausen,* which made a happy companion to his *Slave Ship* and the Francis Bullard prints.

Mrs. Horatio Nelson Slater, a daughter of William Morris Hunt, offered in 1910 to furnish a room above the library to provide a gallery in memory of her father, to contain principally works by him. In order to reach this attic floor, high above the main galleries, a passenger elevator was built. The William Morris Hunt Memorial Gallery, opened on 4 March 1914, permitted the showing of all of his paintings and drawings owned by the museum, pictures permanently deposited by Mrs. Slater — including the *Gloucester Harbor*, which was given her for this purpose by Mrs. John L. Gardner — as well as paintings lent by the Hunt Estate and by owners outside the family.

With the expiration of Jean Guiffrey's leave from the Louvre on 31 March 1914 and the outbreak of war in August, energetic collection ceased again for a time. John Briggs Potter, Keeper of Paintings,

INTERIOR OF THE PALAZZO BARBARO.   Walter Gay.   *Charles Henry Hayden Fund.*
11.1537

FREDERIC PORTER VINTON MEMORIAL EXHIBITION. A 1911 instance of the
temporary adaptation of the Renaissance Cast Court for special exhibitions.

was again the only staff member of what had been described since
Guiffrey's arrival as the Department of Paintings. The rest of Western art continued in the active care of the Misses Flint and Paull
with Frank Gair Macomber's title simplified to the inelegant one of
Honorary Curator (Miscellaneous Collections). The 1912 annual
report first listed a Division of Western Art with Macomber as
Honorary Curator and the ladies still burdened with their descriptive
handles. In the 1914 report the title was changed to Department of
Western Art, with Hervey Edward Wetzel (Harvard A.B. 1911),
a student of Persian and Indian art, added as Associate of the Department. This evolution had followed to some extent the interests of
members of the Visiting Committees, for from the beginning there
had been three separate groups for Western Art. The committee for
paintings, of which Dr. Arthur Tracy Cabot was chairman, had
included Holker Abbott, Mrs. Robert Dawson Evans, Mrs. Walter
Scott Fitz, and the painter Edmund C. Tarbell. Dr. Denman W.
Ross, who was almost singlehandedly responsible for the fast growing
collection of textiles, was chairman of a separate Western Art:

Textiles Committee, while J. Templeman Coolidge headed a Western Art: Other Collections Committee.

The presence on the latter committee of such pioneer collectors of early American decorative arts as Dudley Leavitt Pickman, Henry Davis Sleeper, and Charles Hitchcock Tyler led to increased showing of local works. In 1906 the Museum of Fine Arts held a loan exhibition of 336 pieces of early American silver, and published a catalogue with an introduction on Massachusetts silversmiths by R. T. H. Halsey. (It might be noted that the simultaneous Hudson-Fulton Exhibition at the Metropolitan Museum had contained 273 pieces.) When the new museum opened, a selection of the 233 pieces of silver, lent by twenty-three Massachusetts churches, was displayed in the Eighteenth Century Room. A note in the February 1910 *Bulletin* reported that letters had been sent to many other local churches inviting deposits of further pieces, particularly those that were seldom if ever in current use. In less than two months twelve more churches

CORFU: LIGHT AND SHADOWS. Water color by John Singer Sargent, 1909. *Charles Henry Hayden Fund. 12.207*

responded. During the summer of 1911 a loan exhibition of about 1,200 pieces was shown in the Rotunda. The catalogue, which reproduced about a third of the objects, contained an essay on Connecticut silversmiths by George M. Curtis of Meriden, which was a counterpart to Halsey's essay of 1906 on Massachusetts craftsmen. With such evidence of growing interest, some churches made outright gifts of their silver. The October 1911 *Bulletin* announced the gift of a Joseph Edwards beaker of 1768 by the First Congregational Church of Hanover, Massachusetts. Previously the only pieces owned by the museum had been eight given by the West Church in Boston upon its dissolution in 1892. In May 1912 the New South Church of Boston gave eight pieces of communion silver. Although lack of material in its own collection and of space for the proper showing of loans had hampered any attempts to display satisfactorily either European or American furniture, an exhibition of *Colonial Furniture and Glass*, lent by Francis H. Bigelow of Cambridge, was arranged in the Forecourt Room from the end of May to 1 November 1912. This first effort at showing furniture was described and illustrated in the August 1912 *Bulletin*.

Gardiner Martin Lane, President since 1907, died at the age of fifty-five on 3 October 1914. Within the month, Morris Gray (Harvard A.B. 1877, LL.B. 1880), who had been a member of the board since 1902, was elected to fill the vacancy. As the new painting galleries were about to be opened, Gray concluded his first report with a statement of needs apart from annual subscriptions. These were an Administration Fund of at least $1,000,000 in order to pay all annual operating expenses, including those of the new wing; larger funds for the purchase of works of art; and a fund of $100,000 for the development of the Library. But having said this, he concluded:

> While I think it suitable to express in this way certain of the needs and opportunities of the Museum, I think it entirely unsuitable to appeal to friends of the Museum at this time for these large contributions of money. The great shrinkage of income and principal due to financial conditions and the very grave need of humanity, not only on this side of the water but on the other bid us stand aside.

Yet even in the present stress there must be people in the community who are so much interested in the Museum that, despite their generosity to these deeper needs, they may still be able, still be willing to give to the Museum. If such there be I am certain that I speak for the Trustees when I say that the Museum will feel only a deeper gratitude for gifts at this time.

CHAPTER X

The Evans Wing and Paintings

The second stage of construction, which enlarged the exhibition space of the Museum of Fine Arts by 40 percent, was completed only five years after the first, through a single gift. It will be recalled that Guy Lowell's plan had called for a block of picture galleries, fronting on the Fenway, connected with the existing building by a Tapestry Gallery leading out of the Rotunda. Mrs. Robert Dawson Evans had written Gardiner M. Lane on 8 May 1911 offering to give the picture galleries called for in this plan, with no other stipulation than that a tablet be placed on the stairway indicating that the building was given in loving memory of her husband who had been briefly a trustee of the museum.

This gift has made the name of Robert Dawson Evans familiar to thousands of Bostonians for more than half a century, but as he was not included in the *Dictionary of American Biography* little has been remembered of his remarkable career, which exemplified the opportunities open to the imaginative and the industrious in the last third of the nineteenth century. Although born in St. John, New Brunswick, on 30 September 1843, he was brought to Boston soon after birth when his family, like so many others from the Maritime Provinces, crossed the frontier into New England. After attending public school in Boston, Evans became a clerk in the Hall Rubber

Company. In spite of being only seventeen when the Civil War broke out, he enlisted in the 13th Massachusetts Volunteers, was commissioned captain in a black regiment, but was so badly wounded in the second battle of Bull Run that he was invalided home for good. He returned to a job with Charles M. Clapp's Aetna Rubber Mills in Jamaica Plain. In 1867 he married Maria Antoinette, the daughter of Mr. and Mrs. David Hunt; three years later he became a partner in Clapp, Evans and Company, which operated the Aetna Mills. The American Rubber Company which he organized in 1877 with a capital of $200,000 was one of the concerns later embraced by the United States Rubber Company which, on its formation with a capital of $50,000,000, was the largest industrial concern of its time. Evans became president of this giant in 1892 and continued until 1898 when he retired from the rubber business.

He was not long idle, for the following year he became interested in copper mining. He participated in the reorganization of the United States Mining Company, operating in Utah, of which he was president for seven years, which later became controlled by the United States Smelting, Refining and Mining Company of which he was a director. He also became president of the Yuba Consolidated Gold Mines Company, a California enterprise promoted by John Hays Hammond, which many years later proved remarkably beneficial to the Museum of Fine Arts. As he had collected paintings by Reynolds, Romney, Lawrence, Turner, Nattier, and Van Dyck, he was elected a trustee of the Museum of Fine Arts on 23 May 1907. His service was brief, for having been thrown from a horse he died on 6 July 1909, aged only sixty-five. Soon after his death, Mrs. Evans gave the museum in his name as well as hers the Savoy replica of the celebrated Van Dyck portrait of *Charles I of England with his Queen and Children*, the original of which, painted in 1632, is in the Royal Collection at Windsor.

Two years later Mrs. Evans proposed to give the picture galleries as an even greater tribute to her husband. It was at first contemplated that this wing be connected with the Rotunda only by a temporary two-story fireproof corridor. As plans were drawn, Mrs. Evans warmed to her work, adding in 1912 $325,000 to her initial gift of $500,000. The provision in 1913 of a reserve fund of $175,000 increased her final commitment to $1,000,000. As a result it was possible to substitute the Tapestry Gallery with a Lecture Hall below for the proposed temporary corridor and to elaborate considerably the new Fenway façade. Lowell's original drawings had suggested simply a modest pavilion in the center with smaller ones at the ends with large expanses of blank wall on the main floor, for the picture galleries were to be lighted from above. The revised plan called for a colonnade of twenty-two Ionic columns, 50 feet high, surmounted by an attic ornamented by three symbolical reliefs of two figures each. The central panel representing Sculpture, by Bela L. Pratt, enclosed a field containing the name of the building. The eastern relief, by Richard H. Recchia, personified Architecture, and its western counterpart, by F. W. Allen, Painting.

Excavation having begun in the last days of 1911, it was hoped to open the building during the first week of 1914. Delays in shipment of materials from Europe because of the war required postponement first to January and then to February 1915. The former painting galleries to the east and west of the Rotunda were closed during September and October 1914 to permit their transformation to new uses. By removing the pictures from the original building, the Department of Chinese and Japanese Art gained the whole of the southwest wing as well as the four galleries west of the Rotunda. To give that department undisputed occupancy of the ground floor as well, the Director's offices were temporarily removed to the area west of the Crypt (where they still are fifty-five years later), displacing picture storage and the Superintendent's stock room. The office of the Secretary and the study rooms for Western Art, including textiles, were shifted to corresponding rooms east of the Crypt, which had hitherto housed the Department of Prints. The Lawrence and Bremgarten rooms were shunted off to the ground floor of the Evans Wing, where they were in no greater harmony with their neighbors than they had been in proximity to the Japanese Garden. The large gallery to the east of the Rotunda was assigned to the Nearer Orient collections, while the two former picture galleries to the east of it became available to the Department of Egyptian Art. The subsidiary corridor leading from the Rotunda to the Egyptian galleries was hung with Peruvian, Coptic, and primitive textiles. These transfers having been accomplished during the summer and autumn of 1914, the Evans wing was formally opened with an evening reception on 3 February 1915. During the following week when no admission was charged, some twenty thousand visitors swarmed in.

The block on the Fenway had a frontage of 325 feet and a depth of 105 feet, while the connecting wing, which was 55 feet wide, ran for 155 feet between the two buildings. As with the Huntington Avenue building the exterior walls were faced with Crotch Island granite, while straw-colored brick was used for walls that would give on interior courts in the completed scheme. From the central Fenway entrance, a monumental stairway rose in a semicircular hall of Indiana limestone. On the landing, where the stairs separated into two reverse flights, right and left, was a tablet with the following inscription:

IN LOVING MEMORY OF
ROBERT DAWSON EVANS
1843–1909
MERCHANT, FINANCIER, AND PATRON OF ART
A TRUSTEE OF THIS MUSEUM
BUILT BY HIS WIFE, MARIA ANTOINETTE EVANS

On the main floor an Ionic colonnade supported a half-dome.

Although the stairway provided direct access from the Fenway to the picture galleries, the normal approach of a general visitor to the museum would be on the main floor, from the Rotunda by way of the 40-foot-high, Tapestry Gallery, 100 feet long and 33 feet wide, which was lighted by twelve clerestory windows on each side, with sills at 27 feet from the floor. Here the walls were of French travertine, the pavement of Tennessee marble, and the ceiling rested on heavy transverse beams, supporting smaller lengthwise oak beams. Here there was space to hang even the largest tapestries in comfortable relation to each other. Although the gallery was bound to serve as a thoroughfare, long benches down the middle of the room, permitted visitors to linger. Outside, the gallery was flanked by open loggias that for many years never served the slightest useful purpose. Of late, however, they have furnished providential accommodation

EVANS MEMORIAL WING. The Fenway façade as completed in 1915, before the addition of the Decorative Arts Wing.

for the portable stoves needed by caterers whenever a dinner is served in one of the museum galleries!

The doorway at the northern end of the Tapestry Gallery led to the semicircular stair hall of the Evans Wing and the axial corridor that divided the picture galleries. Across the corridor from the stairway landing, directly over the Fenway entrance, was a central gallery (VII), 24 feet, 8 inches wide by 36 feet, 4 inches long, walled with Indiana limestone and floored, like the corridor and stairway, with Tennessee marble. On each side of this were an oblong and a square gallery (VI and V to the west, VIII and IX to the east) running along the Fenway, and at each end of the axial corridor were large rectangular galleries (IV to the west, X to the east) extending the depth of the building. The galleries along the Fenway were all 34 feet wide, the width that had been ascertained as most desirable in the tests for light made in the temporary Experimental Gallery in 1903–1905; the oblong ones (VI and VIII) were 56 feet long. These were lighted by arched skylights, with a diffusing loft

below a gambrel roof with solid center and steep glazed sides. The
end galleries (IV and X), which were 36 feet wide and 80 feet long,
had flat skylights. In all of these the walls were hung with fabrics
woven in solid colors — soft green, rose crimson, or gray-green — in
patterns shown only by difference in texture. South of the corridor
the rooms were only 20 feet wide and the ceilings 18 feet high, rather
than 29 or 30. Those to the east (XI and XII) were skylighted and

THE TAPESTRY GALLERY IN 1928.

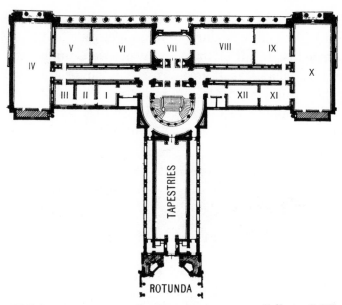

EVANS MEMORIAL WING, MAIN FLOOR PLAN. Galleries I–III
are side-lighted; IV–XII top-lighted; the Tapestry Gallery has
clerestory light.

hung with a brownish neutral stuff; those to the west (I, II, and III)
were paneled in oak and lighted by windows.

The small paneled rooms, designed for primitives, were the beginning of a chronological circuit extending from galleries I through
XII. Galleries I to VI were initially assigned to older paintings, VII
to English masters of the eighteenth and nineteenth centuries, and
VIII through XII to more modern work. The eastern half of the
axial corridor formed a Sargent Gallery, originally hung with water
colors by John Singer Sargent; the western half a Boit Gallery, similarly used for showing the work of Edward D. Boit. The opening
was celebrated by an extensive loan exhibition, in which paintings
owned by Mrs. Evans were hung in gallery V, and a number of
French pictures lent by Mrs. Henry C. Angell and others, as well as
American paintings from Copley, Stuart, and Allston, through
William Morris Hunt and Winslow Homer to Frank Duveneck, John
Singer Sargent, and Frank W. Benson were temporarily shown.

The east end of the ground floor of the Evans Wing provided
admirable quarters for the Department of Prints. Seven exhibition

EVANS MEMORIAL WING, GALLERY V, IN 1930. The west wall of the present P–5, looking through to P–4.

EVANS MEMORIAL WING, GALLERY II, AS ORIGINALLY BUILT. The paneled partitions that created three small galleries were removed in 1930.

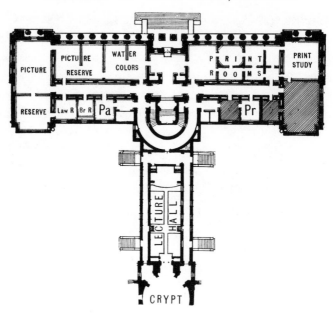

EVANS MEMORIAL WING, GROUND FLOOR PLAN.

rooms occupied the area below painting galleries VIII and IX. Here it was possible to hang framed prints upon walls of appropriate dimensions to the best advantage. For the opening the first Print Room was devoted to a selection of the finest engraved portraits, while the six smaller rooms contained Charles Meryon's *Eaux-fortes sur Paris*, Turner's *Liber Studiorum*, Dürer woodcuts, prints by Martin Schongauer, contemporary etchings, and works of the "Men of 1830." Along the axial corridor cases contained the tools used in the several processes of printmaking, with modern French and German color prints hung above them. At the east end of the wing (under painting gallery X) were the Study Room and workroom of the department; on the other side of the corridor, the print library and the curator's office. The department also used the curving corridor behind the main staircase to hang twenty selected impressions of Piranesi's *Vedute di Roma*. In the basement were two intaglio presses and a printing press for woodcuts, where Associate Curator Richter could instruct art students anxious to improve their knowledge of the processes of printmaking.

To the west of the Fenway entrance the space corresponding to the Print rooms was assigned to water colors and picture reserve. Across the corridor was the office of the Keeper of Paintings and, for want of any better spot to place them after their ejection from the southwest wing, the Bremgarten and Lawrence rooms. The end rooms (below painting gallery IV), although ultimately designed for picture reserve, were temporarily used to slake the increasing interest in early American decorative arts and furniture. Here in 1915 was exhibited a collection of English and American furniture of the late seventeenth and early eighteenth centuries, lent by Dwight W. Prouty, and other pieces owned by Miss Theodora Lyman. American portraits were hung on the wall, and in a bookcase was shown a collection of Waterford glass lent by Mrs. H. G. Otis.

On the ground floor in the connecting wing a Lecture Hall seating 450 persons occupied the space directly below the Tapestry Gallery. (Safety regulations subsequently reduced the capacity to 365.) The inclined floor gave a good view of the 20- by 30-foot stage, which could be adapted for concerts and plays. This room was lighted by French windows from the cork-floored corridors that flanked it on the other side, which provided direct communication between the Evans Wing and the Crypt of the main building. A booth above the main entrance at the south of the Lecture Hall provided for projection of slides without stumbling over a lantern in the main aisle.

In 1914 Mrs. Walter Scott Fitz, the mother of Edward Jackson Holmes, had given the museum not only one of the great treasures of the Classical collection, the gold and ivory statuette of the *Minoan Snake Goddess*, but an octagonal panel by Fra Angelico. This enchanting diminutive painting of the *Madonna and Child*, with angels, saints, and a donor in a flowering meadow, had once been owned by the French sculptor and collector Baron Henri de Triqueti, who had advised the Boston Athenæum in the early eighteen seventies on purchases made with the insurance received after the loss of the Lawrence Collection in the Boston fire. When his collection was sold in Paris in 1886, the panel passed to Mr. Edouard Aynard of Lyons, on whose walls it hung until 1913. This enchanting gift greatly enhanced the museum's representation of late medieval Italian painting.

MADONNA AND CHILD. Fra Angelico. *Gift of Mrs. Walter Scott Fitz. 14.416*

The spacious flexibility of the Evans Wing inspired both gifts and purchases of paintings. Soon after the opening, Mrs. Fitz, who until her death in 1929 was a constant benefactor of the museum, gave three Italian primitives which were installed in the oak-paneled gallery I, near the Fra Angelico. These were a *Madonna and Child* by Barnaba da Modena, a head of the Magdalen by Segna di Buona-ventura, and a saint of the school of Simone Martini. A cassone front with a battle scene by a follower of Paolo Uccello was purchased in Paris through the Francis Bartlett Fund in 1915, while a Sienese panel of the *Marriage of St. Catherine* (then attributed to Lippo Memmi, now thought to be the work of his follower, Barna da Siena) was bought from the Sarah Wyman Whitman Fund. In 1916 Mrs. Fitz added a tiny (7 1/2 by 5 1/2 inches) panel of the *Crucifixion* by Lippo Memmi.

French nineteenth-century paintings that had been purchased by various Bostonians as "contemporary art" came to the Museum of Fine Arts in considerable numbers during the second decade of the twentieth century. A Corot landscape of 1870 was received in 1913

by the bequest of Francis Bartlett; a somewhat larger one of 1872–
1874, *Souvenir d'un Pré de Brunoy*, was given in 1916 by Augustus
Hemenway in memory of Louis and Amy Hemenway Cabot. In 1917
the extensive collection of paintings and pastels by Jean François
Millet made by Quincy Adams Shaw (1825–1908) was given by
his children, Quincy A. Shaw, Jr., and Mrs. M. Graeme Haughton.

A year after his graduation from Harvard College in 1845, Quincy
Adams Shaw had accompanied his friend and relative Francis Parkman along the Oregon Trail. After exploring the Rocky Mountains,
he turned eastward, spending the winter of 1849–50 in Egypt and
Palestine and the following seven or eight years in Paris, where his
sister, Mrs. William Batchelder Greene, was living. Through his
friend William Morris Hunt, who was then studying painting in
Paris, Shaw also found his way around the artistic world. The painters of the Barbizon School, who were still not fully appreciated by
their compatriots, received early encouragement from American
collectors, attracted to their work through Hunt's enthusiasm. In the
early fifties Martin Brimmer had bought Millets through Hunt, all
of which eventually reached the Museum of Fine Arts. The largest
sum that Millet had received down to that time was the 500 francs
paid by Brimmer in 1852 for *Buckwheat Harvest*, which was brought
to Boston and lent to the Athenæum's 1854 exhibition. Altogether
Martin Brimmer bought eight Millets, three of which he gave to the
Museum of Fine Arts for the 1876 opening. The other five were
received thirty years later in 1906 after the death of his widow.
Some of these were already familiar to Bostonians from their inclu-
sion in Athenæum exhibitions of 1854, 1855, 1859, and 1860.

Quincy Adams Shaw was married in Boston in 1860 to Pauline
Agassiz, daughter of the Swiss scientist Louis Agassiz, whose migration to Harvard in 1847 had led, among other things, to the founding
of the Museum of Comparative Zoology. During a wedding trip to
Paris, the Shaws first met Millet. In 1862 they built a house near
Jamaica Pond, where the family lived until his death in 1908. Shaw's
life combined in a manner peculiar to nineteenth-century Boston a
taste for the wilderness with appreciation of the elegances of Europe,
the ability to wrest a fortune from Western mines and an inclination
to live quietly as a neighbor of Francis Parkman by Jamaica Pond,

surrounded by works of art acquired through a very personal taste. He bought land in the region of Lake Superior and organized the Hecla Mining Company, and in 1866 bought land on the Michigan shore of Lake Superior. Under the inspired superintendency of his brother-in-law, Alexander Agassiz, the Calumet and Hecla properties became not only the greatest copper mine in the world but declared the largest dividends which any metal mine in the world has ever divided. Years later, Alexander Agassiz wrote, "If Quin had ever known when he was beaten we should never have pulled the thing off." But as neither of these men ever knew when they were beaten, Alexander Agassiz wound up as an eminent zoologist and oceanographer, who combined the direction of his father's Museum of Comparative Zoology with the affairs of the Calumet and Hecla Mining Company, while Quincy Adams Shaw not only greatly aided that museum but collected the Millets and Renaissance sculpture that eventually enriched the Museum of Fine Arts.

In the early seventies Quincy A. Shaw began to collect Millet's work. On 8 January 1872 the artist wrote to Sensier: "An American gentleman and lady, M. and Madame Shaw, of Boston, came a little while ago to ask me for a picture which I have promised to paint for them. They chose *The Priory of Vauville* as the subject from among the drawings they saw here." In 1874 Shaw bought from William Morris Hunt five important Millets that had escaped destruction in the Boston fire of 1872 through the fortunate circumstance of their being in Hunt's house rather than his studio. During the next twenty years Shaw added oil paintings, pastels, and drawings until he had assembled what constituted the largest collection of Millet's work in one place. He had further bought some nineteen pieces of Italian Renaissance reliefs and busts that included the work of Donatello, Bartolommeo Bellano, the Della Robbias, and other sculptors, which Wilhelm von Bode, of the Kaiser Friedrich Museum in Berlin, considered "any museum might envy him." Bode, who had visited Shaw in Boston, wrote thus of the collection:

It was in his modest home in Jamaica Plain, surrounded by beautiful scenery, that I first learnt to appreciate fully what the *paysage intime* in France can produce; of Jean François Millet, Mr. Shaw possessed such an abundance of oil paintings, pastels, and finished drawings as can hardly be found in all the Museums and private collections in France. These show the master's art on so many sides and on so high a level that here I first became fully conscious of the commanding superiority of this master over all the painters of our modern times.

During his lifetime Quincy A. Shaw had given the 26 oil paintings, 27 pastels, and 3 etchings by Millet and the pieces of Renaissance sculpture to his children to be transferred to the Museum of Fine Arts when two rooms should be provided for their exhibition. Until the Evans Wing was completed, no appropriate space was available, but on 29 March 1917 the gift was formally accepted, and the collection installed in picture galleries XI and XII, where it remained for some forty years. When this permanent exhibition opened on 18 April 1918 a catalogue of the Quincy Adams Shaw Collection was published, which illustrated all the works of art described in it. The addition of Shaw's 53 oils and pastels to the dozen already in the collection made the Museum of Fine Arts pre-eminent in the world in the representation of Jean François Millet.

In 1917 Dr. Denman W. Ross once again gave the museum all the works of art that he had deposited since his previous omnibus gift. While this contained much of value for nearly every department, the painting galleries benefited by 35 pictures, including works of Pietro Longhi, Tiepolo, a Romney portrait, a very fine Dutch still life, and water colors by Dodge Macknight and Leon Bakst. Through a similar gift of works previously loaned by J. Templeman Coolidge, the museum acquired title to an immense *Boar Hunt* by Frans Snyders that had hung as a loan since 1889. In the same year Mrs. W. Scott Fitz gave an octagonal Umbrian marriage salver, attributed by Osvald Sirén to Giovanni Boccati da Camerino, which represented on the obverse the *Meeting of Solomon and the Queen of Sheba* and on the reverse a winged *Cupid with Cornucopias*. By bequest of Charles Francis Adams, who had died in 1915, the museum received the very attractive Copley portrait of his grandfather, John Quincy Adams, painted in 1795 when (aged twenty-seven) he was

JOHN QUINCY ADAMS. John Singleton Copley,
1795. *Bequest of Charles Francis Adams.*
17.1077

Minister at The Hague. In the same year two Renaissance portraits
by Vittore Carpaccio were purchased, as was the vividly mannered
My Uncle Daniel and His Family by the contemporary Spanish
painter Ignacio Zuloaga. My first sight of the latter at the age of
twelve was a traumatic experience; a decade later when I came to
know Spain the group portrait seemed entirely reasonable.

Although the war prevented easy contact with European sources,
one important French picture, Gustave Courbet's *La Curée* was
purchased in 1918 from the Henry Lillie Pierce Fund. This scene
of hunting the roebuck in the uplands of the Jura near Courbet's
native village of Ornans (Doubs) had been shown at the Salon of
1857. It had been bought in 1866 by a group of Boston artists, of
which William Morris Hunt was a member, called the Allston Club.
Within three days the artists had raised the purchase price of $5,000
and were able to display their treasure in the clubroom, advertised
by a large banner over the sidewalk. This was the first Courbet
acquired in the United States. As the artist was then a storm center

in Paris, this appreciation of his work by American painters gave him singular pleasure. In a series of articles on "Boston Painters and Paintings" in *The Atlantic Monthly* for 1888, William Howe Downes described Courbet's reaction:

> Armand Gautier was with him on the evening that he received the money for the picture, and he relates that Courbet cried out, "What care I for the Salon, what care I for honors, when the art students of a new and a great country know and appreciate and buy my works?" Gautier adds that Courbet's rural simplicity and frugality never forsook him, and he never took a cab; so he (Gautier) pinned the money in Courbet's vest, and as the artist climbed upon an omnibus he said it was the proudest day of his life.

Soon after its purchase by the Allston Club, *La Curée* was acquired by Henry Sayles, who lent it to the Museum of Fine Arts in 1877,

EVANS MEMORIAL WING, GALLERY X. The west wall of the present P–10, after 1917, showing Zuloaga's *My Uncle Daniel and His Family*.

LA CUREE. Gustave Courbet. *Henry Lillie Pierce Fund.*
18.820

the year of Courbet's death and the year after the opening of the
Copley Square building.

The painter Jean-Léon Gérôme reacted violently to the acceptance
by the French Government in 1894 of some of the contemporary
paintings from the Caillebotte Collection then offered to the Luxem-
bourg, concluding that "we live in an age of decadence and im-
becility." He had not seen the collection, but as he believed it to
include work by M. Monet and M. Pissarro, it was clear to him that
"if the Nation has seen fit to accept this sort of *muck*, what it needs
is a complete moral regeneration. This is anarchy, pure and simple,
and nothing is done to put an end to it." Some Bostonians shared
Gérôme's violent aversion to the Impressionists; others liked them.
Alexander Agassiz, reporting to his mother from Paris on 9 March
1901 of his purchase of a Rosa Bonheur *Royal Tiger*, which would

go splendidly with a *Lion* that he already owned, gave a clue to his reactions to the Impressionists as well as those of his brother, his sister Mrs. Henry Lee Higginson, and his brother-in-law Quincy Adams Shaw, when he wrote:

> There are some of the modified impressionist landscape painters here whose things I like very much also, so I indulged in a couple. There was one by Monet I would have bought, but Max could not stand it, though he acknowledged it was the best of its kind he had seen. I dare say Ida would have appreciated it, but Quin feels about them much as I do — he would not give them house room. The only way to have them is about a mile off — then they are superb. They suggest anything and everything you can fancy. It is astonishing what a lot of pictures are sold here to go to America. We seem to be cleaning up the picture market as fast as they are produced.

But Peter Chardon Brooks thought better of Monet in 1891 than Maximilian Agassiz did a decade later, for Bishop Lawrence's sixteen-year-old daughter Marian (Mrs. Harold Peabody) noted in her diary:

> After dinner Uncle Peter showed us all his new pictures by a man named Monet which have just arrived. He has always had a house full of paintings of the Barbizon School, but these are very different and *very* impressionistic so they cannot be hung near the others. He had them in the front hall and all up and down the long staircase. I thought they were lovely, so light and sparkling and sunny.

Denman W. Ross obviously agreed with the young Marian Lawrence, for in 1892 he lent the museum Monet's *Ravin de la Petite Creuse*, painted in 1889. The first Monets to be owned by the Museum of Fine Arts were this picture and two others that were included in Dr. Ross's large general gift of 1906. A fourth, *Bras de Seine, près Giverney*, painted in 1897, was given by Mrs. W. Scott Fitz in 1911.

The year 1919 was an *annus mirabilis* in gifts of French painting, for it brought three substantial collections as well as distinguished individual pictures. The forty paintings of the Henry Clay and Martha Bartlett Angell Collection, the gift of Mrs. Angell, included not only six Corots, four Daubignys, and a Millet, but the first examples of Eugene Boudin — *Beach near Scheveningen* (1864) and *Marine, Bordeaux, 1873* — and Camille Pissarro — *Village on the River* (1873) — to be owned by the museum. Among the twenty pictures of the John Pickering Lyman Collection, given by Miss Theodora Lyman, were two Monets — *Massifs de Fleurs à Vetheuil* and *Sur la Côte à Trouville*, both of 1881 — a second Pissarro, *Morning Sunlight on the Snow* (1895), and the museum's first Sisley. Alexander Cochrane, a trustee from 1913 to 1919, bequeathed Gilbert Stuart's portrait of Governor James Sullivan of Massachusetts, a Corot landscape, Monet's *Les Nymphéas, Paysage d'Eau* (1907), as well as a Monet and a Renoir of the *Grand Canal in Venice*. This first Renoir to be owned by the Museum was joined within 1919, the year of the artist's death, by a second, *La Seine à Chatou*, given by Arthur B. Emmons of Newport, Rhode Island.

A sixteenth-century portrait of Françoise de Longwy by Corneille de Lyon was purchased from the Francis Bartlett Fund in 1919, while Sargents of different generations improved the American holdings of the Department of Paintings. Two delightful Boston genre scenes by Henry Sargent (1770–1845), *The Tea Party*, and

THE TEA PARTY and THE DINNER PARTY. Henry Sargent. *Gift of Mrs. Horatio Appleton Lamb in memory of Mr. and Mrs. Winthrop Sargent. 19.12 and 19.13*

DAUGHTERS OF EDWARD DARLEY BOIT. John Singer Sargent, Paris, *1882. Gift of the daughters in memory of their father. 19.124*

The Dinner Party, were given by Mrs. Horatio A. Lamb (in memory of Mr. and Mrs. Winthrop Sargent), while the daughters of Edward Darley Boit gave (in memory of their father) the group portrait that John Singer Sargent (1856–1925) had painted of them in 1882. *The Road*, a wartime French sketch by John S. Sargent was purchased in 1919.

The Museum of Fine Arts took a bold step into unfrequented Spanish medieval territory by buying in 1921 the Romanesque mural paintings from the apse of the Catalan church of Santa Maria de Mur in the province of Lérida. Indeed only a few years earlier no one suspected that Catalan Romanesque mural painting existed. A group of learned and energetic Catalan nationalists that included the architect Josep Puig i Cadafalch and the art historian Josep Pijoan

MURAL PAINTING FROM THE APSE OF SANTA MARIA DE MUR. Catalan, 12th century. *Maria Antoinette Evans Fund. 21.1285*

had formed the Institut d'Estudis Catalans in Barcelona in 1907. Wishing to do something immediately that might gain them support from the local government, they tried to conjure up a project that would attract the attention of the learned world. In many remote Catalan villages, especially in the foothills of the Pyrenees, small rubble Romanesque churches with semicircular apses, built in the eleventh and twelfth centuries, were still standing relatively unchanged, save for an occasional coat of interior whitewash or the addition of a gold retablo that completely masked the original apse. Puig and Pijoan, being imaginative men, reasoned in the abstract that there might be medieval mural paintings somewhere under whitewash or behind retablos. They went off to the mountains to explore, and found that their guess was correct. There were indeed Romanesque mural paintings in a number of country churches, more extensive and better preserved than anything of a comparable period elsewhere in Europe. Thus in 1907 the Institut d'Estudis Catalans hurried into print the first fascicule of a series entitled *Les pintures murals catalanes*, which created the anticipated murmur of excitement not only in Barcelona but among foreign medievalists. This new learned body, having won its right to popular support, soon built up a library, began the publication of Puig i Cadafalch's *L'arquitectura Romanica a Catalunya*, and a host of other scholarly studies on all aspects of the history, archaeology, philology, and literature of Catalonia. This is one instance where a nationalist revival paid rich scholarly dividends.

Publicity of any kind about valuable works of art is bound to attract thieves, miscreants, and art dealers. If improperly safeguarded objects are not stolen, they are likely to be bought and spirited away from the places where they belong. The mural paintings of Santa Maria de Mur were published in the fourth fascicule of *Les pintures murals catalanes*. Before long someone bought them, removed them carefully from the walls, got them across the Pyrenees into France, and shipped them to New York. It was not too difficult, for the village was not only close to the frontier, but was then accessible only by a mule track. When it was discovered that these murals had left Spain, steps were taken immediately to safeguard those of other remote churches by removing them from the walls and taking them to Barcelona. In a very short time the Museo de la Ciudadela in Barcelona contained an exhibition of Romanesque mural painting unrivaled in the world. The door was locked after only one had escaped, and this one came to Boston.

Looking back after nearly fifty years, the purchase of the Mur paintings in 1921 seems almost incredibly prescient and imaginative. Arthur Kingsley Porter (1883–1933), who was to become the Apostle of the Spanish Romanesque to the United States, had only come to Harvard as Professor of Fine Arts the previous year. His earlier books had dealt with France and Lombardy, and he was only beginning his studies in Spain. The murals themselves were too austere and unfamiliar to have any immediate appeal even to those who loved the Middle Ages through Italian panels with gold backgrounds. They were, moreover, expensive to buy, transport, and install. Yet they were brought to Boston and successfully installed in a simulated chapel created by slicing off one end of gallery IV of the Evans Wing. By the spring of 1923 they were on exhibition; an extensive description appeared in the *Bulletin* of the following June. The Santa Maria de Mur paintings were not only the first of their kind to reach the United States but the only ones that are ever likely to, thanks to the care with which the other examples are now safeguarded in Barcelona. In this instance the Museum of Fine Arts was several laps in advance of art historians as well as of popular taste. Consequently, four years before I first went to Spain to begin work on my *Spanish Romanesque Architecture of the Eleventh Century* (London: Oxford University Press, 1941, reprinted 1969) I was already thoroughly acquainted with the mural paintings from one of the remote mountain churches that I was to describe.

Another Spanish acquisition of 1921 that has doubtless given greater pleasure to visitors than the Romanesque murals was the Velázquez portrait of the *Infanta Maria Theresa*, given by Mrs. Edwin Farnham Greene in memory of her parents, John Howard and Charlotte Peabody Nichols. This portrait shows a daughter of Philip IV of Spain, born in 1638, at the age of fourteen or fifteen, some seven years before she became the Queen of Louis XIV of France. It was sent to Vienna in 1653 in an earlier effort to further the marriage of the Infanta, and remained there until January 1921, when it left the Kunsthistorisches Museum in exchange for other paintings; in December of that year it was purchased from its new owners and given by Mrs. Greene to the Museum of Fine Arts.

Although Mrs. Robert Dawson Evans died on 16 October 1917,

ST. DOMINIC KNEELING BEFORE A CRUCIFIX. El Greco.
Maria Antoinette Evans Fund. 23.272

her generosity lived after her, for the Maria Antoinette Evans Fund
(principal and income unrestricted), established in 1922 under the
provisions of her will, eventually brought the museum double the
million dollars that she had given in her lifetime for the construction
of the picture galleries. From this fund was purchased in 1923 the
museum's second El Greco, which represents *St. Dominic Kneeling
before a Crucifix.* Like the portrait of Fray Felix Hortensio Palavicino,
which so attracted John Singer Sargent, the St. Dominic had powerfully appealed to nineteenth-century artists. Jean François Millet,
who had owned the latter painting (which must have been one of the
first El Grecos to leave Spain) until his death in 1875, kept it in his

studio "to put himself in tune." It was then long in the possession of Edgar Degas, being sold with the residue of his studio in 1919.

Degas, whose housekeeping habits were always confused, made more utilitarian use of St. Dominic than had Millet, according to Richard Wilbur's "Museum Piece," which the poet assures me is soundly documented.

> The good gray guardians of art
> Patrol the halls on spongy shoes,
> Impartially protective, though
> Perhaps suspicious of Toulouse.
>
> Here dozes one against the wall,
> Disposed upon a funeral chair.
> A Degas dancer pirouttes
> Upon the parting of his hair.
>
> See how she spins! The grace is there,
> But strain as well is plain to see.
> Degas loved the two together:
> Beauty joined to energy.
>
> Edgar Degas purchased once
> A fine El Greco, which he kept
> Against the wall beside his bed
> To hang his pants on while he slept.

From the planning stages of the Huntington Avenue museum it had been contemplated that contemporary artists and sculptors would adorn the building and its grounds with their works, on the precedent set by Charles F. McKim during the construction of the Boston Public Library between 1887 and 1895, where Puvis de Chavannes, John S. Sargent, Edwin A. Abbey, John Elliott, Joseph Lindon Smith, Augustus and Louis Saint-Gaudens, Daniel Chester French, and Frederick Macmonnies had blended painting and sculpture with architecture in the best tradition of the Renaissance. Sargent's murals on the end walls of the third-floor gallery of the library had aroused such admiration when the building opened in 1895 that Edward Robinson succeeded in raising $15,000 that would permit the artist to continue his work along the lateral walls of the gallery. This precedent was in the minds of the planners of the Museum of Fine Arts. Moreover, Holker Abbott, who was appointed a trustee of the museum by the Boston Athenæum from 1909 until his election to the board in 1916, was the brother of Samuel A. B. Abbott whose taste and autocratic action during his presidency of the Boston Public Library had assured Charles F. McKim freedom to achieve that superbly decorated building. Furthermore, almost everyone involved in the Museum of Fine Arts was a friend, patron, or relative of John Singer Sargent. But decoration of the museum proceeded more slowly than in the library, where city funds provided the mainstay of construction and operation.

J. Randolph Coolidge, Jr., in describing the architectural scheme of the new museum in 1907, had remarked of the huge forecourt that "future benefactors of the Museum must provide for the enrichment of this space with statuary, architectural fragments, fountains, benches and other accessories to form an easy and delightful introduction to the wealth of the choicer objects that are sheltered within the building." Alas for noble aspirations, parked automobiles have long formed the dreary and undelightful introduction to the building from Huntington Avenue, although one piece of contemporary sculpture was placed in the center of the court in 1913. The sculptor Cyrus E. Dallin, born in Utah when villages were still protected from Indian attacks by adobe walls, conceived early in this century a series of four statues depicting the attitude of American Indians toward the intruding white man. The first, *The Signal of Peace*, representing their friendly meeting, is now in Lincoln Park, Chicago. The second, *The Medicine Man*, representing the red man's suspicion of the white invader, found a home in Fairmount Park, Philadelphia. The third, *Protest*, shown at the St. Louis Exposition, represented the warfare of tribesmen against settler, while the fourth, *The Appeal to the Great Spirit*, since 1913 in the museum's forecourt, symbolized surrender, not to human enemies but to a higher friend. The fourth statue, which received a gold medal at the Paris Salon of 1909, was done far from the plains, in Arlington Heights, Massachusetts, where the sculptor lived in his later years. Recently Mrs. Arthur Wells Jones of Point Pleasant, Pennsylvania,

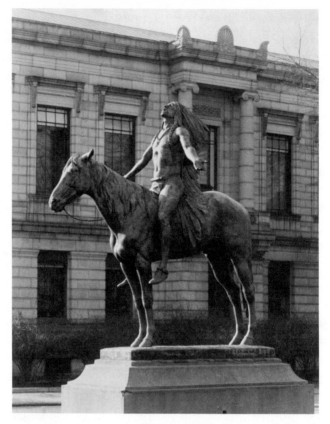

THE APPEAL TO THE GREAT SPIRIT. Bronze, Cyrus E.
Dallin. Since 1913 in the Forecourt of the Museum of
Fine Arts.

wrote to say that she had a special feeling for the Museum of Fine
Arts because Dallin had used her family's carriage horse as a model
for the Indian pony in *The Appeal to the Great Spirit*. He was a
neighbor of Mrs. Jones's parents, "and whenever he was commissioned to do an equestrian statue he borrowed our horse 'Prince' —
a Kentucky thoroughbred, and changed him into an Indian pony."
The group attracted such enthusiasm in Boston that in 1911 a subscription was opened to purchase it for the park system. A gift from
Peter C. Brooks completed the fund on condition that the work be
placed in the museum forecourt. In recent years its presence has
occasionally aroused skeptical comment from passers-by whose sense
of history is too feeble to make them aware that modernity evaporates

overnight. In the arts, as in everything else, the adjectives "modern," "contemporary," and "present day" are as inane as they are inaccurate.

Although the block of rough stone over the Huntington Avenue entrance has awaited a sculptor for sixty-one years, the Evans Wing was, as we have seen, adorned with sculptured reliefs when completed in 1915. John Singer Sargent returned to Boston from England in 1916 after an absence of thirteen years to complete the decoration of the Boston Public Library gallery, which had been awaited for more than two decades. At the suggestion of Arthur Fairbanks, the Director, the museum trustees contracted with Sargent to decorate the dome of the Rotunda. The problem was difficult, for this "slice of architecture" was so very architectural that the coffered

HUNTINGTON AVENUE ENTRANCE IN 1920.

THE ROTUNDA WITH SARGENT MURALS IN 1921. A comparison with page 233 will show the extensive reconstruction
involved in providing Sargent with space to decorate.

dome had to be rebuilt in order to give Sargent surfaces upon which
to paint. During his long absence from Boston, Sargent had practically given up portraiture in oils and was increasingly occupied with
water colors. As the Rotunda dome, even when rebuilt, gave little
opportunity for great murals like the frieze of Prophets and the
Crucifixion in the Boston Public Library, he thought in terms of
sculptural rather than pictorial decoration. As David McKibbin has
described it,

> He had a model of the dome made and originally intended to do
> the four large elliptical panels in relief and colour; but on studying
> the lighting, he found that there was not enough direct light to
> justify the use of the third dimension, as the modelling of the upper

parts would be invisible. He therefore abandoned his first intention and these panels were consequently painted; while the bas-relief treatment was reserved for those parts of the dome receiving more direct light. In order to find a suitable moulding which would not cut off this source of light and cast a shadow, Sargent experimented with many different types, moulding and casting them in plaster and trying them out on the model which his architect friend Thomas Fox had constructed for him. Afterward when he had solved the problem, Mrs. Gardner collected these sample strips of moulding from his studio and constructed a fireplace hood for her house in Brookline, occasioning a pleasantry from Sargent to the effect that if "architecture is frozen music" he would like to be around when the fireplace melted.

In 1917 Sargent rented his late friend Frederic P. Vinton's studio in Newbury Street so that Thomas A. Fox might have space to construct the models upon which he was to base his decoration. By the end of May 1918 work with the model and small-scale studies was practically completed in the studio, while reconstruction of the dome at the museum had reached a point where plain surfaces, substituted for the coffering, were ready to receive Sargent's moldings, enrichments, bas-reliefs, and the painted decorations. Between May 1919 and July 1920 were completed, cast, and put in place the bas-reliefs of *Eros and Psyche, Dancing Figures*, the *Three Graces*, and *Aphrodite and Eros* that were to stand in pedimented frames, as well as the reliefs of *Fame*, a *Satyr and Maenad, Arion*, and the *Education of Achilles* that were to be placed above the frames. Between February and October 1921 Sargent painted the circular compositions of *Ganymede, Music, Astronmy*, and *Prometheus*, as well as the four large elliptical paintings of *Apollo and the Muses; Architecture, Painting, and Sculpture protected from the ravages of Time by Minerva; Classic and Romantic Art*; and *The Sphinx and the Chimaera*. Thomas A. Fox in a descriptive pamphlet prepared for the unveiling on 20 October 1921 particularly noted that "all the modelling, not only of the compositions themselves but of the details, as well as all the painting of the canvases, was actually done by the artist himself without the usual and supplementary aid of assistants."

APOLLO AND THE MUSES. John Singer Sargent decoration of the Rotunda.

President Morris Gray observed in his 1921 report: "The decorations have been very deeply and very generally appreciated for themselves, and in addition, they give a joyous welcome that the former cold, sombre, and forbidding walls failed entirely to give." Consequently, Sargent was requested to consider continuing the decorations over the main stairway. In this segment of the "slice of architecture" there was even less surface to decorate than in the Rotunda, as Sargent found when he came to grips with the problem. On 20 January 1922 he wrote Thomas A. Fox:

> The photographs you sent me of the Museum Staircase make me feel that decorating it is rather hopeless unless they will allow of some alterations as they did in the Dome. As it is there are no spaces for painting but those shallow strips along the skylight and that postage stamp of a lunette over the library door.
> I have thought of a scheme that would I think make the place much handsomer and would give at least three good spaces for painting *across* the axis of the Staircase.

THE ROTUNDA WITH SARGENT MURALS (detail).

I am sending you under separate cover two photographs, one a rough plan and one a sketch in perspective of the effect I propose from the bottom of the stairs. Neither of these are absolutely correct but are mere indications.

In the first place I don't see the necessity of that enormous skylight going the whole length of the staircase. I should think that the middle part might be vaulted across to afford a good space for painting and the skylight left across the lower and upper ends. Then I would like the walls which enclose the two parallel corridors that run from the Library to the Rotunda on each side of the Staircase to be replaced by columns so that from below one would look through two porticos as it were and see the light of the walls of the two long rooms of casts.

I think this would spread out the effect and take away that monotonous look of a tunnel that makes the staircase so ugly.

Then lastly I should like to see the six columns spaced differently, one at each end and two groups of two in between. This would leave wider intervals to see through and perhaps six ceiling surfaces to paint in the corridors. Those ceilings would get a lot of reflected light from the plaster cast walls and would be worth decorating whereas now they are in the dark and invisible from the staircase as the columns are so close together. I think if those corridors were opened out as I suggest the effect would be much handsomer and would have a suggestion of those vistas in Genoese palaces.

When you get these photographs please put your brains to thinking whether these changes would be an improvement for the eye, then whether the changes could be made without bringing the building down on one's head. The latter point ought to be ascertained before frightening the Trustees. If it is an improvement and *if* it is workable . . . show my sketches to say Mr. Morris Gray. As the staircase and walls stand at present I don't see any opportunity for decoration.

I realize that the architectural changes I propose are vaulting over the middle part of the skylight, taking away the enclosing walls to the corridors, changing the spacing of the 12 existing columns and making 13 others for the other sides of the corridors — hardly more than they did in the Rotunda.

The last phrase is an understatement worthy of an Italian Grand Duke contemplating alterations in his baroque palace! To propose reshuffling a dozen great Ionic columns in this lordly manner illustrates the risks of dealing with artists, but it seemed to trouble the trustees as little as it concerned Sargent. In 1922 the Museum of Fine Arts was running a deficit of over $40,000 and charging to unrestricted capital funds almost half of the quarter of a million spent for the purchase of works of art, yet Morris Gray was evidently unfrightened, for he simply stated in his 1922 report that "arrangements have been made by the Museum with Mr. John S. Sargent for his decoration of the ceiling above the main stairway and the adjacent corridors." Obviously art was art, and artists must be obeyed, regardless of vulgar considerations. So Sargent spake, as in Genesis i, "and it was so."

He was quite right. The stairway *did* look better; it was less of a tunnel, but for many months it was enclosed by temporary partitions while all the structural changes were being made. Sargent worked partly in Boston, partly in London. David McKibbin's meticulous research even establishes the order of some of the work, for he notes in his *Sargent's Boston* that was prepared for a 1956 Museum of Fine Arts exhibition:

> We are able to date some of the work done in Boston from the fact that Sargent selected three models from the Ziegfeld Follies which was playing in the city. These three girls posed for the Danaïdes, carrying their water-jars in procession up to the boundless amphora, above the entrance to the Museum Library, and they appear again as the Hesperides in the ceiling panel in which Tom McKellar, one of the models employed by Sargent in all his decorations, posed for the Atlas.

The decorations were completed in the winter of 1924–25, but on 15 April 1925, on the eve of his departure for Boston to oversee their installation, Sargent died in his sleep in London. Everything had been so carefully and precisely planned that the decorations and paintings fitted easily into place. On 3 November 1925 they were unveiled, simultaneously with the opening of a memorial exhibition of Sargent's work. In the color scheme of golden ocher on a blue background and in technique they simply extended the earlier adornment of the Rotunda, as was appropriate, but in these last works the artist became more purely decorative, with larger figures and more dramatic movement. On the vault over the staircase, the mythological schemes of the Rotunda were continued by two large paintings, *The Winds* and *Apollo in his Chariot with the Hours*, separated by the reduced skylight. Over the Library entrance is a large lunette in which the Ziegfeld chorus girls, disguised as *Danaïdes*, pour water into a great vase-shaped fountain, while below are three small panels of *Philosophy, The Unveiling of Truth*, and *Science*. On the ceiling of each corridor leading from the Rotunda to the Library are three paintings, a square panel at each end and a round one in the center. On the left the subjects are *Orestes, Phaeton*, and *Hercules and the Hydra*; on the right *Perseus on Pegasus Slaying Medusa, Atlas and the Hesperides*, and *Chiron and Achilles*. The Ziegfeld girls as Hesperides have cast off all disguises and doze, intertwined in seductive and revealing poses; fortunately Atlas is too absorbed by his burden to be tempted

THE MAIN STAIRCASE WITH SARGENT MURALS IN 1925. A comparison with page 222 will show the reconstruction involved in carrying out Sargent's wishes.

to pay appropriate attention to them. At the bases of the vault above the columns are six vivid reliefs of naked athletes hurdling over garlands with a vitality and exuberance that suggests the pleasure Sargent had in this, his last completed work.

David McKibbin tactfully appraises his hero's decorations in the following judicious terms:

Sargent's murals have not met with universal acclaim. Many would agree with one of the most eminent art critics living today, who, after seeing the decorations in the rotunda of the Museum,

DANAÏDES. John Singer Sargent, lunette over Library door.

pronounced them "very ladylike." But the fact remains that the Museum decorations present one of the rare instances in which a painter has been permitted to modify the architectural character of a building in order to achieve a desired relation between architecture, sculpture and painting.

As a child I had reveled in the murals of the Sargent Gallery at the Boston Public Library, which still give me pleasure. But I remember vividly after nearly forty-five years my bitter disappointment on first

ATHLETES HURDLING OVER GARLANDS. John Singer Sargent, reliefs over main staircase

seeing the Museum of Fine Arts staircase. The decorations seemed to me, as Sir Winston Churchill is reported to have said of a man named Bossom, "neither one thing nor the other."

From his election as President in 1914, Morris Gray had regularly concluded his annual report with a few pages of reflections on the life of beauty, the education of the spirit, exaltation, the real value of art, and similar abstract and elevated themes. Unlike most Boston lawyers and trustees, Morris Gray was something of a poet. In 1923 a thirty-two page pamphlet of extracts from these final pages of his reports was published under the title of *The Museum and the Public: Selections from the Recent Writings of Morris Gray, President of the Museum, Reprinted at the Request of the Trustees of the Museum.* In the same year the Marshall Jones Company published his *The City's Voice: A Book of Verse,* delightfully designed by D. B. Updike and printed at the Merrymount Press. Had he been President when the Sargent murals were unveiled, he would undoubtedly have discussed them in his 1925 report. But on 17 July 1924 he resigned his office on account of ill health, although he continued as a trustee until his death on 12 January 1931. Arthur Fairbanks having also resigned as Director on 28 February 1925, by the time the 1925 report came round no one thought to mention the completion of the Sargent decorations.

CHAPTER XI

The War and the Years
Following

With the migration of paintings to the Evans Wing, the galleries west of the Rotunda came within the province of the Department of Chinese and Japanese Art and provided room for the suitable exhibition of early Chinese paintings and sculpture. Although the name of the department had been enlarged to include China in 1903, it will be recalled from Chapter IV that a decade earlier when Fenollosa had arranged an exhibition of Chinese Buddhist paintings of the eleventh and twelfth centuries from the Temple Daitokuji of Kyoto, ten of these had been purchased (half by the museum and half by Denman Ross) to provide the temple with funds for necessary repairs. During Paul Chalfin's curatorship, he would occasionally pick up Chinese objects at reasonable prices at the Yamanaka and Matsuki auction sales in Boston, using income from the James Fund. Denman W. Ross's 1906 gift of objects previously loaned to the museum included the five Sung paintings from the Temple Daitokuji that he had bought in 1893, as well as other Chinese paintings, bronzes, porcelains, and enamels.

With the coming of Okakura-Kakuzo, who believed so strongly in the unity of the East, the collecting of Chinese and Tibetan objects was intensified. Dr. Ross generously helped, as always, in every way possible. So, from the time of his appointment as chairman of the

KWANNON. Marble, Chinese, T'ang
dynasty. *Special Subscription Fund,*
1907.

department's Visiting Committee in 1906, did Edward Jackson
Holmes and his mother, Mrs. W. Scott Fitz. In 1907 from the Special
Subscription Fund that they had instigated, Okakura-Kakuzo purchased a T'ang marble torso of a *Kwannon*, found among the ruins
of a temple of Shensi province, Chinese bronze vases of the Chou
and early Han dynasties, 109 bronze mirrors that represented the
evolution of that form in China from the early Han through the Ming
dynasties, 7 Han pottery vases, and 35 stone carvings of the sixth and
seventh centuries that showed the transition from the Han style to
the Greco-Indian and the subsequent amalgamation of the two.
Frank Gair Macomber, who had prepared the catalogue of the
tapestry exhibition of 1893, lent and subsequently gave his un-
paralleled collection of early Chinese pottery.

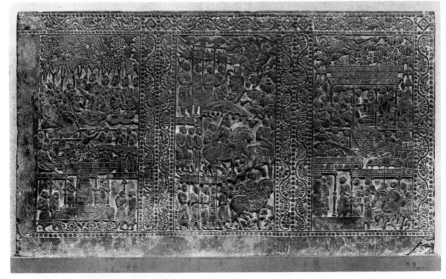

TOMB SCULPTURE RELIEF. Stone, Chinese, Northern Ch'i dynasty. *Gift of Denman W. Ross and Gardiner M. Lane. 12.588*

Through the contagion of Okakura-Kakuzo's enthusiasm, the department's holdings expanded in many areas. When in Boston he would often ask groups of ladies to tea parties in his office and set them to sewing silk bags for pieces of Japanese lacquer while he talked to them enchantingly about Oriental art. Kojiro Tomita who, on his arrival in Boston, stayed with Okakura in his Hemenway Street apartment, recalls one evening when he waited up until 4:00 A.M. for his host's return from an evening with Mr. and Mrs. Holmes at 296 Beacon Street. The three enthusiasts had become so immersed in museum business that they talked nearly until sunrise. When the Holmeses asked Okakura to buy them something particularly fine for their own collection during one of his visits to Japan, be brought back an exquisite little bronze gilt Korean *Buddha Bhaisajyaguru (Yaksa)* of the eighth century, which Ned Holmes eventually gave the museum in 1932 in memory of his mother.

When Denman W. Ross gave in 1913 the superb fifth-century stone Bodhisattva in memory of Okakuro-Kakuzo, he lent an engraved stone slab of the Han dynasty, and his young friend and traveling companion Harvey E. Wetzel lent a Buddhist memorial stela of

THE BUDDHA BHAISAJYAGURU (YAKSA).
Bronze, gilt, Korean, Silla dynasty. *Gift*
of Edward Jackson Holmes in memory of
his mother, Mrs. W. Scott Fitz. 32.436

A.D. 554. The following year Ross joined with three other trustees — Gardiner M. Lane, Alexander Cochrane, and George Robert White — in giving three Chinese tomb sculptures of the Han dynasty. A heroic-size stone Kuan-yin of the early seventh century and a life-sized pottery figure of a Lo-han were purchased through the Francis Bartlett Fund in 1915, while Ross gave a late sixth-century limestone sculpture of the Buddha and two Bodhisattvas standing against an ornamented aureole.

This was a remarkable year in Oriental acquisitions of many kinds, for 22 Chinese paintings were purchased, ranging in date from the twelfth to the seventeenth centuries, as were a Japanese bronze head of a Buddha of the Kamakura period. A great series of Japanese Nō-drama costumes was bought partly with museum funds and partly by gift of William Sturgis Bigelow, who also gave (as did Denman W. Ross) a number of fine Japanese color prints. A small Chinese limestone sarcophagus of the T'ang dynasty, of unusual perfection and great historic interest, was purchased in 1916. When Dr. Ross on 1 March 1917 repeated his omnibus gift of all objects

STONE MEMORIAL STELA. Chinese,
West Wei dynasty, 554 A.D. *Bequest
of Hervey Edward Wetzel. 19.125*

lent by him at the time, the Chinese and Japanese Department
gained, among other things, 88 Chinese, 31 Japanese, and 3 Tibetan
paintings, 4 pieces of stone sculpture, 39 bronzes, 44 sword guards,
51 porcelains, and 14 jades. As always, one is left breathless by the
quality, quantity, and variety of this one man's collecting.

Francis Gardner Curtis, who had become an Associate in the
department in 1906, died on 29 November 1915, leaving a bequest
of $25,000 restricted to the purchase of especially fine Oriental
objects. This was expended in 1917 on a group of Chinese paintings

AVALOKITESVARA (KUAN-YIN).
Limestone, Chinese, Sui dynasty.
Francis Bartlett Fund. 15.254

that was dominated by Ch'ên Jung's picture of *Nine Dragons*, a Sung dynasty masterpiece of the highest quality, perfectly preserved, and accompanied by an authentic record of appreciation covering the picture's life from the year 1244 when it was painted. Early in 1916, a few weeks after Curtis' death, John Ellerton Lodge, a son of Senator Henry Cabot Lodge, was appointed Curator, and Kojiro Tomita was promoted to be Assistant Curator of the Department of Chinese and Japanese Art. Although Lodge was appointed Director of the Freer Gallery at the Smithsonian Institution in 1921, he combined that

LADIES PREPARING NEWLY WOVEN SILK (details). Chinese scroll, full color on silk, by Emperor Hui-tsung (1082–1135). *Chinese and Japanese Special Fund.* *12.886*

THE NINE DRAGONS (detail). Chinese scroll, ink and slight color on paper, Sung dynasty, dated 1244. *Francis Gardner Curtis Fund.* *17.1697*

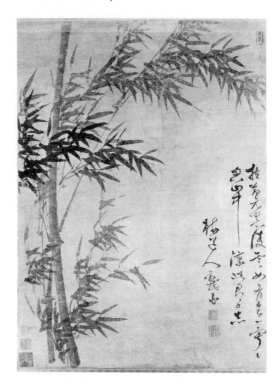

BAMBOO IN THE WIND. Chinese paper *kakemono*, by Wu Chên, Yuan dynasty, early 14th century. *Special Chinese Fund.* 15.907

post with his Boston curatorship for a decade, spending four to six months of each year in Washington. In 1931, when he resigned from the Museum of Fine Arts to devote his entire time to the Freer Gallery, he was succeeded as Curator by Kojiro Tomita.

Thanks once again to Denman W. Ross, the Museum of Fine Arts in 1917 became the first in America to organize a section of Indian art. The 1913 exhibition of his recent acquisitions, mentioned in Chapter IV, had included 151 Persian and Indian paintings and drawings, which by January 1915 had been given to the museum. In 1914 these were joined by 171 Persian and Indian paintings purchased through the Francis Bartlett Fund and special contributions. This remarkable collection, assembled by Victor Goloubew, a Russian living in Paris, and for some years lent to the Musée des Arts Decoratifs, was regarded as the finest of its kind in Europe. Dr. Ross then not only purchased the Rajput and Mughal paintings, Jaina manuscripts, and small Indian bronzes assembled by Dr. Ananda Kentish Coomaraswamy (1877–1947), but persuaded the collector to follow his possessions to Boston and become Keeper of Indian Art in the new section that was created in 1917 within the Department of Chinese and Japanese Art.

This remarkable man, the son of Sir Mutu Coomaraswamy and an English mother, had been born in Colombo, Ceylon, on 22 August 1877. As his father, the first Asiatic to be knighted and the first Ceylonese to be called to the bar in the reign of Queen Victoria, died when his son was still an infant, Ananda Coomaraswamy was educated in England, where he received a doctorate in science from the University of London. Returning to his native island at the age of twenty-five as Director of the Mineralogical Survey of Ceylon, he not only did distinguished scientific work but initiated the movement for national education, the teaching of the vernacular in all schools, and the revival of Indian art and culture. His *Mediaeval Sinhalese Art*, published in 1908, and its 1913 sequel, *The Arts and Crafts of India*

TORSO OF A YAKSI. Sandstone, Indian, Sānchī, 1st century B.C. *Ross Collection.* 29.999

HALF OF PEDIMENT. Stone, Indian, Mathurā, 1st–2nd centuries A.D. *Charles Amos Cummings Bequest Fund. 26.241*

and Ceylon, established his stature as an art historian, but with the passage of years he turned increasingly to philosophy. In his English manifestation he was profoundly sympathetic to the artistic, political, and social views of John Ruskin and William Morris; in the preface to *The Arts and Crafts of India and Ceylon* he wrote: "The Hindus have never believed in art for art's sake; their art, like that of mediaeval Europe, was art for love's sake." Like Okakura-Kakuzo he moved effortlessly between East and West, blending the higher aspects of both worlds in his conception of art as an integral part of daily life. Sister Nivedita, an Englishwoman who had become a disciple of Swami Vivekananda, characterized Okakura as "the William Morris of his country"; similarly, when *Mediaeval Sinhalese Art* appeared she acclaimed it a classic.

Ananda K. Coomaraswamy had offered to give his collection to the government of India on condition that a suitable museum be built for it at Banares. As the majority of Indians were then as impervious to the revival, regeneration, and interpretation of traditional Indian art as the Japanese had been to theirs in the eighteen seventies and eighteen eighties, this offer came to nothing. Instead Coomaraswamy followed Okakura to the Museum of Fine Arts, where he spent the last thirty years of his life. As he fully shared Okakura's conviction that "Asia is one," it was highly appropriate that a collection begun with Japan, extended to China, should now embrace India. The passageway from the Rotunda to the Oriental wing became an Indian Corridor, where were assembled Buddhist and Hindu stone sculptures and bronzes, Jaina manuscripts, Rajput and Mughal paintings, textiles, jewelry, and metalwork to the total of 440 objects, with 1,130 more reserved for study. As Coomaraswamy pointed out in his first report,

> The Museum now possesses the materials for a logical presenta-
> tion of Asiatic art as a consistent whole — a unity in the sense
> which Mr. Okakura so often insisted upon. It is precisely the art of
> India, linked as it is on the one hand with that of Persia, and on

THE HOUR OF COWDUST, KRISHNA BRINGING HOME THE HERDS and RAS LILA, THE MILKMAIDS FOLLOWING KRISHNA. India, Rajput paintings, 18th century. *Ross-Coomaraswamy Collection.* 22.683 and 17.2618

the other hand with that of China — the whole foundation of Chinese Buddhist art being formally Indian, — which needs to be represented in any museum pretending to deal fundamentally with the art of the Far East; and it is only due to various accidents that the art of India, which is to so great extent an art of *sources,* has been so long neglected.

In 1922 the collection of Persian and Mohammedan art, which had been roosting uneasily in the Department of Western Art, was transferred to the charge of Dr. Coomaraswamy, who thenceforth became Keeper of Indian and Mohammedan Art. By gift some very handsome objects had been received over the years, such as the twelfth- or thirteenth-century Persian bowl from Rhages, decorated with the signs of the zodiac, that Mrs. J. Montgomery Sears had given in 1909 in memory of a dead son. But probably the most spectacular of the transfers was an Indian wool carpet of the early seventeenth century, in which is woven a landscape with figures and mythological beasts, given to the museum in 1893 by Mrs. Frederick L. Ames in the name of her late husband. This greatly admired and often reproduced carpet, which is a major monument in the history of Mughal art, excited enthusiasm among artists well before it

BOWL WITH SIGNS OF THE ZODIAC. Persian, 12th or 13th century, from Rhages. *Gift of Mrs. J. Montgomery Sears in memory of her son. 09.103*

WOOL CARPET. Landscape with Figures and Mythological Beasts. Indian, Mughal, early 17th century. *Gift of Mrs. Frederick L. Ames in the name of her husband. 93.1480*

reached Boston. In 1882, when Mr. and Mrs. Ames were apparently thinking of buying it in London, they asked the architect Henry Hobson Richardson, who had created most of the buildings in the Ames enclave at North Easton, to find out what he could about its importance. Richardson applied to William Morris, who replied from Kelmscott Manor on 11 July 1882 (in a letter now in the museum's files):

> I examined carefully Messrs. Durlacher and Marks' Carpet; it is a very rare and fine work of art: it belongs to the highest class of this kind of works, of which necessarily very few specimens are left, and is a noble example of that class . . . . It is in extraordinarily good condition; there is an unimportant mend or two in it, and the black, of which there is but a little has been eaten down to the warp by the chemical action of its dye, as always happens when a carpet is of this age: the rest of the surface is just as it came from the loom. The color of the carpet is as perfect as these things generally are; its design striking and original as a piece of drawing. The design is a most curious example of that mixture of Persian and Chinese that is found in the Persian art of the time of Shah Abbas the Great, when there was so much intercourse between the two countries by the overland carriage trade; and the carpet must be considered from the historical point of view a most valuable specimen of this art . . . I should say that [it] is unique . . . Altogether it must rank very high among the half dozen of these splendid pieces which have been in the market of late years, and seems to me simply invaluable. Might I venture to suggest that some record of it should be made and published for the benefit of students of art. Some of the chromolithographs are so good nowadays that a reproduction of a good and careful drawing of it would be of great service to those who are interested in such matters.

With so remarkable a scholar as Ananda K. Coomaraswamy in charge, and with Denman Ross's collecting continuing at its normal pace, the possessions of this new section multiplied like the loaves and fishes. In 1923 Coomaraswamy published a *Portfolio of Indian Art*, consisting of 108 heliotype plates of which 4 were in color, and parts I and II of a *Catalogue of Indian Art*. The first of these was a general introduction to the collection, while the second dealt with sculpture. Part IV, *Jaina Paintings and Manuscripts*, was published in 1924; part V, *Rajput Painting* in 1926; part VI, *Mughal Painting*, in 1930, while in 1927 Karl W. Hiersemann of Leipzig published Coomaraswamy's *A History of Indian and Indonesian Art* in both an English and a German version.

Few scholars in any field have thought more profoundly or written more prolifically than Ananda K. Coomaraswamy. He was physically and intellectually a unique ornament to the Museum of Fine Arts for three decades, although only intermittently a methodical curator. A tall, spare man, with an ascetically beautiful bearded face surmounted by a leonine shock of hair, he had proceeded from mineralogy to art history before he arrived in Boston. As a mind like his never rests, he continued through aesthetics to metaphysics, and in his later years had become rather completely a philosopher and theologian, who spoke the languages of Yoga and of Thomas Aquinas with unconscious transition between East and West. In *The Transformation of Nature in Art*, published by the Harvard University Press in 1934, he analyzed the community of theory behind medieval European and Asiatic art. Of this period, Dr. Eric Schroeder, who worked as a volunteer in the department has written:

Most of my first day was spent down in a cellar storage among dusty unexhibited objects; but when I emerged at the end of the darkened winter afternoon to speak to Mr. Tomita, the Curator of the Asiatic Department [as it had been renamed in 1927], Coomaraswamy walked into Mr. Tomita's office and sat down to listen. Some of the antiquities had interested me; and I was expatiating upon them with enthusiasm. Mr. Tomita, who disapproved of Dr. Coomaraswamy's negligence in his purely curatorial functions, observed pointedly that it would be a very good thing if someone would put that storage in proper order, for it had long been a disgrace. There was a short silence. Then Dr. Coomaraswamy's rather mumbling tones emerged from the shadow beyond the lamplight.

"Perhaps one of these days I ought to take a run down and have a look at the old place," he said, like a London stockbroker remembering after the lapse of many years the ivy-mantled home of his ancestors.

What irony! It was not only the sublime detachment from what other people expected of him which delighted me, but rather the incongruity of this efflorescence, this perfectly aimed quotation from Edwardian conventionality, from the surface of a personality so unconventional and so unsentimental. Laughing, I looked toward the speaker. The lenses of his large spectacles gleamed, and his cigarette end glowed; I could more dimly see through the thin beard lines of laughter drawn about his painfully fastidious mouth. He was sitting back, his legs crossed with the elegance only possible to the very thin; and his head was tilted in the cock of a connoisseur as he enjoyed the effect of his humor. In that moment I knew that whatever I thought about him I should like him.

Dr. Schroeder tells how before long he and Coomaraswamy were constantly engaged in argument, "for I was trying to revive the art-historian who had become extinct in the philosopher, and he was determined to evoke the philosopher in an immature art-historian."

His concern with Museum objects and their history, with dating and attribution, was now slight, though his memory retained astonishingly much of his old great learning in this respect. Taste and expository ingenuity in the galleries he called "window dressing" and left to others who cared more than he. These others were, very properly in a Museum, a majority; and they tolerated Ananda's philosophic dogmatism unconvinced. One day at lunch we were going at it hammer and tongs, Ananda maintaining the essentially metaphysical character of artistic production and I asserting the frequent and significant predominance of moral and natural motive, he citing texts and I adducing works and circumstances, he pointing out the continuity in all traditional cultures of metaphysical reference in symbols, I challenging him to explain on any such grounds so characteristic a form as for instance the panegyric in Mediaeval Persia. Our table-companions at last found a spokesman in the Director of the Museum [G. H. Edgell]. "I don't want to hurry you," he said politely, "but when you two have *quite* finished splitting that particular hair, will you take time out to pass me the salt?"

In 1931 when Mr. Tomita was appointed Curator of the Asiatic Department, Dr. Coomaraswamy's title was changed to Fellow for Research in Indian, Persian, and Mohammedan Art, which was better related to the manner in which he then exercised his mind. So it remained until his sudden death on 9 September 1947, a little more than two weeks after the celebration of his seventieth birthday; he might with equal appropriateness have been designated as "resident guru" of the museum. On his death, Aldous Huxley, who knew him only through his books and correspondence, spoke of "that extraordinary combination of vast learning and penetrating insight which gave to Coomaraswamy his unique importance as a mediator between East and West."

Going back thirty years to the period of Ananda Coomaraswamy's arrival at the Museum of Fine Arts, successive issues of the *Bulletin* contained his accounts of the hitherto little known treasures of Rajput and Mughal painting, the Buddhist bronzes from Ceylon, Nepal, and Tibet, the Burmese glazed tiles, the Gandhara and Cambodian sculpture that had come to the museum, chiefly through Dr. Ross's active generosity. Through the death of Hervey Edward Wetzel on 14 October 1918, the museum lost a friend, who had he lived might have carried on Denman Ross's role for another generation. Born in Detroit on 2 February 1888, he entered Harvard College with the class of 1911. As he was an only child and as both his parents died while he was an undergraduate, he found himself with considerable means. Although he returned to the Graduate School of Business Administration, he was soon diverted from business to the study and collecting of art through the friendship of Edward Forbes and of Denman Ross, with whom he went to Asia and Europe in 1912–13. He was appointed an Associate of the Department of Western Art in 1914. In 1916 he returned to Asia to study and search for objects. On his return he became a Ph.D. candidate in the field of Persian and Mohammedan Art, and learned Arabic. Although the museum offered him the active charge of its Persian and Mohammedan collections, he went instead to Plattsburg, New York, for a course of military training. Disqualified for army service because of a weak heart, Wetzel went to France with the Red Cross, where he died of pneumonia, as Oric Bates had in an army camp a week earlier.

By his will Hervey Wetzel left the Museum of Fine Arts the great Chinese stela that he had lent earlier, and a considerable part of his collection, as well as $100,000 to be spent in the purchase of a few objects of supreme interest and importance. With this fund was bought in 1920 a glorious twelfth-century wood sculpture overlaid with color and gold of the Kuan-yin P'u sa. In the same year a collection of Chinese and Japanese works of art formerly owned by Okakura-Kakuzo was acquired through the generosity of William Sturgis

THE BODHISATTVA AVALOKITESVARA (KUAN-YIN). Wood,
Chinese, Sung dynasty, 12th century. *Hervey Edward Wetzel
Fund. 20.590*

Bigelow and Okakura's heirs, supplemented by appropriations by the
museum. The department was further enriched by numerous gifts
from Dr. Bigelow and from the estate of Henry Adams. Not long
afterward Mrs. W. Scott Fitz gave a large bronze dedicatory group of
the *Buddha Amitabha and attendant divinities* of the Sui dynasty,
dated 593 A.D. This remarkable group had been brought to the United
States in 1911 and had been offered to the Museum of Fine Arts,
which had regretfully foregone it because of the exorbitant price
asked by the dealer who had it. Eleven years later Edward Jackson
Holmes saw it again in Vignier's shop in Paris, and cabled the museum, which was greatly interested in having it. Thus in 1922 his

mother bought and gave the bronze group, even though the asking price was still so high as to require her to borrow money in order to do so. In 1927 it was discovered that six subsidiary bronze figures from this same group were in the possession of Charles Rutherston of Bradford, England. Although Mr. Tomita went to England in an effort to secure them, the owner was unwilling to sell at a possible price. During the Second World War the figures were sent to the United States and were lent to the Museum of Fine Arts. At the end of the war the complete group was for the first time exhibited, and was published in its proper form in the June 1945 *Bulletin*. Finally in 1947, after two decades of negotiation, Edward Jackson Holmes purchased the six figures and gave them to the museum to complete his mother's gift of a quarter of a century before.

Japan in the twentieth century could still make collectors out of Bostonians, for a visit there in 1909 caused William Stuart Spaulding (Harvard A.B. 1888) and his younger brother, John Taylor Spaulding, to become enthusiastic over Japanese prints. Although

DEDICATORY GROUP, BUDDHA AMITABHA (O-MI-TO) TRINITY AND ATTENDANTS. Bronze, Chinese, Sui dynasty, dated 593. *Gift of Mrs. W. Scott Fitz and Edward Jackson Holmes.* 22.407

they acquired in this trip only a single fine print by Hiroshige, they soon were recognized among the leading print collectors of the world, for they maintained the highest standards of quality and condition. They would often buy an entire collection only to secure a very few desirable prints. The six thousand that they gave in 1921 were a magnificent addition to the earlier gifts in the field from Bigelow and Ross.

When Lacey Davis Caskey became Curator of the Department of Classical Art in 1912, he began work on a catalogue of Greek and Roman sculpture in the museum, which was eventually published in 1925. Arthur Fairbanks, whose *Athenian White Lekythoi* had appeared in two volumes in 1907 and 1914, began work in 1915 on a catalogue of pottery. His *Catalogue of Greek and Etruscan Vases: Part I, Early Vases preceding Athenian Black-figured Ware* appeared in 1928, three years after Fairbanks had retired from the museum. The handbook for high-school students that he published in 1915, entitled *Greek Gods and Heroes as Represented in the Classical Collections of the Museum*, revised by George H. Chase in 1948 and improved in format with successive printings, has survived for fifty-five years as a useful introduction for beginners.

Dr. Chase, a much loved Classical scholar who was for many years John E. Hudson Professor of Archaeology at Harvard and Dean of the Graduate School of Arts and Sciences, as well as by Harvard appointment a museum trustee from 1918 to 1945, had published in 1908 a catalogue of the Arretine pottery that James Loeb (1867–1933), the founder of the Loeb Classical Library, had for a time lent to the Fogg Art Museum. In 1914 Chase began work upon a similar volume describing the Museum of Fine Arts collection of this material. His *Arretine Pottery: A Catalogue of the Collection in the Museum* was published in 1917 with the aid of a generous gift from Loeb. In 1919 George H. Chase gave eight Lowell Lectures that the Harvard University Press published in 1924 under the title of *Greek and Roman Sculpture in American Collections*, a delightful book that sketched the history of ancient sculpture with illustrations from the holdings of Boston and other American museums. He was a minute little man, full of learning and human kindness; as a graduate student I took a reading course with him on Greek vases simply for the pleasure of seeing him once a week. As I then passed as a medievalist, this had little to do with my main purpose, but I have seldom learned more or enjoyed myself more in a comparable period of time.

The artist Jay Hambidge (1867–1924) had developed early in this century an ambition to discover the technical bases of design. After studying Greek remains in Sicily, he advanced the theory that both in the symmetrical forms of nature and in Greek art there existed a "principle of proportion" that is not only constant but capable of mathematical expression. As his theory developed, he differentiated between "dynamic" and "static" symmetry. In the former, which he found in nature and in Greek art, he believed "the measureableness of symmetry is that of area and not line." He believed that classical artists carefully and exactly fixed the limits of their composition, but within these bounds worked freely. As Denman W. Ross was one of the supporters of Hambidge's theory, Lacey Caskey in 1918 undertook a study of the forms of the Attic black-figured and red-figured vases in the Boston collection to determine how far their evidence might be of assistance.

During the last seven months of the year, Caskey laid aside his work on the sculpture catalogue to devote himself to this investigation. Some 250 vases were measured and their proportions determined, while full-size elevations of 120 were drawn, with Hambidge frequently present for consultation. Two hundred more were drawn and analyzed the next year, and by September 1920, when Caskey was given six months' leave of absence for recuperation from this geometrical orgy and for study in Greece, the manuscript of his *Geometry of Greek Vases* had gone to the printer. This analysis of 185 vases in the collection was published in 1922. The volume gave joy to Hambidge, who only survived two more years, and was useful in itself for its accurate drawings of the shapes of vases. The first formal catalogue to be issued, however, was *Attic Vase Paintings in the Museum of Fine Arts* by Caskey and J. D. (later Sir John) Beazley, Lincoln Professor of Classical Archaeology at Oxford, the first part of which appeared in 1931.

Although the pace of collecting never returned to that of the decade 1895–1904, which was interrupted by the need of husbanding resources for the construction of the present building, the De-

SNAKE GODDESS. Gold and ivory, ca. 1600–1500 B.C., as reassembled and as received. *Gift of Mrs. W. Scott Fitz. 14.863*

partment of Classical Art has grown steadily through the activities of its succession of learned and alert curators. There have been some acquisitions as unique and exciting as any of the Warren era, such as the arrival in 1914 of the diminutive gold and ivory statuette of the *Snake Goddess*, which is the most refined and precious object to have survived the ruin of Minoan civilization. This remarkable gift of Mrs. W. Scott Fitz was painfully reconstructed at the Museum of Fine Arts from hundreds of ivory slivers and gold fragments, obtained in a cigar box from a Cretan peasant who was a passenger in a steamship bound from Piraeus to Boston in 1913. Another remarkable acquisition was the seventh-century gold *Libation Bowl*, dedicated at Olympia by the sons of Kypselos, tyrant of Corinth (655–625 B.C.), which was purchased in 1921 with income of the Francis Bartlett Fund. Denman W. Ross's 1917 general gift of previous loans included an archaic Greek limestone statue of a man of the sixth century B.C., while a similar gift of J. Templeman Coolidge added to the collection a particularly lovely Hellenistic marble fragment of the torso of a young girl. It has earlier been noted that the great collection of engraved gems, to the assembly of which Edward P. Warren had devoted his later years, was purchased between 1921 and 1927 with the aid of the Francis Bartlett Fund.

Morris Gray, who had urged in his 1915 President's report that a museum should exhibit its works of art "in such a way and in such an environment as to enable the beholder not merely to see them more perfectly, but — and this is a very different thing — to enjoy them more deeply," spoke with pleasure the following year of the changes that had been made in the Classical wing to enhance the exhibition of the Boston counterpart to the Ludovisi Throne. An alcove had been created near the east end of the Fifth Century Room to isolate this fine piece under top light, and changes made in the doors leading from this gallery to improve the new exhibition. In mentioning this, Morris Gray expressed the hope that the staff will place seats there,

LIBATION BOWL. Gold, Greek, from Olympia, late 7th century B.C.
Francis Bartlett Fund. 21.1843

FIFTH CENTURY GREEK ROOM AS ALTERED IN 1916.

and personally, I hope that it will place there the color — perhaps in the form of a couple of large bay trees — that is needed to bring out the warmth and beauty of the object. Assuming that the Museum does this, it will suddenly convert an object which hitherto the public have usually passed almost without notice into one of the great, and deservedly great, features of the Museum — one that will be far better known, one that will be far more enjoyed.

Arthur Fairbanks in the 1916 Director's report to the trustees mentioned other changes under consideration in the classical department,

the object of which is to increase the visitor's enjoyment of the works of art by giving them a more attractive setting. That many of our galleries have seemed cold and bare is quite generally agreed. The correction of this fault, and in particular the definite changes that have been proposed, in so far as they do not involve too great an expenditure of funds much needed for other purposes, are urged on your attention.

Conflicting demands upon limited funds always cause confusion. The events that followed in the Department of Classical Art are an instructive example of what can occur when one embarks upon "window dressing" without the ready means to carry it through.

The Classical wing had been deliberately designed with a series of galleries that would provide a chronological progression from archaic Greece to the Greco-Roman period without the slightest possibility of going astray. There were in consequence but two doors from the exhibition rooms to the gallery that looked down on the Classical court. Although admirable for logical historical exhibition, for scholarly study, and indeed for popular instruction, this plan was not necessarily conducive to the aesthetic rapture that entranced Morris Gray, for he wrote in 1916:

> The exhibition galleries of museums open out of each other usually. This gives a certain stately effect and enables the better handling of crowds on free days; and it may well be wise, and indeed necessary. Yet it entails a certain corridor use of the rooms, which constantly disturbs the man who is rapt in the contemplation of a work of art and tends to give him, unfortunately, a restless, hurried feeling. Here and there in the different departments museums would do well to exhibit some of their greatest works of art in alcoves or rooms to be entered presumably only by those interested.

In the Classical wing nothing had been sacrificed to "stately effect," for although rooms led out of each other, doors had been placed for use rather than the creation of distant vistas. But the construction of the alcove for the Boston Throne had required the blocking of the previous passage from the Fifth Century to the First Marble rooms and the opening of new doors to the Graeco-Roman Gallery. Thus the notion was developed of transforming the two Marble Rooms into one stone-faced gallery, measuring 27 by 40 feet, which would be accessible only from the Graeco-Roman Gallery and consequently no longer on a direct line of travel. This was undertaken in 1916, although it involved moving at least once, and sometimes two or three times, some 1,800 objects, not all of which were light. Lack of funds and wartime shortages prevented the completion of the work for nearly five years. During this period the best Greek marbles were placed wherever possible, many of them out of historical sequence and in unfavorable light. In 1919 Arthur Fairbanks plaintively reported: "For two and a half years the marble room has been abandoned and the confusion has continued. Even though the cost of refitting this room suitably should prove large, it is a misfortune to delay it any longer than necessary." The mess continued for some time, for although work was resumed in 1920 it was not completed until the summer of 1921. Even then the walls were only plastered, rather than faced with stone, as architect Gordon Allen's original plan had called for. This experience discouraged for many years further architectural tinkering with the Classical galleries.

Ananda K. Coomaraswamy, who was around while all this was going on, stated ex cathedra in his provocative little book *Why*

THE GREEK MARBLE ROOM AS COMPLETED IN 1921.

Exhibit Works of Art? that "it is not the function of a museum or of any educator to flatter and amuse the public." Yet during the presidency of Morris Gray much thought, time, and money was lavished upon efforts to attract a "public," the extent of whose interest in the museum was never completely clear. Money, as always, continued in short supply, for as the Evans Wing had added over 40 percent to the exhibition space of the museum, annual operating expenses were bound to increase accordingly. Thus in the 1915 President's report, Gray noted:

> The running expenses of 1915 were $162,480.91. These cannot be reduced materially by added economies. They can be reduced by closing a substantial part of the Museum and by giving up a substantial part of its force. But this would mean a great reduction in the service to the public. Moreover, it would entail presumably a loss of public interest, and it might well cause a diminution in gifts and bequests which would injure the Museum far more than the current deficits do.

Accordingly he reiterated the need, previously expressed in 1914, of an Administration fund of at least $1,000,000 to achieve a position where the incomes of that and of existing unrestricted funds would, with the annual subscriptions, pay all normal running expenses. Mrs. Evans had asked that the $88,751.44 remaining from her gift for the construction of the wing, be placed in such a fund. Moreover the trustees voted to transfer there approximately 75 percent of unrestricted moneys received by current bequests. Thus $170,500 was earmarked from recent bequests of Miss Katherine C. Pierce, Miss Sarah E. Simpson, Francis Skinner, Edward Wheelwright, and Miss Caroline L. W. French. From these two sources the Administration Fund received some $359,000. Morris Gray pointed out that the remaining 25 percent of these recent bequests would be used for the purchase of works of art, so that "those who give unrestrictedly should have their generosity shown, not only in the financial accounts that are read by the few, but in works of art that are seen by the thousands who year after year visit the Museum."

Thanks to the Evans Wing many more thousands appeared. The 1914 attendance of 205,109 increased by more than a quarter in

1915 to 267,211, and 1916 showed only a modest drop to 265,409. Although income steadily improved, operating expenses were always a lap or two ahead. In 1915 the income was $112,719, and outgo $162,480, the deficit $49,761; in 1924 the comparable figures were $232,082 and $258,137, and the deficit was $26,055. The highest deficit of this decade was $67,855, the lowest $25,220. This kind of financing, so oddly prophetic of the New Deal, continued blithely in the hope that the more was spent on public services, the greater would be the eventual reward; in short, it was confidently hoped that virtue would some day pay. It did not seem to do so in 1917, for attendance dropped to 224,735 and annual subscriptions from $41,267 to $36,491. Nevertheless, Morris Gray, who, like Henry Noble Mac-Cracken of Vassar College, persisted in referring to himself as "Your President" made an impassioned plea for abolishing the admission fees, which had produced $15,909 in 1917. His report for that year concluded:

> In these tragic days the Museum should be opened free to all who wish the help that art is privileged to give; free entirely, or, if that be deemed unwise, free to a much greater degree than it is at present; and this not merely because it would increase presumably the number of visitors, but rather because it would develop a deeper interest in the Museum through the substitution of equality of privilege in place of the constant differentiation between those who pay and those who do not pay — that equality of privilege which goes far towards making a great public library the intellectual home of the people. Many arguments can be made against this proposition, perhaps the strongest is the additional expense at this time of heavy deficits. It is true that the money received through paid admissions would be lost; but this, amounting as it does to less than 3 percent of the running expenses, is a small matter. It is true, also that the money received from annual subscribers might be materially lessened; and this would be serious, because the subscriptions amount now to about 20 percent of the expenses. Yet be that as it may, the question is far greater than the question of money. It is a question of rendering the greatest service at the time of the world's direst need. Although unaided by State and city, let us not, at least in these days, sell the service that it is possible for the Museum to render. Let us swing the doors wide and make the entrance as free

as is the entrance to the parks of a great city. As they give the beauty of nature, let us see to it that the Museum gives, as far as in it lies, the beauty of art; let us make that beauty free to all.

This appeal suited the wartime mood of Boston. On 17 January 1918 the museum became free, all seven days of the week. It was not possible immediately to judge the reaction, for owing to a shortage of coal a large part of the building had to be closed during January and February, while the influenza epidemic in October required complete closing for more than three weeks. Thus, although the 1918 attendance was only 212,281, that of 1919 was 280,189, slightly more than the number that had turned up in 1910 when the new building was still a major novelty. Thereafter the rise was steady: 288,312 in 1920, 319,895 (1921), 330,243 (1922), 383,746 (1923), and 406,427 (1924). In 1919 annual subscriptions only crept up lightly to $37,484 but the year was a rich one in bequests and gifts of paintings, as has been noted in Chapter X. Morris Gray believed firmly in the "soft sell," for although he badly wanted more annual subscriptions or an increased Administration Fund, he wrote in his 1919 report:

> Your President believes that the Trustees should present the needs of the Museum clearly and strongly to the public generally, and should stand upon that appeal. Endowed with full knowledge the individual should be left to untrammelled decision. Your President does not believe in the institution of a "drive" similar to those so successfully used at times for other great charities, especially for those of broader public interest and understanding and, in the case of colleges particularly, of a deep hold upon the affection of graduates. It is true that the aggressive and widespread personal solicitation of the "drive" might bring in a good deal of money that no other method could obtain. Yet the Museum stands in a certain sense apart from other great charities. Those who give money to it are generous, but few. They are interested in the Museum and they know its needs. At the same time they are people that receive and answer many appeals. Under these circumstances it is neither wise nor suitable that they should be approached by personal and influential solicitation and urging. It is true that they might give more. But the Museum does not desire contributions from them or from

others that are in any degree reluctant or forced. It desires only contributions that are made for the cause and solely for the cause that the Museum serves.

Incidentally your President believes that the Trustees will do more wisely to concentrate their personal efforts upon the development of interest in the Museum. Indeed, the interest will bring the gift.

As the key to this approach depended so greatly upon the personal efforts of the trustees, it would be prudent at this time to consider who they were in 1919. Charles W. Eliot, the only surviving Founder of 1870, had retired from the presidency of Harvard a decade before and was, at eighty-five, in dignified seclusion in Cambridge. Denman W. Ross, the next senior in election (1895), was exploring new frontiers, collecting and giving superb objects to the museum as vigorously as ever; Charles Sprague Sargent (1900) continued to direct the Arnold Arboretum. Morris Gray (1902) was a lawyer and private trustee of the pattern so usefully familiar in Boston, looking after his own and other people's property and giving generously of his time to public institutions. Edward Waldo Forbes (1903) had for a decade been director of the Fogg Art Museum at Harvard. Thomas Allen (1909), painter, was chairman of the Council of the Museum School and of the Art Commission of the City of Boston. There followed two self-made men, elected in 1911 with obvious hopes of possible benefits to be received: Thomas Nelson Vail, President of the American Telephone and Telegraph Company, and George Robert White, head of the Potter Drug and Chemical Company, the manufacturers of Cuticura soap. Alexander Cochrane, an industrialist who was elected in 1913, had died on 10 April 1919, bequeathing to the museum desirable French paintings noted in Chapter X. Augustus Hemenway (Harvard 1875), who had given the Hemenway Gymnasium to the university in 1878 and was, after Gardiner M. Lane's death, the chief supporter of the Harvard – Boston Egyptian Expedition, had joined the board in 1913.

In 1915 three trustees were elected: William Crowninshield Endicott (Harvard A.B. 1883), lawyer and private trustee; George Peabody Gardner, who has previously been mentioned in connection with the Print Department; and William Endicott (Harvard A.B. 1887).

The last-named was the son of William Endicott, a Founder and second President of the museum, and himself a banker with Kidder Peabody and Company. Although both Endicotts were much of an age, black-bearded, and lived near each other in Marlborough Street, they were not closely related. William C. Endicott and George Peabody Gardner were, however, both first and second cousins of each other through the Peabody family's delight in marrying relatives. Holker Abbott, a stalwart of the Copley Society and Tavern Club, had been elected in 1916 after earlier service as a representative of the Boston Athenæum. When Francis Lee Higginson resigned as Treasurer and trustee early in 1917, William Endicott succeeded him as Treasurer. When he went off to France on behalf of the Red Cross in the summer of 1917, William Crowninshield Endicott took over the finances, which he ran in dictatorial manner for nearly two decades. On the death of Abraham Shuman in 1918, his place was filled by Henry Lee Shattuck (Harvard A.B. 1901, LL.B. 1904), one of the few old Yankees to hold his own in the rough-and-tumble of city and state politics, a future treasurer of Harvard College; he was among other things a collector of early American prints and paintings. Dudley Leavitt Pickman (Harvard A.B. 1873), also elected in 1918, was the grandson of a Salem shipmaster and merchant and a collector of European and Chinese porcelains, while Henry Forbes Bigelow, who replaced Alexander Cochrane in 1919, was an architect, who had enlarged the Boston Athenæum building in 1913–1915 and otherwise shown a subtle understanding of New England architecture.

As representatives of Harvard, the Classicist Professor George Henry Chase, had in 1918 joined Dr. William Sturgis Bigelow (1891) and J. Templeman Coolidge (1902). J. Randolph Coolidge, Jr. (1899) and Alexander Wadsworth Longfellow (1904) still represented the Boston Athenæum, but in the company since 1917 of Charles Knowles Bolton, its librarian, who had considerable interest in New England paintings and antiquities. The Massachusetts Institute of Technology had appointed its President, Richard Cockburn Maclaurin, since 1909; Edward Jackson Holmes, devoted friend of the Department of Chinese and Japanese Art, since 1910; and, from 1916, Desmond Fitzgerald, hydraulic engineer and collector, who in 1913 built an art gallery near his house in Brookline for his paintings and Korean and Chinese pottery and porcelains. To complete the list, the Trustee of the Lowell Institute, A. Lawrence Lowell (1900) had been since 1909 President of Harvard University.

Denman Ross's classmate and lifelong friend, Dean L. B. R. Briggs, is reputed to have said, when asked how one could change President Lowell's mind when it was made up, "I don't know. I'm not Nelson Perkins. I can't put my hands on his shoulders, push him into the corner, and say 'Now, shut your idiotic mouth and listen to some sense.'" Harvard Corporation meetings in the years when Lawrence Lowell, Thomas Nelson Perkins, Charles Francis Adams, and Bishop Lawrence were four out of the seven present must, on occasion, have resembled a gathering in Valhalla with gods noisily clouting each other over the head with sledge hammers. So, one suspects, may have some of the deliberations of the trustees of the Museum of Fine Arts, for this was a company of strong individualists of decided opinions, notably deficient in "tame cats," "consensus men," and wasters of time. In particular the Treasurer, William Crowninshield Endicott, could shift with the speed of light from a ferocious growl to a contagious laugh. He was the benevolent autocrat, if not president, of nearly every organization concerned with the past of New England. He could be a highly genial companion. His ideas were generally excellent, but if he did not like something there was no doubt of his opinion. During his service as Treasurer (1917–1936) of the Museum of Fine Arts, he seldom remained silent; if he disliked a work of art approved for purchase by the Committee on the Museum he was quite capable of exercising a unilateral veto by failing to pay for it.

Arthur Fairbanks in 1919 called the attention of the trustees to various needs beside the completion of the Marble Room that should be undertaken if funds could be found. In the interests of economy even the care of the building had been somewhat stinted. It would be desirable to organize occasional loan exhibitions of high standard if funds were available for the necessary assistants, for transportation, and for insurance. Funds were needed for publication, for administration, for purchases, and also for more curators. On this point he wrote:

While I believe the Museum has reason to be proud of its Staff, at several points it is still inadequate. We have no Curator or Keeper who is an authority on mediaeval and renaissance art; the Keeper of Paintings prefers not to assume responsibility in connection with the purchase of American paintings; and in the absence of Dr. Reisner in Egypt, he should again be represented here by a scholarly Assistant Curator.

The need of a curator with scholarly competence in the Middle Ages and Renaissance was particularly felt, for various pieces of Gothic sculpture had been given or purchased at the end of the war. Indeed the Gothic Room had been arranged only in the previous spring to display these new acquisitions.

In June of 1919 Morris Carter, who had been Assistant Director since 1913, resigned in order to work full-time for Mrs. John L. Gardner at Fenway Court; for thirty years following her death in 1924 he was the first Director of the Isabella Stewart Gardner Museum. Morris Carter's post at the Museum of Fine Arts was filled by the appointment of Charles Henry Hawes, a graduate of the University of Cambridge (M.A. 1902), who after extensive travel in the East and some experience in business in England had become Professor of Anthropology at Dartmouth College. Before coming to Boston he had married one of the most distinguished classical archaeologists of her time, Harriet Boyd, a graduate of Smith College who in the early years of the twentieth century had excavated the Cretan city of Gournia. From 1919 to 1922 Hawes served also as Bursar; in 1924 his title was changed to Associate Director.

Henry Preston Rossiter (University of Toronto A.B. 1909) was appointed Assistant Curator of the Print Department in March 1919. During several years as a teacher and in business in Canada he had become interested in prints and engravings. When he joined the Canadian Army at the outbreak of the First World War, he proved during a musketry course at Ottawa to have extraordinary speed in operating machine guns and when blindfolded, an unanticipated ability to take one apart and put it together again in fewer seconds than anyone had ever done it before. Although as a platoon and company commander in France he had little opportunity personally to operate a machine gun, the Ottawa training had a curious influence upon his subsequent career. During the musketry course he had become familiar with a marvelous instrument called the Marenden Range Finder. About a year later in France, he chanced to dine at Brigade Headquarters with the inventor of the instrument. During dinner General Marenden told Rossiter how, during extended service in Persia, he had come to love and collect Persian pots. It was a revelation to discover that one could be interested in art without forfeiting the character of officer and he-man. Until that dinner Henry Rossiter had never mentioned his interest in prints to anyone; thereafter his visits to print dealers when on leave in Paris became less surreptitious. After demobilization as a Major at the end of the war, he determined to make a career of museum work in this field. Two years after coming to Boston, he resigned to become Curator of Prints at the National Gallery of Canada in Ottawa. As FitzRoy Carrington resigned later in 1921, Henry Rossiter was persuaded to return to Boston, after only a little over a year's absence, to become Acting Curator of Prints on 1 September 1922. In October 1923 he became

THE JUDGMENT HALL OF PILATE. Anonymous engraving, Florentine, 15th century. *Maria Antoinette Evans Fund. 31.1206*

ST. JOHN THE BAPTIST IN THE WILDERNESS. Engraving by
Master E. S., German, 15th century. *Maria Antoinette Evans
Fund. 31.1208*

Curator, a post that he filled with outstanding energy, imagination, and distinction for the next forty-four years. In the decade following the end of the war, when many great continental collections were being dispersed, he made extraordinary purchases for the Print Department at European auctions. Although the more than four decades of his curatorship were notable for remarkable acquisitions in all fields of printmaking, the hunting was particularly rewarding in the twenties. But the thirties were not without their significant discoveries. In 1931, for example, a number of important early prints were obtained at auction sales in Europe through the Maria Antoinette Evans Fund. In this group early Italian engraving was brilliantly represented by the anonymous fifteenth-century Florentine *Judgment Hall of Pilate*, which Arthur M. Hind described as "the largest and most important of all fine manner prints." The impression acquired, which is the only complete one known, came from the

Ducal Museum, Gotha. An equally remarkable example of almost contemporary German work was the circular engraving, dated 1466, of *St. John the Baptist in the Wilderness*, which is one of the most charming and celebrated works of Master E. S., active ca. 1440–1468. Of this print, Henry P. Rossiter wrote in the October 1931 *Bulletin*:

> It was not unknown in its generation, for artists freely appropriated its parts, a flower here, a figure there, so that long before the century had passed it had cropped up piecemeal in various forms. Because of its exquisite detail, its size and circular shape, some think that it was intended as a design for a paten. Whether this is true or not, there can be little doubt that the author did not take over his stock of ideas or his art ready-made.

Two acquisitions of 1932 were indeed *incunabula incunabulorum* of printmaking. Of *The Queen of Stags*, a fifteenth-century playing card for a game whose pack comprised five suits — Flowers, Wild Men, Birds, Stags, and Beasts of Prey — the Curator wrote in the *Bulletin* for October 1932:

> From the Stephen Bullard Fund the Museum has purchased an important engraving by the Master of the Playing Cards, who, while probably not the inventor of engraving, emerges in the first half of the fifteenth century as its earliest known practitioner. Mere seniority might easily raise the veriest hack into prominence; but this master will bear scrutiny for his talent alone. With a firm grasp of design he brings to this work a creative mind and a practised, unflagging hand, so that anyone confronted by his complete series of playing cards — anyone whose boundaries in art do not coincide with the metropolitan cab radius — stands in grave danger of being charmed by their originality and zest. Cultivating his bent, he turns a bright eye toward nature, an eye so vivacious that his beasts, birds, flowers, fanciful wild folk and comely worldlings take life as animate things. He draws expressively the features of his well modelled heads, while his court card figures, whether in motion or repose, are so regally savoring their rôles, so gracefully and graciously at ease, that the fifteenth century player must have been a dull fellow who could not have wished himself of their world.

THE QUEEN OF STAGS. Engraving by Master
of the Playing Cards, German, 15th century.
Stephen Bullard Fund. 32.482

The second of these extraordinary acquisitions, Boccaccio's *De la ruyne des nobles hommes et femmes*, published by Colard Mansion at Bruges in 1476, is the first printed book to be illustrated by copper engravings. The museum's copy, bought through the Evans Fund, is one of three known examples in which have been pasted all nine of the illustrations by an anonymous Flemish artist (known as the Master of the Boccaccio Illustrations). It is the only known copy in which the engravings have been colored by hand, to simulate the effect of illuminated miniatures. If the printed book were to become the poor-man's manuscript, mass-produced, the engraver had the technique for supplying an economical substitute for illumination.

The staff of the Department of Western Art changed completely at the end of the war. The importance of its collection of textiles,

GIOVANNI BOCCACCIO, *De la ruyne des nobles hommes et femmes*. Published by Colard Mansion, Bruges, 1476, with engravings by the Master of the Boccaccio Illustrations. *Maria Antoinette Evans Fund. 32.458*

BOCCACCIO RETELLING THE STORY OF ADAM AND EVE. Detail from the Bruges 1476 edition. *Maria Antoinette Evans Fund. 32.458*

which had grown so substantially through the gifts of Denman W. Ross, was recognized in 1900 by the appointment as Assistant in Charge of Miss Jenny Brooks, a sister of Professor Edward S. Morse's devoted secretary, Margaretta Brooks. She was succeeded in 1904 by Miss Sarah Gore Flint, who having been born in Arequipa, Peru, now and then Hispanicized her name to Sarita. In September 1918, not long after her marriage to the physician-ornithologist Dr. Charles Wendell Townsend, who was her sister's widower, she resigned and was made Adviser to the Department. Her niece and stepdaughter, Miss Gertrude Townsend, a graduate of the Museum School, was soon after, on the recommendation of Denman Ross, appointed Assistant in Charge. As with Henry P. Rossiter, the choice was a fortunate one, for more than fifty years later, after long service as Curator, Miss Townsend is still busily at work in a field of which she possesses unique knowledge.

Miss Flint's friend and traveling companion, Miss Florence Virginia Paull, who had come to the Copley Square museum in 1895 as extra help to address envelopes and had become General Loring's secretary, was appointed Assistant in Charge of Other Collections in the Department of Western Art on 12 July 1909. Miss Paull had helped considerably with the catalogue of the 1906 American silver exhibition, while that of the 1911 exhibition was almost entirely her work. The largest collection of American and English pewter shown at one time was on display from 8 November 1916 until 15 January 1917. Over five hundred pieces, dating from the seventeenth to the early nineteenth centuries, lent by seventy owners, were exhibited, and a list of American pewterers prepared and put on sale. When William Lindsey in 1916 gave as a memorial to his daughter, Leslie Lindsey Mason, lost in the *Lusitania* sinking, the extensive collection of old musical instruments gathered by the Reverend Francis W. Galpin of Harlow, Sussex, Miss Paull arranged an exhibition of them that was described in the October 1917 *Bulletin*. To the considerable variety of objects that fell in her bailiwick, Mohammedan as well as European until the former passed to Dr. Coomaraswamy's charge, an increasing number of early American artifacts were added. Two Colonial doorways from the Eben White Tavern, Hatfield, Massachusetts, which were bought in 1916, suggested the idea of creating a "special Colonial installation" in the basement of the Evans Wing, below the Picture Reserve, where (as noted in Chapter X) a loan exhibition of American furniture was temporarily shown. As paneling was also available, it was proposed to cut a connection between the two floors, which would permit installing a Colonial staircase and balusters.

In 1918 Miss Paull married Henri Léon Berger, who carried her off to Hartford, where she became General Curator of the Wadsworth Athenaeum. With a Visiting Committee containing such collectors as Dudley L. Pickman (chairman), Charles Hitchcock Tyler, Henry Davis Sleeper, Francis Hill Bigelow, and William Crowninshield Endicott, it was natural to seek as her successor someone who would actively pursue the interest in American decorative arts that was steadily growing. Thus in May 1919 Edwin James Hipkiss, an architect who had become especially interested in Colonial art, was appointed Keeper in the Department of Western Art. This choice clearly reflected the turn of thought summarized in the section "The Colonial Department" of the 1919 President's report, where Morris Gray wrote:

> The Museum has long desired to gather together beautiful objects of Colonial art and to exhibit them in a fitting setting. With this in view it has recently acquired a distinguished house [the Jaffrey house in Portsmouth, New Hampshire] of the Colonial period — about to be torn down. It proposes to remove the stairways, mantelpieces, doors, windows, panels, and other portions of the interior deemed desirable, for installation in the Museum when funds permit; and after that removal to sell the house and land.
>
> A great collection of beautiful objects of Colonial art would undoubtedly interest the public through its artistic merit and its historical value. But it would have a larger value; for it would tend to develop the appreciation of beauty in the home through a close comparison of the objects of Colonial art that the individual sees in the Museum with the objects for similar purposes that he himself possesses. Nor would that development stop in the home, but through awakened appreciation it would lead gradually to the more difficult appreciation of yet higher forms of art. The desire for beauty in the home is fundamental.

Such a collection would be far more effective if exhibited in the environment of the period. Now the opportunity to purchase good interiors of Colonial houses is not frequent to-day; so it should be availed of as it arises, even although exhibition must be deferred through lack of funds. The purchase of this particular house is largely due to the active interest and generosity of Mr. Charles H. Tyler and Mr. J. Templeman Coolidge, supplemented by an appropriation by the Trustees.

Arthur Fairbanks echoed the hope that these rooms, built into some section of the building, might give a suitable setting to exhibit Colonial portraits, furniture, silver, and glass, adding that "no lesson the Museum can teach is practically more important than this lesson, drawn from our own history, of the meaning of art for the home." Fairbanks reiterated the plea in 1920 with the remark that "such a series of galleries would greatly interest our visitors, and the influence of such exhibitions on taste in home decoration might be large."

In 1922 the museum bought the interior finish of "Oak Hill," a house designed by Samuel McIntire about 1800 for Mrs. Nathaniel West, daughter of the Salem merchant Elias Hasket Derby, which had come on the market following the death in 1921 of Mrs. Jacob Crowninshield Rogers, who had occupied it since 1879. Miss Martha C. Codman, a great-granddaughter of Elias Hasket Derby, not only contributed generously toward the purchase but gave many pieces of furniture originally contained in the house. "Oak Hill," despoiled of its trim, served as a Xaverian Juniorate until it was demolished and its fine trees chopped down to make way for the North Shore Shopping Center in Peabody. The following year Mrs. Edward Foote Dwight gave, in memory of her parents, George and Sarah Elizabeth Eddy Parsons of New York, a Tudor paneled room of 1490, while the museum bought an English Georgian room.

With paneling and furniture piling up in storage, there was a general desire for a new wing, in which everyone could happily play house. During 1924 a committee of the trustees, of which Dudley L. Pickman was chairman, raised $572,100 from approximately one hundred friends of the museum, and excavation was begun. This was an admirable achievement. It gave general pleasure, yet it represented running with the pack in a manner hitherto unfamiliar to Boston. In the previous half-century the Museum of Fine Arts, thanks to collectors like Bigelow, Weld, Warren, Ross, and Bullard, and to the incomparable archaeologist Reisner, had pioneered in its collecting of Japanese, Classical, and Egyptian art, of textiles and prints; in attracting to its staff Okakura-Kakuzo and Ananda K. Coomaraswamy it had set a standard seldom equaled anywhere. Now in the nineteen twenties it was succumbing to the current passion for "period rooms," with which Americans everywhere lusted to endow their local art museums. The superb assembly of European decorative arts in the Pierpont Morgan Wing of the Metropolitan Museum, opened in 1918, followed by the construction of the adjacent American Wing, which opened on 10 November 1924, had a profound effect upon frequenters and friends of museums elsewhere, even in Boston. It was in due course to have its apotheosis in the Henry Francis du Pont Winterthur Museum.

When the Huntington Avenue building was being planned in 1904, Matthew S. Prichard had raised the possibility of one or more actual rooms to illustrate the art of Colonial New England as a means of perpetuating "in this way some record of the local genius." He spoke, however, of "the sacrifice of one or two contemporary paintings" to such an interior as not too great, even though "their individual value would be lost . . . in enhancing the effect of the room." Now, two decades later, the possibility of achieving at small cost of space and funds such an act of local artistic piety was suddenly likely to expand far beyond the boundaries of New England, if the gift of the Tudor room of 1490 was any harbinger of things to come.

The proposed new Western Art building would connect the Classical wing with the Evans painting galleries in much the manner envisioned by Guy Lowell's original plan, but once again construction was being undertaken before the income from endowment permitted a balanced budget for the operation of the existing buildings, for there was a deficit of $26,054 in 1924. As the devil hates holy water, even the most conservative Boston treasurer is uncomfortable with a credit balance at the end of a year's operations, lest the institution's friends be discouraged from further gifts through the misapprehension that no more money is needed. It must be admitted that, although there had been a deficit every year since the move to Huntington Avenue, there was little risk of a visit from the sheriff, for each year a substantial sum had been spent on the purchase of works of art — since 1921 only once below a quarter of a million dollars a year — which could have been curtailed in case of actual need. But the theory was to buy while the buying was good, and to increase public services, in the hope that this would eventually produce further gifts and bequests.

Free admission had been introduced in 1918. Free concerts were tried on three evenings in 1920, the expense of which was contributed by a few friends of the museum, and which were attended by an average audience of nearly 2,200. The semi-centennial of the museum's incorporation was celebrated only by a public reception on the evening of 6 December 1920, for as Morris Gray wrote:

> In approaching this matter they [the trustees] felt that the Museum is a great civic institution endowed by private generosity, but dedicated to the service of the public. Under these circumstances they did not wish to limit their invitations to the annual subscribers, or, indeed, to any yet larger class in the community. They wished to invite all those, rich and poor, educated and uneducated, who have the right, the equal right, to come to the Museum — the public. They believed that the celebration of this anniversary should be shared by all in the unity of a common ownership.

The only publication commemorating the anniversary was a 38-page paper-covered pamphlet by Benjamin Ives Gilman, entitled *Museum of Fine Arts Boston, 1870–1920*, suspiciously resembling in style and content what professional fundraisers nastily term "a brochure."

Two or three free concerts a year by the Boston Symphony Orchestra, the Harvard Glee Club, or the New England Conservatory Orchestra were continued for some years, always through private gifts. In 1923 the experiment was tried of providing motor-bus trips to bring classes from the Boston public schools to the museum. Although 2,537 children were brought in one hundred classes from twenty-six schools at a cost of $1,320, the experiment was not

GEORGE ROBERT WHITE. Charcoal drawing, John Singer
Sargent, 1917. 30.504

resumed in the autumn of 1924 for want of funds. While the summer story-telling to children from playgrounds and settlement houses
that had been begun by the gift of Theodore N. Vail might have come
to an end on his death, it was made permanent through the anonymous gift in 1922 of the Carolina Sumner Freeman Fund of
$75,000, the income of which was restricted to maintaining this
practice.

The self-made George Robert White, who in 1915 gave the museum a portrait of John Howard Payne (author of "Home, Sweet
Home") in the role of Hamlet, and who was often offended that his
fellow-trustees paid little attention to his suggestions to spend more
on maintaining the museum grounds, is said once to have complained: "I wish that some day one of you gentlemen would accept at

least one of my recommendations." As he had given $1,000,000 for a new building of the Massachusetts College of Pharmacy, it was somewhat disheartening to discover on his death in 1922 that, though he had bequeathed $100,000 to the Museum of Fine Arts, he had left $5,000,000 to the city, the income of which was to be used "for creating works of public utility and beauty, for the use and enjoyment of the inhabitants of the City of Boston." Later the museum benefited greatly by the generosity of White's sister, Mrs. Frederick T. Bradbury, but in 1922 it did not seem that attempts (in Coomaraswamy's phrase) "to flatter and please the public" necessarily won support from self-made millionaires for essential museum functions.

In 1924, just as the funds for the construction of the new wing had been raised, there began a changing of the guard that, in its completeness, recalls the sequel of the "battle of the casts" two decades earlier. On 17 July 1924 Morris Gray resigned as President "on account of ill health," although he remained a trustee until his death on 12 January 1931. Although Thomas Allen was immediately elected his successor, he died on 25 August 1924; consequently, George Peabody Gardner was elected President on 10 October 1924 to serve until the next annual meeting. On 5 August 1924 Benjamin Ives Gilman, Secretary of the Museum since 1894, submitted his resignation, also to take effect at the annual meeting. When the trustees assembled on 15 January 1925 they had not only to find a President but a Director, for Arthur Fairbanks resigned on that day, after eighteen years' service. The uncommunicative announcements made at the time provide no clue to these changes, nor does the page-long account of Fairbanks' service that appeared in the April 1925 *Bulletin*. As the minutes of the trustees and the museum files are equally unrewarding, one can only surmise possible explanations for this rather clean sweep.

The recurring theme of Morris Gray's ten reports as President is the attraction of the public, by one means or another. His 1921 report ended with a section, "The Museum and the Public," full of emotionally charged rhetoric, that concluded:

It is especially the opportunity and the privilege of museums of fine art to awaken the love of beauty so that the eyes may see and the heart shall feel. And out of that awakening perhaps the master will be born who shall embody in imperishable art the vision of a great nation. So that ages yet to come shall stand before its inspiration. Today men are wont to say that the nation should turn its back on the war and face the dawn of a great commercial prosperity. They are wrong, for the nation that forgets the spiritual ideals of the last few years and seeks only material prosperity faces not the dawn, but the night. It is not commercial prosperity; it is spiritual ideals that await the coming of the master.

Arthur Fairbanks concluded his report in the same volume by calling attention to the duty of the museum to future generations in these more sober words:

The opportunities of the last fifty years have enabled us to secure collections of permanent value, and similar opportunities cannot recur to the same extent. The two great sources on which museums have drawn, private collections, and excavation, are becoming exhausted. High prices paid for works of art in recent years are fundamentally based on the gradually lessening supply coming into the market. The duty of the Museum to future generations means first, that the great art of the past must be preserved; not that it must be preserved unseen, but that it must be exhibited with primary consideration of its safety. It means, secondly, that additions to the collection should be made not so much for present effect on our public today as for an enduring effect today and during generations to come. In other words, the limited funds at our disposal should be spent for objects which we believe to be of the finest quality, and therefore of the most lasting value. And, thirdly, it means that the work of the Museum Staff should be directed not so much toward an effect on our public in any given year as with a view to the effectiveness of the Museum through a long future.

Difficult questions are before us — questions of purchase, questions as to exhibition, questions as to what our public wants, questions as to what men are pleased to call the "efficiency" of an institution like this Museum. In facing such questions I commend to your attention the long view of our opportunities and our responsibilities.

Arthur Fairbanks' report for 1924, his eighteenth and last, submitted to the meeting at which he resigned, concludes with a kind of summary of the changes that have taken place during his tenure of office. The amount of invested funds has nearly doubled; the amount received from annual subscribers has risen from $17,966 in 1906 to $62,969 in 1924.

> The running expenses of the Museum, which were $79,278 in 1906, have been kept down to $239,378 in 1924, though the building to be maintained is nearly four times as large, the cost of fuel and other supplies has practically doubled, and the increased cost of living has necessitated larger salaries for the staff and higher wages for the employees.

He cites the increase in collections through the gifts of Bigelow, Weld, and Ross, the excavations of the Egyptian expedition, and the gifts of money that permitted Okakura to buy in the East and Guiffrey in Europe, and observes that "many European prints of unusual quality were secured; and a few great pieces have been purchased for other departments, for example, the Renaissance tomb of Catherine Savelli, the Catalonian fresco, and the Chinese statue of Kuan-yin."

Although the Renaissance tomb is here cited in the same breath as the Romanesque mural paintings and the great Kuan-yin, there is otherwise a curious reticence about it in museum publications. In the laconic list of acquisitions from 3 April through 1 May 1924, published in the June 1924 *Bulletin*, there appears under Western Art, Sculpture, the following entry:

> 24.149. Gothic altar from Chapelle Royal, Pau, French, fourteenth century. 24.150. Renaissance tomb monument of Maria Catherina Sabello, by Mino da Fiesole. Purchased from the Maria Antoinette Evans Fund.

Now the first of these acquisitions was illustrated and described in the same issue of the *Bulletin* in an article by Charles H. Hawes, entitled "French Gothic Altarpiece," which stated that it "is reported to have been concealed during the troubled times of the French Revolution," and was found a few years ago on a farm near Pau. No further reference to the Mino da Fiesole tomb appeared, however, until the April 1937 *Bulletin*, when it became the subject of an illustrated article by Edwin J. Hipkiss, William J. Young, and G. H.

GOTHIC STONE RETABLO. Catalan, from Anglesola, province of Lérida. *Maria Antoinette Evans Fund. 24.149*

TOMB OF CATERINA SAVELLI. Italian marble, by Alceo Dossena, 20th century, in the manner of Mino da Fiesole. *Maria Antoinette Evans Fund. 24.150*

Edgell, entitled "A Modified Tomb Monument of the Italian Renaissance." There it stated that the tomb was exhibited for three years after its acquisition in the Stone Room of the Evans Wing, and transferred in 1928 to the fifteenth-century Italian Gallery of the new building in readiness for its formal opening in November. "In planning this important occasion it was deemed best to withdraw from exhibition so impressive an example of sculpture which had become the subject of strong controversial opinion." The general conclusion of all this is that the tomb "was an original of the fifteenth century, rebuilt, partially re-cut, with certain additions or substitutions that did not belong to the original monument."

The sculptor Joseph A. Coletti tells me that in April 1925, while studying at the American Academy in Rome on a Sachs Fellowship from Harvard, he received a letter from Edward W. Forbes, enclosing photographs of certain details of this tomb, asking him to compare them with well authenticated works of Mino da Fiesole. He did so and reported that he thought it was derived rather too closely for comfort from the tomb of Francesco Tornabuoni in Santa Maria sopra Minerva in Rome. He reported this, and subsequently met the Italian sculptor Alceo Dossena, who told him that the Boston tomb was his work rather than that of Mino da Fiesole. Indeed the principal monograph on this versatile twentieth-century Italian artist — *Alceo Dossena, Scultore* by Walter Lusetti (Rome, 1955) — who could carve as readily in the style of archaic Greece as of the Renaissance, reproduces the Boston tomb of Caterina Savelli as one of Dossena's works, the author noting that "some of these statues were sold without his knowledge to American museums, authenticated by some of the most eminent archaeologists of Europe."

Museum committees are always reluctant to admit that they have made expensive mistakes. So, although Edward Forbes and his Harvard colleague Paul J. Sachs, who had been elected a trustee of the Museum of Fine Arts in 1932, were convinced by Joseph Coletti's report of Dossena's authorship, the tomb simply remained in limbo until it was resuscitated in the spring of 1937 with an explanation that, like the curate's egg, it was only partly fresh. The only book on Dossena owned by the Boston Athenæum is the catalogue of an auction sale of his sculptures in earlier styles that was held at the

National Art Galleries, Inc. in New York on 9 March 1933. This comes from the library of William Crowninshield Endicott, whose only possible interest in the subject could have been the so-called Mino da Fiesole tomb at the Museum of Fine Arts. His own tastes did not run to that kind of thing, and I can deduce that he would have gone to the trouble of obtaining the catalogue only to reinforce a previous conviction that the tomb of Caterina Savelli was by Dossena.

This is all guesswork, but it is not beyond the bounds of possibility that the various resignations of 1924 and 1925 are not unrelated to the Treasurer's having made the welkin ring about the purchase of this tomb, which he might, by one of his intuitive flights, have concluded to be a "damn fake." Further support for this surmise comes from the conjunction of his death on 28 November 1936, while still Treasurer, and the publication of the attempted rehabilitation in April 1937.

Arthur Fairbanks' final report had concluded with a dignified and well-reasoned statement on the relations of trustees and staff in museum administration, which began,

> The art museums which have grown up in such numbers in America recently ordinarily owe their origin to some rich collector or group of collectors. The motive of the founders is ideal — a desire to give to others the satisfaction in works of art which has come to the collectors themselves. At this stage the art museum is a public institution in intention and in its service, but not in its administration.
>
> The spirit of philanthropy, however, which maintains our colleges and universities in America, has led to a phenomenal development of art museums out of this initial stage. As the museum grows in size and importance, its organization inevitably changes and its ideals are modified. A staff is developed to take the work of administration under the trustees, to study the collections and make them more useful to the community, to give expert advice as to purchases and gifts of works of art. And the very ideals of the museum change. The effort to increase the collections generally becomes an effort to raise the standard of the collections by adding fewer and fewer objects, and only those of high quality. The preservation of works of art for future generations becomes a matter of first importance.

He pointed out the way in which the museum comes to depend upon its curators in the same sense that the university depends upon its faculty for its teaching and research, continuing,

> With these changes the task of the trustees of the Museum becomes no less, but rather greater, though it is far different from what it was at first. Instead of handling the details of administration, the care and the wise use of growing funds occupy their attention. They have the ultimate responsibility for securing and using a staff of experts. They decide on the purchases recommended to them. They must finally pass on the policy of the institution and the ideals it seeks to carry out. In this they are successful under modern conditions only as they secure a staff whom they respect in the field of work belonging to the staff, and only as they retain the respect of the staff for themselves in the exercise of responsibilities which are theirs.

Fairbanks' statement of the proper division of responsibility in such an institution is as valid now as then. Had there been in 1924 a curator with special knowledge of the Middle Ages and the Renaissance, as he had recommended five years earlier and as there is today, the Savelli "Mino da Fiesole" tomb would hardly have been purchased. Such a curator would very probably have sniffed out its origins as Joseph A. Coletti did. Moreover he would have recognized that the genuine Gothic limestone carving purchased at the same time was not French at all but part of a Catalan *retablo*, originally in the church at Anglesola in the Spanish province of Lérida. Within two years after its acquisition in Boston, its origins were recognized by the Catalan medievalist J. Pijoan, who published an account of it in the Barcelona periodical *Gaseta de les Arts* of 15 September 1926. Had this been known in time, the price might well have been lower, for in 1924 Spanish medieval sculpture was only just beginning to be appreciated outside of the country.

Benjamin Ives Gilman, in his last official communication, dated on Saint Sylvester's Day 1924, just five years after his talk in the Gothic Room, recorded his conviction of "the precedence of influence over growth" when he wrote:

The Museum of Fine Arts in Boston would have a distinguished future, even though not another painting or sculpture or work of the minor arts were ever to enter its doors. The imperative duty left to it would consist in the effective display of its contents to the eyes and minds of successive generations of visitors, more and more unable to appropriate without aid the magnificent legacy it offered them from a receding past.

CHAPTER XII

The Decorative Arts Wing
and the Depression

At the annual meeting of 15 January 1925, the trustees elected the youngest of their number, Thomas Jefferson Coolidge (1893–1959) as the sixth President of the Museum of Fine Arts. Although only thirty-one at the time, he had already been a member of the board for four years, having been elected a trustee on 20 January 1921 to fill the place of Thomas N. Vail. This great-great-great-grandson of Thomas Jefferson was neither artist nor collector, but an officer of the Old Colony Trust Company, founded by his father in 1890, with wide business interests. In November 1914, as a senior in Harvard College, he had within a week distinguished himself by the unlikely combination of running 98 yards for a touchdown against Yale in the first game ever played in the Yale Bowl and being elected to Phi Beta Kappa. He was graduated *magna cum laude* in mathematics in June 1915, and had served overseas as a Major of Field Artillery before settling down to banking in Boston. A big, handsome, extremely able man, he was at the same time modest and reticent. He would clearly bring sound judgment to an institution that had been sailing close to the financial wind; moreover, he would be around for many years to come. To fill the vacancy on the board created by the death of Thomas Allen, the architect William Truman Aldrich was elected a trustee. The general balance of the board re-

EDWARD JACKSON HOLMES AND THE MUSEUM STAFF. Front row, left to right: Kojiro Tomita, Charles Henry Hawes, Edward Jackson Holmes, John Briggs Potter, Ashton Sanborn. Back row, left to right: Henry Preston Rossiter, Dows Dunham, Lacey Davis Caskey, Ananda K. Coomaraswamy, Edwin James Hipkiss, Hanford Lyman Story.

mained much as it had been in 1919, for the vacancy created by the death of George Robert White in 1922 had been filled by the election of Edwin Farnham Greene, who was in the textile business.

As Arthur Fairbanks' resignation was accepted at the same meeting, to take effect on 1 March 1925, a new Director had to be found. In the manner of two decades earlier, when J. Randolph Coolidge, Jr., had filled the gap after Edward Robinson's resignation, Edward Jackson Holmes, a trustee since 1910, was on 16 April 1925 appointed Director *pro tempore*, without salary. Charles H. Hawes continued as Associate Director. Cyrus Ashton Rollins Sanborn (Harvard A.B. 1905, A.M. 1908), a Classical scholar known by the second of his given names, who had been Librarian of the museum since 1922, was appointed Secretary in place of Gilman. Ashton

Sanborn, who had in the past been an Assistant in the Classical Department and had helped Dr. Reisner prepare for publication some of the reports of the Egyptian expedition, continued in charge of the Library. As Benjamin Ives Gilman, who had inaugurated the Docent service in Copley Square, resumed charge of instruction after the resignation of Huger Elliott in 1920, Henry Hunt Clark, Director of the Department of Design in the Museum School, was appointed Supervisor of Instruction in July 1925. In October the Vicomte Simon de Vaulchier joined the staff as Assistant to the Director, but resigned the following year.

Edward Jackson Holmes had, as we have seen, been closely associated with the museum before he became a trustee. He shared the interests of his mother, Mrs. W. Scott Fitz, who had given many notable objects to the museum; he and his wife traveled widely and collected in many fields. Although an amiable and charming man, he was not a decisive or impetuous administrator, as one member of the staff discovered when Holmes paced the floor of his office for ten minutes trying to decide between the adjectives "big" and "large" in a piece of dictation. Unlike Randolph Coolidge, who had withdrawn from his temporary post at the end of his covenanted year, Ned Holmes discovered that he liked being Director and wished to stay at it. As this seemed to suit his colleagues, who were doubtless more at home with him than they would have been with a strange scholar, he was appointed permanent Director on 21 January 1926. He held the office until October 1934 when he was elected President in place of T. Jefferson Coolidge, who had resigned because of his appointment as Undersecretary of the Treasury. When Holmes became Director he withdrew from the board of trustees; as Desmond Fitz-Gerald died during 1926, the Massachusetts Institute of Technology appointed two new members, William Emerson, Dean of its School of Architecture, and Edwin Sibley Webster of the engineering firm of Stone and Webster. President Eliot, the last of the original incorporators of 1870, died in 1926, as did Dr. William Sturgis Bigelow, who had been appointed by Harvard for forty-five years. In Dr. Bigelow's place Richard Cary Curtis (Harvard A.B. 1916, LL.B. 1921) was designated, while the board elected to Eliot's vacancy George Harold Edgell (Harvard A.B. 1909, Ph.D. 1913), Professor of Fine Arts at Harvard and since 1922 Dean of the Faculty of Architecture. In 1934 when Holmes became President, Edgell succeeded him as Director of the Museum of Fine Arts. It seems wise to explain this game of musical chairs in one place, lest the reader become confused by the Protean metamorphoses of these two men.

Four years passed between the fundraising and ground-breaking of 1924 and the opening of the new wing on 14 November 1928. During this time a variety of materials were bought for specific uses in the installation of exhibits. In 1925, for example, seventeenth-century woodwork was obtained from the Browne-Pearl House in West Boxford, Massachusetts, and from the oldest part of the Manning House in Ipswich, while an English four-lancet stained glass window with figures of the apostles of about the year 1435, coming from a chapel at Hampton Court in Herefordshire, was purchased through the Maria Antoinette Evans Fund. In the same year Henry Davis Sleeper, the creator of "Beauport" in East Gloucester, gave his collection of Paul Revere silver. The twenty-two pieces, given in memory of his mother, Maria Westcote Sleeper, were unusually well documented, for the succession of owners of each from the time of making to the present had been established by Sleeper. The name of the Department of Western Art was in 1926 changed to the Department of Decorative Arts of Europe and America, and the title of Edwin J. Hipkiss altered from Keeper to Curator; accordingly, the building under construction was henceforth known as the Decorative Arts Wing. At the same time, Miss Gertrude Townsend was designated as Keeper of Textiles within the department: in 1930 she became Curator of an independent Department of Textiles.

The new wing extended east from the Egyptian galleries, ran north parallel to the Tapestry Gallery, and then west to join gallery X of the Evans Wing; by doing so it created the first of the two large interior courts contemplated in Guy Lowell's original plan. Only on the Fenway side was it to be two rooms deep and faced with a granite façade. Its other arms consisted of a single series of period rooms or galleries, opening out of each other; these were one room deep, with the court walls of brick and the outside walls of temporary stucco, for it was contemplated that another line of future galleries would be added beyond. These would have the granite façades requisite for the

DECORATIVE ARTS AND EVANS MEMORIAL WINGS IN 1951.

completion of the final form of this portion of the building. On the main floor the Decorative Arts Wing would be reached from the Rotunda by the eastern subsidiary corridor, to be used for the display of framed textiles. On this level the European arts were to be exhibited. The American rooms were to be installed on the ground floor and on a still lower level that, although equivalent to the basement, was well lighted from the interior court.

In the early stages of construction Mrs. Frederick T. Bradbury, the sister of George Robert White, the Misses Hannah and Grace Edwards, and Mrs. W. Scott Fitz proposed that the forthcoming interior court become a garden, and offered to bear the cost of making it. Accordingly, the landscape architect Arthur A. Shurtleff (known to us in later years by his self-imposed spelling of Shurcliff) created a simple but dignified plan, in consultation with the Director and a committee of architects including William T. Aldrich, Henry Forbes Bigelow, and (until his death in 1927) Guy Lowell. Although the garden was accessible from the new wing, the two principal entrances were through French windows in the Lecture Hall corridor, which

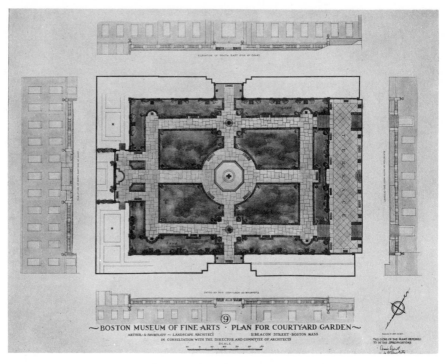

PLAN FOR COURTYARD GARDEN.

gave on a broad paved terrace, bounded by a balustrade pierced by two flights of steps leading down. In the center on the level reached by the steps was an octagonal fountain, surrounded by a flagged area with seats. The terrace balustrade was continued on the three other sides of the court, with paved paths and grass plots protected by hedges filling the lower level. Space was provided for the installation of sculpture and for trees and shrubs in pots. This happy development gave a secluded area, well screened from city noise and traffic, where visitors might relax in good weather. At any season, however, it offered a pleasant prospect from the windows that looked on to the court.

More than fifty rooms and galleries in the wing made it possible for the Department of Decorative Arts to exhibit for the first time, in chronological sequence, its varied collections. The planning for these exhibits became the solemn responsibility of an installation committee of which the architect Henry Forbes Bigelow was chairman, which met thirty-six times between 24 February 1926 and 9 October

COURTYARD GARDEN WHEN RECENTLY COMPLETED.

1928. The members were William T. Aldrich, J. Templeman Coolidge, and Dudley L. Pickman, with the Director, Associate Director, and Treasurer participating *ex officiis*. Edwin J. Hipkiss as Secretary kept meticulous minutes that would have satisfied a Saint Simon at Versailles. As with the trustees of the Boston Public Library, who had solemnly voted on 15 November 1892 "that *Sanitas* be the form of water-closet bowl to be adopted for use in the new Public Library building," no detail was too insignificant to be considered by this body of tasteful gentlemen. The perfection of a seventeen-word dedicatory inscription required correspondence with Professor Bliss Perry and Morris Gray, as well as discussion at no less than eleven meetings. Members of the staff, other than the Curator in his capacity of Secretary, never participated in these august deliberations. Although Miss Gertrude Townsend, Keeper of Textiles in the department, might submit fabrics, suitably framed, for consideration, she was at no time invited to attend a meeting of the committee.

After eleven meetings, the material and pattern of the stone floor

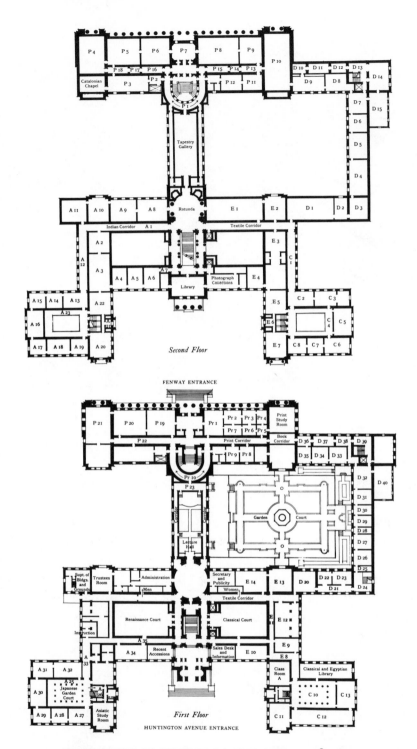

Second Floor

FENWAY ENTRANCE

First Floor

HUNTINGTON AVENUE ENTRANCE

FLOOR PLANS OF MUSEUM OF FINE ARTS, 1928–1941.

PORTAL OF CHURCH OF SAN MIGUEL AT UNCASTILLO. Spanish, 12th century.
Francis Bartlett Fund. 28.32

for the Gothic Gallery, was finally determined. In this room (D–1),
the first on the main floor to be entered from the corridor that led
from the Rotunda, were hung eight recently acquired fragments of
tapestries woven for Cardinal Ferry de Clugny between 1480 and
1483. Here the stone Gothic retablo from Anglesola was exhibited,
with various capitals and architectural fragments. The assembly and
installation of a Spanish Romanesque portal from the church of San
Miguel at Uncastillo in the province of Zaragoza, purchased from the
Francis Bartlett Fund in 1927, temporarily defied the ingenuity of

the committee, for it had arrived in 215 packing cases of unmarked stones, weighing 24 tons, with no other guide to its reconstruction than a photograph of the doorway before demolition. By the autumn of 1930, however, this fine monument had been reassembled on the west wall of the Gothic Gallery.

A Kingsley Porter's *Spanish Romanesque Sculpture*, being when published in 1928 the first comprehensive study of that subject, noted the presence in Boston of this portal. Its acquisition by the Museum of Fine Arts the previous year represented, like the purchase in 1921 of the mural paintings from Santa Maria de Mur, a bold foray into uncharted waters. I suspect this early interest in Spanish Romanesque to have been an enthusiasm of Charles H. Hawes, the Associate Director. In 1927 the museum also bought twelfth-century mural paintings of the *Last Supper* and the *Three Marys at the Sepulchre* which once adorned the Spanish Mozarabic *ermita* of San Baudelio de Berlanga in the Castilian province of Soria. These were installed in the Evans Wing in the "chapel" that had been created for the paintings from Santa Maria de Mur. The entire Romanesque decoration of San Baudelio de Berlanga was removed and brought to New York in 1920, where it was offered for sale as a whole. When the owners despaired of selling the entire group, the

THE THREE MARYS AT THE SEPULCHRE. Spanish mural paintings from San Baudelio de Berlanga (Soria), 12th century. *Maria Antoinette Evans Fund.* 27.786

DECORATIVE ARTS GALLERY D–5 AS ORIGINALLY INSTALLED.

Museum of Fine Arts purchased these two panels with the aid of the Maria Antoinette Evans Fund; others were subsequently purchased by the Metropolitan Museum and the Indianapolis Museum.

Adjoining the Gothic Gallery a smaller room (D–2), suggesting a private chapel, was devised as a setting for the recently purchased English fifteenth-century stained glass window. There followed a series of large galleries (D–4, 5, 6, 7) in which the decorative art of Italy, Spain, the Netherlands, and England from the fifteenth century through the seventeenth century was exhibited, each being restricted to a single nationality. Here textiles, furniture, sculpture, pottery, glass, silver, wrought iron, and leatherwork of each country were placed in harmonious groupings, designed to show both the spirit of the time, the interrelation of the various forms of art, and the stylistic influences of one country upon another. These galleries were lighted by windows that looked onto the court. Three smaller rooms with skylights (D–10, 11, 12) were devoted to the decorative

DECORATIVE ARTS GALLERY D–11
AS ORIGINALLY INSTALLED.

arts of France and Italy in the eighteenth century. The Hôtel de Montmorency panels and the two large Bouchers from the Deacon house were in D–11, while the Athenæum Panninis hung in D–12 in the company of contemporary consoles, mirrors, and other Italian furniture.

The rooms thus far mentioned have been conventional museum galleries of some flexibility, adapted to any changes of exhibition that might be called for over the years. However, the Decorative Arts Wing also contained a number of "period rooms," whose dimensions were governed by permanent installation of paneling or other architectural elements; these were to be furnished with objects that it was hoped might approximate their original contents. The earliest of the English period rooms was the Tudor interior of about 1490 from Somersetshire, which was built into gallery D–14, at the northeast corner of the new wing, in such a way that not only the exterior of the windows could be seen but visitors could enter the room itself. Chronologically this was followed in gallery D–8 by the State Morning Room of Hamilton Palace, Lanarkshire, Scotland, of about 1690, which was one of two rooms given by Mrs. Frederick T. Bradbury in memory of her brother, George Robert White. The Installation Committee was so eager to work with Mrs. Bradbury in the White Memorial rooms that on 11 March 1926 it considered the possibility of beginning to set them up even before the completion of the building. The oak paneling from Hamilton Palace, built by Charles, third Duke of Hamilton, from designs by the Scottish architect James Smith, clearly required an ornamented plaster ceiling. Various designs were discussed; by 24 April 1928 one was achieved that met the

DECORATIVE ARTS GALLERY D–12 AS ORIGINALLY INSTALLED.

ROOM FROM HAMILTON PALACE. *Gift of Mrs. Frederick T. Bradbury in memory of George Robert White. 24.25*

approval of the committee and Mrs. Bradbury, who then proceeded to purchase from the P. W. French and Company of New York furniture that was considered suitable for the period of the room. An Ispahan rug of the early seventeenth century was placed on the floor, while on the walls were hung English paintings and the great early sixteenth-century Flemish tapestry of the miracles of Saint Claude, originally in Knole House in Kent, that George Robert White had bought in 1916 when some of the collections of J. Pierpont Morgan were dispersed.

Between the Hamilton Palace Room and the connection with the Evans Wing, there followed (because of memorial proximity though out of logical sequence) another room given by Mrs. Bradbury — a white and gold early Louis XVI salon (D–9), whose walls were enriched with mirrors and tapestry panels after designs by Christophe Huet. As Mrs. Bradbury was prepared to buy whatever was needed for the furnishing of these memorial rooms, the committee determined on 14 December 1926 to have dummy chandeliers made and placed here to determine what should ideally be sought in the market. The majestic speed of deliberation is indicated by the minutes of the twenty-seventh meeting, held on 17 February 1928.

It was voted to ask P. W. French and Company to send two French chandeliers for the Louis XVI Salon to Boston for trial in the room.

The use of one old chandelier and one modern copy in order to get a pair was considered and

It was voted that an old pair or two old chandeliers matching approximately were desired for this room, and that P. W. French Company be so notified.

Finally on 12 August 1928 a scheme for hanging the crystal chandeliers was approved and "chain #108 ½–213, to be furnished by Bigelow Kennard and Company was selected."

LOUIS XVI SALON. *Gift of Mrs. Frederick T. Bradbury in memory of George Robert White. 24.270*

Time and expense were minor considerations in this effort, to judge by a letter of 16 February 1927 from Robert Samuels of P. W. French and Company concerning modern chairs with antique coverings offered by Mrs. Bradbury.

> Mrs. Bradbury and the late Mr. George R. White were always interested in the beautiful and old, but at times some of the old frames would be too rickety for use, and the old coverings were mounted on new frames. There are not very many pieces of this kind, and knowing how keen Mrs. Bradbury is to have the installation of the William and Mary room and the Louis XVI room be beyond criticism of any kind, we are most certain that Mrs. Bradbury will replace some of the modern frames with old pieces that are suitable. In fact we have been commissioned to be on the lookout for pieces of the choicest kind, that would be adaptable for the two rooms in question.

The impression that one derives from reading the minutes of the Installation Committee is that of tasteful amateurs, working with donors and dealers to achieve something satisfactory to the twentieth-century eye, rather than the effort of scholars to produce a documented record of the past. It suggests "playing house" in the manner dear to committees of local historical societies rather than the meticulous reconstruction that Classical or Egyptian curators would have attempted with material in their areas. George A. Reisner dealt more conscientiously with ancient Egyptian furniture. One must in fairness remember that carefully documented historical investigation of the decorative arts is a phenomenon of the second half of the twentieth century. Most earlier writing on the subject accepted the opinions and hearsay of collectors and dealers in lieu of facts to be squeezed from inventories, contemporary descriptions, and craftsmen's account books and records.

The next room in the English sequence was a fine Chippendale interior of about 1750 from Woodcote Park, Epsom, Surrey, given with appropriate furnishings by Eben Howard Gay. On the ground floor were three small Louis XV rooms, two of which were purchased, and one given by Guy Lowell; the American rooms occupied the remainder of that floor, as well as all of the exhibition space on

LOUIS XV SALON FROM
CHATEAU DE LA MUETTE,
PASSY. *Charles A. Cummings
Fund.* 24.357 Removed and
sold in 1959.

the lowest level of the wing. In this series the visitor could proceed from the seventeenth-century Essex County rooms through an interior of 1730 from the Orne House at Marblehead, a room of 1740 from Fiskedale in Worcester County, to a parlor from the George Jaffrey House in Portsmouth, New Hampshire, representing the style of 1750. For the turn of the century there were the Samuel McIntire parlor, dining room, and bedroom from "Oak Hill" in Peabody, an 1803 room from Bath, Maine, with French scenic wallpaper, given by Dudley L. Pickman, and a room of similar period with scenic paper of the seasons given by Dartmouth College from a house that it owned in Hanover, New Hampshire.

The John Singleton Copley portrait of Paul Revere at work and the later Gilbert Stuart portraits of Revere and his wife were given in 1930 by Joseph Warren Revere, William Bacon Revere, and Edward Hutchinson Robbins Revere. During the nineteenth century the Copley portrait had been consigned to the attic of the family house in Canton, for the Reveres of the time did not relish the sight of their ancestor in his shirtsleeves, at work on a teapot. They infinitely pre-

ROOM FROM IPSWICH, MASSACHUSETTS, ABOUT 1675.

ROOM FROM JAFFREY HOUSE, PORTSMOUTH, NEW HAMPSHIRE, ABOUT 1750.

MCINTIRE PARLOR FROM OAK HILL, PEABODY, MASSACHUSETTS.

ferred the Stuart portrait in which he had his coat on and presented
a more dignified appearance. Indeed the donors of 1930, as small
boys a good many decades before, had used the Copley as a target for
their air rifles, though fortunately without too expert marksmanship.
Now happily the portrait emerged from limbo, and was placed with
the Stuarts in an eighteenth-century room from the Jaffrey House,
newly installed on the Court Floor to display not only the Sleeper
Collection of Revere silver but 94 pieces lent by Mrs. Nathaniel
Thayer (Pauline Revere) a great-granddaughter of the silversmith.
The latter collection became the property of the museum in 1934
by bequest of Mrs. Thayer.

The Director in 1931 reported that "the excitement of the year"
was the bequest by Charles Hitchcock Tyler, a member of the Visiting Committee, of examples of early American furniture, silver, and
prints, "so fine in quality and so great in number that it will take

PAUL REVERE. John Singleton Copley and Gilbert Stuart. *Gifts of Joseph W., William B., and Edward H. R. Revere.* 30.781 and 30.782

months even to examine them." In the seventeenth-century American group Tyler had three great cupboards, three Connecticut chests, a Hadley chest, early chairs, two covered with Turkey work, wall clocks, and the finest wrought-iron candlesticks received by the museum. The eighteenth century was represented on a similar scale, and there were fine English and Dutch pieces as well. A memorial exhibition of portions of the collection was held at the end of 1932 before the pieces went to their permanent destinations in the Decorative Arts Wing.

The expansion of the Visiting Committee to include such enthusiastic collectors as Frederick J. Bradlee, Jr., Hollis French, Eben Howard Gay, and Dr. and Mrs. William H. Baltzell, Mrs. Nathaniel Thayer, Chauncey C. Nash, Dwight Blaney, and Hermann F. Clarke had led to proportionate developments in the collection, inspired by the new wing and the euphoria of the 1930 Tercentenary celebration of the Massachusetts Bay Company's arrival in Boston. In spite of the Depression, and the prudent resolve of the trustees to engage in no major expansion of the building, a modest addition to the Decorative Arts Wing was made in 1930–31, from designs of William T.

Aldrich. This provided space on the lower floor for the Leslie Lindsey Mason Collection of Musical Instruments, on the ground floor for an English Georgian room of 1748 from Newland, Gloucestershire, given in memory of Dr. William Hewson Baltzell by his wife, and on the main floor an additional gallery for general exhibition. The term "decorative arts" was interpreted in the broadest sense, for in 1928 J. Templeman Coolidge lent, and in 1932 gave, his collection of ship models. Another great Flemish tapestry from Knole, depicting the *Passion of Christ*, was given in 1929 by Robert Treat Paine, 2nd, in memory of his son, Walter Cabot Paine. This was thought to have been the gift of Archbishop Warham, and is known to have hung

SCENES FROM THE PASSION OF CHRIST (detail). Wool and silk tapestry, Franco-Flemish, late 15th century, from the chapel at Knole. *Gift of Robert Treat Paine, 2nd, in memory of his son, Walter Cabot Paine. 29.1046*

in the chapel at Knole at the time of its surrender to Henry VIII in 1537. There it remained until the summer of 1928 when it was removed to be sent directly to Boston. In 1933 an extraordinary collection of English silver of the sixteenth, seventeenth, and eighteenth centuries was received as an anonymous gift in memory of Charlotte Beebe Wilbour (1833–1914), the daughter of the Reverend Edmund M. Beebe of Springfield, Massachusetts.

In the spirit of the Massachusetts Bay Tercentenary, the museum held a loan exhibition of one hundred Colonial portraits from 19 June to 21 September 1930, which is commemorated in an illustrated catalogue prepared by Philip Hendy, who had been appointed Curator of Paintings on 1 May. Three years earlier he had resigned the post of Assistant to the Keeper of the Wallace Collection in London to undertake the cataloguing of the paintings in the Isabella Stewart Gardner Museum. Young, learned, and full of ideas, he had based himself in Florence but had traveled widely between Madrid and Budapest in preparing the catalogue, for he had no intention of publishing second-hand opinions. He wished to see for himself. What he saw did not always convince him of the correctness of attributions accepted by Mrs. Gardner and Bernard Berenson. Consequently, when his manuscript was submitted to the trustees of the Isabella Stewart Gardner Museum, of which the founder's somewhat irascible nephew, Harold Jefferson Coolidge, was President, the fur flew. When Philip Hendy's *The Isabella Stewart Gardner Museum: Catalogue of the Exhibited Paintings and Drawings* was handsomely printed in 1931 by the Merrymount Press, Morris Carter in an introductory note wrote: "The catalogue is largely a record of the author's convictions, and is in many ways the most personal catalogue yet published by a museum. While the Trustees are not responsible for the opinions expressed, they gladly take full responsibility for giving them the opportunity for publication offered by this catalogue." In the preface it is noted that all the attributions are Hendy's save for that of *Christ Bearing the Cross*, which he attributed to Palma Vecchio, but which remains under the name of Giorgione. On this point Harold Coolidge had obviously set his feet.

As William C. Endicott was a trustee of the Museum of Fine Arts as well as of Fenway Court, and as Harold J. Coolidge was not, Philip

Hendy was, upon completion of his catalogue, invited to move a few hundred yards down the Fenway, where there had not been a Curator of Paintings since Jean Guiffrey returned to the Louvre in 1914. John Briggs Potter, appointed Keeper of Paintings in 1902 held the fort in the department as he had before and after Guiffrey's three-year term as Curator, although in 1928 his title was changed to Advisor to the Department. A cherished bit of museum folklore would have it that Philip Hendy was considerably puzzled during his first days in office by the feeling of being shadowed, as if he were in Moscow. Wherever he went in the Evans Wing or in the basement store-rooms he had the impression of being followed by a strange man, who turned out, of course, to be Potter. Through a slip in Ned Holmes's administrative arrangements, neither the old Advisor or the new Curator had been warned of each other's existence! Any problems of protocol were soon solved by changing Potter's title to Fellow of the Museum, and listing his name high up on the staff roster with the Director, Secretary, and Registrar, rather than in the Department of Paintings. On Potter's complete retirement in 1935, he was made an Honorary Fellow of the Museum, a post he held until his death on 13 September 1945.

Philip Hendy made a number of physical changes in the Evans Wing. The partitions separating rooms III, IV, and V were removed, and a single gallery created, on whose rough plaster walls the earliest paintings in the collection were hung. With William T. Aldrich he devised plans for dividing the long east and west corridors of the Evans Wing into three sections each, to form new exhibition spaces for small pictures. Fresh fabrics were applied to gallery walls, and pictures generally hung in a single line. He made a careful examination of stored paintings, many of which had been badly varnished or repainted. After some of these had been cleaned and studied they appeared as entirely respectable works by Gainsborough, Bonifazio, Van Dyck, and Tintoretto. On his recommendation the Roger van der Weyden St. Luke drawing the portrait of the Virgin was sent to Berlin in March 1932 for expert cleaning by Dr. Helmut Ruhemann. It returned handsomer than ever, and, through its exhibition in the late summer at the Kaiser Friedrich Museum, fully accepted by Max Friedlander, Hulin de Loo, and Emile Renders of Bruges as the

EVANS WING CORRIDORS AS ALTERED BY PHILIP HENDY AND
WILLIAM T. ALDRICH.

original by Roger's own hand, from which several other versions of
the picture had been copied.

In October 1933 Philip Hendy resigned the curatorship, after
three and a half years, and returned to England, where he became
successively Director of the Leeds Gallery, Slade Professor of Fine Art
at Oxford, and Director of the National Gallery. In 1950 he was
knighted. The Department of Paintings remained without a head
until the summer of 1934 when George Harold Edgell, a trustee and
Dean of the Harvard Faculty of Architecture, agreed to become
Curator of Paintings on a half-time basis. Although a number of
paintings were purchased in the late twenties and early thirties, even
more remarkable pictures came by gift. A Tintoretto portrait of
Alessandro Farnese was given in 1927 by Mrs. W. Scott Fitz and
Robert Treat Paine, 2nd. Manet's full-size sketch for *The Execution
of Maximilian* was given in 1930 by Frank Gair Macomber, while

the following year Robert Treat Paine, 2nd, gave Edgar Degas' extraordinary portrait of the *Duke and Duchess of Morbilli*. And in 1931 were lent some of the pictures owned by John Taylor Spaulding, who was as remarkable a collector of European paintings as he was of Japanese prints.

The extent and quality of the gifts to the Department of Decorative Arts, only a few of which have been mentioned earlier in this chapter, indicate the response to the construction of the new wing. But any addition to buildings, unaccompanied by substantial endowment, creates problems, and while this wing was being built, the museum was faced with a totally unanticipated crisis. In March 1926 the City of Boston's Building Department let it be known that the Museum School, completed in 1909, being technically of "temporary construction" could no longer be used after the close of the school year 1926–27. T. Jefferson Coolidge reported the problem:

> This decision forced the Museum to take immediate steps for the erection of a new and permanent structure, which had been contemplated for many years but postponed through lack of funds. A piece of land, situated on Museum Road, well adapted to the needs of the School, was purchased, and the building has already reached its first story. It will be of inexpensive construction, but well designed, with excellent light, and carefully planned to meet the needs of more than three hundred students. The entire outlay will approach $400,000. This will involve the Museum in a very serious expenditure and lay a heavy burden upon its resources, unless friends interested in the School or in art education generally will defray part of the expense.

When the School of the Museum of Fine Arts moved to its temporary building beside the museum in Huntington Avenue in 1909 it was in its thirty-third year. Its instructors were a remarkably able group of highly respected artists, who got on well together. In the Department of Drawing and Painting Edmund C. Tarbell and Frank W. Benson taught painting, Philip L. Hale drawing from life, William M. Paxton drawing from the cast, and Bela L. Pratt modeling, while C. Howard Walker directed the Department of Design. The four painters were held in high national esteem. Benson and

Tarbell had taken over in 1890 following the death of Otto Grundmann; Hale had joined them in 1893 on his return from Paris, while
Paxton came along in 1906. The close relation between these men
made their instruction unusually effective. Art schools in general
suffered from having to pay their own way from tuition. To achieve
this they had to enroll a large body of students that necessarily often
included the untalented seeking to fill vacant hours or able young
women waiting to get married. Normally in an art school with a
couple of hundred pupils of varying abilities, criticism would have
been perfunctory and uncoordinated, but here instruction came
closer to attaining the superior ideal of private study with an artist.
Young ladies filling time learned something, and graduates who went
on to careers often held important teaching posts in other institutions,
or earned substantial incomes, particularly from portraiture. The
harmony of this scene had been rudely interrupted in 1912 when
the Museum of Fine Arts, which had imported Huger Elliott from the
Rhode Island School of Design as the first Supervisor of Educational
Work, gave him an additional charge to reorganize the Museum
School.

Hitherto the school had always managed its own affairs quite informally under the direction of a Council, chiefly of outside friends
and supporters, on which the President and Director of the museum
and J. Templeman Coolidge sat as representatives of the trustees. In
1912 Thomas Allen had been twenty-eight years on the Council and
its chairman for the previous nine. Being both a painter and a man
used to managing large financial interests, he was exceptionally
valuable in this post. Hitherto as long as the Museum School stayed
solvent and maintained standards, the museum let it alone. Now
Huger Elliott was appointed Secretary of the Council and Director
of the Department of Design, over the head of C. Howard Walker,
who had established it in 1884, in addition to taking charge of
educational work at the museum. In September 1912 Elliott began
an administrative reorganization of the school. The four painters
rightly protested what they regarded as the intrusion of a nonpainter
into their highly specialized field. The school year of 1912–13 became immediately an unhappy one. Tarbell and Benson resigned in
December 1912 and Paxton and Walker in April 1913. At the end

of the year only Philip L. Hale remained of the old group of painters; though in sympathy with his colleagues, his career had become primarily that of teaching. Although Frank W. Benson accepted a three-year appointment as a visiting instructor, and in 1917 joined the school's Council, as Tarbell did later, the old harmony of instruction was shattered. Moreover the successors of the departed painters were men of lesser stature. The appointment as Tarbell's successor of Frederick Andrew Bosley proved unfortunate, for, although an outstanding pupil at the school from 1900 to 1906 and the holder of its Paige Scholarship in 1906–1908, he did not fulfill his earlier promise and was inept as a teacher. Although Bela L. Pratt continued to teach sculpture, he died in 1917.

The death of Thomas Allen on 25 August 1924, only a few weeks after his election as President of the Museum of Fine Arts, removed the greatest single element of continuity in the life of the Museum School, for he had become a member of its Council in 1884 and had been its Chairman since 1902. To compensate for this loss, Edmund C. Tarbell was persuaded to become Chairman of the Council on 18 February 1925. So matters stood in the spring of 1926 when the museum was confronted with the necessity of providing a new building for the school. This was promptly undertaken, and was completed in time for use at the beginning of the school year in September 1927. It was one of the last works of Guy Lowell, who died on 4 February 1927, while it was still under construction. Although the appeal to friends produced contributions of $50,576 for this purpose, more than $400,000 of museum funds had to be expended for land, construction, and equipment. Of necessity the museum itself had made its first major financial commitment at a time when the school was in a period of transition, with less unity of direction than in its first half-century. Moreover the Depression was only a little way ahead.

In 1930 Tarbell and Benson resigned as members of the Council, although they continued as honorary members until 1931 when they completely severed their connection with the Museum School. T. Jefferson Coolidge in the museum report for the latter year laconically described what amounted to a complete break with the past continuity of the institution.

The School of the Museum has passed through a very important year. It suffered the loss by death of Mr. Philip L. Hale and by resignation of Mr. Henry Hunt Clark, Mr. Leslie Thompson and Mr. Frederick A. Bosley.

Mr. William James was elected Chairman of the School Council — a position which had been temporarily held by myself. Messrs. Rodney J. Burn and Robin Guthrie, both trained in the Slade School of Design, were appointed instructors in painting and drawing and Miss Ethel Williams was appointed as instructor in the Department of Design.

The Council looks forward with interest and confidence to the success of the school under its new leadership.

Unhappily these expectations were not fulfulled. The new Chairman, a painter who had taught at the school from 1913 to 1926, proposed asking Augustus John in London to recommend artists to take charge of the painting department. The Council agreed, although the painter, Harry Sutton, Jr., one of its active members, resigned in consequence and Tarbell and Benson withdrew from their honorary association. Augustus John's nominees, who arrived in 1931, did not prove to be the anticipated messiahs. In 1932 Coolidge reported less optimistically: "The Museum School has a difficult problem ahead. The attendance has shrunk and the expenses are greater than the income." The number of full-time students had dropped from 207 to 131. A year later he observed that the school's expenses had been cut to a point where there will be no loss, "except for the fact that the Museum will probably receive no return for the money it invested in the school building." The national "new deal" had its local counterpart in the Museum School in 1934 with the importation of Alexandre Iacovleff, a Russian émigré painter living in Paris, as the head of the painting department.

T. Jefferson Coolidge's reports as President were always simple and direct, without reflections on art, as has been seen in his comments on the Museum School. He made it clear that money was needed, and expressed succinct pleasure when it came in. The annual subscriptions, which had been $61,703 in 1925, rose steadily until in 1929 they amounted to $94,487. Naturally they fell after the stock market crash, but less rapidly than might have been expected, for they produced $82,014 in 1930, $68,459 in 1931, and $48,277 in 1932. Only in 1933 and 1934 was approximately $34,000, a figure lower than the $43,849 of 1910, received. The Depression did less damage in the Museum of Fine Arts than in most places, partly because of a shrewd Treasurer and even more because of the steady influx of bequests. The certified public accountant's report for the year 1931 notes laconically:

In 1929, prior to the drop in security prices, the Trustees disposed of a substantial portion of the Museum's common stock investments. Proceeds of sales were credited to the investment accounts of the respective issues to the extent of reducing to nominal values the book cost of remaining shares and the remainder of the proceeds was placed in a Reserve.

The late James Melville Hunnewell, who succeeded William C. Endicott as treasurer of the Colonial Society of Massachusetts in 1931, once remarked to me that when he took over the society's affairs he was surprised to find almost no stocks and bonds, but a great deal of cash, with which he was subsequently able to buy a number of desirable securities at very reasonable prices! The auditor's report suggests that at the museum William C. Endicott had also viewed with distaste the astronomical values of stocks in the spring and summer of 1929 and had acted as a prudent Boston trustee should.

Beginning in 1922 with a payment of $575,000, the wholly unrestricted legacy received from Mrs. Robert Dawson Evans had by 1935 amounted to some $2,500,000. Normally annual payments of $150,000 were made by her estate, although more was received in some years and less in others. But a considerable number of smaller bequests had materially increased the funds available for operating expenses, even though costs always kept enough ahead of the income to produce a theoretical annual deficit, that could have been avoided by buying fewer works of art. Including the $150,000 from Mrs. Evans, $299,551 was received in 1925, $271,175 in 1926, $172,746 in 1927, and $191,583 in 1928. In 1929 the bequests mounted to $543,573, and in 1930 to $399,779, thanks to the will of George Nixon Black of Boston and Ellsworth, Maine, who not only left important examples of English, American, Dutch, and French furniture and silver of the seventeenth and eighteenth centuries and an unrestricted fund of $150,000, but a residual bequest that eventually brought in over $500,000. Of the 1930 total $92,214 had been an initial payment under the will of Mrs. Frederick T. Bradbury, who had died on 4 April 1930 and whose bequest of half the residue of her estate brought in $4,234,514 the following year. President Coolidge, reporting in 1930 the prospect of this gift, observed,

> Mrs. Bradbury has signified in her will that, when the trustees see fit, they shall build a wing with a large portion of this money. I feel, however, that it would be unwise for the Museum to take this action for some years to come. The building of the new wing is only half the cost — an equal sum would probably be needed for maintenance — and even with this magnificent gift, our financial condition would not warrant an important addition to our building. We need the income to relieve us from deficits and to enable us to use unrestricted funds, which have hitherto been reserved for running expenses, for the purchase of works of art. I believe it is far better to improve the quality of our collections rather than to increase the size of our exhibits and I feel certain that in so doing we would not be acting contrary to Mrs. Bradbury's desires.

Legacies of $152,893 were received in 1933 and $210,552 the following year. The greatly increased sums of $1,175,108 in 1934 and $884,276 in 1935 represent the establishment of the Helen Osborne Gary Fund of $362,620, whose income was restricted for the support of the museum or the purchase of pictures or other works of art, and the Charles Potter Kling Fund of $601,834, income restricted to the purchase of tapestries and early Italian paintings.

Beginning in 1927, the museum began to be closed on Mondays. Although this six-day week saved some $8,000 in extra wages, it was not purely a measure of economy, for it provided a useful opportunity for cleaning and maintenance work in daylight hours, as well as giving curators one day when they could be reasonably free from the interruptions of casual inquiries. Staff salaries were raised in 1929, notwithstanding the increased expense of operating the Decorative Arts Wing. In October 1932, when it seemed that the Depression would reduce the estimated income for 1933 from $550,000 to about $400,000, salaries were reduced from 5 to 10 percent. An accompanying statement expressed the belief that, in spite of the reduction in dollars, the purchasing power would be as great as in 1929. When it was discovered that the rising cost in living expenses during 1933 disproved this theory, the salary cuts were restored.

As it would be obviously unwise to add further to the building in the predictable future, it became imperative to see that the best use was made of the space that existed. Consequently, in 1931 Frederick J. Bradlee, Jr., a collector of furniture who was a classmate of the President's and a member of the Visiting Committee of the Department of Decorative Arts, joined the staff for two years to look at the institution with a fresh eye. Designated by the odd title of Museum Representative, this able and witty man applied good sense and an inspired tongue to the solution of practical problems. He thought it absurd that there was no connection on the ground floor between the Evans and the Decorative Arts wings; a door was cut and new wall space obtained for showing prints. He saw visitors adrift, wondering where they were; floor plans, with text admirably set by the Merrymount Press and stars marking the spot of installation, were placed in various parts of the building. Appalled by the clatter and commotion caused by children drawing in the large cast courts, he tried to find a place in the basement for these classes. As the space that his eye lit upon was full of still more plaster casts, never exhibited since the move from Copley Square, he took steps to get rid of them. Schools and colleges were offered any that they wanted, F.O.B. Boston. When all possible casts had been disposed of in this way, sledge hammers and dump trucks got rid of the remainder.

For a number of years the west court, containing Renaissance casts, had been used for temporary exhibitions that were held by means of screens upon which pictures could be hung. This was a poor improvisation at best; once F. J. Bradlee started housecleaning, it seemed only sensible to clear out the plaster inhabitants of the court altogether, and convert this large area into proper exhibition rooms. The shade of Isabella Stewart Gardner must have applauded this decision; if Matthew Stewart Prichard ever heard of it, he must have smiled wryly. From plans of William T. Aldrich a floor was placed across the court at the level of the Rotunda. On this main floor were created two skylighted galleries, the larger one square and the smaller one rectangular, and a staircase leading to the ground floor, where five small artificially lighted rooms were constructed, which were also directly accessible from the corridors near the Huntington Avenue entrance. This admirably flexible plan permitted visitors to move freely between both floors when a large exhibition required the use of all seven galleries. It was equally practical to have two exhibitions at the same time, one on each floor. These galleries were first used on 3 October 1934 for an exhibition arranged by the Guild of Boston Artists. Although Classical casts still lingered in the east court, their years were numbered.

Before these convenient galleries were available, space had to be improvised elsewhere for an exhibition arranged from 12 January to 28 February 1932 in honor of the eightieth birthday of Dr. Denman W. Ross. As he had given approximately 11,000 objects in the previous forty-nine years, only a selection of them could be shown in the nine galleries that had been cleared for this unique tribute. Anne Webb Karnaghan, in charge of museum publications, opened an account of the Ross Collection in the February 1932 *Bulletin* thus:

> One of the penalties of forming a great collection of art is that the collector lays himself open to discovery. His collection is the mirror of his mind as surely as the masterpieces of Western music and art disclose the individualities that produced them.
>
> A single object in the distinguished collection with which Dr. Denman W. Ross had enriched the Museum during a period of almost half a century offers a key to the man and his work; the entire collection but multiplies the disclosure made by a single object. He has served his fellow men and has found personal satisfaction in the apprehension of life in its myriad manifestations in art, and in the acquisition of those forms acceptable to his taste. The fulfillment of these impulses is revealed in a collection which provokes at once philosophic reflection and aesthetic experience.

Mrs. Karnaghan quoted some of Dr. Ross's observations, published in the December 1913 *Bulletin*, that have been included in Chapter

PARAKEET ON BLOSSOMING PEAR BRANCH. Chinese painting, Sung dynasty. *Gift of Denman W. Ross. 30.461*

IV. She also drew upon recollections of travels in the East that he had included in a tribute to Hervey E. Wetzel in the then current *Bulletin* of the Fogg Art Museum. These deserve attention.

We wanted to see everything everywhere: nature, life, people, and things. Our interest was in the world of vision and our purpose was to discover what is best worth seeing in every kind. We were particularly interested in works of art, in buildings, sculptures, and paintings and in the objects of the so-called minor arts and crafts. Among the things which were for sale we proposed to buy what we liked best and wanted to add to our collections. We interviewed the dealers everywhere. We visited their shops and they came to us with their offerings. In collecting we proceeded regardless of archaeological or historical considerations. We were not archaeologists. We were not historians. We were simply lovers of order and the beautiful as they come to pass in the works of man supplementing the works of Nature. Order is mathematical and ought to be obvious.

The beautiful is as you like it. Regarded as a reflector of colour in light, the work of art is good, bad, or indifferent. Our aim was to select and to collect the best.

By seeking the beautiful always in the best of its kind, Denman Ross had acquired a collection that would have driven him out of house and home had he not constantly passed his possessions along. Down to 1932 there were in the Museum of Fine Arts through his continuous gifts approximately the following: 95 paintings and sketches in the Department of Paintings, 47 prints and drawings in the Print Department, 11 objects in the Egyptian and 13 in the Classical Department, 492 in the Department of Decorative Arts, 4,006 textiles and 6,162 objects in the Department of Asiatic Art; moreover he had given some 1,500 objects to the Fogg Art Museum, where he was Honorary Keeper of the Ross Study Series and Honorary Fellow. Figures are dry fodder, but the illustrations chosen by Mrs. Karnaghan for her article convey a clearer picture. They were: the Chinese sixth-century stone sculpture given in memory of Oka-kura-Kakuzo; the twelfth-century Japanese painting *Ichiji-kinrin*; the *Disciples of Buddha* by the twelfth-century Chinese painter Lin T'ing-kuei; an eighteenth-century Japanese garment; an eleventh-century Chinese painting of women in a pavilion with children playing below it; a seventh-century A.D. South Indian stone carving of Durga; the battered but wonderfully beautiful torso of a Yaksi from Sanci, of the first century B.C.; a leaf from a Persian Shah Namah of about A.D. 1310 depicting Alexander slaying the dragon; a Rajput painting of the *Hour of Cowdust*; an Italian late medieval brocade of the *Noli me tangere* scene; a seventeenth-century Indian silk and gold weaving; a Peruvian embroidery of the early Nazca period (fifth to sixth century, A.D.), incredibly well-preserved; a Persian brocade of the sixteenth century; a Coptic tapestry of the fourth to fifth; a Chinese Sung Dynasty bowl; the head of a French Gothic angel; the marble bust of a Roman of the Antonine period; a late medieval Spanish *Coronation of the Virgin*, given in memory of Samuel Dennis Warren; Claude Monet's *Les Falaises des Petites Dalles*; Whistler's *Old Battersea Bridge*; and, last but not least, a recent addition, a Chinese scroll painting of *Portraits of Emperors*, attributed to Yen

PORTRAITS OF THE THIRTEEN EMPERORS (detail). Chinese scroll, color on silk, attributed to Yen Li-pên, 7th century. *Ross Collection.* 31.643

Li-pên (died 673 A.D.) that Kojiro Tomita described in detail in the same issue of the *Bulletin*.

The scroll of the Emperors had been an outstanding feature in an exhibition of Chinese paintings held in Tokyo in 1929, to which noted collectors in China and Japan lent their treasures. When Denman Ross saw a small reproduction of it, he at once told Kojiro Tomita to try and get it from its owner in China. The price proved so high that Dr. Ross's lawyer pointed out that, even though comfortably off and a bachelor, he simply could not spend such a sum at one time. As he was determined that the scroll should be obtained for Boston, he borrowed a substantial sum against collateral, while the museum advanced the remainder of the price, which he subsequently repaid. The Emperors now adorn the Museum of Fine Arts solely because of Denman Ross's conviction that money was not important enough to save when it could be used for Chinese paintings.

To me at least Denman Ross clearly emerges as the most remarkable single figure in the first century of the Museum of Fine Arts. This eightieth-birthday exhibition was no means the end. For some years he had been closely tied to Cambridge by the long illness of his cousin, Miss Louise Nathurst, who lived with him. After she died, he set out for Europe, where he reveled in museums and dealers' galleries. I saw him briefly at the Savoy Hotel in London, happy as a child to be seeing everything everywhere once again. He returned safely home, but set out once more the following year. This time he died, suddenly of a cerebral hemorrhage, in London on 12 September 1935, in his eighty-third year. His long-time friends at Yamanaka and Company provided a rare and appropriate T'ang pottery jar for the homeward journey of his ashes. Without him, the remainder of this history is bound to be duller.